AFTER THE FLOOD

ALSO BY ROBERT POLITO

At the Titan's Breakfast:
Three Essays on Byron's Poetry

A Reader's Guide to James Merrill's The Changing Light at Sandover

Savage Art:
A Biography of Jim Thompson

Doubles

Hollywood & God

EDITED COLLECTIONS

Crime Novels:
American Noir of the 1930s and 1940s

Crime Novels:
American Noir of the 1950s

David Goodis:
Five Noir Novels of the 1940s and 1950s

Kenneth Fearing:
Selected Poems

The Everyman Dashiell Hammett

The Everyman James M. Cain

The Complete Film Writings of Manny Farber

Manny Farber:
Paintings & Writings
(with Michael Almereyda and
Jonathan Lethem)

AFTER THE FLOOD

INSIDE BOB DYLAN'S MEMORY PALACE

ROBERT POLITO

Liveright Publishing Corporation

A Division of W. W. Norton & Company
Independent Publishers Since 1923

Printed in the United States of America
First Edition

For information about special discounts for bulk purchases, please contact W. W. Norton Special Sales at specialsales@wwnorton.com or 800-233-4830

Manufacturing by Lakeside Book Company
Book design by Daniel Lagin
Production manager: Lauren Abbate

ISBN 978-0-87140-293-6

Liveright Publishing Corporation, 500 Fifth Avenue, New York, NY 10110
www.wwnorton.com

W. W. Norton & Company Ltd., 15 Carlisle Street, London W1D 3BS

Authorized EU representative: EAS, Mustamäe tee 50, 10621 Tallinn, Estonia

10 9 8 7 6 5 4 3 2 1

for Kristine

for Michael Chaiken

for The Friend

". . . Remember?—"

—James Merrill, "The Book of Ephraim"

CONTENTS

PREFACE

SHADOWS ARE FALLING

No, not *that* Bob Dylan.

My course in *After the Flood: Inside Bob Dylan's Memory Palace* arcs—roughly—from 1991 to 2024. That is, here you'll encounter only Dylan's *second* thirty years—again roughly, for that annual tally runs to a little over thirty-three—of his astonishing, but what to call it, though? Others fix on . . . *Dylan's Journey* . . . *Dylan's Great Adventure* . . . even . . . *Dylan's Odyssey*. Anyways, Bob Dylan's second thirty years—roughly—of creating music and writing songs, along with his concerts, books, films, radio shows, television, interviews, tributes, and visual art. A wayward course, yet with edges and borders. *After the Flood* more precisely arcs from his Grammy Lifetime Achievement Award on February 20, 1991, at Radio City Music Hall in New York City through his 2021–2024 *Rough and Rowdy Ways* tour.

Even now, over six decades on, most Dylan stories—and not just *A Complete Unknown* (2024)—tend still to accent 1961 through 1966, amid postscripts for *The Basement Tapes* (1967–1968), or the Rolling Thunder Revue tour (1975–1976), and consign the alleged blur of anything/everything since to a sketchy coda. As the *lifetime achievement* award efficiently insisted on that long ago, drizzly Grammy night, Dylan's extraordinary vocation as a vital and indispensable creative force looked and sounded over: already a remote legend, when, so surprisingly, so strangely, he was about to start all over again.

"We are always striving in the wake of prior narratives," as John Keene proposes in *Punks*. Shadows, ghosts. After his arrival in New York in January 1961, Dylan—as he remembered for *Chronicles, Volume One*—"did everything fast. Thought fast, ate fast, talked fast and walked fast. I even sang my songs fast." His first week in the city, he performed at Café Wha? and Izzy Young's Folklore Center, and met Woody Guthrie at Sid and Bob Gleason's house in East Orange, New Jersey. By mid-February, he wrote "Song to Woody," by April was opening for John Lee Hooker at Gerde's Folk City, and by November recorded his debut, *Bob Dylan*. In 1962 he wrote and recorded most of *The Freewheelin' Bob Dylan*, and toured England, where he appeared in a TV play, *Madhouse on Castle Street*. In 1963, he released *Freewheelin'* and completed another album, *The Times They Are A-Changin'*. By 1964, he was ready for *Another Side of Bob Dylan*, and then over an incandescent fourteen months—give or take—recorded *Bringing It All Back Home*, *Highway 61 Revisited*, and *Blonde on Blonde*.

The Bob Dylan of *After the Flood: Inside Bob Dylan's Memory Palace* rarely moved fast. During the 1990s, some seven years separated his two albums of original songs—*Under the Red Sky* (1990) and *Time Out of Mind* (1997). Four more years to *"Love And Theft"* (2001). Five more to *Modern Times* (2006). Eight years between *Tempest* (2012) and *Rough and Rowdy Ways* (2020). This Bob Dylan is a man in his early fifties through his early eighties who revitalized himself and his art with a fresh, brilliant, intensified collage style of crafting songs; vast, staggering concert tours—over three thousand shows from 1991 through 2024; writing books—*Chronicles, Volume One* (2004) and *The Philosophy of Modern Song* (2022); creating a movie, *Masked And Anonymous* (2003) and inspiring other movies, *I'm Not There* (2007), *No Direction Home* (2005), and *A Complete Unknown*; hosting a weekly radio program, *Theme Time Radio Hour* (2006–2009); and exhibiting his paintings and welded sculptures in galleries and museums across America, Europe, and Asia. Yet the high-speed Dylan of 1961 into 1966 is inescapably also a presence here, if foremost as one of those many looming and falling shadows—to reinvent himself, as I will quote Dylan later, "It was important for me to come to the bottom of this legend thing." Of course, those second thirty-odd years alone would surpass the lifetime achievements of approximately anyone else I could summon for resonant parallels—whether musicians, composers, poets, novelists, philosophers, or painters. I don't readily see parallels for those second thirty years. (Whom might *you* care to nominate? Conceivably Melville . . . ? Stravinsky . . . ? Wittgenstein . . . ? None *exactly*.) In a *Chronicles, Volume Two*, I would welcome a ramble around the 1990s: those David Bromberg Chicago folk covers sessions in June of 1992; more solo folk covers for *Good as I Been to You* and for *World Gone Wrong*, released in October 1993, as he returned and repurposed his singing voice; those hundreds of far-flung live shows, across small towns as well as notable metropolises, as he tested that voice; and finally all those intriguing unfinished song lyrics in his archive at the Bob Dylan Center in Tulsa, Oklahoma, during the years prior to *Time Out of Mind*. If a *Chronicles, Volume Three*, hopefully an invigorating dive into Dylan's re-immersion in American history—the Civil War, Reconstruction, Jim Crow, and the War of 1812—for *"Love And Theft"* through *Tempest*. If a *Volume Four*, maybe the poignant, spirited exchanges between Dylan's laid-back *Nobel Lecture* (2017) and his rigorously retrospective *Rough and Rowdy Ways*.

Perhaps inexorably, I will later also quote F. Scott Fitzgerald's rueful axiom from *The Last Tycoon* apropos of "no second acts" in American lives, although I recognize that he was probably contemplating stage dramas with not two, but three acts—exposition, development, and denouement—and wasn't wholly repudiating mortal second chances. (By that triad play design, Dylan's "lost" 1980s should comprise his official second act; still, 1991 through 2024 isn't—again, not *exactly*—stock denouement.) As I detail in *After the Flood: Inside Bob Dylan's Memory Place*, Dylan's acceptance speech for that 1991 Grammy Lifetime Achievement Award seized my attention, and I immediately started listening closely to him again after a decade—roughly—of not closely listening. The writing of this book then ultimately proved feasible only through a gift second chance of my own, after an ominous illness, corrosive treatments, and multiple radical surgeries.

Secrets, signs, tokens, clues, omens, marks, tools—a ghost language. But *accounting for* 1991 through 2024, as in my forthrightly and confidently *explaining* how he managed to do all he did, especially after those "lost" years? No way. Explaining often is critical shorthand for explaining away. *After the Flood: Inside Bob Dylan's Memory Palace* is a reconnaissance mission: No decisive accounting of Bob Dylan is realistic for decades, at least until family, friends, and collaborators publish their books. Tulsa's staggering Bob Dylan Archive was invaluable to my researches, particularly for the chapters that engage song lyrics and albums. I was involved in the archive and Bob Dylan Center nearly from the outset, even got to participate in the conversations that led to the selection of architects, and the decisions to publish a catalog. But if there's a Rosebud sled in Tulsa, I never found it. The rough-draft and alternate-take Dylan of his sublime archive is at least as slippery, resistant, and mysterious as any other Dylan. From his earliest folk covers in 1960, he manifested a singular mix of inspiration and study, lore and improvisation. As his first manager, Terri Thal, recalled to Ray Padgett:

> One of the things that Bob had, and I didn't realize this until a couple years ago, Bob had and still has, I presume, a kind of odd ability to take in information. He can retain the parts of it that he wants, discard the parts of it that he doesn't want, and tuck away parts of it for future use. Which most people, I think, can't do. They lose it. They don't remember it. If they want it, they can't pull it out. He can.

All the more intensively, from 1991 through 2024 he enlarged, amplified, and escalated folk process beyond music to encompass poems, novels, films, memoirs, and those American and classical histories underwritten in blood. The Dylan of his Tulsa archive isn't just a blazing, mercurial, ingenious reviser of his own words and melodies but also a conscious, sly artist who demonstrably thinks, feels, listens, reads, watches, remembers, and then works incredibly hard to imagine, exteriorize, and embody, as though the prerogatives and powers of his art abide in his never forgetting. It's as if Dylan memorized everything, and it's all there in the songs he sings.

Another shadow, another ghost language. My form here is an abecedarium, a form that—as far as I now can cast back—I first encountered in "The Book of Ephraim," the alphabetical initial foray of James Merrill's *The Changing Light at Sandover*, his trilogy of long poems in communication with the dead and the "other world" over a homemade Ouija board. An abecedarium allowed me to be topic-driven when rundown or recap was needed, but scrupulously chronological when timing instead was crucial. Sometimes a telescope, sometimes a microscope. As A to Z was my frame, my guide—from "Murder Most Foul" in chapter A through "Key West (Philosopher Pirate)" in chapter Z—was *Rough and Rowdy Ways*, Dylan's concentrated succession of glimpses into the sources and dynamics of his art, his glimpses of flesh and spirit, technique and intuition, memory and making—and for me far more candid, generous, and revelatory than his ceremonial *Nobel Lecture*. Later in *Sandover*, Merrill will ask Mirabell, one of his otherworldly interlocutors, a "composite voice," part batwing angel, part subatomic particle, "Is memory soul?" For "Ephraim," though, he is circumspect, wary, casually punning. "Nothing we can recollect is missing," Merrill ventures in *his* chapter Z. "Yet nothing's gone, or nothing we recall."

"Shadows are falling," as Dylan sings on *Time Out of Mind*. Suspicions. Echoes. Glimmers. Traces. Loss. Death. Still more ghosts. Oh, *that* Bob Dylan. "It's not dark yet, but it's getting there."

AFTER THE FLOOD

A

STAY SAFE, STAY OBSERVANT . . .

Admittedly, lies, fear, muddle, fury, the dead and their ghosts, were everywhere. Admittedly, everything was pretty fucked up.

This is what I remember, by way of situation.

Shortly after midnight on March 27, 2020, when Bob Dylan dropped his surprise single—"Murder Most Foul"—America, the world, and my body tracked multiple, interlocking crises. Coiling through some 16 minutes, 55 seconds, the song was his longest ever, and his only release of original writing since *Tempest* in 2012. The front page of the *New York Times* the next morning would read, "JOB LOSSES SOAR; U.S. VIRUS CASES TOP WORLD," as CNN signaled "Trump's approval up amid coronavirus concerns." Compounding insinuations of apocalypse, California's governor Gavin Newsom would soon declare a parallel climate "state of emergency," and wildfire season promised to reel into the worst of recorded history. By year's end, some 9,917 fires scorched more than four million acres, accelerating flash floods and mudflow. "Murder Most Foul" was the first of three such stealth releases—"Multitudes" followed on April 17; "False Prophet" on May 8; and ultimately an entire new album, *Rough and Rowdy Ways*, on June 19. Juneteenth: the holiday that memorialized the date Union Army General Gordon Granger posted the order that "informed . . . the people of Texas . . . all slaves are free." By then, June 19, 2020, witness videos would record Minneapolis police officer Derek Chauvin as he pressed George Floyd to the ground, and knelt on his neck for at least 8 minutes and 15 seconds, even after Floyd lost consciousness and paramedics arrived. Floyd's murder would inspire the largest racial justice collective actions in the United States since probably the civil rights movement.

While I was in Tulsa, researching this book at Dylan's archive, and introducing a dear friend, the writer Lucy Sante, at a reading sponsored by the Bob Dylan Center and Magic City Books, the World Health Organization declared COVID-19 a global pandemic. Until we secured flights home, Lucy and I worried—fantasized—accepted—that we'd be trapped in Tulsa for the duration, the city then in high throttle, often honorably, sometimes disgracefully, towards the centennial of the Tulsa Race Massacre of 1921, a year into the future.

We returned to New York just fine, but I knew something was wrong. By early June I would be diagnosed with a precarious illness that over subsequent months would demand manifold drug therapies and serial surgeries. One operation persisted fourteen hours, a sort of sci-fi marvel of science, internal engineering, and medical dedication, contra all the coeval dystopian breakdowns of that first COVID year. As in a seventeenth-century poem by John Donne, George Herbert, or Andrew Marvell, the fraught human body is a microcosm, a mirror to the larger disintegrating world spirit. Many of us started to feel like we were living in the future, a future predicted by scientists and historians, but that arrived faster than expected. But who would live to see that future through?

Dylan's dead-of-night note that attended "Murder Most Foul" appeared to acknowledge the pervasive civic tumult—as though his new record might actually engage the specific American instant, a prospect at least as startling as the song, for by consensus Dylan had vacated this stance in 1964, when he told Nat Hentoff no more "finger-pointing songs," and "I don't want to write for people anymore. You know—be a spokesman."

> Greetings to my fans and followers with gratitude for all your support and loyalty across the years. This is an unreleased song we recorded a while back that you might find interesting. Stay safe, stay observant and may God be with you.

A "while back" turned out to mean . . . February. So named for the scene early in *Hamlet* when the ghost of the king commands his son to "Revenge his foul and most unnatural murder," the song takes as a point of inflection the assassination of President John F. Kennedy, whom "Murder Most Foul" will also dub "the king." (Closer to home, Congressman Ben Butler of Massachusetts declared at Andrew Johnson's 1868 impeachment trial that "By murder most foul [Johnson] succeeded to the Presidency, and is the elect of an assassin to that high office, and not of the people." Dylan is captivated by America's presidents—on "Must Be Santa" he even augmented the routine list of reindeer with a rhyming litany of chronological commanders-in-chief: "Eisenhower, Kennedy, Johnson, Nixon, . . . Carter, Reagan, Bush, and Clinton.") As Dylan eases into his opening lines, revelation vies with deception, facts with rhetoric, and doggerel tilts into brute eloquence:

> *'Twas a dark day in Dallas—November '63*
> *The day that will live on in infamy*
> *President Kennedy was riding high*
> *A good day to be living and a good day to die*
> *Being led to the slaughter like a sacrificial lamb*
> *Say wait a minute boys, do you know who I am?*
> *Of course we do, we know who you are*
> *Then they blew off his head when he was still in the car*

"Murder Most Foul" is, first, the story of a killing, which Dylan depicts as an execution, and, then, a catalog of the plangent reverberations for a nation—as he later sings—in "slow decay." Dallas strictly speaking *was* dark when Kennedy arrived, rainy and gray, and from the outset Dylan embeds the assassination inside prior American cataclysmic cruxes: Native American ethnocide (referencing the Oglala Lakota saying, "a good day to die") and Pearl Harbor, via Franklin Roosevelt's "Day of Infamy" speech. But 1941 was also the year Dylan was born, and his song is just as cannily personal as it is historical. His memoir *Chronicles* recounts his mother's avid response to a Kennedy campaign visit to Hibbing, Minnesota, six months after Dylan left for Minneapolis and the University of Minnesota. "He gave a heroic speech, my mom said, and brought people a lot of hope," Dylan wrote. "I wish I could have seen him." Kennedy also figured into one of Dylan's first public controversies when, on December 13, 1963, he ruffled his Emergency Civil Liberties Committee hosts in New York after they bestowed upon him their annual Tom Paine Award—for civil rights efforts—by remarking that "I saw some of myself" in Lee Harvey Oswald. More recently, Dylan included paintings of Oswald and Jack Ruby in his "Revisionist Art" series (2011–2012), both modeled after reconfigured *Life* magazine covers. On his twenty-first-century albums, *"Love And Theft"* (2001), *Modern Times* (2006), and *Tempest*, Dylan circulated several conspicuously political songs, among them "High Water (For Charley Patton)," "Cry a While," "Sugar Baby," "When the Deal Goes Down," "Workingman's Blues #2," "Ain't Talkin'," "Scarlet Town," "Tin Angel," and "Tempest." During an interview with novelist Jonathan Lethem, he might jest, "You know, everybody makes a big deal about the sixties. The sixties, it's like the Civil War days. But, I mean, you're talking to a person who owns the sixties. Did I ever want to acquire the sixties? No. But I own the sixties—who's going to argue with me?" Still, on "Murder Most Foul" Dylan thwarts readymade nostalgia, an easy revisiting of the storybook sixties and his golden "spokesman" moment. Instead, mixing and juxtaposing voices, lingos, and tones, he traces the decline of America over the trajectory of his own lifetime through the kaleidoscope of the Kennedy assassination.

Greil Marcus once proposed that the "engine, the motor, of Dylan's best work is empathy." The empathy that prompted him as a young man to identify even with Oswald here disperses any single dominant narrator into a hypnotic succession of irreconcilable speakers: a dazed JFK; his smug killers ("Thousands were watching, no one saw a thing . . . Greatest magic trick ever under the sun"); clueless Oswald ("I'm just a patsy like Patsy Cline"); genial Nellie Connally, echoing the last words Kennedy heard ("You can't say Dallas doesn't love you"); Mary Pinchot Meyer, JFK's rumored lover, herself later murdered, also execution-style; exponents of indignant reason ("Don't worry Mr. President, help's on the way"); playboy, police buff Ruby ("I'm in the red-light district like a cop on the beat"); and finally the devil, who transforms the assassination site into Robert Johnson's crossroads: "Dealey Plaza, make a left hand turn / Go down to the crossroads, try to flag a ride / That's the place where Faith, Hope and Charity died."

As Dylan logs the assassination and its aftermath, he insistently intertwines politics and culture, history and religion. He calls up November 22:

The day that they killed him, someone said to me, "Son,
The age of the anti-Christ has just only begun."
Air Force One coming in through the gate
Johnson sworn in at two thirty-eight

He glances at Parkland Hospital, and Kennedy's autopsy:

I'm leaning to the left, got my head in her lap
Oh Lord, I've been led into some kind of a trap . . .
They mutilated his body and took out his brain
What more could they do, they piled on the pain
But his soul was not there where it was supposed to be at
For the last fifty years they've been searching for that
Freedom, oh freedom, freedom over me
Hate to tell you, Mister, but only dead men are free
Send me some loving—tell me no lie
Throw the gun in the gutter and walk on by

For this net of loose talk tightening to verse, Dylan can sound random—his quicksilver associations—and formal: rhyming couplets, intricate stanzas, deft repetitions. Here the president links a recent ideological pivot ("I'm leaning to the left") to Jackie cradling him in the death car, while around them a tune from *My Fair Lady*, "On the Street Where You Live," slides into "Oh Freedom!," a Reconstruction-era spiritual that Joan Baez performed at the 1963 March on Washington. Kennedy's own anguished voice stiffens into the icy charm of his shooters, ultimately to arrive at a sort of choral lament for his missing "soul," and the nation's, equal parts Little Richard, Dione Warwick, the Everly Brothers, gangster movies, and Jessie Jackson.

Throughout, Dylan just as aggressively—and casually—blurs eras, movements, and historical figures: the sixties, nineteenth-century English Romanticism, the Civil War, Shakespearean kings, the fifties, Jim Crow, and the Bible. During the introductory movement, his shrouded titles and misty, half-remembered phrases from a broken world conjure up a meditation on impermanence, where the present is all there is. Then, his fragments sharply coalesce into a marathon radio playlist, a chanted litany of requests to DJ Wolfman Jack, perhaps broadcasting from across the Mexican border on station XERF, with a signal so powerful the Wolfman could reach Canada:

Play me a song, Mr. Wolfman Jack
Play it for me in my long Cadillac
Play that Only the Good Die Young
Take me to the place where Tom Dooley was hung
Play St. James Infirmary in the court of King James
If you want to remember, better write down the names
Play Etta James too, play I'd Rather Go Blind
Play it for the man with the telepathic mind
Play John Lee Hooker play Scratch My Back
Play it for that strip club owner named Jack
Guitar Slim—Goin' Down Slow

Play it for me and for Marilyn Monroe
And please Don't Let Me Be Misunderstood
Play it for the First Lady, she ain't feeling that good

Over seventy-five, maybe eighty songs in all: and not only songs, for the Wolfman apparently plays movies, Broadway shows, and books, too. Radio is the medium of "Murder Most Foul," and perhaps Dylan's preferred medium as well. In *Chronicles* he recommends New Orleans radio, suggesting "WWOZ was the kind of radio station I used to listen to late at night growing up, and it brought me back to the trials of my youth and touched the spirit of it. Back then when something was wrong the radio could lay hands on you and you'd be all right." On "Murder Most Foul" Dylan himself is also a sort of medium; as the songs unspool he might as well be taking down messages from the dead over a Ouija board. During a 1997 interview, he related the radio to Orpheus in the underworld, with an echo of Jean Cocteau's *Orphee.* "Well, America was tied in with the radio when I grew up . . . Radio stations were all over. It was a large area and transmitters could transmit thousands of miles. . . . The radio connected everybody like Orpheus or something. . . . When I grew up, that's what you listened to."

Despite Dylan's stately vocals, and the elegant trio of keyboards (Alan Pasqua, Fiona Apple, and Belmont Tench), "Murder Most Foul" is a farrago of slippery locomotion. History implodes into puns—Guy Banister and David Ferrie, the alleged assassins at the center of New Orleans District Attorney Jim Garrison's Kennedy investigation, are introduced as though they were hit tunes by British Invasion bands: "Slide down the banister, go get your coat / Ferry 'cross the Mersey and go for the throat." Similarly, the Warren Commission, and its single-bullet theory: "You got me dizzy Miss Lizzie, you filled me with lead / That magic bullet of yours has gone to my head." History erodes metaphor—"When you're down on Deep Ellem put your money in your shoe / Don't ask what your country can do for you." "Deep Ellem Blues" is a song with a pedigree stalking back to the 1920s. Dylan even recorded a version during the sessions for his 1992 album of covers, *Good as I Been to You*. But Deep Ellem is also a historic Black Dallas neighborhood. History saps cliché—"Living in a nightmare on Elm Street" may sound rote, except Kennedy actually was gunned down on Elm Street.

So many songs, poems, novels, films, and gags. Subtexts align like filings around a magnet. Elizabeth Bishop famously said she preferred poems that register the "mind in motion" rather than "at rest," and nowhere in "Murder Most Foul" does Dylan's mind relax. His couplets—stitched together by a rhyme—typically saunter in contrary directions. That magnificent liturgy of American popular culture since the Second World War? Dylan's vocals mourn as he celebrates—those unrivaled accomplishments in the arts were solace and distraction. Wolfman Jack's "speaking in tongues" is babble and prophecy. Easy for a listener to go missing in the claustrophobic torrent of names and associations on "Murder Most Foul," and many earnest annotators did. That might be the craftiest twist of Dylan's design: his song forces us into the paranoia of conspiracy theorists, running down clues, Easter eggs, synchronicities, accidents, and suspicions, a dead-end Pynchonesque quandary. Pynchon's *The Crying of Lot 49* calculated our "extended capacity for convolution," and Dylan here mocks and cautions us together. Tag the quotations, he dares us. Overlook the coup.

Yet touchstones of his twenty-first-century music survive his formidable now-you-see-it, now-you-don't skepticism. Following *Modern Times* and *Tempest*, "Murder Most Foul" restages American history as the history of crime. Through the aperture of the Kennedy assassination, Dylan scans minstrelsy—"Black face singer—white face clown / Better not show your faces after the sun goes down"; the Civil War—"Play the Blood Stained Banner"; and Jim Crow—"Take me Back to Tulsa to the scene of the crime." Echoing *"Love And Theft,"* he situates race as the nucleus of the American dynamo, and racism as the original American sin. And all through "Murder Most Foul" he accents the urgency of memory: "If you want to remember, better write down the names." In this Dylan resembles James Baldwin, who warned, "History is not the past, it is the present. We carry our history with us. We are our history. If we pretend otherwise, we are literally criminals." But by reminding us in "Murder Most Foul" where the bodies are buried, Dylan is circling back to another locus classicus of memory, Cicero's *de Oratore*:

> There is a story that Simonides was dining at the house of a wealthy nobleman named Scopas at Crannon in Thessaly, and chanted a lyric poem which he had composed in honor of his host. . . .
>
> The story runs that a little later a message was brought to Simonides to go outside, as two young men were standing at the door who earnestly requested him to come out; so he rose from his seat and went out, and could not see anybody; but in the interval of his absence the roof of the hall where Scopas was giving the banquet fell in, crushing Scopas himself and his relations under the ruins and killing them; and when their friends wanted to bury them but were altogether unable to know them apart as they had been completely crushed, the story goes that Simonides was enabled by his recollection of the place in which each of them had been reclining at table to identify them for separate internment; and that this circumstance suggested to him the discovery of the truth that the best aid to clearness of memory consists in orderly arrangement.
>
> He inferred that persons desiring to train this faculty must select localities and form mental images of the facts they wish to remember and store those images in the localities.

Who's calling for those records from Wolfman Jack? "What is the truth and where did it go," Dylan, or someone, asks, maybe the ghost of JFK, or anyone's ghost. Probing the afterlife of a grave crime, "Murder Most Foul" radiates a twilight kingdom that by the close feels posthumous. "I can't remember when I was born and I forgot when I died," as Dylan will sing later on *Rough and Rowdy Ways*. The final request is for Wolfman Jack to play the song we're already listening to, and which presumably then will broadcast into eternity.

Amidst the national debasement, corruption, and murdered magistrates—other songs will rouse Lincoln, McKinley, Nixon, and Julius Caesar—Trump is nowhere, and everywhere. In his only interview about *Rough and Rowdy Ways*, with historian Douglas Brinkley for the *New York Times*, Dylan hinted at his concerns, aspirations, and contexts. His album wasn't "nostalgic," but contemporary, current. "I don't think of 'Murder Most Foul' as a glorification of the past or some kind of send-off to a lost age," he apprised Brinkley. "It speaks to me in the moment." Of George Floyd and Black Lives Matter, he confided, "It sickened me no end to see George tortured to death like that. It was beyond ugly. Let's hope that justice comes swift for the Floyd family and for the nation." COVID-19 impressed him as a "forerunner of something else to come. Extreme arrogance can have some disastrous penalties." Correlating "Murder Most Foul" to a folk tradition of "songs about people," Dylan broached yet another assassinated president, "Mr. Garfield." Replying to Brinkley's question about the obvious intimations of mortality in his new songs, he intensified the stakes. "I think about the death of the human race . . . I think about it in general terms, not in a personal way."

During that charged spring of 2020 as I replayed *Rough and Rowdy Ways*, a notion took hold, a notion Dylan himself all but conceded in the incisive candors, pivots, and speculations of his talks with Brinkley: the album is his acknowledgment of his 2016 Nobel Prize in Literature. A few days before the Swedish Academy deadline, Dylan finally did deliver a Nobel Prize Lecture, as required, on June 4, 2017. He spoke his solid, rhythmic prose over Alan Pasqua's piano, à la Jack Kerouac and Steve Allen. Yet his official address proved lax: summaries of classic books—*Moby-Dick*, *All Quiet on the Western Front*, *The Odyssey*—and a misattribution of some lyrics by a later songwriter to Charlie Poole.

Rough and Rowdy Ways, I came to believe, is his real Nobel Lecture—a lecture from inside his own forms and idioms, from inside the same artistry that earned Bob Dylan the Nobel Prize. On two songs, he even references the gold medal he received at a private ceremony in Stockholm. When in "My Own Version of You," Dylan's mad biological engineer boasts, "I want to do things for the benefit of all mankind," he's impishly glossing a line adapted from the *Aeneid* and inscribed on the back of the Nobel Prize medal: *Inventas vitam iuvat excoluisse per artes* (or in William Morris's 1876 translation of the Virgil original, "and they who bettered life on earth by new-found mastery"). On the medal, the Virgil inscription surrounds a young man sitting under a laurel tree, listening to the Muse, and writing down her song. He is among those in "Mother of Muses" whom Dylan imagines uttering sweet entreaties: "Sing of honor and fame and glory be / Mother of Muses, sing for me."

From his initial 1960s New York press coverage onward, Dylan refused any public clarification of his songs, opting for deadpan, put-on, or ridicule. His twenty-first-century recordings advanced strategies of embodiment; he resisted routine statements and singer-songwriter epiphanies for relentless collage. He might write narratively about the Civil War in "'Cross the Green Mountain" for the *Gods and Generals* (2003) film soundtrack, but ultimately Dylan tended to lodge the legacies of empire, slavery, criminality, sin, the body, desire, and his own autobiography in volatile verbal echo chambers of harmonizing and clashing reverberations: Ovid, Homer, Virgil, and Milton; Shakespeare; Henry Timrod, the poet laureate of the Confederacy; Robert Burns, Lewis Carroll, Mark Twain, F. Scott Fitzgerald, and Flannery O'Connor; Junichi Saga's *Confessions of a Yakuza* and *Memories of Silk and Straw*; Charley Patton, Robert Johnson, Blind Lemon Jefferson, Muddy Waters, Dock Boggs, Leroy Carr, the Carter Family, the Stanley Brothers, Hoagy Carmichael, Bing Crosby, and Billie Holiday; W. C. Fields, the Marx Brothers, and assorted film noirs.

Yet on *Rough and Rowdy Ways*, Dylan also reemerges as a restless, sometimes cordial, often corrosive analyst, agreeing at last to engage—if not fully to explain—the whats, hows, and, possibly whys of his creative life. Suddenly, he sounds direct, or almost. Those intensive collages implied, and even staged, his successive incarnations across six decades of musical self-reinvention. But on *Rough and Rowdy Ways* Dylan could sing, bluntly—albeit while quoting Walt Whitman: "I contain multitudes." Nearly as blunt, "Murder Most Foul" frames an account of his origins in global war, national trauma, and the tilt-a-whirl popular culture of the forties, fifties, and sixties. Making art is the axis of every lyric here, and his catalogs incline also to allegory. "I've Made Up My Mind to Give Myself to You" embraces all at once God, a lover, and Dylan's audience. In "My Own Version of You," his gifts for materializing a fresh world out of shards and scraps of the past tip into Mary Shelley's *Frankenstein*:

I've been visiting morgues and monasteries
Looking for the necessary body parts
Limbs and livers and brains and hearts
I want to bring someone to life—is what I want to do
I want to create my own version of you

"Key West (Philosopher Pirate)" localizes spirit, imagination, and the yearning for transcendence. For "Mother of Muses," Dylan entreats Mnemosyne, the goddess of memory, and categorically affirms the epic aims of *Rough and Rowdy Ways*. "I'm falling in love with Calliope."

"Murder Most Foul" was Bob Dylan's first number 1 song ever on a Billboard chart. No other new music I can remember from that fierce spring and summer—no art of any strain, novel, film, poem—so infiltrated and permeated the furors of COVID-19, George Floyd, climate horror, Trump, and death.

Dylan was about to turn seventy-nine years old, and when the pandemic lifted just enough for him to take *Rough and Rowdy Ways* on the road in the fall of 2021, he would be eighty. During those early virus days, younger musicians again looked to him, for their own COVID projects. Bon Iver performed "With God on Our Side" on a Bernie Sanders Livestream event. Daniel Romano recalled Dylan's 1984 appearance on David Letterman when, backed by the Los Angeles Latino punk band the Plugz, he performed a few songs from his then latest release *Infidels*. Romano eventually re-recorded all of *Infidels* as a raging what if/fuck you: *Do (What Could Have Been) "Infidels" by Bob Dylan & The Plugz*.

Emma Swift and Chrissie Hynde produced the sharpest Dylan lockdown albums. Swift's *Blonde on the Tracks* reached right up to *Rough and Rowdy Ways*, including "I Contain Multitudes" alongside a devastating account of "One of Us Must Know (Sooner or Later)" from *Blonde on Blonde* (1966). Hynde and Pretenders guitarist James Walbourne circulated *Standing in the Doorway* as nine revelatory installments of a *Dylan Lockdown Series*, and for her, too, the adventure originated in *Rough and Rowdy Ways*. "Listening to that song"—she recounted of "Murder Most Foul" during an interview with Tina Benitez-Eves—"completely changed everything for me. I was lifted out of this morose mood that I'd been in. I remember where I was sitting the day that Kennedy was shot, every reference in the song. I called James and said, 'Let's do some Dylan covers,' and that's what started this whole thing."

B

IT WASN'T LIKE IT WAS ANOTHER WORLD . . .

Backdrop: One version of my book's story goes something like this. *Ladies and gentlemen, will you please welcome the poet laureate of rock 'n' roll. The voice of the promise of the '60s counterculture. The guy who forced folk into bed with rock, who donned makeup in the '70s and disappeared into a haze of substance abuse, who emerged to find Jesus, who was written off as a has-been by the end of the '80s, then suddenly shifted gears, releasing some of the strongest music of his career beginning in the late '90s. Ladies and gentlemen, Columbia recording artist, Bob Dylan!*

Well, yes, and no. Or not *exactly*, even if almost a full decade of Dylan live shows opened with stage manager Al Santos intoning this—breezy? vitriolic? clueless?—cartoon of an introduction; and that would be Santos actually and reiteratively intoning it night after night, irrespective of where Dylan was playing (St. Petersburg, Russia, or Florence, Massachusetts), as apparently there was no prerecorded announcement; and that's some 850-plus gigs, starting with the Erie County Fair in Hamburg, New York, on August 15, 2002, and running all the way up to the summer 2012 European tour. Santos's words crib a glib Dylan concert preview by Jeff Miers of the *Buffalo News*, and our poet laureate must have found them sufficiently—hackneyed? infuriating? risible?—to encapsulate for his audiences what I believe is the most sustained, intelligent, and startling second act by an American artist since . . . since at least F. Scott Fitzgerald in his notes for *The Last Tycoon* disavowed such creative revitalizations as impossible.

Dylan *did* own a serious problem at the end of the 1980s, though this problem was his chronic quandary and burden as far back as 1974, when he started touring again after an eight-year pause. How could he entice, even oblige his listeners to forget his incendiary achievements of the sixties, so that he might create innovative new music? That he ultimately would after 1992, and at a reinvigorated stratum of skill, experiment, flair, and surprise congruous with *The Freewheelin' Bob Dylan* (1963), *Bringing It All Back Home* (1965), *Highway 61 Revisited* (1965), and *Blonde on Blonde* (1966) is a signature of this book. Yet few can overlook that by the late eighties Bob Dylan was at times lost, and perhaps—most vehemently and harshly—not even Dylan himself.

Across his twenty-first-century set lists, and during interviews, Dylan can dismiss pretty much anything he released, excluding cover songs, and incidental oddities—"When I Paint My Masterpiece," "Lenny Bruce," "Gotta Serve Somebody"—between *Blood on the Tracks* (1975) and *Time Out of Mind* (1997), jettisoning roughly two decades and a dozen albums, a duration and output that surpasses that of many major artists across entire lifetimes. As Dylan later summarized his disillusionment in the 1980s to David Gates in *Newsweek*, "I'd kind of reached the end of the line. Whatever I'd started out to do, it wasn't that. I was going to pack it in." His seventies and eighties songs, he flatly told *Rolling Stone*, "just don't work." Worse, the prospect of writing bored and irritated him. "Once in a while the odd song will come to me like a bulldog at the garden gate and demand to be written," he admitted to Robert Hilburn in the *Los Angeles Times*. "But most of them are rejected out of mind right away. You get caught up in wondering if anyone really needs to hear it. Maybe a person gets to the point where they have written enough songs. Let someone else write them."

For *Chronicles,* Dylan is even crueler about his eighties writing, recording, and performing—the whole shebang a lullaby of awfulness:

> Everything was smashed. I had no connection to any kind of inspiration. . . . My own songs had become strangers to me, I didn't have the skill to touch their raw nerves, couldn't penetrate the surfaces. It wasn't my moment of history anymore. . . . The mirror had swung around and I could see the future—an old actor fumbling in garbage cans outside the theater of past triumphs. I had written and recorded so many songs, but it wasn't like I was playing many of them. I think I was only up to the task of about twenty or so. The rest were too cryptic, too darkly driven, and I was no longer capable of doing anything radically creative with them. It was like carrying a package of heavy rotting meat. . . .

Dylan's decline through the 1980s is sometimes recast as though all that went awry hinged on a few judgment lapses, and the ace songs he capriciously dropped from the final mixes of his albums. If only, for instance, "Blind Willie McTell" and "Foot of Pride" could have anchored *Infidels* (1983), or "New Danville Girl," his collaboration with playwright Sam Shepard, could have introduced the rush of film dialogue on *Empire Burlesque* (1985): instant, revisionist masterpieces. But anyone who witnessed his harrowing performance at Live Aid in 1985 with Keith Richards and Ron Wood—and an estimated television audience of between 1.5 and 1.9 billion tuned into their headlining set—already saw that "old actor" (at age forty-four!) "fumbling" through "Blowin' in the Wind," as though he were a sweaty pub trouper from a forgotten war in a Pogues lyric.

For much of the decade Dylan retained no backing band of his own, instead relying on the renown and stature of others: Mick Taylor (the Rolling Stones), and Ian McLagen (the Small Faces) in 1984, Tom Petty and the Heartbreakers in 1986, and the Grateful Dead in 1987. In the studio he desperately chased the zeitgeist—enlisting Mark Knopfler of Dire Straits to produce *Infidels* after David Bowie, Frank Zappa, and Elvis Costello demurred; or Arthur Baker for the dance tracks of *Empire Burlesque*, over backing by Petty's crew, Bruce Springsteen's E Street Band, Sly & Robbie, and Lone Justice. In 1985 Columbia released *Biograph*, a five-LP box set of past hits, rarities, and liner notes that at the time suggested a lavish funeral program. That funeral came to pass at Madison Square Garden on October 16, 1992, when an alluring who's who of performers—among them, John "Cougar" Mellencamp, Kris Kristofferson, Stevie Wonder, Lou Reed, Johnny Cash, the Clancy Brothers, Richie Havens, Chrissie Hynde, the Band, Roseanne Cash, Sinead O'Connor, Mary Chapin Carpenter, Shawn Colvin, the O'Jays, Eric Clapton, Roger McGuinn, George Harrison, and the surviving members of Booker T. & the M.G.'s—convened to honor him at the 30th Anniversary Concert Celebration. Only the corpse showed up for the encores, and awkwardly sang along, as a grim Dylan persevered through a medley of prime triumphs, from "Song to Woody" and "Girl from the North Country" to "Knockin' on Heaven's Door." Was it only by coincidence that in a round-robin cycle of guest vocalists he took the lead for the penultimate verse of "My Back Pages"? "My pathway led by confusion boats. . . ."

In another version of my book's story, Dylan resolved his sixties problem with a makeshift yet elegant time warp solution, circumstantial and metaphysical. When in 1988 he embarked on what would eventually be dubbed the Never Ending Tour (NET), he transformed his live sound such that arrangements of any particular song might shift radically from night to night, a counterintuitive traditionalizing of his back catalog that disassociated everything from its original moment. Watching Jerry Garcia and the Grateful Dead blur their present and past was a likely prompt for this simple, seismic sleight of hand. The concerts of performers who tote associations with a specific era—the fifties, punk, disco, as well as the sixties—tend to lurch between breakneck recreations of their anthems and precarious stabs at current efforts. For the Dylan of the NET, the NET that he resumed post-COVID in the fall of 2021, when I saw him perform three sensational shows at the Beacon Theatre in New York, a song he had written in 1963 didn't inevitably register "1963," or necessarily resonate differently from a song he wrote in 1966, 1997, 2001, 2006, or 2020, and casual listeners often waited for the chorus to discover which song it was that they wished to applaud. During the NET, Dylan's local solutions to his sixties catch-22 spiraled into a worldview. Cyclical and recursive; disruptive and transformative. As he recapped his quick-witted move in "I Contain Multitudes," his second single from *Rough and Rowdy Ways*, "Everything's flowin' all at the same time."

A disquisition on time, identity, memory, trauma, and creation, "I Contain Multitudes" continued Dylan's Nobel Lecture. Much as in "Murder Most Foul," he squarely states his premises and observations, rather than hint, circle, riff, or deflect. His title loops back, of course, to Section 51 of "Song of Myself":

> *Do I contradict myself?*
> *Very well then I contradict myself,*
> *(I am large, I contain multitudes.)*

By way of a Walt Whitman nod so transparent as to foreclose any doubt, Dylan signals his obvious links to classic American literature; a couplet later in the song cites Poe, and his stories "The Tell-Tale Heart," "The Black Cat," and "The Cask of Amontillado" in a similar call-your-bluff spirit. He invokes the traditional English lyric—"I sing the songs of experience like William Blake"—and the Irish ballad, too, glancing at "The Lass from Bally-Na-Lee" by Antoine Ó Raifteiri. Yet allusive scraps of other quotes and paraphrases also abound, as Dylan quietly mixes into his grand heritage of model American and European writers the—for him—no-less-classic rockers of the fifties, conjuring Warren Smith, Carl Perkins, and Gene Vincent with give-away phrases, "A red Cadillac and a black moustache . . . Pink pedal pushers and red blue jeans." Through references to David Bowie and Mott the Hoople, Dylan also embraces Whitman's queer subtext: "I rollick and I frolic with all the young dudes."

"I Contain Multitudes" distills the voices of "Murder Most Foul" into an inner drama of multiple selves. Once, during a 2012 interview with Mikal Gilmore, Dylan spurned the common perception of him as "somebody with a lot of phases and identities," countering, "I don't see myself that way." But as far back as *Tarantula*, his mid-sixties collection of prose and poetry, even his own "ghost too / was more than one person." The conceit vitalizes his strongest eighties songs, significantly "Jokerman" and "I and I," and is the crux of Todd Haynes's dazzling experimental Dylan biopic, *I'm Not There* (2007), in which six actors portray him. As Sam Shepard already reckoned in 1977, for the *Rolling Thunder Logbook*:

> Dylan has invented himself. He's made himself up from scratch. That is, from the things he had around him and inside him. Dylan is an invention of his own mind. The point isn't to figure him out but to take him in. He gets into you anyway, so why not just take him in? He's not the first one to have invented himself, but he's the first one to have invented Dylan. No one invented him before him. Or after. What happens when someone invents something outside himself like an airplane or a freight train? The thing is seen for what it is. It's seen as something incredible because it's never been seen before, but it's taken in by the people and changes their lives in the process. They don't stand around trying to figure out what it isn't, forever. They use it as a means to an adventure.

The *adventure*, though, of "I Contain Multitudes" is overhearing Dylan as he sorts through the strangeness of his invention, and his "phases and identities," here not sequential or chronological, but palpable now all at once. "In what disorder we live, how many fragments of ourselves were scattered," Elena Ferrante remarked, "as if to live were to explode into splinters." Whitman's poem is a celebration, and an invitation, "Who wishes to walk with me?," he asks. Elsewhere in "Song of Myself," he could position himself as a vehicle for darker American impulses—"Through me many long dumb voices, / Voices of the interminable generations of prisoners and slaves." But Dylan's vision, perhaps because his self-perceptions are even more entangled in the national past, present, and future, is bleaker. In Section 51, Whitman's leaves and blossoms "wilt," yet he's assured of more. "I have fill'd them, emptied them. / And proceed to fill my next fold of the future." By the start of "I Contain Multitudes" Dylan's are "dying," and unremittingly. "Today and tomorrow and yesterday too / The flowers are dying like all things do." A vivid shorthand triad of proper names indicates some of the diverse profiles of his inner expanse—"I'm just like Anne Frank—like Indiana Jones / And them British bad boys the Rolling Stones"—though Dylan accents his sinister tinges, malice, loathing, and betrayal. "I'll show you my heart," he volunteers. "But not all of it—only the hateful part / I'll sell you down the river—I'll put a price on your head / What more can I tell ya—I sleep with life and death in the same bed." By the finish, Dylan skews Whitman's platonic overture into sexual disgust, and tacit vengeance:

Get lost, Madam—get up off my knee
Keep your mouth away from me
I'll keep the path open—the path in my mind
I'll see to it that there's no love left behind. . . .

"I Contain Multitudes" amplifies specific touchstones of "Murder Most Foul," notably memory. Dylan artfully summons what initially rings as a throwaway line—"Half my soul baby belongs to you"—from a Howard Schwartz short story, "The Angel of Forgetfulness," wherein a rabbi loses his power of recall as punishment for his carelessness. Those clamorous "skeletons in the walls" shade American history into nightmarish catacombs for agitated spirits, as Dylan once again designates a dead president and, suitably for nudges of Whitman, the Civil War. When he sings, "I carry four pistols and two large knives," he's referencing Abraham Lincoln's friend and bodyguard Ward Hill Lamon, as described by Shelby Foote in *The Civil War.*

In *Chronicles*, Dylan framed his own intensive focus on the Civil War during the early sixties:

> I needed to slow my mind down if I was going to be a composer with anything to say.

I couldn't exactly put in words what I was looking for, but I began searching in principle for it, over at the New York Public Library . . . In one of the upstairs reading rooms I started reading articles in newspapers on microfilm from 1855 to about 1865 to see what daily life was like. I wasn't so much interested in the issues as intrigued by the language and rhetoric of the times. Newspapers like the *Chicago Tribune*, the *Brooklyn Daily Times* and the *Pennsylvania Freemen*. Others, too, like the *Memphis Daily Eagle*, the *Savannah Daily Herald* and *Cincinnati Enquirer*. It wasn't like it was another world, but the same one only with more urgency, and the issue of slavery wasn't the only concern. There were news items about reform movements, antigambling leagues, rising crime, child labor, temperance, slave-wage factories, loyalty oaths and religious revivals . . . Lincoln comes into the picture in the late 1850s. He is referred to in the Northern press as a baboon or giraffe, and there were a lot of caricatures of him . . . You wonder how people so united by geography and religious ideals could become such bitter enemies. After a while you become aware of nothing but a culture of feeling, of black days, of schism, evil for evil, the common destiny of the human being getting thrown off course. It's all one long funeral song . . . The suffering is endless, and the punishment is going to be forever. . . . The age that I was living in didn't resemble this age, but yet it did in some mysterious and traditional way. Not just a little bit, but a lot. There was a broad spectrum and commonwealth that I was living upon, and the basic psychology of that life was every bit a part of it. If you turned the light towards it you could see the full complexity of human nature. Back there, America was put on the cross, died and was resurrected. There was nothing synthetic about it. The godawful truth of that would be the all-encompassing template behind everything that I would write.

Whether the Bob Dylan of his first Manhattan winter actually took up residence on Forty-Second Street in such scholastic guise can be for us no more than fanciful retrospective conjecture. Like enough, the account signifies the momentousness of the Civil War for him in the late-twentieth century, continuing into the twenty-first—and the 1860s pervade "The Lost Land" section of *Chronicles*, as well as *"Love And Theft"* (2001), *Modern Times* (2006), *Tempest* (2012), and *Masked and Anonymous* (2003). As the second chapter of his belated Nobel Lecture, "I Contain Multitudes" reiterates the priority of race and the Civil War for his music. Moreover, the song directly speaks to the astonishing scale of his achievement, and the strangeness of how he arrived there, both back in the 1960s and in his unprecedented self-revitalization, starting in 1991. Spontaneity and study, Whitman and Gene Vincent, sex and slavery, Blake and Carl Perkins . . . multitudes.

Consider only his accomplishments over the thirty-year span of this book. In another version of my story, call it the hard-work variant, Dylan took charge, ceased stalking trends, assembled a band, toured relentlessly and, when eventually he renewed his songwriting, produced his own records. From 1992 through the fall of 2024 he performed nearly 3,000 times. Many years he exceeded 100 shows—a career high of 120 concerts in 1995; and that's an average of an appearance every three days. (For context, he performed 72 dates in 1965, his sixties top, and just 48 in 1964.) He toured Japan, China, and South America, performed at the White House and for the pope. And throughout he consistently rose to whatever a live occasion demanded—Woodstock '94, before a crowd of some 350,000; or Nara that same year, fronting a symphony orchestra. Dylan also released a dozen studio albums—*Good as I Been to You* (1992), *World Gone Wrong* (1993), *Time Out of Mind*, *"Love And Theft," Modern Times*, *Together Through Life* (2009), *Christmas in the Heart* (2009), *Tempest*, *Shadows in the Night* (2015), *Fallen Angels* (2016), *Triplicate* (2017), and *Rough and Rowdy Ways*—and realized his strongest critical and popular acclamation since *Blood on the Tracks* (1975) and the Rolling Thunder Revue in the mid-seventies. He wrote a memoir—*Chronicles*. He cowrote and acted in an independent film—*Masked and Anonymous*, and contributed songs to other movie soundtracks. He hosted over a hundred episodes of a weekly radio program—*Theme Time Radio Hour* (2006–2009). He created a label, Egyptian Records, and curated tributes to Jimmie Rodgers and Hank Williams, while joining other celebrations—Johnny Cash, Sun Records, Doc Pomus, and Frank Sinatra. He eulogized dead friends and mentors—Cash, Allen Ginsberg, Jerry Garcia, George Harrison, Little Richard, Warren Zevon, and Petty. Playwright Conor McPherson spun a musical from his songs, *Girl from the North Country*, at the Old Vic in London and the Public Theater in New York, and on Broadway. James Mangold directed a biographical film about his life in the 1960s, *A Complete Unknown* (2024). After the publication of *Drawn Blank*, in 1994, Dylan started to circulate his drawings, paintings, prints, and welded sculptures in catalogs, galleries, and museums. Columbia Records and Dylan's New York office coordinated a parallel musical biography for him through *The Bootleg Series*, revisiting and revamping his every past incarnation across multi-CD volumes, while simultaneously introducing crucial "new" songs to the canon, among them "Blind Willie McTell," "Series of Dreams," "Angelina," "Foot of Pride," and "Dignity." He received every possible music or film trophy—Grammy Awards, an Academy Award, a Golden Globe Award, and the Polar Music Prize; and the more elusive national and international honors that increasingly acknowledged his uniqueness as a creative artist—Commandeur des Arts et des Lettres, Kennedy Center Honors, the Dorothy and Lillian Gish Prize, a Pulitzer Prize, National Medal of Arts, Presidential Medal of Freedom, and the Nobel Prize for Literature.

Fierceness of empathy and memory powered Dylan's extraordinary revival as a writer, performer, and even public figure, albeit of a peculiar hidden-in-plain-sight cast. His vertiginous intuition is that the past erupts into the present, an intuition he then embodies and renders literal through allusion and collage. A phrase he buried in his liner notes for *World Gone Wrong* lodges an implicit credo, "learning to go forward by turning back the clock," although the draft in his Tulsa archive is more pointed and apt: "go forward turn back the face of time or fire a few random shots at the clock itself."

Dylan's late-twentieth- and twenty-first-century albums center projects that probe multifaceted historical subjects—the legacies of minstrelsy, for example, on *"Love And Theft"*—and sometimes flare around hidden sparks: Henry Timrod and Ovid on *Modern Times*; Homer on *Tempest.* Collage proved a late instance of the conscious artistry he famously ascribed to his painting lessons in 1974 with artist Norman Raeben—"He put my mind and my hand and my eye together in a way that . . . I did consciously what I used to do unconsciously." Inventions of decision, as much as magic. In a bravura collaged stanza from "Summer Days," Dylan sings:

> *She's looking into my eyes, she's holding my hand,*
> *She's looking into my eyes, she's holding my hand,*
> *She says, "You can't repeat the past." I say, "You can't? What do you mean you can't? Of course you can."*

Without ever winking, Dylan's puckish, snaky lines dramatize here precisely how he can, in fact, "repeat the past," since his lyric slyly repeats a conversation from *The Great Gatsby.* On *Modern Times* he veers from mediumistic—"I've been conjuring up all these long dead souls from their crumblin' tombs" to self-mocking. "I'm so hard pressed, my mind tied up in knots / I keep recycling the same old thoughts." His paintings, too, pursue riddles in their source photographs (often movie stills), and even *Theme Time Radio Hour* honors a 1940 radio program written by Alan Lomax, directed by Nicholas Ray, and featuring Woody Guthrie.

Poems, novels, films, and songs, whatever else they do, direct conversations with the great dead, and Dylan's ghostwriting after 1992 is the most industrious and far-reaching of his life. Late in the sixteenth century, as historian Jonathan Spence recounts, the Jesuit missionary Matteo Ricci "taught the Chinese how to build a memory palace":

> He told them that the size of the place would depend on how much they wanted to remember. . . . One could create modest palaces, or could build less dramatic structures such as a temple compound, a

> cluster of government offices, a public hostel, or a merchants' meeting lodge. If one wished to begin on a still smaller scale, then one could erect a simple reception hall, a pavilion, or a studio. . . . In summarizing this memory system, he explained that these palaces, pavilions, divans were mental structures to be kept in one's head, not solid objects to be literally constructed out of "real" materials. . . . To everything we wish to remember, wrote Ricci, we should give an image; and to every one of these images we should assign a position where it can repose peacefully until we are ready to reclaim it by an act of memory.

In his art after 1992 Dylan is teaching himself—and us—how to build a memory palace—mental structures, particularly songs, that will house past and present, the living and the dead. For *Chronicles* he concludes his account of going to the New York Public Library to read contemporary newspaper reportage on the Civil War with a spatial image of his memory that shrinks Ricci's elate palace to a roadside storage unit. "I crammed my head full of as much of this stuff as I could stand and locked it away in my mind out of sight, left it alone," Dylan writes. "Figured I could send a truck back for it later."

C

JUST A BLUE-EYED BOSTON BOY

Chronology and facts aside, all might have been different, and deeply sad. Dylan's self-reinvention after 1991, his creative realizations and stately advance from eighties vexation to national treasure, now can look inevitable. But a strange over-promising Mobius strip dynamic informs his resurgence such that the same evidence points to opposing resolutions, depending on whether our vantage is now or 1992. Endless touring—seven years!—with no new songs to perform, only past glories, and the words of other writers. Successive albums of folk, blues, and country covers—*Good as I Been to You*, in 1992, and *World Gone Wrong*, in 1993; at least *Bob Dylan*, his debut thirty years prior, included two original compositions, "Song to Woody" and "Talkin' New York," among the standards. Finally, the tripartite excavation of his Columbia archives—*The Bootleg Series Volumes 1–3 (Rare & Unreleased) 1961–1991*. Back in the early nineties such gestures appeared to announce *That's All Folks!* So many great musicians have wound down with a farewell tour, a cenotaph anthology, and a last roots ramble. Yet in twenty-first century retrospect, those reinvigorated live shows, those resonant covers, and those "lost" masterworks, also were the rudiments of his restoration.

"It was important for me to come to the bottom of the legend thing, which has no reality at all," Dylan told Robert Hilburn in the *Los Angeles Times* in 1992. "What's important isn't the legend, but the art, the work." Early on in this artistic and personal revival, he obviously recognized his crisis, though bottoming out and refocusing on "the art, the work" would demand toil and patience and time. "In the early '90s, the media lost track of me, and that was the best thing that could happen," he would acknowledge to Edna Gunderson in *USA Today* in 2001. "It was crucial, because you can't achieve greatness under media scrutiny. You're never allowed to be less than your legend. When the media picked up on me again five or six years later, I'd fully developed into the performer I needed to be and was in a position to go any which way I wanted."

But first, beyond that glazed zombie of himself at Live Aid, a few more brief episodes for scale and perspective of just how lost Dylan seemed in the eighties:

- During the "We Are the World" recording sessions in January of 1985, Dylan struggled with the melody line, a discomfiture not altogether to his own demerit given both the corniness of the Michael Jackson–Lionel Richie song and the lyrical temerity: Who's that *we*? And whose *world*? Dylan turned to Stevie Wonder for direction and asked him to play it on the studio piano. Wonder then mimicked Dylan to Dylan, who then mimicked Wonder mimicking him for the official take. (See Bao Nguyen's *The Greatest Night in Pop* for the video documentation.)
- In *Hearts of Fire*, a 1987 rock remake of *A Star Is Born*, Dylan shyly, maladroitly plays Billy Parker, an aging musician who walked away from it all to raise chickens, but is now heading to England for an oldies concert or, as he says, "a kind of freak show in a carnival." Dylan, Fiona (Flanagan), and Rupert Everett—all vie for most preposterous here. The film is inadvertently almost salvaged by a sequence where Dylan as Billy drawls to Fiona as Molly, a fledgling singer-songwriter, "I guess I always knew I was never one of them rock-'n'-roll singers who was gonna win any Nobel Prize." *Hearts of Fire* eventually headed to video in 1990, without receiving an American theatrical release. Dylan's Elvis movie. . . .

- When Dylan teamed with the Grateful Dead for six outdoor stadium shows in July of 1987, he forgot lyrics, and often chant-sang those he managed to retrieve in a rheumy splutter. "It was as if we never practiced," Bob Weir protested. The story goes that in February of the next year, Dylan phoned the offices of the Grateful Dead in San Raphael, California, and asked to join the band; but someone among the wary, level-headed Dead vetoed his proposal. A return engagement at Great West Forum in 1989 was nearly as pathetic and scary. Dylan played a version of "Knockin' on Heaven's Door" where he actually sounds like he is dying. The summer stadium stint with the Grateful Dead led to one of his two worst live albums, *Dylan & the Dead* (1989)—the other, also of the eighties, is *Real Live* (1984).
- On tour with Tom Petty and the Heartbreakers, Dylan retained the female backup singers from his prior gospel shows. "I had them up there," he later confirmed, "so I wouldn't feel so bad."
- Dylan's stage look—always a resonant gauge of his moods and aspirations, from the early sixties on—swerved in the eighties from a leather vest, muscle Tee, driving gloves, and dangly earrings combo that implied he hoped he was Keith Richards to a hoodie, cap, and dark glasses disguise that declared he didn't want to be there.
- During an acoustic performance of "Desolation Row" in Melbourne, Australia, on April 5, 1992, Dylan stumbled over the "Einstein, disguised as Robin Hood" verse and apparently started crying as he approached and attempted to sing the lines, "You would not think to look at him / But he was famous long ago." According to concert attendees, he then retreated to the rear of stage, his back to the audience, as the band continued into an instrumental. After Dylan returned for a final verse, he sounded—on recordings of the show—as though about to break down again when he sings, "When you asked how I was doing / Was that some kind of joke?"

The era produced what are arguably his feeblest studio albums—*Down in the Groove* (1986) and *Knocked Out Loaded* (1988)—and, as Dylan recapped in *Chronicles*, "In reality I was just above a club act." That is, if your club leases space at the *Inferno*. Rock bottom of this slow debasement arrived on February 20, 1991, when he was awarded a Grammy Lifetime Achievement Award at Radio City Music Hall. As George W. Bush threatened invasion of Iraq and Kuwait, and Dylan, by his own report ill with a cold and fever, performed "Masters of War," his rendition as furious and unaccommodating as his vocals were undecipherable and nasal. Once he took his plaque from Jack Nicholson, he looked around for an exit, before lingering at the mic to channel nineteenth-century Rabbi Shimshon Rafael Hirsch in the bodily aspect of his late father, Abram Zimmerman:

> Well, my daddy, he didn't leave me too much, you know, he was a very simple man, and he didn't leave me a lot, but what he did tell me was this—[long pause]—He said so many things, you know—[nervous audience laughter]—He did say, son, "you know it's possible to become so defiled in this world that your own father and mother will abandon you, and if that happens God will always believe in your own ability to mend your own ways." Thank you. . . .

This is where I come—or *came back*—in. At my Jesuit high school in late sixties Boston, I fixated on Bob Dylan, more infatuated with him than I was even with Beckett, after John Shea in Honors English class at BC High loaned me *Highway 61 Revisited*. I refused to return it for weeks, flipping the LP over into the night, until my father purchased a copy for me at Jason's Luggage and Music in Quincy Square. For a while I toted my Grove Press Beckett trilogy—*Molloy*, *Malone Dies*, and *The Unnamable*—and my vinyl copy of *Highway 61 Revisited* pretty much everywhere, no matter that the probabilities of securing a tranquil reading perch or a handy stereo were nil. This Dylan obsession survived through the astonishing Rolling Thunder Revue, during which Dylan & Co. played the tiny Harvard Square Theater in 1975, and included a drive to New York in 1971 when he reemerged as a guest of George Harrison at the Concert for Bangladesh. My college freshman literature instructor once volunteered that she was in attendance at Newport in 1965, yet refused to answer whether she was among those who booed Dylan and his electric band, thereby coyly revealing her spot on the wrong side of the story, or so I thought. Divorced twice before she reached thirty, volatility and accommodation were among her clashing modes, sometimes adventurously bohemian, other times the righteous WASP of her classic aspirations, a ghost-like soul as confounding to herself as to others. Whenever I ran into her afterwards, she imparted the forlorn, absorbed air of someone who had just missed a train. Boo? Cheer? Reconsider? Regret? She couldn't say.

Yet at some point in the 1970s I slipped away—*Street Legal*? *Slow Train Coming*? The sway of punk and new wave? The glorious Boston bands scene? I would listen to poet friends who still loved all Dylan delivered—*Down in the Groove*, and *Knocked Out Loaded*, too—and their fidelity dumbstruck me as sorry and cultish. But that bizarre evening at Radio City he confessed his artistic decline as a *spiritual* failing—*defiled*, *abandon*, *mend your own ways*—and as a lapsed Catholic I instantly recognized his torment, his despond, his guilt. Soon after, I started to hunt down what I had missed, official releases first, and then I scoured the Greenwich Village shops that stocked bootlegs. I saw Dylan perform at Jones Beach in July of 1991, and at least once—but often several shows—every year since, until COVID canceled his 2020 tours.

When Dylan for *Chronicles* evokes the performances at Alan Lomax's Third Street loft that first persuaded him that music could concentrate "spiritual experiences"—Roscoe Holcomb, Clarence Ashley, Dock Boggs, Mississippi John Hurt, and particularly Mike Seeger, cofounder of the New Lost City Ramblers—he silently inlays into his memories phrases from *Touchstones: A Book of Daily Meditations for Men*, a recovery self-help book published by Hazelden, the alcohol and drug treatment center founded in Center City, Minnesota. (*Touchstones* also quotes him in the entry for December 21, "He not busy being born is busy dying.") Fascinating, too, that the next step in Dylan's creative revitalization involved two albums of folk, blues, and country songs, that essentially recreate Lomax's bimonthly soirees. As he remembers Seeger—who passed away in 2009—for *Chronicles,* Dylan might as well be describing his aims for *Good as I Been to You* and *World Gone Wrong*: "He played on all the various planes, the full index of the old-time styles, played in all the genres and had all the idioms mastered—Delta blues, ragtime, minstrel songs, buck-and-wing, dance reels, play party, hymns and gospel." And when he remembers Seeger's impact on him in 1961, he might as well be describing his transformative hopes for *Good as I Been to You* and *World Gone Wrong* on his 1991 self:

> Nobody could just learn this stuff, and it dawned on me that I might have to change my inner thought patterns . . . that I would have to start believing in possibilities that I wouldn't have allowed before, that I had been closing my creativity down to a very narrow, controllable scale . . . that things had become too familiar and that I might have to disorientate myself. . . . I can't say I'd seen any performances that were like spiritual experiences until I went to Lomax's loft. I pondered it. I wasn't ready to act on any of it but I knew somehow, though, that if I wanted to stay playing music, that I would have to claim a larger part of myself.

The *Touchstones* entries hidden inside his recollections of Seeger float a parallel mini-narrative:

> June 12: This program is not a map of the uncharted territory. It is a guide for survival in the wilderness. It tells us how to orient ourselves when there are no familiar landmarks and how to learn and grow from the experience.
>
> June 29: Expressing anger does not have to be abusive or rejecting. It can mean we care enough to be fully involved and we will not leave after we express it. We can learn to hear others in their anger rather than attempt to control or evade their message. In the process we are invigorated and feel healthier because we are claiming a larger part of ourselves.

> July 21: Many of us men in this program have a struggle with perfectionism. This is a central spiritual issue. Sometimes we feel ashamed or frightened by our imperfections, or we strive so hard to overcome them that we successfully close our lives down to a very narrow, controllable scale. Spiritual awakening means we have a zest for life and accept our imperfections.
>
> November 1: We may have spiritual experiences in our daily lives that we don't think of as spiritual. For many of us, music lifts us from the practical and mundane circumstances of our lives into communion with the universe. One man may like to listen to country music on the radio, another one might play the piano, and another may go to rock concerts . . . Many of us meet our Higher Power through the music we love.

Dylan saw *Good as I Been to You* and *World Gone Wrong* as "necessary," and a way of circling back to his origins. "But this is where it begins for me," he wrote.

In June of 1992 Dylan attempted to record an album of covers with David Bromberg and a full band at Acme Studios in Chicago, but soon opted instead for solo acoustic and his own production at his Garage Studio in Malibu—*Good as I Been to You* in July and August 1992, followed by *World Gone Wrong* in May and June 1993. At the time Dylan was evidently listening to *Folk Tapes*, a vast personal musical florilegium curated by his New York office, comprising some 560 songs across 22 volumes, a sort of overhauled, updated, and enlarged Harry Smith *Anthology*. *Folk Tapes* spanned from "After the Ball" by Bill Bolick and "I Just Can't Keep from Crying" by Blind Willie Johnson (Volume 1, numbers 1 and 2) to "The Nearness of You" by Connie Boswell and "You Are Too Beautiful" by Dick Haymes (volume 22, numbers 20 and 21), with Jimmie Rodgers close by Jimmy Reed; Blind Willie McTell next door to Liam Clancy; Memphis Minnie neighboring Gene Autrey, Billie Holiday and the Delmore Brothers; Bing Crosby and Big Maybelle, Jerry Lee Lewis and Muddy Waters, Etta James and Hoagy Carmichael, alongside selective contemporaries,

Townes Van Zandt, Tom Rush, Joan Baez, Ian and Sylvia, Sam Cooke, Tammy Wynette, Toots and the Maytals; and loads of Mike Seeger and other members of the New Lost City Ramblers. *Folk Tapes* includes songs he would soon record—"Black Jack Davey," "Arthur McBride," "Sittin' on Top of the World," "Tomorrow Night," "You're Gonna Quit Me," "Canadee-I-O," "Jim Jones," "Hard Times Come Again No More," "Step It Up and Go," and "Diamond Joe" for *Good as I Been to You*); and "The Two Soldiers," "Love Henry," "The Lone Pilgrim," and "Stack A Lee" for *World Gone Wrong.* Also covers he performed in concert, "The Female Rambling Sailor" and "Duncan and Brady," and songs that would inform his own writing decades hence, "Don't Let Your Deal Go Down," "Tell Ol' Bill," "Someday Baby," "High Water Everywhere," and "The Titanic."

"No filmmaker has identified so closely with the history of cinema," Richard Brody observed of Jean-Luc Godard, "and no filmmaker has looked so deeply into it." Transpose film to music, and that's Bob Dylan, especially after 1992. (And as Quentin Tarantino continued the analogy—"To me, Godard did to movies what Bob Dylan did to music: They both revolutionized their forms.") On *Good as I Been to You* and *World Gone Wrong,* Dylan was effectively starting over with a dig into the subtexts of his past, and his soon-to-be future songwriting—exile, sexual betrayal, revenge, class, militarism, work, minstrelsy, aging, money, language, race, and empire—and with revamped song strategies: contending voices, layered ironies, and multiple points of view. On *Good as I Been to You*, Dylan can sound tentative, as though not yet convinced by his experiment, despite shattering spins like "You're Gonna Quit Me," "Hard Times," and "Diamond Joe." *World Gone Wrong*, as the apocalyptic title counsels, is still darker, but more confident and shaped, and came with surprise liner notes. For all their assorted traditions, "Blood in My Eyes" "Delia," and "World Gone Wrong" are each devasting on the enigmas of human desire. Legacies of the Civil War pervade—"Jack-A-Roe" and, particularly, "Two Soldiers," also known as "Blue Eyed Boston Boy," entrenched in the Confederate victory at Fredericksburg, where 18,500 died; and as

Dylan writes in his annotation, "a battle song extraordinaire, some dragoon officer's epaulettes laying liquid in the mud, physical plunge into Limitationville, war dominated by finance (lending money for interest being a nauseating & revolting thing) love is not collateral."

Still, *Good as I Been to You* and *World Gone Wrong* also project a rival music world, the world of the late twenties and early thirties where Black and White song styles briefly converged, historical circumstances he would scrutinize further on *"Love And Theft"* a decade down the line. Dylan approached the creators of the songs he recorded for these albums as Modernists, and as always he smartly refused to differentiate the collages of Charley Patton and T. S. Eliot. "These people who originated this music, they're all Shakespeares, you know. They're Thomas Edisons, Louis Pasteurs. They invented this type of thing. In a hundred years they'll be notable for that."

Dylan also insisted, "I've treated them as if they were my songs, and not like covers." So another practical, hard-work aspect here is that he was diligently teaching himself how to sing again. The adenoidal bleat that comic impressionists invariably muster as "Bob Dylan" also dates from the late eighties. But for these traditional lyrics he burrows down deep into the syllables and stresses as though no one has ever vocalized the songs before and he is articulating the lines as occasion and necessity require. His immersion is as palpable on the many 1992 and 1993 solo acoustic session recordings in his Tulsa archive that he didn't immediately release, nearly fifty more songs across an expansive topography. Memory—sense memory—is pivotal to *Good as I Been to You* and *World Gone Wrong*, as Dylan once compared his later Great American Songbook covers to "method acting." Among the pleasures of the Tulsa archive is listening to him over the successive takes as he imagines, and then reimagines, who exactly might be voicing a song. After a trial go, Dylan will often ask engineer Debbie Gold, "Does that have anything?" His patience, and sense of the long view, is everywhere in the outtakes. He recorded "White House Blues" in 1992, during the *Good as I Been to You* sessions, but not until 2020 and *Rough and Rowdy Ways* would he recast Charlie Poole's song to launch his own "Key West (Philosopher Pirate)."*

Dylan sometimes gives an impression that *anyone* could write his original songs. As he argued during his MusiCares awards speech in 2015, "I learned lyrics and how to write them from listening to folk songs. . . . If you sang 'John Henry' as many times as me . . . you'd have written 'How many roads must a man walk down' too." Well, maybe. Other times, it's as if Dylan can't believe *he* wrote them. As he marveled to Ed Bradley on "60 Minutes" in 2004, "I don't know how I got to write those songs. . . . Ah, 'Darkness at the break of noon / shadows even the silver spoon / The handmade blade, the child's balloon. . . .' Well, try to sit down and write something like that."

Dylan's word for his late songwriting is "trance"—"It's one of those things where you write on instinct," he remarked to Douglas Brinkley in the *New York Times* upon the release of *Rough and Rowdy Ways*. "Kind of in a trance state. Most of my recent songs are like that." Thus, contra the practical, hard-work portrayal of Dylan's slow resurgence after 1992 that I've been sketching here, his own accounts in interviews and *Chronicles* tend to accent myth, allegory, and magic. In *Chronicles*, for his "metamorphosis" on stage in Locarno, Switzerland, in 1987, he's at once an exorcist and Saul on the road to Damascus:

---

* A more complete listing of the other songs attempted during the *Good as I Been to You* and *World Gone Wrong* sessions runs: "My Blue-Eyed Jane," "John Henry's Hammer," "Nothin' in Rambling," "Keep on the Sunny Side," "Worried Blues," "Roving Blade," "So Doggone Lonesome," "Fond Affection," "The Storms Are on the Ocean," "Sinking in the Lonesome Sea," "The Female Rambling Sailor," "Hello Stranger," "Deep River Blues," "I Can't Be Satisfied," "Blow Your Whistle Freight Train," "White House Blues," "Deep Ellem Blues," "Just Because," and "Trouble Blues" for *Good as I Been to You*; and "My Blue-Eyed Jane" (again), "Come By the Hills," "New Someday Baby," "Lying to Me," "Sincerely," "I've Always Been a Rambler," "Drop Down Momma/Momma Don't Allow Me to Fool Around All Night Long," "Don't Sell It (Don't Give It Away)," "21 Years," "Bonnie Light Horseman," "Twilight Time," "Please Baby," "Travelin' Riverside Blues," "Goodnight My Love," "Mary and the Soldier," "Keep on the Sunny Side" (again), "The Longest Train I Ever Saw," "Someone to Watch Over Me," "There Stands the Glass," "Old and Only in the Way," "I've Always Been a Rambler," "Easy Street," "Steady Rollin' Man," "32-20 Blues," "Moon Going Down," and "The Seeds of Love" for *World Gone Wrong*.

> For an instant I fell into a black hole. The stage was outdoors and the wind was blowing gales, the kind of night that can blow everything away. I opened my mouth to sing and the air tightened up—vocal presence was extinguished and nothing came out . . . Figuring I had nothing to lose and not needing to take any precautions, I conjured up some different type of mechanism to jump-start the other techniques that weren't working. I just did it automatically out of thin air, cast my own spell to drive out the devil. Instantly, it was like a thoroughbred had charged through the gates. Everything came back, and it came back in multidimension. Even I was surprised. It left me kind of shaky. Immediately, I was flying high. This new thing had taken place right in front of everybody's eyes. A difference in energy might have been perceived, but that was about all. Nobody would have noticed that a metamorphosis had taken place. Now the energy was coming from a hundred different angles, completely unpredictable ones. I had a new faculty and it seemed to surpass all the other human requirements. If I ever wanted a different purpose, I had one. It was like I'd become a new performer, an unknown one in the true sense of the word. In more than thirty years of performing, I had never seen this place before, never been here. If I didn't exist, someone would have to have invented me.

For a Locarno variant he offered David Gates in *Newsweek*, Dylan added that a line then came into his head. "It's almost like I heard it as a voice. It wasn't like it was even me thinking it. I'm determined to stand whether God will deliver me or not. And all of a sudden everything just exploded. It exploded every which way . . . After that is when I sorta knew: I've got to go out and play these songs. That's just what I must do."

"False Prophet," the third single from *Rough and Rowdy Ways* continues the Nobel Lecture Dylan introduced with "Murder Most Foul" and "I Contain Multitudes," and underscores the spiritual, the mythic, and the allegorical, although across contrary, irreconcilable slants. His departure melody, "If Lovin' Is Believing," the B-side of Billy "The Kid" Emerson's

1954 Sun hit "No Teasing Around," is a song about a man whose lover isn't convinced—"If lovin' is believing, tell me why you don't believe in me"; and Dylan presumably ("no teasing around") is sending up his sixties reputation as an oracle. Still, religious associations proliferate—Egyptian, Jewish, Christian, and Zen. But for a lyric grounded in the holy, "False Prophet" can register almost aggressively violent and cheerless. The final line lodges the song as posthumous—"I can't remember when I was born and I forgot when I died"—a solemn evocation of the Egyptian funerary text, *Book of the Dead*, as are other phrases, "day without end," "anger, bitterness, and doubt," and "I just know what I know."

Dylan echoes the descent down to the land of dead souls in Book 6 of the *Aeneid*: "Hello Mary Lou—Hello Miss Pearl / My fleet footed guides from the underworld." Although his tutors here aren't the Sibyl but a flirtatious woman in a Gene Pitney song (Mary Lou) and Jimmie Rodgers's influential teacher (Miss Pearl Pope), "False Prophet" sustains a concurrent Roman setting. (Incidentally, might he also echo his own "Subterranean Homesick Blues"? "Maggie comes fleet foot. . . ."?) Dylan elicits Augustus—"I'm the first among equals, second to none"—and the Roman civil war—"I'm here to bring vengeance on somebody's head"; and so doing hoists the ghost of yet another assassinated ruler, Julius Caesar. As Rome transitions from republic to empire, the Eternal City bleeds into the Sermon on the Mount, the Psalms, Augustine of Hippo, and John Winthrop's America. "Oh you poor Devil—look up if you will / The City of God is there on the hill."

"False Prophet" contrasts what looks like a futile spiritual quest, "I've searched the world over for the Holy Grail," with what sounds like an archetypal spiritual trial, "I climbed a mountain of swords on my bare feet," as Dylan mobilizes a koan from the thirteenth-century Zen compilation *The Gateless Barrier.* Yet how can a seeker be so certain? Or when a self-styled prophet asserts they "sing songs of love . . . [and] songs of betrayal," what's the difference between betrayal and love for a fallen world? "False Prophet" rewrites "Man of Peace" from *Infidels*—"You know that sometimes Satan comes as a man of peace"—but without the certainty that evil is so promptly distinguished from good. Who's singing "False Prophet" anyways? The devil? God? A street corner crackpot? Amid his dark wood of religious and historical foliage, Dylan places us, his listeners, dead center in the confusion, much as our lives do, and we have to figure it out. His title couldn't be clearer, though not his slippery refrain, "I ain't no false prophet," at least a double, if not a triple negative. Throughout "False Prophet" menace tussles with seductive flattery until they're interchangeable. "You know darlin' the kind of life that I live / When your smile meets my smile—something's got to give."

For this third installment of his Nobel Lecture, that "mountain of swords on my bare feet" koan from *The Gateless Barrier* exemplifies radical empathy. But so does a starker line in the song from the Egyptian *Book of the Dead* that advances a negative-space version of the same concept: "I opened my heart to the world and the world came in." In "I Contain Multitudes" Dylan's empathy yielded largesse, amplitude. There he was a conduit, a conveyor, a delivery system, a medium, and larger than himself, any self. By "False Prophet" such absolute empathy now means he also—in effect—disappears, as though he isn't really a person in an ordinary sense of the word, but instead a spectral presence. As far back as 1966 Dylan told Jules Siegel in the *Saturday Evening Post*, "I see things that other people don't see. I feel things that other people don't feel. It's terrible. They laugh. I felt like that my whole life . . . All I did was write and sing, paint little pictures on paper, dissolve myself into situations where I was invisible."

In Dylan's dazzling liner notes for *World Gone Wrong*, "About the Songs (what they're about)," the marvel is the fluent magnitude of spirit in this music that he hears, frames, and enunciates for us—myths, allegories, and magic alongside history, religion, economics, technologies, sensibility, other tunes, and restless phantoms—even as he vanishes into that music. Here he writes of the opening songs:

> BROKE DOWN ENGINE is a Blind Willie Mctell masterpiece. it's about trains, mystery on the rails—the train of love, the train

that carried my girl from town—The Southern Pacific, Baltimore & Ohio whatever –it's about variations of human longing—the low hum in meters & syllables. it's about dupes of commerce & politics colliding on tracks, not being pushed around by ordinary standards. it's about revival, getting a new lease on life, not just posing there—paint chipped & flaked, mattress bare, single bulb swinging above the bed. it's about Ambiguity, the fortunes of the privileged elite, flood control—watching the red dawn not bothering to dress.

LOVE HENRY is a "traditionalist" ballad. Tom Paley used to do it. a perverse tale. Henry—modern corporate man off some foreign boat, unable to handle his "psychosis" responsible for organizing the Intelligentsia, disarming the people and infantile sensualist—white teeth, wide smile, lotza money, kowtow to fairy queen exploiters & corrupt religious establishments, career minded, limousine double parked, imposing his will & dishonest garbage in popular magazines. he lays his head on a pillow of down & falls asleep. he shoulda known better, he must've had a hearing problem.

STACK A LEE is Frank Hutchinson's version. what does the song say exactly? it says no man gains immortality thru public acclaim. truth is shadowy. . . .

Shadowy. Artist Alice Neel once vouched of the people who sat for her, "I get so identified when I paint them, when they go home I feel frightful. I have no self—I've gone into this other person."

D

. . . WITH TECHNIQUES AND CERTAIN STRATAGEMS . . .

Dylan *live*—or as some of his tour posters will blast the prospect: *Bob DYLAN In Show and CONCERT! DON'T YOU DARE MISS IT!* This charged particle of a topic might run to multiple books, year by year, band by band, concert by concert—and already has. Three volumes of Paul Williams's *Bob Dylan: Performing Artist.* Andrew Muir's *The Razor's Edge: Bob Dylan & the Neverending Tour* and *One More Night: Bob Dylan's Never Ending Tour.* Paolo Brillo's *No Such Thing as Forever: Images from 30 Years of the Never Ending Tour 1989–2019.* Matthew Ingate's *Together Through Life: My Never Ending Tour With Bob Dylan.*

The old stories still alive inside us. This book, even with four letters of my abecedarium allocated to Bob Dylan on stage, could appear disproportionally concentrated on histories, concepts, and material phenomena such as albums, books, films, paintings, lyrics, and drafts. For he himself persistently affirms the primacy of performance for him above all else, including his writing and recording songs. "Anybody can sit in the studio and make records, but that's unrealistic and they can't possibly be a meaningful performer," he lectured Edna Gunderson at *USA Today* in July of 1988, only a month into the Never Ending Tour. "You have to do it night after night to understand what it's all about . . . I love to roll into town in the early morning and walk the deserted streets before anybody gets up . . . Then, of course, there's playing on the stage in front of live people, feeling hearts and minds moving." And in 1993, he enthused about touring to the *New York Post*, "To me, it's a dream come true," Dylan said. "What could be bad about traveling places, seeing different things, moving? It keeps you alive."

. . . he's *moving* . . . we're *moving.* Gertrude Stein outfitted the prototype for Americans and moving during her lecture "The Gradual Making of the Making of Americans":

> I am always trying to tell this thing that a space of time is a natural thing for an American to always have inside them as something in which they are continually moving. Think of anything, of cowboys, of movies, of detective stories, of anybody who goes anywhere or stays at home and is an American and you will realize that it is something strictly American to conceive a space that is filled with moving, a space of time that is filled always filled with moving. . . .

Continually moving . . . and *think of anything*: songs, singers, and listeners. Recalling conversations he'd had with Miles Davis and Frank Sinatra, Dylan told Mikal Gilmore in *Rolling Stone*, "Songs don't come alive in a recording studio. You try your best, but there's always something missing. What's missing is a live audience."

Performance—*moving*—was Dylan's sole public mode of reinvention through the early 1990s, as he reversed the traditional career revival two-step of a surprise "comeback" album followed by a "triumphant" tour. Fragments in his Tulsa archive suggest that Dylan all along was chasing song ideas, yet not completing any lyrics. He revived himself on the road—seven years of touring without new songs, over 660 shows between *Under the Red Sky* (released September 10, 1990) and *Time Out of Mind* (released September 30, 1997). For grounding and contrast, consider that during a parallel span in the decade prior—fall of 1980 to fall of 1987—he performed something like 166 times total. From 1961 through

1966, he played fewer than 250 shows. Dylan inadvertently almost named the Never Ending Tour during a 1989 interview in *Q Magazine*, when he responded "yeah, yeah," to journalist Adrian Deevoy's introduction of the durable tagline—a tagline that plainly annoys him. "By the way, don't be bewildered by the Never-Ending Tour chatter," he detoured during the liner notes of *World Gone Wrong*. "There was a Never-Ending Tour but it ended in '91 with the departure of guitarist G. E. Smith."

OK. The way time keeps knocking at our door. Will this then be my personal response to Dylan live? Well, yes, and no, and depends on what you mean, though how could it not be? But not personal, I hope, in that cloying sense of some thrills and chills along the far-flung geographic byways of *Bob & Me*. Meaning, I guess, that I will write here of my own responses to some concerts I attended—yet hardly those shows alone, as hundreds of Dylan performances can now be accessed, the physical bootlegs of the past century having yielded to online postings, increasingly also transmitting video as well as audio, a completist's frolic, despite efforts to curb cell phones during the *Rough and Rowdy Ways* tours. And meaning: my responses are inside a book that is already personal in lots of other ways, even beyond my choice of subjects, my ingresses and configurations, and the probably obvious intimation that I've read enough Dylan books over the decades to recognize that the lights and darks of the best of them—the worst, too—are self-projections, flesh made word, of what already burned inside a particular writer's skull; projections that could utter some things clearly, forcibly, others not.

For if Dylan contains multitudes, he is also a mirror for multitudes. In the months after my diagnosis, Dylan wasn't touring because of COVID, so no new shows were circulating. I found that I couldn't stop playing Dylan bootlegs from the early 1990s, CDs that I sometimes hadn't revisited since I originally purchased them at little stores around the West Village, Rockit Scientist (then on Carmine Street), Subterranean Records (on Cornelia Street), Generation Records (on Thompson), and Bleecker Bob's. I was working from home—teaching poetry and nonfiction workshops in the New School Graduate Writing Program at night on Zoom; and collaborating days with Michael Chaiken, the first curator of the Bob Dylan Archive, also on Zoom, towards a catalog for the future Dylan Center in Tulsa as we exchanged decisions, text, and captions. For all the intensity and darkness inherent in what we were discovering, this was not so much an impersonal, scholarly dig into a musical archive as it was a wild and powerful immersion in living, for I was then undergoing various medical treatments, before and after my four surgeries. The archive was vast, wondrous, and architectural long before Dylan's papers and recordings were lodged in a physical building, long before any building was chosen and fitted. As Louise Bourgeois once remarked, "When you summon, when you conjure the memory, in order to make it clearer, you pile up the associations the way you pile up bricks to make an edifice. Memory itself is a form of architecture." COVID weirdly made everything possible. Who among us wasn't operating from home? I remember leading Zoom class discussions and attending catalog sessions with our editors while hooked up to portable pumps that discharged chemicals through my system, all the while hoping the tubes winding around and under my clothes weren't visible on camera. The treatments led up to my surgeries, and there were more treatments after. As the toxins worked on my body, I took to wearing a Telluride Film Festival cap—but who wasn't wearing a cool or funny hat on Zoom in the house?

Our aim for the catalog was to double back on Dylan's trajectory since his first performances with the Jokers, the Shadow Blasters, and the Golden Chords in Hibbing and St. Paul from the vantage of how the Tulsa Archive transformed the Bob Dylan story. Will this here, this book, then be a *comprehensive* accounting of Dylan live? Hardly. Successive band personnel, touring itineraries, song spread sheets, all that would instantly overwhelm my four chapters with lists only. Lists are vital, mimetic, interesting. But on those piles of bootleg CDs from the 1990s I was hearing Dylan reassembling himself, sometimes self-consciously, often tentatively and dubiously, across a succession of haphazard individual performances that collectively suggested someone assuming a long view. Battling himself and his audiences to engage all he had accomplished, and squandered.

Working with what he had, and had left, and what might be next. Night after night, in public. A private inventory, a reckoning as much with past success as ongoing loss, alienation, and diminishment. A high-wire act. As Dylan told Gilmore in another *Rolling Stone* interview, "What I do is all done with techniques and certain stratagems. But they're not intellectual ones; they're designed to make people feel something."

Intimacy, cell to cell. So rather than aim for encyclopedic, I'll instead try to focus some emblematic moments of strategy and feeling. I previously quoted Dylan on the rewards of media indifference to him during the 1990s such that on the road—but free of invasive scrutiny—"I'd fully developed into the performer I needed to be and was in a position to go any which way I wanted." To my ears, those circumstances only emerged with reliability (and consistency) for him as a singer and player in 1994, nearly six years into the Never Ending Tour. I'll acknowledge five specific performances: Nara, on May 22; Woodstock, on August 14; the Roseland Ballroom, on October 19 and 20: and his *MTV Unplugged*, recorded at Sony Music Studios on November 17 and 18.

MTV Unplugged and Woodstock were intensively visible—both televised—and with other challenges. On *Unplugged* Dylan was toiling in the shadows of Nirvana, and a live album that sold five million copies after Kurt Cobain's death; and Eric Clapton, whose *Unplugged* sold twenty-six million, and received six Grammy Awards. At Woodstock he appeared on the main stage between Porno for Pyros and Red Hot Chili Peppers. He needed to reach the young audience of over 350,000 who gathered on Winston Farm, west of Saugerties. For both he stood up to a consequential, many-sided occasion in a confident and authoritative style that had eluded him during, say, the deflation of Live Aid. The Roseland shows, and Nara (also internationally televised), were more experimental. But all of these 1994 shows I'm mentioning manifest the revitalized return of his own radical aspirations for himself as a performer as he would later inscribe them inside—of all places!—a description of Perry Como's singing in *The Philosophy of Modern Song*:

> Perry Como lived in every moment of every song he sang. He didn't have to write the song to do it. He may have believed the songs more than some of the people that wrote them. When he stood and sang, he owned the song and he shared it and we believed every single word. What more could you want from an artist?

Note, lived *in*, not lived, and *believed, owned.* He's stressing an emotional and artistic inhabitation of a song, not random autobiography but craft and empathy.

First, Woodstock. Back in the summer of 1969, Dylan had fled from upstate New York just as the original Three Days of Peace and Music commenced on Yasgur's Farm in Bethel. He was on his way to England to perform at the rival Isle of Wight. As an emblem of my own high school Catholic good-boy naiveté, note that I had purchased tickets only for the second and third days of the festival—$7.00 per day, entrance at 10 a.m.—since the opening conflicted with my part-time job at Siegel's Shoes in Quincy Square, where my father also moonlighted weekends from the post office. I was covering employee summer vacations that week. By second day, of course, no one could drive within 350 miles of Sullivan County. As Al Aronowitz, a journalist and Dylan circle confidant who accompanied him to the Isle of Wight, explained, "In essence, the Woodstock Festival was nothing but a call to Bob to come out and play." His introduction for Woodstock 1994 would echo that call. "We've waited twenty-five years for this. . . ."

Dylan's backing band since early 1993 comprised John Jackson on guitar, Tony Garnier on bass, Bucky Baxter on steel, slide, and dobro, and Winston Watson on drums. "Play fucking loud," did someone once shout? Watson especially got the memo, conjecturing that at some gigs they came on "as loud as MC5, most def." Dressed in a black suit that summoned no exact musical era, yet would have appeared smart in any decade over the foregoing century, Dylan was spot-on and imposing from the first words of his first song, "Jokerman." Spurred by Watson, his electric songs—

"All Along the Watchtower," "God Knows," "Highway 61 Revisited"—radiated power, "750,000 watts of Dylan, this must be heaven" as one pay-per-view commentator raved late in the set. She also conceded that, "We were all kind of holding our collective breath to see how he would be received tonight," but by 1994 his rep for fumbling momentous invitations was no longer in sync with his current shows. His ferocity that day accommodated audacious subtleties. As per his panegyric for Perry Como, Dylan was singing from inside every recoiling phrase. He rescued "I Shall Be Released"—no longer a self-congratulatory, singalong anthem, but here a chain of intimate, ill-fated devastations. A trio of acoustic songs at the core of his set could have turned reckless amid all that outdoor space, but the intimate vocal delicacy of "Don't Think Twice, It's All Right," "Masters of War," and especially "It's All Over Now, Baby Blue" concentrated the mosh pits and far-flung caverns of Mudstock, as it came to be called, into a riveted fifty-seat café. Watson later recalled to Ray Padgett, "When Bob plays acoustic guitar, I think it's the most beautiful thing someone could hear." And on most of the loud songs, he also shifted into electric lead, swapping solos with Jackson. My wife and I watched Woodstock 94 among friends whose only recent encounters of Dylan were his stadium fiascos with their beloved Grateful Dead—for them, he was a sad, dissipated clown, and they were confused.

At Woodstock, the stakes multiplied to infinity by international television, Dylan was reminding us—and maybe himself, too—who he once was. Before even the idea of *then*, and *now*, when another world began to whisper to him. And that's exactly how that anxious pay-per-view commentator appraised his performance: "Bob Dylan, very very much loved all across this planet, thank you very much. Now people are finally going, so that's why Bob Dylan is on the same concert bill as Cypress Hill, I get it, 'Everybody Must Get Stoned!'" His *MTV Unplugged* outing in the fall put forward a more conservative claim to the same reintroduction gesture. As at Woodstock, the preponderance of his songs emanated from the 1960s, but this time he intensified the visual cues, slipping on shades and slipping into a mod polka-dot shirt that signaled 1965. His phrasing, too, notably on "Dignity," an outtake from *Oh Mercy* (1989) and one of the most contemporary songs he played, resonated vintage Dylan—though his tone was far from nostalgic fun. Closer to reflective, plaintive. His touring band supplemented by Brendan O'Brien on Hammond organ, he veered from an acoustic recasting of hits—"Like a Rolling Stone," "Knocking on Heaven's Door," and "All Along the Watchtower"—to a span of elegies, personal ("Shooting Star") and collective ("Tombstone Blues," "John Brown," "Desolation Row," "Dignity," and "With God on Our Side"), including a somber "The Times They Are A-Changin'." During rehearsals he played a downcast and gorgeous "I Want You," and framed by Baxter's pedal steel and Garnier's bowed bass totally overturned the original, pausing on key parallel phrases, "wasn't born . . . to lose you," "not afraid . . . to look at her," and "where I'd like to be . . . but it doesn't matter," as though abandoned on an island a ruined lifetime away from his desires.

Often in *The Philosophy of Modern Song,* Dylan criticizes songwriting that engages only a single topic or mood. "Everything is too full now," he argued, "we are spoon-fed everything. All songs are about one thing and one thing specifically, there is no shading, no nuance, no mystery." For that transposed "I Want You," for instance, he cracked open some hesitations in the introductory verse—perhaps, "The silver saxophones say I should refuse you"—and shifted the song so that it now insinuated the opposite of what the "want you" lyric appeared to affirm. As he wrote elsewhere in *The Philosophy of Modern Song,* "Sometimes songs show up in disguise. A love song can hide all sorts of other emotions, like anger or resentment. Songs can sound happy and contain a deep abyss of sadness." The multiform subjects and tones in a Dylan song will prompt radical and contradictory live interpretations. Quantum entanglements, every feeling with a trillion eyes; Winston Watson correlated this crosscurrent in his stage craft to Miles Davis. Dylan is careful, though, to distinguish his various dynamics. As he told Jonathan Lethem in *Rolling Stone,* "You've probably heard it said that all the arrangements change night after night. Well, that's a bunch of bullshit, they don't know what they're talking about. The arrangements don't change night after night. The rhythmic structures are different, that's all. You can't change the arrangements night after night—it's impossible."

Rhythmic structures. Such experimentation infused all aspects of the two shows I attended at the Roseland Ballroom in '94. Dylan repeated a number of songs from *Unplugged* and Woodstock, and the overall arc of his current tour stayed the same: a midway three-song acoustic interval folded into an electric opening and finish. But the Roseland set lists didn't clutch so much to sixties favorites—embracing, at least, *Blood on the Tracks*—and his interplay with the band was even more close and improvisational. The spectrum of tones was broad, credible, and alluring: "Maggie's Farm" both nights might smack of the Clash, but "Tangled Up in Blue" was impish on Wednesday, and tense and touchy on Thursday. There were radiant acoustic run-throughs—"One Too Many Mornings" and "It's All Over Now, Baby Blue" the first show; "The Lonesome Death of Hattie Carroll" and "Boots of Spanish Leather" the second. Smart syncopated leads—"Most Likely You Go Your Way (And I'll Go Mine")" one night; "All Along the Watchtower" the next. Across the concerts he carried off some of his most resistant live songs: "Positively Fourth Street," "Joey," and "Like a Rolling Stone." Throughout, his surprising, fresh phrasing joined wit to exigency and crisis. As his Perry Como ordinance demanded, Dylan *owned* each vocal, abiding in a lyric line by line, at times syllable for syllable. At Roseland he wasn't reminding anyone of his former anything. He projected a sort of imaginary tomorrow where every one of his songs had somehow happened at the same time as every other one of his songs. When in the encores of the Thursday show, Neil Young and Bruce Springsteen joined him on stage for "Rainy Day Women #12 & 35" and "Highway 61 Revisited," the occasion felt the inverse of his 30th Anniversary Concert, just two years prior. That night Dylan had looked like he could use some propping up from his famous pals. Here, by extending the invitation to play with him, he appeared to be doing them the favor.

We wish for maps that never existed, will never exist. Nara was still more Utopian, and maybe more unexpected, too. Over three nights

Dylan participated in "The Great Music Experience," a UNESCO Cultural Development Project at the eighth century Buddhist temple of Todai-ji in Nara, Japan, site of the world's largest bronze Buddha statue. Each night he performed three songs, "A Hard Rain's A-Gonna Fall," "I Shall Be Released," and "Ring Them Bells," backed by some Western musicians, including Jim Keltner and Phil Palmer, but also by the New Tokyo Philharmonic Orchestra conducted by Michael Kamen. This was Dylan's first time singing with a classical orchestra—the first time singing required him to heed a score, the first time his own voice wasn't intrinsically the lead instrument. This was a time-honored domain of professional singing he supposedly couldn't do. But "A Hard Rain's A-Gonna Fall" in the only country to experience the atomic bomb? Then, "I Shall Be Released," and "Ring Them Bells"? Souls of the vaporized dead. Dylan was serious, rapt, consumed. Coming off stage on the third night, he reportedly gushed that he hadn't sung so well for fifteen years. "Because all my life, people have been following me," he explained later to "The Great Music Experience" executive producer Tony Hollingsworth. "In this case Michael was conducting. I had to fall in line . . . You know an orchestra doesn't wait for you." Fifteen years back? That would roughly be, give or take, the Rolling Thunder Review.

Nara, Woodstock, Roseland, and MTV *Unplugged*—all were different, all with distinct hazards and opportunities. For each, though, Dylan did what he needed to do. In his Locarno mythic version of his reinvention, those extraordinary live skills should have fallen upon him from on high in 1988, at the launch of his as yet unnamed Never Ending Tour—and though, fascinatingly, his 1988 shows were visibly stronger, visibly more compelling, his reliability soon subsided. Wasn't 1991 probably his worst year live ever? His delivery lapsing into mumbles and slurs, as during a big band performance of "Like a Rolling Stone," for instance, at David Letterman's *10th Anniversary Special* in 1992. In the hard-work variant of his reinvention, by contrast, the years leading up to 1994 find Dylan nearly always trying, with erratic results. Sometimes dazzling, but not steadily. Sometimes awful, yet not invariably. A band of his own, extended tours, his return to harmonica, a dry run at lead guitar, presumably other personal modifications as well: he was mobilizing a future where recently there was only his receding past. Still, online you can click through websites with names like "Best of the NET" and "Five Brilliant Live Performances . . ." of any year from 1988 through 1993, only to hear him mistaking speed for intensity, shouting for conviction, or just singing foggy, rheumy, and nasal. Force—and forced, too. Not that there aren't wonders preserved in those digital anthologies and annuals. "Boots of Spanish Leather" at Jones Beach, in 1988. "Shot of Love" at Stadio Comunale in Livorno, in 1989. "Tight Connection to My Heart (Has Anyone Seen My Love)" at Hammersmith Odeon, London, in 1990, and "Disease of Conceit" with him on piano three nights later, also at Hammersmith. "Idiot Wind" at The Warfield, San Francisco, in 1992, with Jerry Garcia on guitar. "Gates of Eden" at the Huntsville Convention Center, Alabama, in 1993.

Dylan's Perry Como adage again is a shrewd augury for these early '90s revelations. When any Dylan performance is off, the predicament usually isn't so simple as a rushed or adenoidal vocal. An off-performance tends to indicate that on a given night he isn't *living in* the song, doesn't *believe* it, and can't *own* it. Off-performances might further be interpreted as Dylan focusing on himself rather than on what he might be singing. In an array of off-performances across the early '90s—the notorious 1991 Stuttgart concert heads critical lists, yet there were copious others—he can sound like someone who used to be Bob Dylan staging not an individual song but his own amorphous pain, his sadness, grief, regret, disgust, and disarray. "The heart will break, but broken live on," Byron wrote in *Don Juan.* Dylan's body is also his archive, and at assorted early '90s concerts he was a slouched figure in a shapeless checked wool sports jacket. His live dynamic is another apostrophe along his empathy/disappears index. When he's on, Dylan empathizes so intensively and absolutely with a song that he disappears inside the instant-upon-instant disclosure of it. In *The Philosophy of Modern Song,* he resists opportune paraphrase for this radical implication and deep-down vocal embodiment. Writing of Uncle

Dave Macon's "Keep my Skillet Good and Greasy," he recalls, "Sometimes people ask songwriters what a song means, not realizing if they had more words to explain it they would have used them in the song." And writing of Nina Simone's "Don't Let Me Be Misunderstood," he notes, "Like any piece of art, songs are not seeking to be understood. Art can be appreciated or interpreted but there is seldom anything to understand."

Just as on his early '90s studio albums, for live performances too he turned first to folk, blues, and country covers to relight his way. When his own songs eluded him, there was a guess, a hunch, a conviction that the tradition would guide him back to performing. "Eileen Aroon," "Wild Mountain Time," and "Barbara Allen" in 1988. "Lakes of Pontchartrain," "Trail of the Buffalo," and "In the Pines" in 1989. "When First Unto This Country" and "Pretty Peggy-O" in 1990. "Golden Vanity" and "Roving Gambler" in 1991. "Little Moses," "Female Ramblin' Sailor," and "The Girl on the Greenbriar Shore" in 1992. "Weeping Willow" and "I'm Moving On" in 1993. After my diagnosis, and during the first months of my treatments, his folk, blues, and country covers on far-flung bootleg compilations I once upon a time hunted down years before in the Village were the Dylan live performances I listened to at home: *Golden Vanity*, *20/20 Vision*, *A Highway of Diamonds Vol. 3*, *One Timers*, *Under the Covers*, *More Hard to Find*, and an astonishing 9 CD box set, *The Genuine Never Ending Tour Covers Collection 1988–2000*. Dylan gleaning night by night who on stage he might now wish to be.

. . . 1995, 1996, 1997. If everything before somehow led to 1994, the years immediately after were even more impressive, thrilling, and—his new curveball—dependable. The shows I saw. The Paradise Lost Tour with Patti Smith at the Beacon Theatre, December 11, 1995, and their tender duet on "Dark Eyes." A solid outing in Poughkeepsie, May 1, 1996. A magnificent turn at Wolf Trap, August 24, 1997, after Larry Campbell replaced John Jackson on guitar. Alan Lomax was among the crowd. "There is a distinguished gentleman here who came," Dylan told us. "I don't know if many of you have heard of him. Yes, he's here, he's made a trip out to see me. I used to know him years ago. I learned a lot there, and

Alan . . . Alan was one of those who unlocked the secrets of this kind of music. So if we've got anybody to thank, it's Alan. Thanks, Alan."

After 1994, Dylan honored his debts. He rose to any demands. In 1995, a concert for the opening of the Rock and Roll Hall of Fame in Cleveland, and an eightieth birthday tribute to Frank Sinatra, where at "Mr. Frank's" request he sang "Restless Farewell," accompanied by his touring band and a string section. In 1996, the Prince's Trust Charity Concert in Hyde Park, London, as Ron Wood and Al Kooper joined him. A space of time that is filled always filled with moving.

In 1994, 104 shows. In 1995, 116. *Dependable.* Yet the risk? Ladies and gentlemen, please welcome the Rolling Stones . . . Paul McCartney . . . the Beach Boys . . . Bob Dylan. Five, six, and now closing in on seven years without an original song. Henceforth just another upright but spent oldies act? *Dependable.* Over? Promising? Then, by the spring and early summer of 1996, one began to hear whispers about him trying out tunes at soundchecks, tunes for his own new songs that—as it turned out—would have much to say to all those folk, blues, and country covers.

E

THE PALACE OF PAIN

Everything Dylan put into practice after his ". . . so defiled in this world . . ." throwdown at the 1991 Grammys led to *Time Out of Mind*, and moreover *needed* to lead there. Six years later this album of incandescent and bleak new writing was the achievement necessary to vindicate his otherwise irresolute albums of covers and those otherwise hesitant circuits of touring his old songs. Yet the album just as crucially also took on the burdens of his history. "I've been drinking—drinking forbidden juices / I'm thinking—can't live anymore on lame excuses," as he wrote on a draft manuscript page for "Dirt Road Blues," now preserved in his Tulsa archive. "I try to remember how I got here," as he wrote on another manuscript for "Million Miles." I've already mentioned my high school and college fixation on Beckett: *Time Out of Mind* is the country blues record Beckett might have made had he made country blues records: those magnificent sentences telling you all those dire things.

Time Out of Mind frames an implicit arc from the opening line of "Love Sick"—"I'm walking through streets that are dead"—right through the aspirational, otherworldly transcendence of "Highlands." Everywhere Dylan stresses loss, regrets, desperation, and fitful lurches from futile motion to torpid immobility. Again and again he mentions walking, but this is not your gallant flaneur spurred by curiosity and discovery. Instead he walks frail, insignificant, shabby, miserable. Song after song vies for the most stunned and dead-end articulations. On "Not Dark Yet," he sings, "Every nerve in my body is so vacant and numb," and "I ain't looking for nothing in anyone's eyes." In "Tryin' to Get to Heaven," he counsels, "When you think that you've lost everything / You find out you can always lose a little more." Words, often clumsy words, that Dylan left on the cutting room floor were more anguished and stalemated. As he wrote towards "Cold Irons Bound"—"It's too late to communicate or connect with anyone . . . I don't want to know the future / I don't want to know a lot of stuff . . . I see thru myself and don't like what I see." Or towards "Can't Wait"—"It's getting harder to disassociate." As he worked towards "Million Miles"—"I used to be good / I'm sliding by."

Thoughts that caress images of ruin and destruction. I read that draft language when I flew to Tulsa after the sale of Dylan's papers and recordings to the George Kaiser Family Foundation was announced to a startled music press on March 2, 2016. By the time I arrived early the following year, curator Michael Chaiken already was in position, but no one else yet had been permitted to consult the archive beyond Michael and some others at Dylan's New York City office, such as Jeff Rosen and Parker Fishel, who helped assemble and organize it. Once in Tulsa I visited the Woody Guthrie Center, the GKFF's initial foray into collections, research, and museums, where I found lyrics, notebooks, and displays, along with references to my own late friend Sis Cunningham, Guthrie's Oklahoma co-conspirator in the Almanac Singers, and Dylan's editor at *Broadside*. When Dylan himself later stopped by the Woody Guthrie Center he was riveted by a document that also intrigued me—Guthrie's handwritten captions for the photographs in *Weegee's People*. "I didn't know Woody could be so funny," he said. I also drove by Tulsa's Central City High School, where I knew writers Joe Brainard and Ron Padgett had graduated in 1960. Brainard was president of the Art Club and corresponding secretary of the Key Club, and he designed *Tom Tom*, the annual yearbook. Incidentally, George Kaiser was part of that Central City High School class. (Kaiser stands just two students away from Brainard in the Key Club senior photo.)

On a Monday morning Chaiken and I met for coffee at Antoinette's on North Main Street, in a downtown neighborhood these days designated the Tulsa Arts District, but known then as the Brady Arts District, around the corner from the former Brady Theater (now the Tulsa Theater) that served as an internment camp for Black citizens during the Tulsa Race Massacre of 1921, when mobs of Whites attacked them, torching their homes and businesses. (As Dylan sang in "Murder Most Foul" on *Rough and Rowdy Ways*, "Take me back to Tulsa to the scene of the crime.") Today, Brady Street, named originally after Klansman Wyatt Tate Brady, is Reconciliation Way, albeit amid occasionally baffling signage that then tied the thoroughfare to another Brady, a figure with no particular claims on Tulsa, the Civil War photographer Mathew Benjamin Brady.

After reading through a short "Finding Aid" for the Bob Dylan Archive, then housed at the University of Tulsa's Gilcrease Museum, I requested two files: "miscellaneous" 1990s writings and his drafts for *Time Out of Mind*. A surprise of the ample '90s folder was the swarm of songs never completed. Beyond a computer printout of Leonard Cohen's "A Thousand Kisses Deep" dated to January 13, 1999, few items could be affixed to a specific moment. Were any songwriting efforts prior to *Time Out of Mind*? The folder also confusingly held "'Cross the Green Mountain," recorded in 2002 for the soundtrack of *Gods and Generals*; and "Tell Ol' Bill," recorded in 2005 for the soundtrack of *North Country*. Yet there was plenty of rueful wreckage in the mood of *Time Out of Mind*—"I can hold death awhile at arm's length," he had written, in a prescient salute to Shakespeare's *As You Like It*. On envelopes, torn notebooks, Mariott and Omni pads, and violet memo pages, Dylan set down lines, stanzas, choruses, and occasionally titles: "Last Rose of Summer," "Technology of the Heart," "Rules & Regulations," and "Altar of Pride." The most clairvoyant words here, though, aren't a faux song lyric, but a sort of scribbled note to self. "Read Ovid." By 2006—at least—Dylan would of course read

Ovid, skillfully layering into the songs on *Modern Times* reverberations of *Tristia*, *Black Sea Letters*, *Amores*, and *Cures for Love*.

When I turned to the *Time Out of Mind* holdings in the archive, I already knew from session outtakes on *Tell Tale Signs: Rare and Unreleased 1989–2006* (*The Bootleg Series Vol. 8*, 2008) that a song Dylan didn't include on the album, "Marchin' to the City," shared a number of lines with "'Til I Fell in Love with You," and a few more with "Not Dark Yet," and that another jettisoned song, "Dreaming of You," overlapped with "Standing in the Doorway." The multiple versions of "Can't Wait" on *Tell Tale Signs* contained passages that never reached the official release, as well as text Dylan later found a place for in "Sugar Baby" on his next album, *"Love And Theft."* In the drafts, though, the scale of these roving lyrics was momentous, and bewildering. Grouping and reordering pages, and mapping as many of the far-flung lyric migrations as I could in the Zarrow Reading Room absorbed much of an alluring week. Classicists and medievalists appeal to ur-poems—poems thought to be a prototype or precursor to a later poem. Behind *Time Out of Mind* I found a half-dozen more ur-songs besides "Dreaming of You" and "Marchin' to the City," each curiously in a more finished state than drafts of the songs they ultimately advanced. He always was a radical reviser—a hallmark of *The Bootleg Series* is how fundamentally a song might evolve from take to take; but never in my experience as rigorously as here. Dylan's strongest album in decades wasn't so much written as rewritten.

For instance—

- "Cold Irons Bound," his fierce, atmospheric blues of spiritual and erotic incarceration, springs from a pair of ur-songs, "Maybe You Should Forget Me" and "The King of Them All." Dylan worked on two pencil drafts of "Maybe You Should Forget Me" before apparently shifting over to "The King of Them All," which survives only as a typed but incomplete and presumably late transcription. All feature the line, "I'm beginning to hear voices and there's no one around," but both versions of "Maybe You Should Forget Me" operate without a consistent refrain, whereas "The King of Them All" repeats, "The king of them all is starting to fall." One sheet of "Maybe You Should Forget Me" spins quicksilver variations:

This—

I'm beginning to hear voices and there's no one around
Life is repeating itself. The fields have turned brown
I've seen all I want of the damage that's been done
I'm gonna walk the highway til I connect to someone

Then—

All the cats are wearing hats and things are coming unwound
I'm beginning to hear voices but no one's around
Show me to the road, point me to the sun
The days are brutal. The misery's begun
I'm walking in a foggy mist
It's almost like I don't exist.

Dylan also rejects a line that a few years later he would remember for "Things Have Changed"—"Only a fool in here would think he's got anything to prove."

- The taut, formal poise of "Tryin' to Get to Heaven" on *Time Out of Mind* evolves out of the convergence of two other ur-songs, "Until I Saw You" and "All I Ever Loved Was You," each a love ballad. Couplets of "Until I Saw You" also drifted into—or emerged from?—"Dreaming of You," that ur-song behind "Standing in the Doorway," yet the lyrics mainly seem to have led Dylan to "All I Ever Loved Was You," which he then toiled over for three drafts, before reshaping it as "Tryin' to Get to Heaven." Along the way he ventured a hybrid that mixed verses of "All I Ever Loved Was You" and the chorus of "Until I Saw You," and one draft is essentially "Heaven" with an "all I ever loved was you" refrain. "Until I Saw You" combines first-person stanzas—"I wanna take you with me. You're the one"—with crime novel stories about someone named Charlie and his wife. Dylan tipped in some spiritual recovery language, too—"Hour by hour there's a higher power and there's a higher purpose too."

- "Standing in the Doorway" did emerge from "Dreaming of You," yet appears to have originated as still another ur-song, "I Could Never Be Satisfied (With Anyone Less Than You)." The trajectory here parallels "Tryin' to Get to Heaven" as an *almost* conventional romantic ballad—"Your love is my link to the outside world, no other love will do / And I could never be satisfied with anyone less than you"—radiates through several drafts of a related song, "Dreaming of You," en route to a fresh, even startling final form that retains elements of both derivations. A page of "Dreaming of You" asserts "There are no visionaries," and that "There's a moody death in every eye that pretends that it can see." Another page positions the figure "walking thru the summer nights jukebox playing low" as standing in "The Palace of Pain," and intensifies the urgency of memory for Dylan.

Interestingly, there are no discrete drafts in the Tulsa archive for "Tryin' to Get to Heaven," and "Standing in the Doorway," only for the ur-songs backing them. All this ancestral flesh and such vein-tangled snares. Daniel Lanois, who produced *Time Out of Mind*, often mythologizes his introduction to the songs. "Bob Dylan read me the lyrics to *Time Out of Mind* in a hotel room in New York City," he wrote in *Soul Mining: A Musical Life*. "He asked if I thought we had a record, and I said yes. I hadn't heard a note or any melody, but an overwhelming sensation came over me. I was stunned by the power of the lyrics. Bob had written from a perspective that few had seen. Decades of life experience and testimony lay on the pages in front of me. The myth that rock 'n' roll belonged only to youth was about to be shattered by the steel blue eyes of the man himself. The darkness of the lyric was even darker than me."

As I pored over the manuscripts in Tulsa, I wondered what Dylan read to Lanois that night? By other accounts he created "Make You Feel My Love" in the studio, which would mean that at least four of the eleven songs on *Time Out of Mind* probably didn't then exist, or pulsated only as secrets inside those ur-songs. Did he read "'Til I Fell in Love with You," or "Marchin' to the City"? "Standing in the Doorway," or "I Could Never Be Satisfied (With Anyone Less Than You)"? "Tryin' to Get to Heaven," or "Until I Saw You"? Lanois might have heard nearly every word Mr. Steel Blue Eyes ultimately sang, though not in their definitive *Time Out of Mind* settings.

Dylan is often lauded as the first—and leading—modern singer-songwriter. But except in the strictest sense of a singer who writes his own songs, his songwriting propensities couldn't be more inimical to the practices and effects of the classic singer-songwriters Dylan is habitually so designated alongside—writers as gifted and individual as Joni Mitchell, Leonard Cohen, Paul Simon, James Taylor, and Carole King. Standard singer-songwriter modus operandi follows the plot of a James Joyce short story: a recollected experience prompts a hard-won epiphany, as the singer (or their character stand-in) resumes life, scarred but transformed. Details of Dylan's songs, by contrast, are fluid, and such opportune and paraphrasable insights are routinely deflected, baffled, and resisted, including for many songs on *Blood on the Tracks*, his album that hooks closest to the singer-songwriter template. As far back as *Highway 61 Revisited* he could frame a song as a network of equivocal episodes conjoined by a refrain. His strategies mirror the shell games that the Oulipo novelist Harry Mathews styled "situations," where an author's own point of view is incidental. As Matthews told the *Brooklyn Rail*, "I think situations are more important than plot or character . . . as you may have noticed there is very little character development in real life." And as he expanded in another interview in the *Paris Review*, "I had tried writing works involving psychology and characters and all that, and the results were terrible. In [Raymond] Roussel I discovered you could approach prose the way you do poetry. You don't approach it from the idea that what you have to say is inside you. It's a materialist approach, for want of a better word. You make something. You give up expressing and start inventing."

Singer-songwriters, to borrow Matthew's contrast, express, whereas Dylan instead tends to exteriorize consciousness, and make. As he told Martin Scorsese in the Rolling Thunder Review documentary, citing George Bernard Shaw, "Life isn't about finding yourself, or finding anything—it's about creating yourself." Moreover, in *Time Out of Mind*—and for his subsequent albums of the twenty-first century—Dylan increasingly focused fragments across which any illusion of a single interior narrative voice disappears. Over drafts and outtakes of *Time Out of Mind* in the Tulsa archive, the fragments drift from song to song until he can devise a striking situation for them. Sometimes it's as if the record were all one song, and Dylan its ghostly vessel. That "forbidden juices / lame excuses" couplet from the "Dirt Road Blues" manuscript was relocated to a "Can't Wait" outtake, before Dylan cut it. A remarkable free-writing page juggles forays that will vitalize "Love Sick," "Dirt Road Blues," "Highlands," "Mississippi," "Million Miles," and "Things Have Changed," along with a shoulder-shrugging caveat, "Can't feel a thing / What will I sing," and more notes to self. An adjacent page trashes psychology more savagely than Mathews. According to Lanois the drifting fragments persisted even after the record was ostensibly finished, so much so that he needed to devise a process for integrating Dylan's transfers. "He started turning up . . . with lyrical amendments and entirely new stanzas that [engineer Mark] Howard and I worked in, couplets floating from song to song until they found their most potent home. We had to technologically mimic the leakage in Bob's vocal to insure his insertions were flawlessly made to fit."

The Tulsa archive drafts for *Time Out of Mind* also show Dylan revising away from anything faintly autobiographical or personal. His work sheets for "Highlands" divulge many erasures and nuanced readjustments—instead of "listening to Neil Young," the drafts indicate Charlie Parker; and a mention of "watching ivy league boys" and a nod to Harvard's official school color, "where the crimson currents flow," specify more obviously that the "Boston town" restaurant where he's ordering breakfast is really in Cambridge. What survives are his puns—"The twang of the arrow and the snap of the bow"—puns that possibly point to the (now shuttered) Café Pamplona at the intersection of Bow and Arrow Streets in Harvard Square, close by those "green pastures of Harvard University," as he commemorated Ric von Schmidt and Club 47 on his first album, *Bob Dylan*. Yet mainly Dylan excises the explicit stanza about an exhausted, aging musician on never-ending tour:

I'm sitting in the dressing room 'til it's time to play
Payday's coming and I'm willing to pay
Days are passing and the days just turn into years
Sometimes I feel I just want to smash up all the mirrors

Indeed, all those ur-songs point to an erotic grief that draft by draft, fragment by fragment, Dylan abstracted into the intensive spiritual desolation that is the signature of *Time Out of Mind*. In "I Could Never Be Satisfied (with Anyone Less Than You)," he wrote "Your beauty looked into my soul. I was a stranger passing thru." Everything there is "crumbling," and the cause is plain: "Nobody in this crumbling world could ever make me feel the way you do / I could never be satisfied with anyone less than you." By the third track, "Standing in the Doorway," and some smart nicks from "Dreamin' of You," romantic heartache is still core, but Dylan has thickened the lovelorn scenario into a metaphysical noir:

Maybe they'll get me and maybe they won't
But not tonight and it won't be here
There are things I could say but I don't
I know the mercy of God must be near
I've been riding the midnight train . . .

As he worked from "All I Ever Loved Was You" into "Tryin' to Get to Heaven," different refrains, despite reciprocal particulars, transform all. For "All I Ever Loved Was You," the dilemma is love:

When I was in Missouri, they would not let me be
I was never in any great hurry, you only see what you can stand to see
Never trusted anybody to tell me what they knew
Right from the beginning all I ever loved was you

But by "Heaven," life, the whole universe, is the snag:

When I was in Missouri
They would not let me be
I had to leave there in a hurry
They only saw what they let me see
You broke a heart that loved you
Now you can seal up the book and not write anymore
I've been walking that lonesome valley
Trying to get to heaven before they close the door

Dylan's self-inventory on *Time Out of Mind* is pointed and scathing, but deflected, even allegorical, not confessional. As Dylan wrote on a draft manuscript: "The night is coming down and I just won't be able to get far enough away from myself"—a line that he would remember and adapt for "Things Have Changed."

Time Out of Mind is simultaneously a culmination, Dylan's late career breakthrough, and his departure point for the coming new century. He recorded the album with Daniel Lanois in Oxnard, California, during the fall of 1996, and in Miami, Florida, in January of 1997, with post-production back at Oxnard that spring. For all the innovations and wonderments here, by choosing Lanois he was in a sense hedging his wager on his own resurgence. Lanois helped craft his last triumphant collection of original songs, *Oh Mercy*, in 1989, and Dylan was continuing his 1980s habit of relying on producers with strong and distinctive sounds. "I listened to a lot of old records Bob recommended," Lanois recalled, "Charley Patton, dusty old rock 'n' roll, blues. [Drummer] Tony Mangurian and I played along to those, then I built loops of what we did, and then abandoned these sources; a hip-hop technique. I brought these loops to Bob, and we built demos around them." The model was Beck, whom Dylan told Lanois he admired. In interviews, and his memoir *Soul Mining: A Musical Life*, Lanois is circumspect, discreet. Engineer Mark Howard is less so. "There was a situation where Bob wouldn't talk to Dan for a while. Dan would walk in and say, 'Wow, this is sounding great!' And Bob would turn to me and say, 'Did you hear something?' And I'm sitting there, like 'Oh, no . . .' He was kind of playing, but it was intense." Drummer David Kemper remembered a strained session for "Cold Irons Bound":

> I had come in early that day, and going through Miami Beach, it's all this Cuban influence. And I heard this disco record with a Cuban beat, and when I got to the studio, I sat back at the drums and I slowed the beat down, and turned it upside down, and I was just playing, and there was nobody there. No one was expected for a half hour. So I was playing this drum beat, and then Bob snuck up behind me and said, "What are you playing?" . . . I said It's a beat, I'm just writing it right now. "Don't stop it. Keep doing it." And he went and got a yellow pad of paper and sat next to the drums, and he just started writing. And he wrote for maybe ten minutes, and then he said, "Will you remember that?" And I said, yeah, I got it. And then he said, all right, everybody come on in, I want to put this down.
>
> Well I got it in my head, and by then everyone had arrived and tuned up. And take one, he stepped up to the microphone, and "I'm beginning to hear voices, and there's no one around." And I think we did two takes, and then he said, all right, let's move on to something else. I remember Daniel Lanois wasn't happy; he didn't like it. It was one of his guitar breaking incidents. He said to Tony and I: "The world doesn't want another two-note melody from Bob." And he smashed a guitar. So I thought, well, there goes my chance of being on this record. Next time I saw Daniel was at the Grammy Awards, because we had performed that night, and all of a sudden, Male Vocal Performance of the Year, came from that song—the one that Dan was adamant wouldn't get on the record.

Dylan trusted his musicians, and they're a dazzling lot—Kemper, Keltner, Baxter, Cindy Cashdollar, Brian Blade, Jim Dickinson, Augie Myers, Duke Robillard, Bob Britt, Tony Garnier, and Lanois, among others. Prior to a take of "Tryin' to Get to Heaven" that I heard in Tulsa, Dylan says, "Alright, everybody do just what they want, it's the same tempo." In the recordings you can hear him in the studio assembling the music exactly as he did the lyrics, in bits and pieces. After a version of "The King of Them All," he asks, "Let's see if that fits the lyrics." And after another take, "I'm not so happy with that bridge, let's try another one." After a version of "Standing in the Doorway," he pauses, "Maybe we could stick it to the other one." Much as the lyrics, the music migrates. You can listen as the melody for the "The King of Them All" veers into "'Til I Fell in Love With You," or as the band dry-runs the arrangement for "Tryin' to Get to Heaven" through multiple instrumental renditions of "All I Ever Loved Was You." As Dickinson marveled of *Time Out of Mind*, "Bob had an orchestral concept, this thing of too many instruments . . . It's hard to describe. Dylan was standing singing four feet from the microphone, with no earphones on. He was listening to the sound in the room. Which is the sound that did not go on the record. I truly never saw anything like it. He was in unspoken control of 23 people."

On *Time Out of Mind,* Dylan started to hone his collage approach to songwriting, probing the tactics he would intensify across his twenty-first century albums. In "Highlands," for instance, when he revised those "crimson currents" into "Aberdeen waters," he reinforced the dialogue the song directs with Robert Burn's 1789 poem, "My Heart's in the Highlands," itself shaped from a still older Scottish song. But Dylan characteristically both beckons Burn's transcendent yearning and subverts it. His "wherever I go" is now also the empty, cynical peregrination of a disillusioned and out-of-touch rock star on tour. And at another axial moment in "Highlands," Dylan spryly invokes Henry Rollins, the former Black Flag singer and author. Watching some young men and women cavort on the banks of the Charles River, his dispirited wish—"Well, I'd trade places with any of them in a minute if I could"—echoes a similar moment in Rollins's *High Adventures in the Great Outdoors*. Dylan thus morphs knowledgeably into his younger as well as his older poet-musician confrère.

For "Tryin' to Get to Heaven," Dylan absorbed a vast cortège of folk, blues, and spirituals beyond his own ur-songs, songs by Furry Lewis, Byron Arnold, Woody Guthrie, Blind Willie Johnson, Fats Domino, the Carter Family, Elizabeth Cotton, and many more collected by Alan Lomax. But his drafts don't reveal origins. Rollins once more frames the spectral colloquy, as though the singer needed at least one flesh-and-blood voice to anchor the exalted ghosts. Dylan's "Heaven" is crowded with spirits. Again songs, poems, shade a conversation with the dead.

"Mississippi" and "Red River Shore"—why would he leave two of the finest songs of the sessions off *Time Out of Mind*? Here, too, drafts and outtakes are no aid, such strong writing and commanding takes, many included on *Tell Tale Signs* and *Fragments* in *The Bootleg Series*. But "Red River Shore," whether aimed at a Muse and/or a distant Minnesota love, really doesn't tally with the Beckett rue tone. "Mississippi" might be more complicated—for the song palpably "fits." Could it be so simple that "Mississippi"—or a line from it—was too plainly about the high-wire act Dylan was endeavoring here? And that he didn't want to read review after review that concluded, "You can always come back, but you can't come back all the way"?

Save the song for the next record. What started in shame and mortification six years prior at the 1991 Grammy Awards was the 1997 Recording Academy Album of the Year. Dylan accepted his Best Album Grammy next to Lanois, along with a memory, and an acknowledgment. "I just want to say that one time when I was sixteen or seventeen years old, I went to see Buddy Holly play at Duluth National Guard Armory and I was three feet away from him, and he *looked* at me. And I just have some kind of feeling that he was—I don't know how, or why—but I know he was with us all the time we were making this record in some kind of way. In the words of, you know, the immortal Robert Johnson, the stuff we got'll bust your brains out, and we tried to get that across. . . ."

F

. . . A GHOST IN LOVE . . .

False impressions. Figments. Fragments. Phantoms. First, a flashback—though not to February 20, 1991. Instead, a little later, some five weeks *after* Dylan took the Radio City Music Hall stage and received a Grammy Lifetime Achievement Award with his self-lacerating "so defiled in this world" acceptance speech. To March 26 of the same year, when Columbia Records issued *The Bootleg Series Volumes 1–3 (Rare & Unreleased) 1961–1991*, the collection which would start to reconfigure the past he seemed at the Grammys to be running away from, and that maybe had run away with him.

Columbia's timing was so in sync with his honorific that a limited deluxe edition might as well have come with a 24k Bob Dylan Gold Plated Retirement Pocket Watch, except the set was a wild surprise, too. A chronological review of thirty years of music, the faux black-market three-CD (or five-LP) box accentuated rarities and lost songs—fifty-eight in all, none officially released—and charted an alternative recording career for Dylan, shading a parallel ghost world of wonders. His *genuine* shadow kingdom. For those of us who had lost touch after the 1970s there was a hint of a different artist, tentative, experimental, alert to accident, captivated by process, as well as a hint of all the other songs that eventually would turn up, are still turning up. Not long after, my attention caught as much by the disclosures on *The Bootleg Series Volumes 1–3* as by his radioactive Grammy performance, I sought out my first Dylan bootleg CD—my first under-the-counter, contraband bootleg CD—on Thompson Street in the West Village, a live recording from 1981 titled, prophetically, *Stadiums of the Damned*.

There is the kick of the illicit, and the rarer kick of illicit *knowledge*. Bootleg recordings embody both. You'd tell yourself as you departed the shabby purchase site, I am not meant to have this; and later as you listened alone in your tiny apartment, I was not meant to hear—overhear—this. Now that in the twenty-first century, virtually every Dylan concert is retrievable on the internet, that kick of an illicit physical *object* might clock as quaint as Prohibition moonshine. Or television. Back then his Columbia releases ran to nearly thirty studio albums. Yet on any given afternoon around Thompson, Sullivan, Jones, West Third, and Bleecker Streets there was a variable stock of Dylan bootleg CDs roughly five to ten times the span of his official catalog. Commercial but unlicensed, bootlegs traversed an underground, though scarcely clandestine, economy along the outskirts of fandom. Bootlegs weren't pirate recordings—counterfeit copies of lawful goods—just as those bootleg stores weren't really haunts of the most zealous Bob collectors, until his Tulsa archive a still more crepuscular, if arguably purer, network of swapped tapes and photographic reproductions of the young Dylan's marginalia in Woody Guthrie's *Bound for Glory*. Still, all through the 1990s, federal agents routinely raided bootleg stores, seizing every CD on the premises, busts that tended only to interrupt but not halt the weekly influx of fresh titles. Cannier stores took to mixing their bootlegs among Italian and Japanese imports. After 9/11 a rumor circulated through those Village dens that thousands and thousands of bootleg CDs stored in FBI evidence lockers under the World Trade Center were among the inadvertent casualties of the downtown terrorist attacks. "I'm guessing," one of the more hardboiled Village proprietors snorted as he pulled out some Dylan bootlegs he'd set aside for me, "I'm guessing the FBI has bigger things on its mind right now."

The myriad ghosts of dead sins and delights. Bootlegs once flaunted hand-stamped sleeves, xeroxed (if any) credits info, and vinyl that visibly degenerated during play. During my freshman year of college, I bought a copy of *Great White Wonder* in a Harvard Square head shop—a farrago of Minneapolis home sessions, studio outtakes, and Basement Tapes; as far as I know, the earliest Dylan bootleg. By the '90s, however, bootlegs tended to top official releases in style, verve, and authority: meticulous annotation, lavish booklets, often quality sound, and clever titles: *Violence of a Summer's Dream*, *All Hallows' Eve & More*, *Golden Vanity*, *Going Going Guam*, *After the Crash*, and *Boots of Spanish Treasure*. Enterprising scholarship percolated throughout Dylan's ghost world. Starting in 1990 with *Performing Artist: The Music of Bob Dylan, Volume One, 1960–1973*, Paul Williams vividly refocused him as "foremost a performing artist, as opposed to a composer or songwriter" across three volumes that ventured to map some forty years of the live shows that comprised the terra incognita of Dylan bootlegs. In 1997, Greil Marcus rooted his plangent vision of the "old, weird America" of Harry Smith and Bob Dylan not in the official 1975 Columbia Records sixteen track collection, *The Basement Tapes*, but in a spectacular five-CD bootleg set of 103 songs, *The Genuine Basement Tapes*.

Observe that *Genuine*. Dylan bootlegs originated as a taunt, an aesthetic and moral curative. Released three years after the singer disappeared in 1966, and three months after *Nashville Skyline*, *Great White Wonder* emerged out of a critique that implied he had lost his way, and no longer could recognize his own strongest work. "DYLAN'S BASEMENT TAPE SHOULD BE RELEASED," ran the headline in *Rolling Stone* for a cover story, "The Missing Bob Dylan Album." Dylan was muddying a once-clear picture with strange new music, and the bootleggers knew best, that critique went. Slipped inside *Great White Wonder* was a sentimental but hostile conjecture that somewhere else—back in the past, or on some secret tape—the genuine Dylan endured.

An entire phantom universe of once and future bootlegs, alongside the popular legend of Dylan masterpieces and Dylan betrayals. Some shadow releases inevitably circled his catalog like spectral moons, restoring songs and dazzling alternate takes to *The Freewheelin' Bob Dylan*, *Blood on the Tracks*, *Infidels*, and *Oh Mercy*; or capturing sharper, more decisive concerts from the tours documented on his official live albums. *The Bootleg Series Volumes 1–3,* Dylan's own generous insider retrospective, prompted a phantom rival of a trio of three-CD packages, called (what else?) *The Genuine Bootleg Series*, a chronological anthology of 157 additional "lost" recordings. When Columbia finally issued *The Bootleg Series Vol. 4: Bob Dylan Live 1966, The "Royal Albert Hall" Concert* in 1998, bootleggers would match and raise it—first with eight CDs of coruscating 1966 shows, and then a twenty-six-CD box.

Volumes 1–3 was only the inkling of that vast shadow world. Over the decades, the official bootlegs would of course win out—how might even the most cunning or corrupt rum runner compete with Columbia vaults? ("Some of these bootleggers, they make pretty good stuff," as he sang in "Sugar Baby," "Plenty of places to hide things here if you want to hide them bad enough.") Twenty-six black-market CDs from 1966? In 2016 Columbia's Legacy Records released *The 1966 Live Recordings*, a thirty-six-CD box of every known recording from Dylan's tour. 103 black-market Basement songs? In 2014, Legacy Records issued *The Bootleg Series Vol. 11: The Basement Tapes Complete*, 138 tracks and 115 distinct songs. As I write, *The Bootleg Series Vol. 17: Fragments—Time Out of Mind Sessions 1996–1997* (2023), *The Complete Budokan 1978* (2023), and *The 1974 Live Recordings* (2024) are the most recent, though I know others are on their way. For *Volumes 1–3,* each of the CDs counted individually, while later sets amalgamated: two CDs for *Vol. 4*, six CDs for *Vol. 11*, and as many as eighteen CDs for *The Bootleg Series Vol. 12: The Cutting Edge 1965–1966*. (Larger sets came in multiple editions, with a telescoped *Best of* and a sprawling *Deluxe* or *Collector's* alternative.) Legacy Records also launched major Dylan retrospective boxes outside *The Bootleg Series*—including that thirty-six-CD *1966* box; a fourteen-CD *Bob Dylan—The Rolling Thunder Revue: The 1975 Live Recordings*; and that twenty-seven CD 1974 box.

Scale. During the roughly thirty Dylan years chronicled in this book, he recorded six new albums of original songs: *Time Out of Mind*, *"Love And*

Theft," Modern Times, Together Through Life, Tempest, and *Rough and Rowdy Ways*. That's not counting covers, whether folk, blues, Christmas, or Sinatra, and not counting album reissues; still, six CDs, a poet's respectable, engaged, and vibrant book publication schedule, or a novelist's. But across those same three decades, Dylan's Legacy Records ghost world, *The Bootleg Series* and assorted kissing kin, overlayed on top of those six albums of new songs something approaching—depending on your math—146, perhaps 149, maybe even 151 CDs of excavations into his musical pasts. *The Bootleg Series* motions towards Dylan's full career, with a box on his gospel years, *The Bootleg Series Vol. 13: Trouble No More 1979–1981*, and another on the gloomy 1980s, *The Bootleg Series Vol. 16: Springtime in New York 1980–1985*. The predominant focus, though, tends to conjure other periods: the 1970s of *Blood on the Tracks, Desire*, and the Rolling Thunder Revue; his artistic revival, starting in the 1990s; and (inescapably) the 1960s.

Classifications. There are at least two categories of releases in and around *The Bootleg Series*—sets aimed at completists, and those designed to recalibrate what you thought you knew. Obvious completist actions:

- the 1966 and the 1975 boxes
- *The Cutting Edge*
- *The Basement Tapes Complete*
- *Vol. 5: Bob Dylan Live: 1975, The Rolling Thunder Revue*
- *Vol. 6: Bob Dylan Live 1964, Concert at Philharmonic Hall*
- *Vol. 7: No Direction Home: The Soundtrack*
- *Vol. 9: The Whitmark Demos: 1962–1964*
- *Vol. 14: More Blood, More Tracks*
- *Vol. 15: Travelin' Thru, 1967–1969*
- *The Complete Budokan 1978*
- *The 1974 Live Recordings*

Everything, or at least an illusion of everything. But everything, inversely to obsessiveness, doesn't necessarily inspire repeated, or even second listens, and everything rarely reevaluated. Other sets in *The Bootleg*

Series instead recalibrated previous eras. *Vol. 10: Another Self Portrait (1969–1971)* reexamined one of Dylan's most contentious and banished albums, *Self Portrait* (1970), and played up an astute, revisionist essay by Greil Marcus, author of the notorious "What is this shit?" review in *Rolling Stone. Vol. 13: Trouble No More* reconsidered his polarizing Christian albums, *Slow Train Coming* (1979), *Saved* (1980), and *Shot of Love* (1981) as defiant, thrilling live experiences—agile, passionate recitals by Dylan and his backup singers; a terrific gospel-rock band. *Vol. 1–3* didn't so much revisit his tenure with Columbia as reposition it, and heighten his canon of indispensable songs, "Angelina," "Foot of Pride," "Series of Dreams," and "Blind Willie McTell."

This ghost world could have heaped, thwarted, and obliterated Dylan as he strove to reinvent himself on the road during the six years between his "so defiled" Grammys confession and *Time Out of Mind*, his next album of original new songs. (Illicit bootlegs remain the only guide right now to that live resurgence, as there is yet no official documentation of the "Never Ending Tour.") Still, *The Bootleg Series*—counterintuitively—depended on his ongoing revitalization as an artist, for otherwise such elaborate reminders of remote glories would have looked too sad. Following *Volumes 1–3*, a *Vol. 4* wouldn't arrive until after the monumental critical and popular success of *Time Out of Mind.* Curated by Jeff Rosen in Dylan's New York office, *The Bootleg Series* moreover resisted the love/hate prototype of *Great White Wonder* and descendent generations of vinyl, CD, and online contraband that implicitly reproached the singer they also celebrated. Night after night in concert Dylan was transforming his songs such that all years might sound present and vital at once. Rather than a legend of masterpieces and betrayals, where each novel move he made—rock, country, or gospel—either was a breach of faith ("Judas," as the man shouted at him in Manchester in 1966) or a return to the fold ("We've got Dylan back again," as *Rolling Stone* intoned in 1970), there was now only his abiding mastery of all-American music. From inside and outside his formal legend, *The Bootleg Series* mirrored Dylan's traditionalizing impulses on stage and deepened a sense of him as someone inhabiting several time zones synchronically. Choose a date, an episode, an era. Newport, 1965? His 1996 tour? Woodstock? *Self Portrait*? His divorce? His conversion to evangelical Christianity? The 1980s? On *The Bootleg Series* a personal chronology of crises and comebacks dissolved and resolved into music—just music, and more music.

The obvious brilliance of the lost songs on *Volumes 1–3* suggested a workable relation between his two worlds, his past spectral grandeurs and his evolving struggles toward creative renewal, even as the little box set probably also was Columbia hedging a bet on whether he would write again. "Blind Willie McTell," an outtake from *Infidels*, is the most brilliant, as well as the most ghostly—an invocation of apocalypse in the guise of an elegy for a life, and a nation. Built around Mark Knopfler's guitar and Dylan's piano and vocal, and on muted echoes of mournful folk and blues—"The Unfortunate Lad," "St. James Infirmary Blues," and McTell's own "The Dyin' Crapshooter's Blues"—the song retreats and advances simultaneously, the prospect of an immediate death receding back through a montage of American history from the 1930s through Jim Crow, slavery, and the Middle Passage, all bridged by a refrain, "And I know no one can sing the blues like Blind Willie McTell." (Barack Obama would silently embed "Blind Willie McTell" within the opening chapter of *Dreams from My Father*, summoning the "images of another era, a distant world of horsewhips and flames, dead magnolias and crumbling porticos.") Dylan tips his sources towards hurt, corruption, and doom. When near the close he sings, "I'm staring out the window of the St. James Hotel," it's almost as if that hotel is the musical tradition he's momentarily occupying, the rooms and hallways and lobby constructed inside the memory palace melody he's adapting from "St. James Infirmary Blues." For the draft of "Blind Willie McTell" in his Tulsa archive, he started by typing across the page gestures towards his song:

stared at the face of an angel & i learned her features well
charcoal gypsy maidens—they can strut their feathers well
it only reminds me of the day i first heard blind willy mctell

Remarkably, Dylan then apparently typed all five verses, pretty much as he would record them, his light fixes logged in pencil. Starting in 1997, he performed "Blind Willie McTell" at over 225 shows, including a 2012 tribute to Martin Scorsese. Although not technically a lost song, "Every Grain of Sand" (a publishing demo for *Shot of Love*) would also prove crucial to Dylan's future concerts. Once he returned to the road after COVID, nights on his *Rough and Rowdy Ways* tours nearly always concluded with "Every Grain of Sand."

Volumes 1–3 imparted the sultry glow and shock of a great Dylan album. You could hear within it the apotheosis of his own history. For me, *Vol. 8: Tell Tale Signs: Rare and Unreleased 1989–2006* is another retrospective that transmitted a similarly fresh experience. *Tell Tale Signs* probed *Oh Mercy*, *World Gone Wrong*, *Time Out of Mind*, *"Love And Theft,"* and *Modern Times*, along with one-off incidentals, and again the "new" songs startled: "Dignity," "Red River Shore," "Born in Time," "God Knows," "Can't Escape from You," and "Miss the Mississippi." Dylan fleshed out *World Gone Wrong* with covers of "Mary and the Soldier" and "32-20 Blues," and reinforced the significance of *Oh Mercy* with alternate takes of "Most of the Time," "Everything Is Broken," and "Ring Them Bells," and another look at "Series of Dreams." A pair of songs Dylan relegated to movie soundtracks are among the ace rescues here, "Huck's Tune," from Curtis Hanson's *Lucky You*, and especially "'Cross the Green Mountain," from Ronald F. Maxwell's *Gods and Generals*.

An account of Stonewall Jackson and Robert E. Lee over the first years of the Civil War, *God's and Generals* is a stolid prologue to Maxwell's *Gettysburg*, each a Lost Cause film obsessed with ornate period authenticity, yet impervious to any historical recognition that slavery was a factor. Dylan's lyric also doesn't mention slavery. Instead, he worked with fragments of nineteenth-century poems, songs, and hymns, a few by writers as prominent as Walt Whitman ("Come Up from the Fields, Father"), Herman Melville ("The Scout Toward Aldie"), Henry Wadsworth Longfellow ("Daybreak"), and Julia Ward Howe ("Battle Hymn of the Republic"), as well as others obscure to most poetry readers, such as William

Newell ("A New Year's Hymn," "Jared Sparks," and "Serve God and Be Cheerful"), Louisa Jane Hall ("Service in the Hereafter"), Nathaniel Shepherd ("The Roll-Call"), Robert C. Waterson ("The Departed"), Harry L. Flash ("The Death of Stonewall Jackson"), William Gannett ("Sunday on the Hill-Top"), and Henry Timrod ("Charleston"). Many of these framework pieces appear in Alfred P. Putnam's *Singers and Songs of the Liberal Faith* (1875) or in Francis F. Browne's *Bugle-Echoes—A Collection of the Poetry of the Civil War Northern and Southern* (1886).

The voices around this literary table do reference slavery, notably Howe's, and Dylan's polyphonic clangor embraces hymns and poems by dedicated abolitionists (including the pastor poets in Putnam's anthology). But the common denominator is death—pervasive death, tragic death, absurd death. An acid couplet, "Along the dim Atlantic line / The ravaged land lasts for miles behind," intertwines Timrod and Melville, South and North. In Shepherd's "Roll-Call," the names are of young men killed in battle, and all of the *Singers and Songs* poems he convenes are set along the edges of the afterlife. As so often for Dylan death eases into End Times—the "Heaven blazing in my head" and his "monstrous dream" of the Civil War at the opening is overtly the Beast of *Revelations*: "Something came up out of the sea." Still, it's also Yeats in "Lapis Lazuli," projecting ahead from 1936 to the human waste of a looming World War. "Heaven blazing into the head: / Tragedy wrought to its uttermost."

Tell Tale Signs also introduced "Marchin' to the City" and "Dreamin' of You," pivotal songs-behind-the-songs for *Time Out of Mind*, and officially launched Dylan's anxious efforts to revise and repossess the most acclaimed record of his late career—efforts he pursued during subsequent years of live shows and ultimately concentrated into a five-CD box set, *Vol. 17: Fragments: Time Out of Mind Sessions (1996–1997)*, released in 2023. Dylan's reservations often are summarized as disagreements with producer Daniel Lanois, and *Fragments* stages a massive rectification of even mutual decisions, such as Chess-style vocal affects, tape loops, and multi-instrumental orchestration. For the first disc of *Fragments*, engineer Michael Brauer stripped those layers, accenting individual musicians over an orchestral sound, and the result is something like *Time Out of Mind* as if produced by Jack Frost, the pseudonym Dylan would later adopt when he started producing himself.

Hyperactive, spiraling, maybe irreconcilable, *Fragments* doesn't stop there. Across this maze of variant performances the listener is encouraged to dismantle *Time Out of Mind*, and replay the options. We hear a studio translation of the intricate story inside the lyric drafts in his Tulsa archive, all the more intense and elusive since we're listening and not just reading. We now can catch lines, couplets, and verses as they rove from song to song, and not only in such source ur-songs as "Dreamin' of You" and "Marchin' to the City." It's hard to imagine "Not Dark Yet" without "I ain't looking for nothing in anyone's eyes," but Dylan also sings those words in "'Til I Fell in Love with You." We can also hear Dylan as he writes away from the personal—for "Not Dark Yet":

Just being in the same country as her is just making me blue
I got nothing left over of the love that we knew . . .
Well, I can close my eyes and I see her from a long way off
Her lips were so tender, her skin was so soft
I've gone too far down life's beaten track
And I'm praying the master will guide me back

Or on the earliest version of "Dreamin' of You":

Your love is my link to the outside world
And always it will remain . . .
I wish your hand was in mine right now
We could go together well, the road is wide
I squandered the years of my youth
It's a scary thing, the truth
I feel like a ghost in love
Underneath the heavens above
Feel further away than ever before
And it's nothing I know how to explain

From disc to disc as we align a recording timeline, lyric transitions flicker. Song titles, too: "Marchin' to the City" sometimes is "Doin' Alright." But the narrative in Tulsa is still more involved, for there we can eavesdrop on Dylan as he rounds up his music in resistant bits that also prowl song to song. For many songs—"Love Sick," "Dirt Road Blues," "Can't Wait," "Red River Shore," and "Make You Feel My Love"—alternate takes rival, maybe surpass *Time Out of Mind*.

Bootlegs. *Great White Wonder* was a foolhardy stab at a *real*, a *genuine* Dylan, the sage with all the answers. For the Dylan of *Fragments* and *The Bootleg Series*, there are only questions. "How did it feel?" he inquires after a take I heard in Tulsa. "Let's try another one."

G

. . . ROOT CAUSE

Gatsby . . . ? First take note of the obvious, what you already know, or sense as—almost—familiar, and radiate from there. Still, what is F. Scott Fitzgerald doing inside Bob Dylan's *"Love And Theft"*? Smack dab in "Summer Days" there's the onetime James Gatz arguing all over again with Nick Carraway. "You can't repeat the past? / I say, You can't? Of course you can!"

A few lines back, Dylan dropped in on Fitzgerald's sometime friend and tormentor Ernest Hemingway, by way of Jake Barnes and *The Sun Also Rises*: "What looks good in the day at night is another thing." Everything so far sounds smooth, colloquial. Yet why's *he* here—and close by some admittedly curious words from the mouth of Abraham Lincoln? "Sucking the blood out of the genius of generosity." For "Lonesome Day Blues," why *The Adventures of Huckleberry Finn*? "Last night the wind was whispering something, I was trying to make out what it was." Why then rhyme Twain with Henry Rollins? "Yeah, I tell myself something's coming but it never does." And why in the very next verse fire up *the Aeneid*? "I'm going to teach peace to the conquered, I'm going to tame the proud."

Alongside, maybe back of the world we daily experience, suspicions, echoes, and hints soon start to reverberate, take shape. In "Tweedle Dee

& Tweedle Dum," we hear an echo of "A Vision of Poesy" by Henry Timrod—"They walk among the stately trees. / They know the secrets of the breeze." Then—"stab you where you stand," from Edgar Allen Poe's short story "William Wilson." In "Moonlight" we note "the masquerade of birds and bees," from Emerson's essay "The Poet." In "Floater (Too Much to Ask)," Confederate Army General Nathan Bedford Forrest, the first grand wizard of the Ku Klux Klan, hovers by Junichi Saga's *Confessions of a Yakuza*. And Saga's *Memories of Silk and Straw*, too: "Got to get up near the teacher if you can / If you want to learn anything."

A timeless classroom, perhaps a model for the vaulted human brain—might such moments, then, mirror how we learn, remember? In "Bye and Bye," Dylan folds into a melody reminiscent of Billie Holiday's "Having Myself a Time" a vestige of the Roman civil wars, amid other tricky language. The Bible: "I'm gonna baptize you in fire so you can sin no more." Shakespeare's *As You Like It*: "I'm not even acquainted with my own desires." "Po' Boy," too, seems to rally the Bard:

> *Othello told Desdemona, "I'm cold, cover me with a blanket*
> *By the way, what happened to that poison wine?" She says, "I gave it to you, you drank it"*

Yet that stunt, of course, isn't from Shakespeare at all, and instead telescopes the plot of a roughly contemporaneous folk song known variously as "Lord Randall" and "Henry, My Son," even as Dylan launches the song with a sly conjuring of George Griffin's 1866 blackface *Othello*.

"Po' Boy" also distills a sneaky couplet equal parts Baudelaire—"Time and love has branded me with its claws"—and Blind Willie McTell, "Had to go to Florida, dodgin' them Georgia laws." A few of Dylan's *"Love And Theft"* songs will flaunt their melodic prompts by recapping a scrap of the original lyric. "Cry A While" (Sonny Boy Williamson's "Your Funeral, My Trial"); and "Sugar Baby" (Gene Austin's "The Lonesome Road"). For others the ostensible roots of a title might diverge from the wellsprings of the song itself, music and words. "Summer Days" is presumably tagged after Charley Patton's "Some Summer Days," yet with a tune evocative of Big Joe Turner's "Rebecca." In "High Water (For Charley Patton)" a discordant, pace-setting crowd—Patton, Dock Boggs, Clarence Ashley, Wilbert Harrison, Robert Johnson, Bill Bamberger, various nursery rhymes and anonymous ballads, Charles Darwin, George Lewes, Charlotte Brontë, and Louis-Ferdinand Celine, even painters (Aaron Douglas, Romare Beardon, and Roy DeCarava), among other turns and pivots—alternately vie and converge, as ears reel, and our minds lurch.

By the fall of 2001, guests were descending on Dylan's new songs. My favorite among his records over the three decades between *Good as I Been to You* and *Rough and Rowdy Ways*, *"Love And Theft"* initially might be approached as the call-to-order of a fierce trilogy of associated releases that spanning *Modern Times* (2006) and *Tempest* (2012) would refocus and deepen the career rebirth he confirmed with *Time Out of Mind*. Dylan sketched his evolving artistic status with a boxing visual to Jonathan Lethem. "*Time Out of Mind* was me getting back in and fighting my way out of the corner," he said. "But by the time I made *'Love And Theft'*, I was out of the corner. On *this* record I ain't nowhere, you can't find me anywhere, because I'm *way* gone from the corner." The album also announced an astonishing five-year risorgimento, a sustained creative stint that could be lodged honorably aside Dylan's classic triumphs of 1961 through 1966. Starting with *"Love And Theft,"* he would cowrite and act in a provocative topical film, *Masked and Anonymous*; set down an intricate, layered, and indeed charming memoir, *Chronicles*; publish his *Lyrics*; host a lively, musically diverse weekly radio show, *Theme Time Radio Hour*; contribute trenchant songs to movie soundtracks, such as "Things Have Changed," "'Cross the Green Mountain, "Tell Ol' Bill," and "Huck's Tune"; record *Modern Times*; and perform nearly five hundred live shows, including a collaboration with Wynton Marsalis at Jazz at Lincoln Center's 2004 Spring Gala, and an appearance at the Apollo Theater singing Sam Cooke's "A Change Is Gonna Come."

Five years. All of these forays are ambitious, and involved fresh artistic risks. Most also were unexpected, and although each activity was different, individual, there were emphatic overlays. Even more rigorously than *Time Out of Mind,* Dylan's new projects all documented the casual, sometimes startling and disturbing convergences of his own autobiography and the history of America, quickening a stylistic network of loss, projections, longings, ideals, and horrors. Five years. Collectively this divergent handiwork of 2001 through 2006 reactivates the core of his late-phase memory palace.

That sixteenth-century Jesuit in China, Matteo Ricci, following Augustine, Aquinas, and Ignatius of Loyola, emphasized that a memory palace must not be envisioned as a passive repository. His mnemonic system was an instrument for spiritual practice with ancient links to writing, alchemy, and magic. "As for those worthy figures who lived a hundred generations ago," Ricci conjectured, "although they too are gone, yet thanks to the books they left behind we who come after can hear their modes of discourse, observe their grand demeanor, and understand both the good order and the chaos of their times, exactly as if we were living among them." Or as Dylan would sing in "Rollin' and Tumblin'" on *Modern Times*:

> *The night's filled with shadows, the years are filled with early doom*
> *The night is filled with shadows, the years are filled with early doom*
> *I've been conjuring up all these long dead souls from their crumblin' tombs*

Making the dead available to the living, the memory palace proposes a mechanism for rendering all time—past, present, future—modern times. Here Dylan manages at once to describe and incarnate that mechanism, for in this little verse of "Rollin' and Tumblin'" the opening repeated phrases proceed from "Our Willie," an 1865 poem by Henry Timrod, and the final line loops back to Ovid's book of love poems of c. 16 BCE, *Amores*—and both are cut into a blues out of Hambone Willie Newbern and Muddy Waters. That's at least four dead souls conjured up right there.

Yet the history reanimating *"Love And Theft"* is more precise and concentrated, as are the convergences with *Masked and Anonymous.* Both album and film are steeped in the lingos of American carnivals, sideshows, vaudeville, and especially minstrelsy. Director Larry Charles and I visited Dylan's Tulsa archive together during the summer of 2019. He recalled that on their first day of writing *Masked and Anonymous*, Dylan said, " 'I have this box,' and he opened it, and it had stacks of scrap paper, stationery—mostly hotel stationery, like we saw today at the archive. He writes a lot on hotel stationery, especially in those days, I guess, but they were all torn with little things on them . . . aphorisms . . . lines of poetry, names of characters."

Charles described the "same kind of language flowing back and forth between" *Masked and Anonymous* and *"Love And Theft,"* and noted that lines they couldn't fit into movie dialogue found their way into songs. A Mother Goose echo in "High Water (For Charley Patton)" originated, according to Charles, when "one day Bob came in with this line, 'I'm no pig without a wig,' and I'm like, Bob, I have to tell ya, even in a movie like this, this dense, weird movie, no one's gonna understand that line."

Across this zigzag of puns, rhymes, and gags, though, Dylan's new album and the film he was creating simultaneously with Charles radically scaled up the caustic, no-nonsense scrutiny of race and the Civil War he broached on his anthologies of blues, folk, and country covers, *Good as I Been to You* and *World Gone Wrong.* As he reflected later to Mikal Gilmore in 2012 for *Rolling Stone*:

> . . . the United States burned and destroyed itself for the sake of slavery. The USA wouldn't give it up. It had to be grounded out. The whole system had to be ripped out with force. A lot of killing. What, like, 500,000 people? A lot of destruction to end slavery. And that's what it really was all about.
>
> This country is just too fucked up about color . . . Blacks know that some whites didn't want to give up slavery—that if they had their way, they would still be under the yoke, and they can't pretend they don't know that. . . .

> It's doubtful that America's ever going to get rid of that stigmatization. It's a country founded on the backs of slaves. You know what I mean? It goes way back. It's the root cause. If slavery had been given up in a more peaceful way, America would be far ahead today. Whoever invented the idea 'lost cause. . . . ' There's nothing heroic about any lost cause. No such thing, though there are people who still believe it.

"Love And Theft"—the atypical quotation marks plausibly point to Eric Lott's 1993 scholarly book of the same calid, aphoristic title about nineteenth-century American minstrelsy—scrutinizes legacies of that "lost cause." *Masked and Anonymous*, almost as likely was christened from a passage in Dale Cockrell's *Demon's of Disorder: Early Blackface Minstrels and Their World* (1997), dares to imagine the impending, next American Civil War.

First, Dylan's record. During interviews in the fall of 2001 Dylan insisted on isolating *"Love And Theft"* from *Time Out of Mind*, as though over the prior four years of touring his Grammy Album of the Year all the comeback talk had congealed for him. Daniel Lanois bore his most scurrilous grievances here, and Dylan didn't hesitate to ridicule what he now judged as an overwrought soundscape. Asked why "Mississippi" wasn't included on *Time Out of Mind*, he seethed to David Fricke: "The song was's pretty much laid out melodically, lyrically, and structurally, but Lanois didn't see it. Thought it was pedestrian. Took it down the Afro-polyrhythm route . . . Polyrhythm has its place, but it doesn't work for knifelike lyrics trying to convey majesty and heroism . . . Things got contentious once in the parking lot. He tried to convince me that the song had to be 'sexy, sexy, and more sexy.'" Henceforth Dylan would produce his own recordings under the semi-incognito moniker Jack Frost.

Later interviews indicate that Dylan concluded *Time Out of Mind* sounded monotonous, slow, and lugubrious. "I knew that after that record that when and if I ever committed myself to making another record," Dylan told Robert Hilburn, "I didn't want to get caught short without up-tempo songs. A lot of my songs are slow ballads. I can gut-wrench a lot out of them. But if you put a lot of them on a record, they'll fade into one another, and there was some of that on *Time Out of Mind*." Ultimately, Dylan seemed baffled that his 1997 album was taken as a sort of lachrymose memoir. By contrast *"Love And Theft,"* he argued to Edna Gunderson, is "not me dragging around a bottle of absinthe and coming up with Baudelairean poems. It's me using everything I know to be true." Asked by Mikal Gilmore to describe his new songs, Dylan waxed public, not personal. "The whole album deals with power. If life teaches us anything, it's that there's nothing that men and women won't do to get power. The album deals with power, wealth, knowledge, and salvation—the way I look at it. If it's a great album—which I hope it is—it's a great album because it deals with great themes. It speaks in a noble language. It speaks of the issues or the ideals of an age in some nation, and hopefully, it would also speak across the ages. It'd be as good tomorrow as it is today and would've been as good yesterday."

Perhaps only when he came to despise *Time Out of Mind* a little could Dylan write more. Yet his new album wasn't the about-face his cantankerousness declared. For all his quibbles, *"Love And Theft"* essentially intensifies the fragmented and collaged composition cues he floated on *Time Out of Mind*, though this acceleration of scale represented also a broadening of kind. The what-if-I-put-this-next-to-that experiment he assayed on *Time Out of Mind* tended exclusively to layer song lyrics—the multiple signals, for instance, to spirituals collected by Alan Lomax for *The Folk Songs of North America* in "Tryin' to Get to Heaven"; and significantly even the books, verse and prose, that he mainly reverberated were by a songwriter, Henry Rollins.

This restraint has the look of a self-imposed boundary, even a rule. Yet by the time he created *"Love And Theft,"* language of any category, source, and style suddenly proves provocative for Dylan: yes, songs and the books of singer-songwriters, including *A Shot in the Dark: Tennessee Jive* (2000), a Nashville retrospective box set put out by Bear Family Records, but now also novels, short stories, histories, travelogues, lyric poems, classical epics, nursery rhymes, essays, public speeches, plays, and movies. For just one entry on *"Love And Theft,"* the lead-in "Tweedle Dee & Tweedle Dum," along with Boggs, Johnson, and more than a half-dozen tracks recorded by the New Lost City Ramblers, Dylan mobilizes the Book of Genesis, Poe, Timrod, Lillian Hellman, Tennessee Williams, the minstrel skit *Box and Cox*, Tod Browning's *Freaks*, and Bethany Bultman's *New Orleans*, all to a tune redolent of "Uncle John's Bongos" by the Grand Ole Opry duo Johnnie & Jack. On *"Love And Theft"* Dylan seems particularly drawn to covers—all those folk, country, and blues songs reintroduced by the New Lost City Ramblers; songs that are already patchwork—his "Moonlight" emerges from A. P. Carter's "Meet Me By the Moonlight Alone," itself a hybrid of sundry eighteenth- and nineteenth-century sallies; and to other slippery, alloyed materials—that minstrel *Othello* in "Po' Boy," and *Box and Cox*, derived from an English farce based on a French comedy. So crafty are Dylan's reconstructions for *"Love And Theft"* that I wouldn't be surprised if someday we learn every bit of speech—no matter how idiosyncratic, and Dylanesque—elegantly mirrors another song, poem, film, or novel.

"Love And Theft" should then presage Bob Dylan's consummate vanishing into tradition and history. But over and over in his interviews during the fall of 2001 he insisted on precisely the personal dimensions of his new writing. "I've never recorded an album with more autobiographical songs," he stressed to Gunderson. And to Christopher John Farley in *Time*: "All of 'em. Every single one, every line. It's completely autobiographical." Cryptic? Deflective? Perverse? I've come to feel Dylan in those conversations was honestly, deliberately focusing his motives and aspirations on *"Love And Theft."* Moreover, I don't believe he intended "autobiographical" in any loose spirit—those musical and cultural allusions aren't just his influences, or a representation of the contents of his aging neurons; though they are inevitably that too, of course. And I don't sense he was only reinscribing the rote Whitmanesque transaction of an apparent self-erasure that occasions the return of a vaster, cosmic self; though that move figures in his song-collages. I also don't believe he was merely calling attention

to one of the moments here anyone would style "autobiographical"—the moment when months after the death of Beatty Zimmerman he sings, "I wish my mother were still alive."

"Love And Theft" is a rare record that aims for a total impact. Everywhere contingent on race, minstrelsy, and the Civil War, Dylan's subject is nothing less than the history of American popular music. As Eric Lott argued in his *Love and Theft*:

> One of our earliest culture industries, minstrelsy not only affords a look at the emergent historical break between high and low cultures but also reveals popular culture to be a place where cultures of the dispossessed are routinely commodified—and contested. The heedless (and ridiculing) appropriation of "black" culture by whites in the minstrel show, as many contemporaries recognized, was little more than cultural robbery, a form of what Marx called expropriation, which troubled guilty whites all the more because they were so attracted to the culture they plundered. Indeed, for a time in the late 1840s minstrelsy came to seem the most representational national art. In this way minstrelsy became a sight of conflictual intensity for the politics of race, class, and nation.
>
> If at this juncture we are to understand anything more about popular racial feeling in the United States, we must no longer be satisfied merely to condemn the terrible pleasures of cultural material such as minstrelsy, for their legacy is all around us.

Dylan's album shadows this inside story of American music—on "Summer Days" he sings, "Where do you come from, where do you go? / Sorry, that's nothin' you would need to know." Except that he does need to know, since that inside story is where he originates, his autobiography. Much like those other "guilty whites" Lott memorializes, Dylan obviously adores all the variegated musics he musters to compose *"Love And Theft,"* but he won't overlook their rendezvous with slavery, lynching, Jim Crow, and blackface, won't overlook his own White privileges. As Yeats wrote,

"I must lie down where all the ladders start / In the foul rag and bone shop of the heart."

The poignancy of *"Love And Theft"* is Dylan's acknowledgment across "every line" that no matter how empathetic or enlightened his intentions, as a White blues singer he inescapably operates within a minstrelsy tradition. Earlier in his history he referred to "Desolation Row" on *Highway 61 Revisited* as "a minstrel song through and through," and for Rolling Thunder in 1975 he performed in whiteface. Just before they started recording *Oh Mercy*, he sent Lanois, Mark Howard, and Malcolm Burn a cassette. "Great, we're going to hear some songs," Burn enthused to *Uncut*. "There was this little note: 'This'll give you a good idea.' Dan and Mark Howard and I sat down to listen—and this Al Jolson music started. We were like, 'What the fuck?' So, we fast-forwarded. It was a whole tape of Al Jolson. We looked back at Bob's note: 'Listen to this. You can learn a lot.'" Retrospectively, such gestures suggest Dylan was already working toward consciousness of his own implication in the tortuous racial dynamics he simultaneously rebukes and celebrates on *"Love And Theft."*

Carnivals and circuses loom in Dylan's private mythology, at least as far back as an appearance on WBAI in 1962, when he was twenty, and claimed six years "off and on" of carny travel. Recalling entertainers he encountered in Hibbing, he told Jeff Rosen for Martin Scorsese's *No Direction Home*, "You could see guys in blackface. George Washington in blackface or Napoleon wearing blackface . . . weird Shakespearean things. Stuff that didn't really make sense at the time." During a 2009 talk with Bill Flanagan, Dylan circled back to those sideshows, and associated his carny experiences with the songs he wrote around the civil rights movement:

> Mass media had no overwhelming reach so I was drawn to the travelling performers passing through. The sideshow performers—bluegrass singers, the Black cowboy with chaps and a lariat doing rope tricks. Miss Europe, Quasimodo, the Bearded Lady, the half-man half woman, the deformed, the bent, Atlas the Dwarf, the fire-

> eaters, the teachers and the preachers, the blues singers. I remember it like it was yesterday. I got close to some of the people. I learned about dignity from them. Freedom too. Civil rights, human rights. How to stay within yourself. . . . The stuff off the main road was where force of reality was.

As late as October of 2024, Dylan recommended on his X account Tod Browning's film *The Unknown* (1927), starring Lon Chaney as a carnival knife thrower—"Alonzo the Armless"—and Joan Crawford as Nanon Zanzi, the daughter of the carnival's owner, also Alonzo's secret love, and featured in his act. (Putting forward *The Unknown*, was he also mischievously observing *A Complete Unknown*, then about to enter sneak previews?)

Dylan's civil rights songs of the 1960s delivered observations, commentary, and statements, however speculative, and often ambiguous. His songs on *"Love And Theft"* instead embody, their revelations emerging from the juxtapositions and echoes of his furiously allusive textures.

As he advances a conversation about America and American music where race, slavery, and racism are decisive, he embeds into his lyrics a Who's Who of nineteenth-century writers, politicians, scientists, and philosophers, some directly engaged in the Civil War, others for backdrop: Lincoln, Herman Melville, Timrod, Poe, Twain, Nathan Bedford Forrest, Ralph Waldo Emerson, George Lewes, and Charles Darwin. Across songs of every era Dylan correlates American history with crime—hence his noir flourishes ("Well, I'm stranded in the city that never sleeps"), and the recurrent citations of Junichi Saga's first-person accounts of Japanese gangsters, *Confessions of a Yakuza*. His Ernest Hemingway reference in "Summer Days" is another facet of this noir subtext, as Dylan implants only part of the original sentence, while presumably expecting us to cough up the whole: "It is awfully easy to be hard-boiled about everything in the daytime, but at night it is another thing." The other Saga book, *Memories of Silk and Straw*, assembles voices from the vanished world of prewar Japan, tracing what he terms "the faint shadow of a lost age in their way of life," and I am reminded of Dylan's own words about the American South in the same interview with Bill Flanagan where he saluted carnival folk:

> It must be the Southern air. It's filled with rambling ghosts and disturbed spirits. They're all screaming and forlorning. It's like they are all caught up in some weird web—some purgatory between heaven and hell and they can't rest. They can't live and they can't die. It's like they were cut off in their prime, wanting to tell somebody something. It's all over the place. There are war fields everywhere . . . a lot of times even in people's backyards.

On *"Love And Theft"* Dylan links the American empire to Japan, and to ancient Rome—hence also the whispers of Virgil. Gatsby in "Summer Days" typifies hubris about history, and again I suspect we're intended to complete the transfer. After Gatsby protests "of course you can" repeat the past, Fitzgerald writes, "He looked around him wildly, as if the past were lurking here in the shadow of his house, just out of reach of his hand." Nick Carraway's warning about Daisy just prior to Gatsby's meltdown—"I wouldn't ask too much of her"—merges into a reflection on *Confessions of a Yakuza*—"Tears or not, though, that was too much to ask"—and yields the final line of "Floater (Too Much to Ask)" ("And tears or not, it's too much to ask"), along with that song's working title in the Tulsa drafts: "Too Much to Ask." As Dylan sings in "Sugar Baby," "Some of these memories you can learn to live with and some of them you can't."

Beyond this panoramic, the specifics inside songs are even nimbler, and more generative. On "Bye And Bye," "Floater (Too Much to Ask)," and "Moonlight," Dylan arouses a jovial, parlor-song ambiance, only to have all three lyrics list into menace, abuse, and apocalypse, a cunning stylistic counterpart to those "rambling ghosts and disturbed spirits" under Southern lawns. For "High Water (For Charley Patton)" he foregrounds a banjo as he updates "High Water Everywhere," Patton's two-part blues about the Great Mississippi Flood of 1927, still the most devasting river cataclysm in American history. As Lott remarked in *Love and Theft*, "the rural white tradition, and its commercial issue in modern bluegrass music, inherited much from the minstrel show—not least the black style of banjo playing on which minstrelsy partly traded." Throughout "High Water," Dylan inlays blues and bluegrass, Black and White musicians: Patton, Robert Johnson, Dock Boggs, Clarence Ashley, Big Joe Turner, and Wilbert Harrison. Confederate minstrelsy—"Wait for the Wagon," and "The Boatman's Dance," by Dan Emmett, the composer of "Dixie"—intersects "Po' Lazarus," a prison work song by James Carter that Alan Lomax recorded at Parchman Farm, and one of Dylan's slow-burn couplets pairs the racism of "Wait for the Wagon" with notorious anti-Semite Louis-Ferdinand Celine: "Jump into the wagon, love / Throw your panties overboard." White British rationalists, namely Lewes and Darwin, vainly taunt religion, and Bertha Mason is at once Patton's wife, Bertha Lee, and the madwoman in the attic of *Jane Eyre*. As Dylan sings, "It's rough out there / High water everywhere." His geography, too, is arrestingly at odds—Vicksburg, where Patton was buried; Highway 5, in Mississippi's Benton County, named for Confederate General Samuel Benton; and Clarksdale, home to Johnson, Willie Brown, John Lee Hooker, Gus Cannon, W. C. Handy, Muddy Waters, Frank Stokes, Ike Turner, and Sam Cooke.

In "Tweedle Dee & Tweedle Dum," most of the recollected phrases Black and White, high and low, across music, religion, fiction, plays, and movies that I named earlier convene joke couples, twins, and doubles, but they're gags with a sting. As Scott Warmuth once speculated, Dylan's song suggests a sort of answer record to the Grateful Dead's "Uncle John's Band," his tribute to their tribute to John Cohen of the New Lost City Ramblers, and the founder of the Friends of Old Time Music. The illumination melody for "Tweedle Dee & Tweedle Dum"—"Uncle John's Bongos," the tale of a traditional musician turned beatnik in Greenwich Village—further ties up the Cohen knot. Yet the hip parable Johnnie & Jack recite in "Uncle John's Bongos" is Dylan's story, too, and perhaps Bob & John are the terminal duo of "Tweedle Dee & Tweedle Dum." Once again he inculpates himself in the mechanisms of love and theft, and what Eric Lott called "the racial logic usually hidden in our romantic notions of the bohemian, the Beat, the hipster." For Lott, "a major strain in American bohemia" from Whitman through Carl Van Vechten, Norman Mailer, Tennessee Williams, and Jack Kerouac, "has its origins in blackface performers and enthusiasts."

"Sugar Baby," Dylan's finale on *"Love And Theft,"* revisits "The Lonesome Road," a would-be traditional Black folk song cowritten around Tin Pan Alley in 1927 by Gene Austin and Nathaniel Shilkret. Stepin Fetchit mimed "The Lonesome Road" in the part-silent, part-talkie *Show Boat* (1929), and the song was recorded by everyone from Austin himself to Bing Crosby, Paul Robeson, Frank Sinatra, Louis Armstrong, Sam Cooke, Stevie Wonder, and Willie Nelson. Dylan also possibly slips into "Sugar Baby" a sinister glint of "The Old Folks Started It," aka "The Darktown Strut." But his closing verse circles back to "The Lonesome Road," and there in the guise of honoring and lamenting "love" he speaks to the enchantments, traumas, and sins of his musical traditions:

Your charms have broken many a heart and mine is surely one
You got a way of tearing the world apart, love, see what you've done
Just as sure as we're living, just as sure as you're born
Look up, look up, seek your Maker—'fore Gabriel blows his horn

When a decade later Dylan was challenged by Mikal Gilmore about "the controversy over quotations in your songs from the works of other writers," as if he were a snotty plagiarist and *"Love And Theft"* a humdrum term paper, he countered angrily: "Wussies and pussies complain about that stuff." Then thoughtfully: "I'm working within my art form. It's that simple. I work within the rules and limitations of it. . . . It's called songwriting. It has to do with melody and rhythm, and then after that, anything goes. You make everything yours."

Dylan's *art form* here spans folk process and literary modernism, and the peculiar genius of *"Love And Theft"* is the way one explodes against and into the other. I'm reminded of an exhibition I saw in 2017 at the National Gallery of Art in Washington, *Outliers and American Vanguard Art,* that focused the correspondences across outsider and avant-garde expressions. I'm reminded, too, of when Walker Evans was asked why he photographed the South, and he answered the Civil War.

Lott in *Love and Theft* scans some rare nineteenth-century intervals when "interracial solidarity was briefly and intermittently achieved." For Dylan another such spot of time was the late 1920s and early 1930s; and so many of his favored artists here, as we've seen, hover around 1925 through 1935. Charley Patton and Clarence Ashley, Dock Boggs and Blind Willie Johnson, Jimmie Rodgers and Leroy Carr. In the folk pantheon, as Dylan once told Jon Pareles, "To me there's no difference between Muddy Waters and Bill Monroe." A third such moment for Dylan would be his own adolescence during the 1950s. "This was before folk music had ever entered my life," he recounted to Bill Flanagan in *AARP*. "I was still an aspiring rock 'n' roller. The descendent, if you will, of the first generation of guys who played rock 'n' roll . . . Buddy Holly, Little Richard, Chuck Berry, Carl Perkins, Gene Vincent, Jerry Lee Lewis. They played this type of music that was Black and white . . . When I first heard Chuck Berry I didn't consider he was Black. I thought he was a white hillbilly. Little did I know he was a great poet, too. And there must have been some elitist power that had to get rid of all of these guys, to strike down rock 'n' roll for what it was and what it represented—not least of all it being a Black and white thing."

An American trinity of incandescent, fleeting utopias. The lost paradise that agitates "Lonesome Day Blues," the song on *"Love And Theft"* where Dylan invokes Beatty Zimmerman, however, is domestic, and intimate: "Set my dial on the radio I wish my mother were still alive." His yearning, his grief, arises dead center in the song, five verses on each side. The offhand association of radio and mother rouses all the inspirational and nourishing musics of his life. Dylan's glance in "Lonesome Day Blues" at the *Aeneid*, and the ghost of Aeneas's father as he envisions the Roman empire after the civil wars—"teach peace to the conquered . . . tame the proud"—not only links America and Rome but also situates the song in the underworld, the afterlife. His glances at *Huck Finn*—"My sister, she ran off and got married / Never was heard of any more" and "Last night the wind was whisperin', I was trying to make out what it was"—sharpen his mourning, and summon fresh ghosts, for as Twain writes, "I felt so lonesome I most wished I was dead. The stars was shining and, and the leaves rustled in the woods ever so mournful; and I heard an owl, away off, who-whooing about somebody that was dead, and a whippowill and a dog crying about somebody that was going to die; and the wind was trying to whisper something to me and I couldn't make out what it was, and so it made the cold shivers run over me. Then away out in the woods I heard that kind of sound a ghost makes when it wants to tell about something's that's on its mind and can't make itself understood, and so can't rest easy in its grave and has to go about that way every night grieving. I got so down-hearted and scared. . . ."

For "Lonesome Day Blues," Dylan mined a dark vein of vintage blues, Son House, Blind Willie McTell, Muddy Waters, Leroy Carr, and the Mississippi Sheiks, but also "Sad and Lonesome Day" by the Carter Family, a country lament about the burial of a mother: "Today has been a lonesome day / And it seems tomorrow'll be the same old way . . . Oh they carried my mother to the burying ground." In a further Black and White turnaround, A. P. Carter based his song on Blind Lemon Jefferson's "See That My Grave Is Kept Clean." Dylan of course covered "See That My Grave Is Kept Clean" for his 1962 debut *Bob Dylan*, and again with the Band on *The Basement Tapes*.

Widening circles. Narrowing circles. Inevitably, Eric Lott listened to *"Love And Theft"* and wrote an essay about the strangeness of that encounter for his next book, *Black Mirror*. "So many things cluster here: the people you once clung to, the wrongs you couldn't help . . . the very sources of your energy and your art . . . Race, memory, and music meet . . . You reach back to your roots, you work through your masks, and you find yourself again in the land where the blues began." Lott marveled at what he hailed as the "overall sense of melancholic lift" on *"Love And Theft."*

Well, *maybe*. Or another *yes*, that is also another *no*. "These memories I got, they can strangle a man," Dylan concedes in "Honest with Me." Yet if *"Love And Theft"* finally does ascend to melancholy *and* lift, *Masked and Anonymous* now will only admit the melancholy—only the *strangle*.

H

. . . ONE OF YOUR FATHER'S FAVORITE PERFORMERS . . .

Hell, first with a small "h"—*hell.* Natural disasters: volcanic eruptions, avalanches, floods. Also wars, riots, police beatings, and terrorist raids. A stately crawl along the desolate sidewalks and human wreckage of downtown Los Angeles, shot—director Larry Charles told me—by dangling a documentary camera out a window of their moving film crew van. That opening montage. *Through me you pass into the city of woe.* Over the soundtrack static bleeds into a Japanese-language cover of Bob Dylan's "My Back Pages" by the Magokoro Brothers, and a radio preacher's boom-box sermon: "Will man destroy the earth to move on? Is that his destiny? Ask yourself a question, people, are you humble before God?"

Dystopian fictions usually at least pretend to be set in the future. Near future, distant future, no matter, they *imply* a future. That opening montage of *Masked and Anonymous* casually blurs future, past, and present, cosmopolitan America and what Cold Warriors dismissed as the "Third World." Much as on *"Love And Theft,"* though, it's not the Cold War but the American Civil War that's axial—later in the film we'll listen to "Dixie," hear about Sherman and Lee, and meet a carny knock-off of Abraham Lincoln, along with the more substantial and urgent blackface banjo player Oscar Vogel (Ed Harris). Far from an historical episode bracketed inside safe, reliable dates—say 1861 to 1865—or an impending, hypothetical revanchist Confederacy, the Civil War in *Masked and Anonymous* is ongoing, constant, a sort of Endless Infernal Tour. The story of a dying dictatorial president (Richard Sarafian) and his son Jack Fate (Bob Dylan), the film shapes an extrapolation from the reigns of Nixon, Reagan, Bush, and Bush, with the catastrophes of Vietnam, El Salvador, Nicaragua, Somalia, Afghanistan, and Iraq "coming home to roost," as Malcolm X once observed of the Kennedy assassination, a cinematic projection that with the ascent of Trump, COVID, the Russian invasion of Ukraine, Netanyahu and Hamas, the Supreme Court overturning of *Roe v. Wade*, and climate horrors increasingly looks more realistic than anything breaking now on CNN and MSNBC.

Masked and Anonymous will also eventually acknowledge Hell with a capital "H." As TV producer Nina Veronica (Jessica Lange) tunes into the radio of her on-set trailer:

> Geologists in Trenton are digging the world's deepest hole and have reached the depth of thirty miles. Something went amiss when the drill bit began to rotate wildly out of control. Scientists have measured the temperature down there as up to 3,000 degrees. They have lowered microphones into the pit and heard the sounds of millions of suffering souls. Dr. Samosa, at the project management center, has determined that the center of the earth is hollow. "Hopefully," he says, "whatever is down there will stay down there."

Men perish with whispering sins, silent sins. When at the finish of my previous chapter, I tentatively reaffirmed Eric Lott's "overall sense of melancholic *lift*" for *"Love And Theft,"* I was mistakenly, even imperiously brushing aside the immediate historical surroundings. I mean September 11, 2001, the album's release date. Historical surroundings that of course the album itself couldn't know, despite the presence of an eerie, all but vatic line in "Mississippi"—"Sky full of fire, pain pouring down." Historical surroundings that of course I as a New Yorker will never forget. "Mississippi" is one of those Dylan songs that if it isn't about *everything* at least it is about many things, a procession of separate moments linked by a recurrent chorus remindful of "Rosie," the Parchman Prison work song. "Only one thing I did wrong / Stayed in Mississippi a day too long." For many of us, *"Love And Theft"* is irrevocably bound up in that date. In fact, I was listening to the album that sunny Tuesday morning when a friend phoned, and without saying hello demanded—"Turn on your TV"—and hung up.

"Love And Theft" was the first Dylan album I managed to hear prior to its official release—a gift from another friend, a music journalist, who was inadvertently sent two advance CDs. I turned on the television, *"Love And Theft"* still playing on my stereo, just as hijackers crashed the second plane into the World Trade Center South Tower, and a startled newscaster shouted at the monitor over her shoulder, "Look! Another one!" I lived then in a small apartment on Charlton Street, in Soho, just off Sixth Avenue, and this would have been about 9:03 a.m., as I now glean from one of many internet 9/11 timelines. I had been up late the night before at a celebratory dinner in Café Loup after a New School Writing Program poetry reading, and for the next hour or so I alternated between watching TV and making trips to the street where in the near distance, dead center down Sixth Avenue, the North and South Towers were visible and burning. Sirens. Commiserating, stunned neighbors, including for a while actor Matthew Broderick—I can see his eloquent shoulder shrug; hear his somber, "Can you believe this?" The South Tower collapsed at 9:59, and the North Tower at 10:28.

Charlton Street is a few blocks north of Canal, so I wasn't part of the evacuation of Lower Manhattan, though throngs surged up Sixth towards the West Village, Chelsea, and Midtown with their backpacks, shopping bags, and clothes bundles. Infinite despair. Not until the weekend would I be able to take the bus upstate to rejoin my wife in New Paltz, where she taught Chinese history and film. Infinite wrath. In the aftermath of 9/11 George W. Bush would inaugurate the Patriot Act, drastically expanding the surveillance powers of federal law enforcement, conjure the Axis of Evil, and invade Iraq, amid false claims of Saddam Hussein harboring weapons of mass destruction and al-Qaeda. Decades later, in 2022, when Bush meant to denounce Vladimir Putin for the war on Ukraine, he—accidentally? remorsefully?—condemned the "decision of one man to launch a wholly unjustified and brutal invasion of Iraq." Why this is hell, nor am I out of it.

What I recall most about residing on Charlton Street during those early months after 9/11 is the *smell*, rarely during the daytime, but pretty much every night. Around midnight, or 1 a.m., an odor would abruptly materialize, though it wasn't at all—as one might fear—a stench redolent of the burnt flesh of the nearly three thousand men and women who died that morning; and also not the recognizable miasma of carbonized rubber, metal, and plastic. It was harsh, acrid, all-pervasive—a ghastly aroma all its own, and resembling nothing of my acquaintance since. Despite the PCBs and PAHs in the dust around Ground Zero, the EPA pronounced the downtown air safe to breathe—and this by September 18, scarcely a week after the attacks. Twenty years down the line, cancer lawsuit ads are staples on late-night news TV, although apparently only for New Yorkers who dwelt south of Canal Street. Yet rightly or wrongly from the first night on Charlton Street when I smelled that strange *smell*, I understood that someday as a consequence of living there I would find myself precariously sick.

For all that, the raw, cheerless *tone* of *Masked and Anonymous*, released in 2003—at least by contrast to that boisterous "lift" on *"Love And Theft"*—carries the distinctive whiff of a post-9/11 toxic fume. One discordant marvel of the film is the brilliance of the cast—John Goodman, Jessica Lange, Jeff Bridges, Luke Wilson, Penelope Cruz, Val Kilmer, and Mickey Rourke—their meticulousness, vitality, and dedication, and how casually appalling the characters they inhabit can be. Except for Rourke's Edmund, none is precisely evil; it's more that here, as Ray Davies of the Kinks once sang, "Everybody's in showbiz." The dramatic engine, the MacGuffin of *Masked and Anonymous*, is a televised benefit rock concert, ostensibly for the "victims of the revolution," and featuring just one headliner, Dylan's Jack Fate, who at the outset rots in a strait and dark and foul-smelling prison for long-ago personal crimes against his president father. The concert is merely a charade inside the larger sham. Goodman's promoter, Bridges's music journalist, Wilson's rock star buddy/guitar roadie, Lange's television producer, Cruz's occult girlfriend, Kilmer's carnie animal wrangler: all play out their tragicomic cultural roles, already beaten down, weary, even bored with themselves, as though they don't remember the alternative, if indeed there is another way to live and move through this world.

Uncle Sweetheart (Goodman), described in the script as "a hard drinking, hard living, hard ass combination of John the Baptist and P. T. Barnum," appears to be based on Dylan's second manager, Albert Grossman, down to the girth and glasses. Sweetheart can rally an almost Shakespearean gallimaufry of languages, and also spin rote rock-evangelist patter. To Nina (Lange): "Honey, this here's a benefit concert . . . Bigger than Live Aid or Farm Aid or whatever . . . I'm not making a dime on the action . . . I'm just trying to feed starving children is all." To Fate (Dylan): "I got so much shit happening man, I'm gonna turn this into Woodstock, Altamont, the Beatles at Shea, Live Aid, and the Elvis comeback special all rolled into one." It's Sweetheart who mobilizes Dylan, and a carnival of magicians, contortionists, and historical reenactors—"the greatest human menagerie since the Stone Age." Yet every Sweetheart word is a rococo con, including his later vulnerabilities and confessions; all profits from the benefit will eventually go to reimbursing his debts to the mysterious Percy and Blunt, bag men apparently for Rourke's Edmund, who apparently is the draconian next-in-line for the presidency.

When we first meet journalist Tom Friend (Bridges) during a meeting with his editor (Bruce Dern), he's wearing the hoodie and sunglasses combo twenty-first-century Dylan himself sometimes dons as a street disguise. Later he slips into a cool dress shirt and leather jacket straight from Newport, 1965. Visibly baffled but charmed by his own slithery self, this journalist interviews Fate through monologues masquerading as questions, many of his convoluted, self-consuming tirades rooted in Dylan's '60s press conferences. His editor works for the government, and unlocks an ankle monitor so Friend can go on assignment. Friend is aggressive with Fate: "Zappa, remember him? Now there's a guy who wouldn't take no for an answer . . . He let it all hang out, didn't he? What about you, Jack? Have you ever let it all out?" And racist, too:

> You know the London *Times*, Jack? You been in England lately? You wouldn't recognize the place. Big Ben is there, so's the Tower of London, but it's just a theme park. The English are in the minority in their own country, Jack . . . What Hitler and Napoleon couldn't do has been done in a bloodless coup.

Performing for Fate how he believes a conscientious reporter sounds, Friend, for all the bluster, concedes his futility. "People have always died. So what's new? You can't abolish death. Writing about it doesn't change anything."

Bobby Cupid (Wilson) is trickier to locate. On his way out of prison, Fate phones Cupid, who instantly abandons his job and life for his old pal and mentor. In Dylan's history, maybe Bob Neuwirth? But Cupid's hallmarks—his snakeskin jacket, the vintage guitar he claims "Blind Lemon" originally used to perform "Match Box Blues," even his name—all emanate from Valentine "Snakeskin" Xavier, the White blues guitarist Marlon Brando played in *The Fugitive Kind*, the 1960 Sidney Lumet film based on Tennessee Williams's *Orpheus Descending*, itself a revision of an earlier play, *Battle of Angels*, that Williams took up again after watching Elvis Presley. (On *Tempest* Dylan will quote *Battle of Angels* for "Long and Wasted Years.") Cupid tells Fate he received the guitar from "this old boy's house in Dallas . . . Blind Lemon gave it to him when he was leading him around." In Dallas, around 1912, Lead Belly met Blind Lemon Jefferson, and they traveled and performed together. In *The Fugitive Kind* Xavier's guitar is signed by Lead Belly, as well as by Blind Lemon Jefferson, and like his snakeskin jacket the instrument serves as his erotic talisman.

Brando's Xavier exemplifies the Beat hipster, his love for blues and alertness to civil rights soused in Williams's sour early rock 'n' roll colonialist fantasy of Blacks as a source of carnal deliverance and domestic menace. (A woman attracted to Xavier's "walk" and his "guitar" in *The Fugitive Kind* discovers that her husband once set fire to her family wine garden after her father "sold liquor to Negroes," and in his crazed jealousy of Xavier he then torches her own store.) *Masked and Anonymous* tempers Xavier's tacit minstrelsy, and shrouds Cupid's nostalgia for blues—"This is one of the guitars that started it all"—inside his reflex romanticism of any art. "Hemingway, now there's a guy who could write," he tells Tom Friend. Or, to Fate: "Let's go to the South Seas. Let's go where Gauguin went."

As the producer, Nina Veronica (Lange) initially seems the only participant at all anxious about creative standards for the TV special, or its moral integrity. "Uncle Sweetheart, an entire society is counting on you to raise some money for them," she chides Goodman's character. Yet she's happy to pass on to Fate any network demands for a contractual playlist of readymade protest songs: "Revolution," "Street Fighting Man," "Won't Get Fooled Again" "Riot in Cellblock #9," "Ohio," "Eve of Destruction," "Kick Out the Jams," and "Jailhouse Rock." Dylan and Larry Charles here orbit Elvis Presley's celebrated 1968 "Comeback" special, which NBC and Colonel Tom Parker planned as a Christmas show, and I wouldn't be surprised if director Baz Luhrmann screened *Masked and Anonymous* before he recreated the tensions around Presley, Parker, and NBC in *Elvis* (2022). For the network—and the government—protest is a brand, and "charity," Nina learns, "is like any other business." She never forgives Fate not playing her network playlist. "Sounds like a lot of songs," he says.

Pagan Lace (Cruz), Tom's partner, similarly appears to inhabit the ethical and spiritual center of *Masked and Anonymous*, though her prayers, altars, cards, and wisdom are also the manifestations of her chronic OCD. The carnival animal wrangler (Kilmer) demonstrates what appears to be heroism and an otherworldly sleight of hand, yet his spiels obviously are memorized, and he loses his place, repeats himself. Even Mrs. Brown

(Susan Traylor), whose "lovely daughter" (Tinashe Kachingwe) sings "The Times They Are A-Changin,'" spurs derision. "My daughter has memorized all of your songs," she boasts to Fate. But when asked why, she admits, "'Cause I made her, that's why." Folk music as child servitude—a final turn of the screw Uncle Sweetheart endeavors to obscure. "What do you think of that, Jack?," he asks. "Used to be she'd be sweating away in some factory, underage. . . . Anyway, she wants to sing her little heart out."

Sweetheart, Tom Friend, Bobby Cupid, Nina Veronica, Pagan Lace, Mrs. Brown, her daughter—each one is tainted, dubious. In a scene Charles filmed but ultimately cut, Friend and Lace visit a fortune teller, who counsels them:

> Every commitment, every truth, every ideal, everything of beauty, all these things are being stripped away. You are living in a world where all the jewels, diamonds, pearls, and rubies have been replaced by queer replicas.

Queer replicas. Sweetheart's "menagerie," a caustic emblem of this showbiz drift. "Here they are, Jack." Jean Darkness, Dali the Rubber Girl, Eddie Quicksand with Milo, and The Great El Mundo with Ella the Fortune Teller. "At our service. . . . "

Alongside, step right up, Pope John Paul II, Mahatma Gandhi, and Abraham Lincoln. "Our shooting gallery of beloved world leaders," Sweetheart cracks. *Masked and Anonymous* started out as a totally different project: a comedy series for HBO. "Dylan was an inveterate movie watcher," Larry Charles told me in Tulsa. On his tour bus in the '90s, he had a TV with a VCR. "At this particular period in his life he was watching a lot of Jerry Lewis," Charles recalled. "He was completely entranced by Jerry Lewis, and he said to Jeff Rosen, his manager, I'd really like to do a comedy series, and Jeff was like, really? And he's like yeah . . . Bob was kind of groping a little bit in the late '90s, before he found the next phase of his career." Charles, as it happens, is a "distant cousin" of Jeff Rosen's. "We had not spoken to each other since I was five or six years old," but they reconnected as adults through Eddie Gorodetsky, a writer and mutual friend who would briefly appear in *Masked and Anonymous*. "Jeff knew I did *Seinfeld*," Charles continued, "and so when this comedy idea came along he called me up and said, 'Would you be interested in sitting down with Bob?'" Charles's expectations were minimal. "My thought was this is so cool, I'm gonna have one meeting with Bob, and I'll be able to brag to all my friends."

Charles and Dylan met at the Eighteenth Street Coffee House in Santa Monica, a coffee shop/boxing club that "Bob owned there." As Charles recounted:

> We just sort of immediately started talking about the project. A very weird day—the first thing his assistant said, you guys want something to drink? And I said yes, I'll have an iced coffee, and he said, I want something hot, I want a hot beverage. And when they brought the hot beverage and the iced coffee, he immediately grabbed my coffee and started drinking the ice coffee. So now I'm in a *Curb / Seinfeld* situation here, I'm meeting Bob Dylan for first time and now he's stolen my drink. You know, do I say something, or do I let it slide? And I was going to let it slide because things were going so well now . . . we're actually working. About halfway through, he goes, why aren't you drinking your drink? And I said, because you stole it, you stole my drink, you're drinking my drink, and he cracked up. That kind of broke the ice to a large degree, and we started writing.

They wrote together in a cubicle at the back of the coffee shop by the boxing gym, Dylan chain-smoking throughout. "One of the first things Jeff told me was don't call him Dylan, don't ever call him Dylan, just always call him Bob. Cause he's Bob, you know, Dylan is your problem to figure out." At their first coffee, Dylan said to Charles, "'I have this *box*,' and he opened it . . . stacks of scrap paper, mostly hotel stationery . . . He said I don't know what to do with all this, he just spilled it out on the table, and I started picking through it and going, well . . . Uncle Sweetheart, this could be the name of a character, you know, Tom Friend, that's the name of a character, Jack Fate, that could be the name of a character, and here's a line that person could say, this person could say that, and he was like, you can do that? And I was like, *yeah*, and we started doing basically a Burroughs cut-up version of the script, taking the script and sort of pasting."

Charles described the concept of the half-hour HBO series as "basically this kind of a Buster Keaton cypher type of character, very stone-faced, very detached, walking through this surreal comic landscape, and using reference points from his songs." When the time came to sell the series to HBO, "Jeff and I said to Bob, you know if you go to the meeting we'll sell the project right in the room, they won't have the balls to say no to you." According to Charles, Dylan didn't want to attend, but reluctantly agreed. "I remember meeting at Century City, and at that time I wore pajamas all the time, I don't know why . . . and I would look like a patient wherever I went. Bob showed up . . . in full Western villain regalia, black hat, black duster, black boots, black gloves, a studded black shirt . . . and the two of us strutted into HBO, and everybody's like, what the fuck is this?"

Chris Albrecht, the then chairman and CEO of HBO was waiting for them. "He's so excited, as most people are, so excited to meet Bob that he can't help but gush and point to his wall and say, look I have my original Woodstock tickets right there. And Bob said, *uh, I didn't play at Woodstock*, and then he walked past all of us to the other side of this gigantic office with these big floor-to-ceiling windows, and he stared out the window for the entire meeting after that. The vibe in the room was very tense as I tried to pitch this comedy project and every now and then I would try to get Bob engaged . . . and he wouldn't even turn around to acknowledge that the other people were there." Still Charles and Rosen proved right—HBO couldn't refuse Dylan, and they sold the series anyways. "We walked out of the meeting, Jeff, my manager Gavin Palone, myself, and we were clicking our heels. We couldn't believe that we pulled this off. Bob seemed very pensive and unhappy, and I said, what's the matter? And he was like, I don't want to do it anymore, and I was like, what's wrong? '*It's too slapsticky.*' "

The HBO series by Charles's account might suggest a musical version of Samuel Beckett's *Film*, his 1965 short that featured Buster Keaton, though Charles's summaries of his conversations with Dylan—Dylan's deadpan, Charles's run-on—prompt other Beckett pieces, *Endgame*, *Krapp's Last Tape*, even *Molloy*. Charles remembers Palone trying to talk him out of continuing to work with Dylan. But he was adamant. "You don't understand, for me I'm on the Bob Dylan train, I'm lucky enough to be on this train, I'm taking it to the final stop, I'm not getting off, I don't care what happens." He told Dylan, "Look, I'm prepared to do whatever you want to make this work, and he was like, *okay*. We went back in, and we started writing what became the *Masked and Anonymous* script, folding some of these things into it."

When they returned to the Eighteenth Street Coffee House, Dylan now stretched beyond his box of hotel stationery, and instigated fresh writing. "He was very fertile during this period," Charles marveled. "He'd come in with these incredible monologues. He'd say, I wrote this last night . . . and I didn't want to change a word." According to Charles, Dylan drafted the character monologues that drive *Masked and Anonymous*, and it then fell to him to slot them into scenes:

> I sort of had to be the dramaturge . . . I had to decide who's saying that, why are they saying that, who are they talking to . . . Most of those great monologues, the John Goodman monologues, the Luke Wilson monologues, the Tom Friend monologues, the Jessica Lang monologues . . . *The Fugitive Kind* and the snakeskin jacket, the Blind Lemon Jefferson guitar . . . most of those monologues in some form or another came from him, and then scenes around them would be fashioned by me.

Dylan often surprised Charles—particularly when, for instance, "out of the blue one day" he came in with Tom Friend's '60s media harangues. Together they focused a dramatic situation, preserving the Dylan deadpan affect, the Dylan reference songs, and even some of the corny jokes of the HBO series, but the emphases shifted, the spirit darkened. "A lot of what he wrote," Charles noted, "you know the Andrew Jackson stuff, the biblical stuff about Ezekiel and the wheel . . . the prophetic stuff . . . or just a weird story about a trailer park . . . they were redolent of a Third World America . . . a post-Apocalyptic America . . . I started to fashion a story . . . he's the Prodigal Son, his father's a dictator, so we started to put together that sort of structure . . . the benefit concert, because that would be a corruption of the process in the story, but also an opportunity to showcase the band . . . we combined a number of different things."

Charles called their screenplay a "treasure map," and as on *"Love And Theft,"* Dylan's monologues for *Masked and Anonymous* excavate strata of subtext. The invocations, even distortions of religious impulses here nonetheless flaunt authoritative sources—Genesis 37:19; Matthew 5:14 and 15:11; and Saint Cyprian's "Letter to Donatus Concerning God's Grace." The name Edmund calls up *Lear*, and a character named Prospero (Cheech Marin) paraphrases the *Agamemnon* of Aeschylus. Fate checks into the forlorn Whitman Hotel. The inflections of Uncle Sweetheart's rollicking trickster razz—"As long as I keep talking I know I'm still alive"—encrypt John Quincy Adams, Kenneth Patchen, and Blind Willie McTell. Bobby Cupid echoes Paul Auster on America from *Moon Palace*: "The land is big out there. After a while it starts to swallow you up." Tom Friend channels Orwell, but also a sideshow photography book, *In Search of the Monkey Girl*. Along the way, Dylan and Charles absorbed some of their evident Modernist models for collaged prose: Patchen's *Journal of Albion Moonlight*, John Dos Passos's *U.S.A.*, and (inevitably?) Burrough's *Naked Lunch*.

Across *Masked and Anonymous*, America's past distills into a cavalcade of crime, and Charles told me that in their preparation for filming he and Dylan screened numerous film noirs and westerns, including *Kiss Me Deadly*, *The Killing*, *Key Largo*, *Gun Crazy*, *The Fugitive*, *Los Olivados*, *Enamorada*, *Django*, and *Texas, Adios*. "That look, like everything else in the movie, is a synthesis," Charles observed. Their locations—seductive, and mystifying—are "another layer." Fate's prison cell was a bear cage in the old Griffith Park Zoo, site also of the bus scene by a derelict Red

Car Station. Nina operates inside the Scottish Rite Masonic Temple on Wilshire. The president's palace was once a synagogue in East Los Angeles. Sweetheart's office, and the lobby where Fate phones Cupid, were in the same abandoned downtown building. "So all these places we found in Los Angeles," Charles said. "One day we were driving around, and I saw these steps, and I had that image of when [Jack Fate] needs to go see his mother, and I thought his mother could be in a graveyard up there, and that'll be a cool kind of crane shot following him up those stairs."

Dylan "was the true casting director of *Masked and Anonymous*," Charles recounted, "for as soon as the word went out that Bob Dylan was going to make a movie we couldn't stop people from wanting to get involved." On set, Charles primed each of the actors on their backstories—backstories that often weren't even in the original three-and-a-half-hour draft screenplay. "Bob's not concerned about the why's, but for me as a director dealing with actors I needed to give them some kind of why, so they understood what they were driving at. I gave them all backstory, you know, that they could bring to the performance."

Syntheses. Contrasts. Songs across languages and musical traditions. A dense, multi-angled script rendered talkative, even as if spontaneous, by ace actors. The fluid camera. *Masked and Anonymous* does not so much advance a plot as coordinate sequences. Early on, Dylan's "Blind Willie McTell" plays as Fate's bus snakes past the ravages of downtown Los Angeles. From the bus Fate flashes back to his childhood, a frolic with his father and mother on faded Super 8 film, and remarks in a voiceover, "Once he was a real father, full of love, compassion, and forgiveness, but that didn't last too long. . . . From the cathouses and gambling joints he rose to the top rung of civilization, President of this godforsaken nation." (The stage direction in the screenplay reads, "Think JFK and John John.")

Quick cut to Cupid's bar, where he takes Fate's call and "He Was a Friend of Mine" is on the jukebox: "Jack, I didn't think I'd ever hear from you again after that night." Inside the bus station now, Fate cradles the pay phone receiver. Another quick cut—Nina fights with Sweetheart about whether Fate will show, as Francesco De Gregori sings "If You See Her,

Say Hello" in Italian, and Sweetheart reassures Nina, "How do you know he's not like Claude Rains in that movie *The Invisible Man*?" Fate arrives at the Whitman Hotel, and the desk clerk gives him what he claims is the room Nixon occupied the night of the infamous "you don't have Nixon to kick around anymore" news conference. In the elevator Fate again flashes back, this time to a different hotel: his adolescent rendezvous with his father's mistress (Angela Bassett). Over the bed in his room at the Whitman looms a large portrait of the president, and he dials the palace, only to get a recording. He pulls another scrap of paper from his jacket, phones his father's sickroom, but hangs up. Then, another flashback to his meeting with his father's mistress, and another voiceover: "In my father's world you do not take what's his, not his gold, not his silver, not his woman. I thought I was doing it for my mother. I thought I was doing it for my country. Ultimately I knew I was doing it for me."

Cut to Fate entering a bar where Sweetheart sells him on the benefit concert: "A patriotic rhapsody. . . . Imagine yourself being reincarnated in the Civil War in Babylon. . . . You put your career back on track. . . . Make a little money, and save the world all at the same time." Sweetheart introduces Fate to the band he's put together for him, the Simple Twist of Fate, "the best and only Jack Fate cover band in the world." Fate then performs "Down in the Flood," backed by his own tribute combo. Simple Twist of Fate: Larry Campbell and Charlie Sexton on guitars; Tony Garnier on bass; George Receli on drums, Dylan's sharpest touring band, at least since the Hawks in 1966. Every song was done in one take. "These guys were so tight, they're on the road all year round, they knew how to play the song in their sleep. And that's how this band was . . . so we chose to shoot it that way," Charles said. To capture the songs Charles filmed as "rehearsals" for the benefit concert by Fate and Simple Twist, the crew screened tapes of local country and western television from the 1950s, along with the Johnny Cash show on ABC from 1969 through 1971. During the strongest runs, scenes collide and converge much as stanzas of a Dylan lyric. "When you see Porter Wagner and those kind of guys in these elaborate costumes, most of the music was shot in one take, going from Porter to the guitarist to the pedal steel to the stand-up bass, moving around and not cutting."

Charles shot twenty-two songs in full. Those that made it into the commercial release incline towards apocalypse, Hell with a capital "H": "Down in the Flood," "Drifter's Escape," and "Cold Irons Bound." "Dixie"—composed circa 1859 by Daniel Decatur Emmett, a blackface minstrel from Ohio—is the conspicuous curve, though Dylan had introduced the song in concerts during 1990 and 1991, and it entered *Masked and Anonymous* first as a band "warmup" that they then resolved to film. Before "Dixie" became a Confederate anthem, the song served as a walkabout—the concluding dance number in a minstrel show, and a Northerner's faux folk fantasy of a freed slave's nostalgia for the Southern plantation of his boyhood. Lincoln played "Dixie" at rallies, and when he announced Lee's surrender. Rewritten often, particularly during the Civil War—and notably as "Dixie to Arms!" by Albert Pike, a Boston-born journalist, poet, and Confederate brigadier general and envoy to the Native American nations—the song spans the musical and historical whorls Dylan tracked on *"Love And Theft."* Against the smug "protest" of the network playlist, "Dixie" is the jab of a finger in your eye, in the eye of America, and in the eye of this movie, to put you ill at ease, and shake you up a little. There's no easy way to hear it.

In a later Dylanesque succession of scenes, Tom Friend confronts Fate about Hugh Hefner, and Janis Joplin, "The Judy Garland of rock," as the singer shaves in his trailer: "You're supposed to have all the answers." Next, dressed up to go on stage, Fate intersects a carny visual pun, *Man Eating Chicken*. (Pull back the tent flap: a bucket of crispy fried chicken drumsticks.) *Masked and Anonymous* then returns to the Civil War, Reconstruction, and Jim Crow. On the steps of some scaffolding over the stage, Fate encounters the ghost—or is it?—of the blackface minstrel Oscar Vogel (Harris). "I was one of your father's favorite performers once," Vogel then tells Fate. "Everything was going great as long as you kept your mouth shut. But he was doing things that were wrong, your father. His desire for retaliation and revenge was too strong. . . . I had the show.

I had a forum. So I spoke out. It's not what goes in the mouth it's what comes out that counts. They said it was an accident. Some even said it was a suicide. . . ."

Fate is performing on stage at the benefit concert with Simple Twist of Fate—"Cold Irons Bound"—when Edmund announces the death of the president, and his own new agenda:

> At the moment we are giving people a new identity, erasing the collective memory. We are rewriting the history books. Nothing was more important to our President than bringing peace to this war-torn country. Peace, a lasting peace, can only be achieved through strength. So, in my first act as the new President, as the leader of the new government, this new regime, we will begin immediately to deploy troops to the southern regions. We will resume bombing in the jungle. There will be no more violence in the organized media. Real actual violence will take the place of manufactured violence. We will empty the prisons, and we will build the football stadiums. And the evildoers from the prisons will be trampled by wild elephants, mauled by uncaged bears, and pecked to death by screaming eagles. Furthermore, we will alert the rebel leaders that all the negotiations are finished. There will be no more compromises.

At least twice in the screenplay, Edmund is linked to Andrew Jackson. "I'm the man your father wanted you to be," Edmund explains to Fate. They grew up together, but Edmund's father was the palace groundskeeper, his mother cleaned the house, and the family was "illegal." Within the biblical/Shakespearean frame of *Masked and Anonymous*, Fate should be the filial alternative to Edmund's populist autocracy, yet he's at least as tarnished and damaged as Sweetheart, Tom, Nina, Cupid, and the rest. After Edmund mentions the family rise from servitude to the presidency, Fate turns patrician: "I remember your ma, wonderful lady. Used to ask permission before she did anything."

Aspects of Fate intimate a parallel-universe Bob Dylan, albeit with a scintilla of Elvis. (Fate, too, has a dead twin brother.) The sweet Super 8 home movies are dated "Approximately 1941," the year Dylan was born. Fate's music elicits clichés of Dylan journalism, hostile and adoring. Nina wonders, "Will his songs be recognizable?" And Pagan Lace: "I love his songs because they are not precise. They are completely open to interpretation." In the draft script, Oscar Vogel affirms his personal ties to Fate. "Your father would bring you here when you were a child," Vogel tells him. "I'd put you on the show. You'd play your guitar. Sing a song. When I heard you were doing a show here, I thought you might return the favor."

As the ghost whisperer of truth, Vogel is, of course, the most degraded and stigmatized of all. Without mentioning his name, Edmund alludes to him early on, as does Sweetheart, but who is—or was—Vogel exactly? Maybe Dan Emmett, the blackface composer of "Dixie"? Dylan's beloved Al Jolson? More than Jolson himself, though, he resembles Larry Parks, the actor who portrayed Jolson in *The Jolson Story* (1946) and *Jolson Sings Again* (1949). In 1951, Parks testified before the House Un-American Activities Committee. He admitted that he had been a member of the Communist Party, and after giving the dates of his membership as 1941–1945, he begged the committee not to be forced to name others: "Do not make me crawl through the mud like an informer." But threatened with contempt, in a closed session Parks "named names," and after the news was leaked to the press he was blacklisted in Hollywood anyways, and Columbia terminated his contract. At the hearing, he described himself as "probably the most completely ruined man that you have ever seen." Parks was godfather to Jeff Bridges, the actor who plays Tom Friend in *Masked and Anonymous*, and in 2011 Bridges spoke at a memorial service for Parks's wife, the actress Betty Garrett. Still, Vogel might be almost any White singer of Black music since the invention of minstrelsy through rock 'n' roll.

Religion in the film often reduces to a tabloid joke of UFOs, aliens, crop circles, and Roswell. Politics are circuitous, and circular. Over and over, figures from Sweetheart to Friend to Fate ask variants of *Which side are you on?* as though sides made a difference. But as the soldier Fate chances upon during his bus ride over the border reveals, the rebel movement is funded by the government they want to topple.

Fate performs "Cold Irons Bound," but for whom? The benefit concert broadcast is usurped by Edmund's iron-fisted address to the nation. No one outside the negligible studio audience of stagehands and extras hears Fate's song. He is soon arrested again, and on the way back to his strait and dark and foul-smelling prison, when a live recording of Bob Dylan singing "Blowin' in the Wind" plays, and Fate's face fills the screen. With a melody famously rooted in "No More Auction Block," is this the truth-to-power protest of Oscar Vogel's ghostly manifestation? Or . . . more entertainment? As Fate's voiceover concludes without concluding, "I stopped trying to figure everything out a long time ago."

I

. . . AN INVISIBLE WORLD THAT . . .

"I wish someone would have mentioned that to me earlier," Dylan confesses in *Chronicles: Volume One*, referencing the infamous revelation in Rimbaud's "Lettre du voyant" of May 15, 1871, to his friend Paul Demeny. Sometime in 1961 or 1962, "someplace along the line Suze [Rotolo] had also introduced me to the poetry of the French Symbolist poet Arthur Rimbaud. . . . I came across one of his letters called 'Je est un autre,' which translates into 'I is someone else.' When I read those words bells went off. It made perfect sense." Previously in *Chronicles*, Dylan signaled that when he arrived in New York, "There's a lot I didn't have, didn't have too much of a concrete identity either." And long after, recalling a 1987 "going through the motions tour" with Tom Petty and the Heartbreakers, he will admit, "I'd always be making some lame excuse. Actually, I don't know who was making the excuse, since I had closed the door on my own self." But as Dylan continues his meditation on Rimbaud's *voyant* letter, "It went right along with [Robert] Johnson's dark night of the soul, and Woody's hopped-up union meeting sermons and the 'Pirate Jenny' framework. Everything was in transition and I was standing in the gateway."

I don't know who was making the excuse. . . . Who then is *Chronicles* chronicling? And who in turn is the chronicler? Dylan's book opens with a colorful and amusing misperception. He has just signed a publishing contract with Leeds Music Corporation, and founder Lou Levy is steering his young charge through Manhattan—up to the "pocket sized" studio in the Pythian Temple on West Seventieth Street where Bill Haley recorded "Rock Around the Clock," and down to "a red leather upholstered booth" inside "Jack Dempsey's restaurant on Fifty-Eighth Street and Broadway." Levy introduces him to Dempsey, who "shook his fist at me" after myopically confusing him for a fledgling boxer. "You look too light for a heavyweight kid," Dylan remembers the prizefighter cautioning him, "you'll have to put on a few pounds." But Levy clarifies, "He's not a boxer, Jack, he's a songwriter and we'll be publishing his songs." Dempsey, unfazed, responds, "Oh, yeah, well I hope to hear 'em some of these days. Good luck to you, kid."

Scenes, conversations, locales, background, characterizations, perspective, jokes. Who would have guessed that the insistently cagey Bob Dylan would in his sixth decade deliver a casual masterwork of a "you-are-there" memoir? Yet that's just what he accomplished with *Chronicles* in 2004. The book's range is limited: definitely focused, telescoped and thematic. Nothing about *Highway 61 Revisited*, or *Blonde on Blonde*. No *Blood on the Tracks*, Rolling Thunder Revue, or *Slow Train Coming*. Next to nothing about family, wives, or children. No, at a time when Dylan was deep into the activities of reimagining and regenerating himself as a songwriter and performer with *Time Out of Mind*, *"Love And Theft,"* and years of restless, worldwide touring, he nimbly centered some parallel moments from his past. Of the five chapters in *Chronicles*, three circle the roughly ten months between his arrival in New York in January of 1961 and the recording of his debut album, *Bob Dylan*, for Columbia that November. The other chapters summon spells of creative, professional, and spiritual calamity, demanding change, and—if possible—reinvention: *New Morning* in 1970; and *Oh Mercy* in 1989.

Again and again in *Chronicles* across eras and milieus, Dylan puts us right next to him. As Mikal Gilmore enthused for *Rolling Stone*, "He conjures up rooms full of living history, full of the famous and the unknown, and he tells us how they walked, talked, looked, and why they mattered."

Charles Taylor speculated in *Salon*, "What may throw some readers about *Chronicles* is how modest and straightforward it is. . . . Dylan is revealing about the things that matter." Greil Marcus, captivated and thoughtful, suggested, "You can sense the choices between one word and another. This wasn't spoken into a tape recorder or ghost-written. There are lines like him talking about '50s rockabilly artists [who play like they are] navigating burning ships—flashes like that."

Vivid, in the moment, immediate, interior. To save something from the time where he—we—will never be again. Early on, he introduces Fred Neil, then daytime MC at the Café Wha? on MacDougal Street:

> Fred would play for however long he felt, however long the inspiration would last. Freddy had the flow, dressed conservatively, sullen and brooding, with an enigmatical gaze, peachlike complexion, hair splashed with curls and an angry and powerful baritone voice that struck blue notes and blasted them to the rafters with or without a mike. He was the emperor of the place, even had his own harem, his devotees. You couldn't touch him. Everything revolved around him.

He ushers us into the sanctum sanctorum at Izzy Young's Folklore Center:

> Izzy had a back room with a potbellied wood-burning stove, crooked pictures and rickety chairs—old patriots and heroes on the wall, pottery with cross-stitched design, lacquered black candlesticks . . . and a lot of things having to do with craft. The little room was filled with American records and a phonograph. Izzy would let me stay back there and listen to them.

When one cold day Dave Van Ronk walks into the Folklore Center shopping for a guitar, Dylan sticks close, watchful. "He was gruff, a mass of bristling hair, don't give a damn attitude, a confident hunter . . . Izzy took the guitar down and gave it to him."

Elsewhere in *Chronicles* he sketches his emotional awakening upon first hearing some Woody Guthrie recordings in Minneapolis:

> That day I listened all afternoon to Guthrie as if in a trance and I felt like I had discovered some essence of self-command, that I was in the internal pocket of the system feeling more like myself than ever before.

He exposes the origins of his own songs, such as "Dark Eyes":

> I was staying at the Plaza Hotel on 59th Street. . . . As I stepped out of the elevator a call girl was coming towards me in the hallway—pale yellow hair wearing a fox coat—high heeled shoes that could pierce your heart. She had blue circles around her eyes, black eyeliner, dark eyes. She looked like she had been beaten up and was afraid she'd get beat up again. In her hand, crimson purple wine in a glass. "I'm just dying for a drink," she said as she passed me in the hall. She had a beautifulness, but not for this kind of world. Poor wretch, doomed to walk this hallway for a thousand years.

And during a stroll through New Orleans he poignantly adumbrates his rise from the artistic dead, while making *Oh Mercy*:

> The first thing you notice about New Orleans are the burying grounds—the cemeteries—and they're a cold proposition. . . . The past doesn't pass away so quickly here. You could be dead for a long time. The ghosts race towards the light, you can almost hear the heavy breathing—spirits all determined to get somewhere. New Orleans, unlike a lot of those places you go back to and that don't have the magic anymore, still has got it. . . . Around any corner, there's a promise of something daring and ideal and things are just getting going.

Flesh made word. Shadowing Dylan's arrival in New York, the first chapter of *Chronicles* locks together with the last, though the connections are not so much chronological as they are in the spirit of Waverly Place, a street in the West Village that winds and forks until, near Grove Street, Waverly Place intersects itself. By launching his memoir with music publisher Lou Levy, Dylan insinuates that his first chapter, "Markin' Up the Score," will recount his songwriting process, but this is quickly revealed as another false impression. The narrative spur is instead Dylan's need to "find singers, the ones I'd heard on record" and then, as he settles into the city, his yearning to perform at the Gaslight Café, also on MacDougal Street: "It was a club I wanted to play, needed to." As he wanders around the West Village and Soho, sleeping on the couches of his new friends, Dylan crisply portrays some of those singers, Van Ronk, Neil, Richie Havens, and Karen Dalton, along with Tiny Tim, Moondog, and Billy the Butcher, as well as Columbia Records talent scout and producer John Hammond. By chapter's end Dylan still hasn't reached the Gaslight Café, or written a song for Levy to promote, but no matter. "I'd soon be hired to play The Gaslight and never see the basket houses again. . . . But now destiny was about to manifest itself. I felt like it was looking right at me and nobody else." The future is too immense for him to imagine. It will happen, that's all.

In the final chapter, "River of Ice," Dylan is back in Lou Levy's office and, after a brief phone call home to his parents, he serially recreates his transformation from a player of "hard core folk songs backed by incessantly loud strumming" into the author of "It's Alright Ma (I'm Only Bleeding)," "Mr. Tambourine Man," "The Lonesome Death of Hattie Carroll," "Who Killed Davey Moore?," "Only a Pawn in Their Game," and "A Hard Rain's A-Gonna Fall"—to repeat his own future jewel list. Dylan flashes back from the vantage of those revolutionary songs to Duluth, Hibbing, and Minneapolis, and ahead to Greenwich Village, as if retrospectively mobilizing a roadmap of inevitability from chance, desire, and the zeitgeist. How his "destiny"—to repeat the pun he drops twice in *Chronicles*—was "manifest."

In *Chronicles*, Dylan's Bildungsroman starts with carnivals. Carneys, of course, track among the through lines of his imagination, and as he writes of Hibbing, "There were three-ring circuses that came to town a few times a year and full-tilt carnivals complete with human oddities, showgirls and even geeks. I saw one of the last blackface minstrel shows at a county carnival." From carnivals Dylan moves on to the University of Minnesota and the Beats. "I suppose what I was looking for was what I read about in *On the Road*—looking for the great city, looking for the speed, the sound of it, looking for what Allen Ginsberg had called the 'hydrogen jukebox of the world.' " His next phase—also in Minneapolis, around Dinkytown by the university—takes him into the "parallel universe" of folk music:

> A culture with outlaw women, super thugs, demon lovers and gospel truths . . . streets and valleys, rich peaty swamps with landowners and oil men, Stagger Lee, Pretty Pollys and John Henrys—an invisible world that towered overhead with walls of gleaming corridors. It was all there—ideal and God-fearing—but you had to go find it.

Along University Avenue in Dinkytown, Dylan listens to Odetta and Lead Belly records, and encounters singers and folklorists, particularly John Koerner, at whose apartment he learns songs performed by a steadily amplifying radius of folk and blues artists past and contemporary, Charley Patton, Blind Lemon Jefferson, Tommy Johnson, Blind Blake, John Jacob Niles, Dave Van Ronk, Roger Abrams, and—markedly—the New Lost City Ramblers, who would stimulate him all the way through *"Love And Theft"* and *Modern Times*. In the decisive turn of his musical education, Flo Castner, an actress who—coincidentally?—also appeared in Dylan Thomas's *Under Milkwood* at the Walker Arts Center in Minneapolis, then plays those Guthrie 78s for him at her brother's house. As Dylan continues about Guthrie in *Chronicles*:

> Woody's got a fierce poetic soul—the poet of hard crust and gumbo mud. . . . For me, his songs made everything else come to a screeching

> halt. I decided then and there to sing nothing but Guthrie songs. . . . I said to myself I was going to be Guthrie's greatest disciple. . . . I even seemed to be related to him. . . . He looks not unlike my father in my father's younger days. . . . Woody Guthrie had never seen nor heard of me, but I felt like he was saying, "I'll be going away, but I'm leaving this job in your hands. I know I can count on you."

Clouds disperse—until a snide Dinkytown friend, Jon Pankake, "a folk music purist enthusiast" who would eventually write liner notes for the Smithsonian Folkways reissue of the *Anthology of American Folk Music*, informs him of another singer with the same improbable MO, Ramblin' Jack Eliott, and Dylan is "cast into sudden hell." Still, that destiny of his even here stands dauntless and steadfast—"Whatever I heard people say was irrelevant . . . The road ahead had always been encumbered with shadowy forms that had to be dealt with in one way or another." And for the next step of this private songwriting edification he listens to Joan Baez, whom he curiously only writes about prior to their meeting and living together in New York: "A voice that drove out bad spirits . . . The singer has to make you believe what you are hearing and Joan did that."

Baez and Elliott inescapably rouse glimmerings of the Village, and so Dylan quits Minneapolis—absconding by other accounts with a few of Pankake's rarest New Lost City Ramblers albums, and "head[s] off to where life promises something more." It's here, then, that "Markin' Up the Score" and "River of Ice" finally crisscross—more glimpses of Van Ronk, Levy, and Hammond, plus introductions to Noel Stookey, Hugh Romney (aka Wavy Gravy), Len Chandler, Paul Clayton, Carolyn Hester, Richard Fariña, and Albert Grossman. But the wild card is his young girlfriend, Suze Rotolo, and as Dylan evokes her in *Chronicles* she proved as crucially influential to his songwriting as anyone before or after. Her sister Carla was employed by Alan Lomax, and she herself worked in the New York Congress of Racial Equality office. It was Suze who acquainted Dylan with the songs of Bertolt Brecht, when they attended a production of *Brecht on Brecht* at the Theatre de Lys on Christopher Street. In 1963 she was the assistant to stage manager and set designer Quinton Raines for a later production of *Brecht on Brecht* at the Sheridan Square Playhouse, and she brought him to rehearsals. In her book, *A Freewheelin' Time: A Memoir of Greenwich Village in the Sixties*, she says that she especially wanted him to hear "Pirate Jenny":

> It is a compelling song of revenge and as sung by Micki Grant, a black woman, it took on another dimension. This was the civil rights era, and listening to her sing the song was a powerful piece of living theater. I knew Bob should not miss it. He sat still and quiet. Didn't even jiggle his leg. Brecht would be part of him now, as would the performance of Micki Grant as Pirate Jenny.

Dylan digs into "Pirate Jenny" for some five pages in *Chronicles*, showing how "I took the song apart and unzipped it," and that Brecht served as a prototype for the elusive songs he craved. "I could see that the type of songs I was leaning towards singing didn't exist, and I began playing with the form, trying to grasp it—trying to make a song that transcended the information in it, the character and the plot."

Suze directed Dylan to what he tags the "collage tableaus" of Red Grooms, presumably during the artist's show at the Tibor de Nagy Gallery in October and November of 1962, and henceforth Grooms is a song template. "What folk songs were lyrically," he reckons in *Chronicles*, "Red's songs were visually—all the bums and cops, the lunatic bustle, the claustrophobic alleys—all the carnie vitality. Red was the Uncle Dave Macon of the art world." According to her memoir, Suze and Dylan also went to MOMA for *The Art of Assemblage* (1961), where they would have experienced collages by Braque, Breton, Cornell, Duchamp, Ernst, Hoch, Motherwell, Picabia, Picasso, Rauschenberg, and Schwitters.

As one of the last planks of his Bildungsroman, John Hammond gives him an advance acetate of Robert Johnson's *King of the Delta Blues*—and Dylan then consecrates eight pages to the shock of hearing him. "From the first note," he raptures, "the vibrations from the loudspeaker made my hair stand up. The stabbing sounds from the guitar could almost break a window. When Johnson started singing, he seemed like a guy who could have sprung from the head of Zeus in full armor. I immediately differentiated between him and anyone else I had ever heard." As with "Pirate Jenny," he rips the songs apart so that he might intuit how Johnson created them:

> I copied Johnson's words down on scraps of paper so I could more closely examine the lyrics and patterns, the construction of his old-style blues lines and the free association that he used, the sparkling allegories, big-ass truths wrapped in the hard shell of nonsensical abstraction—themes that flew through the air with the greatest of ease. I didn't have any of these dreams or thoughts but I was going to acquire them.

With the addition of Rimbaud, courtesy of Suze, Dylan now exhibits his songwriting apprenticeship as complete—or almost. "Soon I'd step in heavy loaded, fully alive and revved up. Not quite yet, though."

Even though in "River of Ice" his great songs are only dispatched in prospect, as destined ambitions, vital principles of what in 2022 he would dub his *Philosophy of Modern Song* are already nascent. One is the astonishing largeness of his vision of folk music. Across *Chronicles*, folk isn't taste, an enthusiasm, affinity, or—Lord knows—a career move, folk for Dylan is simultaneously the vast world and his only tool for probing, comprehending, and managing that world. "Folk songs were the way I explored the universe," he observes of his coffee house days, "they were pictures and the pictures were worth more than anything I could say. . . . Most of the other performers tried to put themselves across, rather than the song, but I didn't care about doing that. With me, it was about putting the song across." And still more adventurously, while listening to the radio in a friend's Soho apartment he affirms that "songs, to me, were more important than just light entertainment. They were my preceptor and guide into some altered consciousness of reality, some different republic, some liberated republic."

Another rudiment of that philosophy involves how he sets his songs—and Bob Dylan—against the history of music and culture. *Chronicles* recurrently frames everyday antitheses—original and traditional, unique and a copy, authentic and spurious, improvised and rehearsed, even truth and lies—and then scuttles and scoffs at any such distinctions. As he praises the New Lost City Ramblers: "At the time, I didn't know that they were replicating everything they did off of old 78 records, but what would it have mattered anyway? It wouldn't have mattered at all. For me, they had originality in spades, were men of mystery on all counts." Hearing Guthrie and demonstrating "self-command" are indistinguishable. Of the tunes he learned from John Koerner, he writes, "I could rattle off all these songs without comment as if all the wise and poetic words were mine and mine alone." Dylan details the cock-and-bull he told Billy James, the Columbia Records publicity head, about his origins and past jobs—"he tried to get me to cough up some facts, like I was supposed to give them to him straight and square"—while on the opposite page he cites John Hammond's admiration of his "sincerity." He informs James that "I didn't see myself like anybody," but then says that he "copied" some of Van Ronk's recordings "phrase for phrase." Across *Chronicles*, writing songs invariably is rewriting other songs. "What I was into was the traditional stuff with a capital T . . . What I usually did was start out with something, some kind of line written in stone and then turn it on its head with another line—make it add up to something else than it originally did." The Dylan of *Chronicles* might sound like an AI algorithm built from T. S. Eliot's "Tradition and the Individual Talent," except that his ecstasy of influence claims are only a wilier variation on the views in his poem "11 Outlined Epitaphs," as far back as 1963: "Yes, I am a thief of thoughts / not, I pray, a stealer of souls / I have built an' rebuilt / upon what is waitin' . . . / a word, a tune, a story a line / keys in the wind t' unlock my mind."

If "Markin' Up the Score" and "River of Ice" rough out a topography of his future songwriting, the third chapter, "New Morning," then catalogs his all-out assault in the late 1960s on pretty much everything "Bob Dylan"—and all the troubles and vexations that he unloosed upon himself with those songs. It's now 1968, as *Chronicles* neatly overskips his incandescent ascent, and he is living in Woodstock with his wife and young family. "I had been in a motorcycle accident and I'd been hurt, but I recovered," he writes. "Truth was that I wanted to get out of the rat race. Having children changed my life. . . . Outside of my family, nothing held any real interest." He presents himself as isolated and hounded—in flight from his fame, his media image, and his purported role in music and society: "Whatever the counterculture was, I'd seen enough of it. I was sick of the way my lyrics had been extrapolated, their meanings subverted into polemics, and that I had been anointed as the Big Bubba of Rebellion." Dylan here resents any exterior attempts to define him, recognizing in hindsight that he "had failed to sense the ominous forebodings" when Ronnie Gilbert of the Weavers introduced him at the 1964 Newport Folk Festival with a convivial, "And here he is . . . take him you know him, he's yours." Similarly, when even his friend and guitarist Robbie Robertson asks him, "Where do you think you're gonna take it . . . You know, the whole music scene," his swift impulse is to cut and run. "I felt like I might have been living in another part of the solar system," Dylan recalls. "It was like dealing with a conspiracy. No place was far enough away."

Meanwhile, his father has died—Abram "Abe" Zimmerman passed away on May 29, 1968—and on his return from the funeral Dylan says that he found a letter from Archibald MacLeish inviting him to write songs for a play, *Scratch*, based on Stephen Vincent Benet's "The Devil and Daniel Webster." In *Chronicles* Dylan and his wife drive to MacLeish's home in Conway, Massachusetts, and he recounts the poet's pronouncements on Eliot, Ezra Pound, Homer, François Villon, Stephen Crane, Douglas MacArthur, and J. P. Morgan. As MacLeish later wrote in a letter, "Now as to Bob Dylan. He proved simply incapable of producing new songs," yet "New Morning," "Father of Night," and "The Man in Me," from *New Morning* originated in *Scratch*. For *Chronicles* he characterizes himself as still in flight—now from the gloom of MacLeish's vision. "Archie's play was so heavy—so full of midnight murder," he writes. "There was no way I could make its purpose mine." But Dylan is clear that in fleeing his fame and image, he was also fleeing his own past descent into the dark of 1966: "I wasn't going to go deeper into the darkness for anybody. I was already living in the darkness. My family was my light and I was going to protect that light at all cost." And he is clear that he is in flight from what he calls the truth. "The play itself was conveying some devastating truth, but I was going to stay far away from that. . . . I didn't want it in my house."

In "New Morning" sometimes that flight—that escape—is literal. After their life in Woodstock veers into a "nightmare," the Dylans move to New York City "in hopes to demolish my identity." Disaster. They go out West. No better. Dylan then samples guerrilla theater, and claims that in order to "remodel the image of me" he'd pour whiskey over his head and walk into a store, "knowing that everyone would be talking." Finally, he admits to a form of artistic suicide, and alleges that *Nashville Skyline* and *Self Portrait* were deliberate muddles. When he releases *New Morning* he goes along with the critical fanfare that it is a "comeback" album, but sardonically motions, "It would be the first of many." So fierce, methodical, and absolute is his blitz on "Bob Dylan" that "New Morning" is tantamount to a dismantling of his encircling Bildungsroman, a virtual anti-memoir inside the memoir. Expanding on a notion advanced by James Alan McPherson, writer Yiyun Li observed that, "Anti-memoirs, for me, are about de-selfing. You have to take yourself out of it, while still writing about things you're concerned with and want to write about. So in the end, an anti-memoir is not really about the author—it's more about the reader." "New Morning" might be said to de-self the Dylan of "Markin' Up the Score" and "River of Ice."

Yet such de-selfing is hardly limited to one chapter of *Chronicles*. Intimations of anti-memoir discompose and destabilize page upon page of his ongoing roman-fleuve. Throughout there's a routine, almost a formula—whenever Dylan sounds, say, most direct, personal, and authoritative, there's likely a bit of mischief nearby. A tiny, subversive worm gnaws through all the citations I described above—accurately, I still believe—as "vivid, in the moment, immediate, interior." When Dylan recreates for us Fred Neil at Café Wha?, his memory is worked up from words and phrases in Sax Rohmer's *The Return of Dr. Fu-Manchu* and Robert Greene's *The 48 Laws of Power.* Izzy Young and the Folklore Center arrive courtesy of Kate Simon's 1959 guidebook *NY Places and Pleasures*, though Simon isn't specifically depicting Izzy at all but "The Typical New Yorker," and not the Folklore Center, but McSorley's Ale House, Howerla's Ukrainian Bookstore, and Surma's Book and Record Shop. His sketch of Dave Van Ronk mashes Simon's invocation of that standard New Yorker into Jack London's "Batard." Dylan's psychic metamorphosis on hearing Woody Guthrie bisects Robert Louis Stevenson's "Story of the Young Man in Holy Orders," and the "sudden hell" he's tossed into after learning about Ramblin' Jack Elliott is also a nod to London. He materializes that woman behind "Dark Eyes" via Geri Hershey's *Nowhere to Run* and H. G. Wells's *The War of the Worlds.* Those cemeteries in New Orleans inter still more Sax Rohmer, with a remnant of Mark Twain. Billy the Butcher wasn't a folk singer but William Poole of Herbert Asbury's *Gangs of New York*, helped along by a dash of Hemingway's "The Killers." MacLeish's conversations with Dylan mostly coincide with the senior poet's edition of *The Complete Poems of Carl Sandburg.* Even Dylan's Lou Levy and Jack Dempsey opening—the recording studio, restaurant booth, and heavyweight gag—all honor Charles Mingus describing far different locales and situations in *Beneath the Underdog.* And anyways, wasn't Dempsey's restaurant farther south down Broadway than Fifty-Eighth Street, in the Brill Building, between Forty-Ninth and Fiftieth?

As Kate Simon jokes in *New York*, "Everything said of the Village is almost true." For Dylan and *Chronicles* the wonder, then, isn't so much you-are-there, as *who* was there? His reminiscences distance through another shrewd refractive tilt. Levy, MacLeish, and Guthrie are each forwarded as a stand-in father; he christens Baez his "counterpart," and that notion animates all his extended reflections, the Beats, Koerner, Chandler, Clayton, Van Ronk, Suze, etc. Over and over in *Chronicles* Dylan makes it clear that he knows that we know that these fathers and counterparts are projections. He recognizes aspects of himself in them? Recognizes aspects of them in himself? Mirror on mirror, down a dim hallway.

Dylan verges on bravura in the finesse of his double vision. His impish second chapter, "The Lost Land," twirls a Pynchonesque novella from the same Greenwich Village lore that fires "Markin' Up the Score" and "River of Ice"—so Pynchonesque that along the way he surreptitiously commemorates *Gravity's Rainbow.* In "The Lost Land" Dylan is crashing on another sofa, but the Vestry Street Federal-style locale is imaginary, as probably are the cryptic custodians of that sofa, a bohemian couple named Ray Gooch and Chloe Keil (amazingly spun from the tiniest of spurs in Lloyd Morris's *Incredible New York* and a 1942 "Hero of the Grid Iron" *True Comic*). The year is 1961, and Dylan again approaches the process of writing songs, but in an abstract, practically allegorical way. "You want to say something about strange things that have happened to you, strange things you have seen," he only vaguely recalls. But he pinpoints the moment when he knew he would eventually "have to write my own folk songs" in his realization that he could never perform traditional music as powerfully as Mike Seeger, his melancholy awakening an echo—as I mentioned previously—of daily entries in *Touchstones: A Book of Daily Meditations for Men*, of the Hazelden Meditation Series. Writing new songs is thus implicitly spiritual. Like desire, his memory never stops, pairing the dead with the living, real with imaginary beings, his dreams with history. The year might be 1961, but his obsessions in "The Lost Land" are up-to-the-minute. When Dylan purports to inventory the books in Gooch's vast library, he casually counts off some of the authors and topics vital to his twenty-first century records: Ovid, Dante, Milton, Greek and Roman history, the Civil War. Correspondingly, when he relays his excursions to the New York Public Library to pore over Civil War newspapers, that reconnaissance reads as his research for *"Love And Theft,"* not *Bob Dylan.* His reactions to those newspapers even mull Dorothy Dineen Volo and James M. Volo's *Daily Life in Civil War America*, a book he couldn't have read before 1998. Time in "The Lost Land" is at a crossroads—"you could feel the old world go and the new one beginning"—yet porous: "Folk songs transcended the immediate culture."

His chapter in *Chronicles* on *Oh Mercy* (titled "Oh Mercy") is still more audacious, as Dylan shapes a multifaceted send-up of our stock therapeutic modern memoir, replete with a sudden crisis, amid surprising consequences; tough resolutions; and assorted remorseful yet joyous insights. The crisis: he "ripped and mangled" his hand in a "freak accident," an episode he interprets symbolically. "I had been kidding myself, exploiting whatever talent I had beyond the breaking point . . . There was a missing person inside of myself and I needed to find him." The consequences: after a destructive half-decade of blocked and wasted years, he is writing songs again. The tough resolution, across multiple, interlocking phases: "In time, my hand got right, but it was ironic. I stopped writing the songs." And, then, in 1989, at Bono's recommendation, he records *Oh Mercy* with producer Daniel Lanois in New Orleans.

As for those thorny insights, he offers three huge epiphanies, all from 1987. During a dismal rehearsal with the Grateful Dead, he disappears into a bar where he discovers a singer fronting a jazz combo:

> Suddenly and without warning, it was like the guy had an open window to my soul. . . . I could feel how he worked at getting his power, what he was doing to get at it. I knew where the power was coming from and it wasn't his voice, though the voice brought me sharply back to myself. I used to do this thing, I'm thinking. . . . It was like I'd forgotten how to button my own pants. . . .

Dylan then narrates that mysterious night in Locarno, Switzerland, when on tour with Tom Petty he "fell into a black hole," and "instead of being stranded at the end of the story, I was actually in the prelude to the beginning of another one." Finally, he gives us the key to his restored guitar playing, an intricate mathematical technique rooted in triplets that he says years ago Lonnie Johnson taught him, and "now all of a sudden it came back to me, and I realized that this way of playing could revitalize my world."

"Oh Mercy" gestures towards all you'd wish for in a Dylan memoir. Doesn't he take us song by song through *Oh Mercy*, divulging the conditions of each composition, and revisiting his sessions with Lanois? Doesn't he pivot private, domestic—telling us that his wife (though not which wife) joined him in New Orleans, and taking us with them when they go on a motorcycle holiday, even mentioning a daughter's school play? All you'd wish for . . . but caveat lector. Yet—again—his phrases shade allusive undertones. Dylan nearly winks at us during his drunken night with Bono that led him to Lanois. "When Bono or me aren't exactly sure about somebody," he allows, "we just make it up. We can strengthen any argument by expanding on something either real or not real." Well, *yeah.* His postil on Johnson's triplets is wilier. Much of his language about the advantages of the guitar system muses on Robert Greene's *The 48 Laws of Power*, specifically around Law 27—"Play on People's Need to Create a Cultlike Following." When Dylan enthuses over Johnson's technique, "You gain power with the least amount of effort, trust that the listeners make their own connections," he's contemplating Green on "The Science of Charlatanism, or How to Create a Cult in Five Easy Steps." Despite the surface rave, his subtext flickers HOAX.

His collages can intensify towards the ends of his chapters. The close of "The Lost Land" brilliantly intersects Mezz Mezzrow and Jack London, and the concluding paragraphs of "Oh Mercy" weave London, Madame Blavatsky, and the letters of Thomas Wolfe; and the book winds down with Joe Esterhas's *American Rhapsody*. Dylan's de-selfing in *Chronicles* is militant, pervasive, and cuts deep. He'll be walking across the yard of his Malibu house, and pause to describe the sea—though the view actually isn't his at all, but Marcel Proust's for *In Search of Lost Time*. Or he'll buy a red flower for his wife—and both flower and wife also live in Robert Louis Stevenson's "Providence and the Guitar." That "navigating burning ships" phrase Greil Marcus adored? Jack London's "The Seed of McCoy." Still, *Chronicles* rarely is so fixed and simple as sheer fabrication, and Dylan's anti-memoir won't entirely cancel his memoir. The most transparently fictional sequences carry what at least read on the page as revelations. "The Lost Land" is where he advances folk songs as his "preceptor and guide" to "reality," and details the influences on his songwriting.

Fabrication. Revelations. As Dylan writes of Ray and Chloe's apartment, "Everything in plain sight," conveniently hiding the word "hidden." Just as in his songs, he scatters throughout *Chronicles* numerous reflexive knots and nuggets that are tempting to decode as emblems for the book. At a folk music party he mentions seeing "the outlaw artist" Robyn Whitlaw, and notes that "years later Whitlaw would be arrested for breaking and entering and stealing. Her defense was that she was an artist and that the act was performance art and, incredulously, the charges against her were dropped." Whitlaw was the invention of art critic Ralph Rugoff for an April Fools' essay he wrote for *LA Weekly*, and one wonders if "performance art" is also Dylan's "defense" for *Chronicles*, and his thicket of collage. Are such collages and *Chronicles* ultimately for him, as he evokes New Orleans, "a great place to live vicariously"? Maybe the trajectory of memoir and anti-memoir lies closer to the description he offers of his song "Disease of Conceit" in "Oh Mercy": "Reality can be overwhelming. It can also be a shadow, depending on how you look at it." Might *Chronicles* hover in his riff on "What Was It You Wanted?," another *Oh, Mercy* lyric? "It's like you set up a thick smokescreen and then put the real action ten miles away."

Can anyone say?

I now resume the little questions I asked earlier about "who" *Chronicles* is about, and "who" wrote it. Irish folksinger Liam Clancy once pronounced Dylan a "sponge." Sponges absorb, and release. But to say something as mock clever as *This is a story about a sponge by a belated, infinitely more sophisticated incarnation of that sponge* would trivialize his anti-memoir as well as his memoir. After all, if *Chronicles* weren't so insistently alive, enthralling, and persuasive as a memoir, the anti-memoir inside it wouldn't matter, could come across as only an abstruse stunt. Instead, though, I see a conscious artist telling us—sometimes circuitously, sometimes candidly; on any page, phrase by phrase in any sentence—what he did, and within the cascading arcs, mobilities, and layers of those pages and phrases and sentences also showing us how he did it, generating a life out of scraps and gems. Each its own world, a hypnotic, many-sided facet of the universal, with "Bob Dylan" as the revelation.

Who then seems a wrong question. During an interview with Bill Flanagan in 2009, Dylan inclined perhaps the nearest we will ever come to such elucidation when he was asked about the recent presidential election, and started talking about Barack Obama's memoir, *Dreams from My Father.* "What struck you about him?" a surprised Flanagan wishes to know, and Dylan responds with a mix of facts, conjectures, qualifications, and framing. "I'd read his book and it intrigued me," he starts. "He's got an interesting background. He's like a fictional character, but he's real. First off, his mother was a Kansas girl. Never lived in Kansas, though, but with deep roots. You know like Kansas bloody Kansas. John Brown the insurrectionist. Jesse James and Quantrill. Bushwackers. Guerillas. Wizard of Oz Kansas. I think Barack has Jefferson Davis back there in his ancestry someplace."

Dylan then turns to Obama's father. "An African intellectual. Bantu, Masai, Griot type heritage—cattle raiders, lion killers," he continues. "I mean it's just so incongruous that these two people would meet and fall in love. You kind of get past that though. And then you're into his story. Like an odyssey except in reverse." He then takes up Obama's prose. "His writing style hits you on more than one level," Dylan continues. "It makes you feel and think at the same time and that's hard to do. He says profoundly outrageous things." Dylan marvels at the strangeness of Obama's fate. "In some sense you would think being in the business of politics would be the last thing that this man would want to do . . . he probably could have done anything. If you read his book, you'll know that the political world came to him. It was there to be had."

> Like a fictional character, but he's real . . . just so incongruous . . . an odyssey except in reverse . . . more than one level . . . feel and think at the same time . . . says profoundly outrageous things . . . there to be had.

Praising *Dreams from My Father,* Dylan seems to be confronting his own *Chronicles.* Obama and Dylan early on possessed a large and precise sense of their own destiny. There's something about each of them that is always thinking of himself and locating himself in other people. In a single line of the victory speech Obama gave in Grant Park on election night in 2008 he was able to summon King, Kennedy, Roosevelt, and Lincoln without exactly quoting any of them. I have never witnessed anything like it—unless it's Dylan embodying America's past inside the textures of his songs and in *Chronicles.* The memory of a collective memory in an individual memory, the lived dimension of history.

Obama appears also to have seen himself in Dylan. For *Rolling Stone* the president remembered the singer's performance at the White House in February of 2010 for "A Celebration of Music from the Civil Rights Movement":

> He wouldn't come to the rehearsal; usually all these guys are practicing before the set in the evening. He didn't want to take a picture with me; usually all the talent is dying to take a picture with Michelle and me before the show, but he didn't show up to do that. He came in and played "The Times They Are A-Changin.'" A beautiful rendition. The guy is so steeped in this stuff that he can just come up with some new arrangement, and the song sounds completely different. Finishes the song, steps off the stage—I'm sitting right in the front row—comes up, shakes my hand, sorts of tips his head, gives me a little grin and then leaves. And that was it. . . .

"That was our only interaction with him," Obama concluded. "And I thought, that's how you want Bob Dylan, right? You don't want him to be all cheesin' and grinnin' with you. You want him to be a little skeptical about the whole enterprise."

J

SOMEONE TOLD ME ABOUT A FAITH HEALER . . .

Just when you thought—well, just what were you *thinking*—and just who is that *you* anyways? Me? Bob Dylan . . . ? Dylan's audience, or whoever was left of it? One? Anyone? Just when all seemed finished, everything was revving up again. *Time Out of Mind*. "Things Have Changed." *"Love And Theft."* After guitarist Larry Campbell joined the band in March of 1997, he "wondered if he had signed on with a nostalgia act," until he heard *Time Out of Mind* on the tour bus. This moment is another opening for my book of reinvention and memory, a moment vital to Dylan's future psychic currents flow. Yet in a human, a literal sense, this book could have stopped there, too. For just as mixing of the album neared completion, Dylan got very sick. "We were somewhere in the Midwest and there was this dust storm," Campbell recounted to *Mojo*, "brown dust mixed with goose shit, coming off the river because it was so dry. . . . Bob went out on his motorcycle, inhaling this stuff." When Dylan complained of chest pains, doctors diagnosed histoplasmosis pericarditis, a potentially fatal infection of the sac around the heart. That May he was hospitalized and forced to cancel a ten-city European tour scheduled for June, to rest up. "I'm just glad to be feeling better," Dylan quipped for a press release. "I really thought I'd be seeing Elvis soon."

Touring, his next phase: from the fall of 1997 to the fall of 2002. Cured, refurbished, Dylan was back on the road within three months. During the almost exactly five years between the release of *Time Out of Mind* on September 30, 1997, and the night of October 4, 2002, when he started to play piano on stage, initiating a core shift in his own performance instrument from guitar to keyboards as well as for his live band sound, he would appear in concert more than 550 times. Writing about Willie Nelson's "On the Road Again" for *The Philosophy of Modern Song*, he intimated the enchantments of touring with a slippery second-person nod-and-wink confession:

> And then there's another song to be written about the real reason you can't wait to get on the road again. Nobody's mad because you didn't take the garbage out, acquaintances don't just drop in unannounced, neighbors don't give you the stink-eye every time the wind shifts.
>
> The thing about being on the road is that you're not bogged down by anything. Not even bad news. You give pleasure to other people and you keep your grief to yourself.

Five years. There is a loneliness that can be rocked. There is a certain loneliness that roams. Something like the collective fear of losing him—"The scary news blowin' in the wind last week was that Bob Dylan, 56, might be dying," as *Newsweek* reported in June of 1997—along with triumphal reviews of *Time Out of Mind* prompted a reconfiguration of his turn-of-the-century status from dubious oddity to international treasure. His first gig upon recovery was in Bologna, Italy, for a crowd of some three hundred thousand young Catholics at the invitation of Pope John Paul II for the World Eucharistic Congress. (The pope, too, resurrected "Blowin' in the Wind" for his sermon: "You ask me how many roads a man must walk down before he becomes a man. I answer: there is only one road for man, and it is the road of Jesus Christ, who said 'I am the Way and the Life.'")

During these five years, Dylan found his way back into visible American culture: Kennedy Center Honors, a Grammy, a Golden Globe, an

Oscar. His concerts moved from mid-sized halls to vast arenas, and he toured with Joni Mitchell, Van Morrison, Eric Clapton, the Rolling Stones, and Paul Simon. He contributed a cover of Dean Martin's "Return to Me" to *The Sopranos* and appeared on *Dharma & Greg.* Dylan's revitalization on the road led to maybe his best band ever—Campbell on guitar, mandolin, bouzouki, pedal steel, and slide; Charlie Sexton also on guitar; Tony Garnier on bass; and David Kemper on drums. Despite the conspicuous gifts of Campbell and Sexton, Dylan was often his own lead guitarist, even while singing, a legacy presumably of his solo folk shows. By the late 1990s, Dylan could play whatever he wanted across his entire back catalog, show after show of revelations. Early acoustic—"John Brown," on June 14, 1998, in Bremen, Germany; "Blowin' in the Wind" on March 16, 2000, in Santa Cruz, California; "Chimes of Freedom," on March 3, 2001, in Newcastle, England; and "Song to Woody" on October 30, 2001, in Green Bay, Wisconsin. Sixties electric—"I Want You" on November 15, 1999, in Ithaca, New York; "Visions of Joanna" on September 24, 2000, in Portsmouth, England; and "Fourth Time Around" on November 8, 2000, in Bethlehem, Pennsylvania. Basement Tapes—"Tears of Rage" on February 22, 1999, in Troy, New York; and "This Wheel's on Fire" on August 20, 2001, in Telluride, Colorado. Gospel—"Gotta Serve Somebody" on October 22, 1998, in Duluth, Minnesota; and "Solid Rock" on April 5, 2002, in Stockholm, Sweden. The eighties—"License to Kill" on June 17, 1998, in Brussels, Belgium; "I and I" on November 10, 1999, in New Haven, Connecticut; "Lenny Bruce" on April 3, 2000, in Cedar Rapids, Iowa; and "Seeing the Real You at Last" on November 19, 2000, in Towson, Maryland. From *Oh, Mercy*—"Shooting Star" on June 27, 2000, in Las Vegas, Nevada; "Where Teardrops Fall" on May 1, 2001, in Asheville, North Carolina; and "Man in the Long Black Coat" on July 22, 2001, in Pescara, Italy. From *Under the Red Sky*—"Born in Time" on February 1, 1998, in Newark, New Jersey; and "Under the Red Sky" on May 1, 1999, in Ischgl, Austria.

Scrutinizing Waylon Jennings's "I've Always Been Crazy" in *The Philosophy of Modern Song*, Dylan situated touring along an inherently palliative continuum of "craziness" and "insanity":

> Therapy works for a lot of people, though entertainers have it easier than most. Instead of having to pay someone an hourly fee to feign interest in listening to them drone on about their lives, a canny performer can reel in an audience, unburden themselves, and receive adulation as well as a nice payday simultaneously. What issues was Elvis working through with thousands of teenage girls calling out his name? What death issues was Screamin' Jay Hawkins coming to terms with, charging people to watch him emerge from a coffin?
>
> . . . People begin acting out to have better stories to tell, to not disappoint their audience, whether it be a thousand teenage girls or a solitary therapist. And that's where it moves from craziness to insanity.

Dylan's own "issues" after the summer of 1997 weren't anymore the viability of his old songs, the skills of his band, or even his health. The achievements of *Time Out of Mind,* and then of *"Love And Theft,"* meant that for the first time in decades—perhaps since the Rolling Thunder Revue—he could now introduce albums of glorious new music that weren't overwhelmed by the sixties classics that still largely shaped his live shows. How might he incorporate this new music? How would new and old flow together, particularly as old and new might be separated by thirty-five years? By 1994 Dylan had traditionalized his live music such that songs no longer flagged particular "Bob Dylans" so much as they shaded a continuous present. What started as an experiment for revivifying past songs now had evolved into a comprehensive worldview that inevitably inflected his new songwriting. No longer in pursuit of any zeitgeist approval, the "timeless" arrangements and lyric textures of *Time Out of Mind* and *"Love And Theft"* marked the culmination of those concert experiments, that postmodern worldview. Yet Dylan appeared reluctant to affirm what he had attained on record, particularly on *Time Out of Mind.* When—down the line—he released *Rough and Rowdy Ways*, he embarked as soon as possible on a world tour that specifically showcased the record. Even for *"Love And Theft"*—inside of two months (give or take) after release he had performed eleven of the twelve songs live. But during his 1997 concerts he managed to roll out just six of the eleven *Time Out of Mind* songs: "Love Sick," "'Til I Fell in Love With You," "Not Dark Yet," "Cold Irons Bound," "Make You Feel My Love," and "Can't Wait." "Million Miles" would debut only in 1998, "Tryin' to Get to Heaven" and "Highlands" in 1999, "Standing in the Doorway" in 2000, and he has never as far as I know played "Dirt Road Blues" live.

Dylan's wariness, and a reluctance to reaffirm his prowess? Arguably, the songs themselves are not the cruxes here. Chances are any resistance to playing them can be attributed to his clashes with producer Daniel Lanois during the recording of *Time Out of Mind* at Criteria Studios. "My recollection of that record is that it was a struggle," Dylan later acknowledged, "a struggle every inch of the way. . . . Repeatedly, I'd find myself compromising on this to get to mat." Lanois threw a chair, according to musicians involved in the sessions, smashed a guitar, and when they left Miami, he and Dylan were barely speaking. Sometimes Dylan's argument with Lanois is narrowed to his preference for "the sound in the room"—"the sound that did not go on the record," as pianist Jim Dickinson attested earlier—over the producer's loops and affects, yet that's at once convincing and too neat. In another vivid Criteria incident, engineer Mark Howard recalled Dylan walking in as Lanois rehearsed "Can't Wait" without him, the producer instructing the players, "You know those are good takes, but I just gotta get that version. I gotta get back to that." In the Tulsa archive, you can overhear Lanois searching for the definitive takes of songs, sometimes even in his own thin travesty of Dylan's voice. But as lines, couplets, and verses migrated from lyric to lyric, the songs on *Time Out of Mind* are radically pliant and ambiguous even for Dylan, and defy such definitives. "Dylan would just shut down," Howard continued. "Bob actually pulled Tony Garnier, his regular bass player, into the room with Dan at one point. He says, 'Tony, have I ever played any song twice exactly the same?' Tony says, 'No, Bob, no.' Bob says, 'See? I don't do that.' And Dan's like, 'Yeah, but that song "Can't Wait" . . .' Bob's like, 'I did it that way, and I'm never doing it that way ever again. I don't do anything the same way twice.'"

From the opening night of his fall 1997 UK tour when he debuted "Love Sick" in Bournemouth, Dylan live would endeavor to reclaim *Time Out of Mind* from Daniel Lanois through a fierce multiyear dismantling and reassembling that would be documented—as we saw—on a pair of entrants in *The Bootleg Series: Vol. 8: Tell Tale Signs* and *Vol. 17: Fragments.* The live tracks from *Time Out of Mind* included on *Fragments* tend to stress speed, power, the fire and brimstone likely a response to Dylan's complaint that in Criteria with Lanois "I felt extremely frustrated that I couldn't get any of the up-tempo songs I wanted." Force and volume proved to be just two of his many forms of revision, as night after night into the next century he remade on stage his comeback album. His in-concert variables for *Time Out of Mind* match any Dylan era in risk and finesse. The fragmentary lyrics and vagrant melodies proved so fluid, so volatile, and so open that a new arrangement could engender a different song. Listeners can log their own favorite surprises and wonders from shows attended and across the internet. But consider, for instance, four contrasting versions of "Can't Wait"—the sardonic bounce of December 8, 1997, in New York; the soft-loud pivots of September 24, 2000, in Portsmouth, almost jazzy despite all the despair in his vocal; harder-edged and helpless on April 24, 2002, in Nuremberg; the astonishing shuffle of June 26, 2019, in Stockholm that recast the refrain as a run of taunts. Three versions of "'Til I Fell in Love with You"—tense and anxious on March 7, 2001, in Osaka; snazzy and swinging on November 27, 2005, in Dublin; witty and sarcastic on June 20, 2015, in Mainz, Germany. Two renditions of "Million Miles"—rueful on February 2, 1999, in Pensacola; seething on November 25, 2003, in London.

My adjectives are approximations, doubtful shorthand for stage dynamics that upended structures and moods. In less than a blink, his songs seemed to change—and Dylan's activity in concerts transformed the more magisterial forays on *Time Out of Mind* too. His performance of "Tryin' to Get to Heaven" on April 7, 1999, in Lisbon insisted on loss, devastation, and the futility of otherworldly aspiration, whereas his ascendant vocals and guitar on November 19, 2000, in Towson conjured a radiant afterlife; then, in Atlantic City on June 6, 2004, his stress was mainly on the struggle, the *tryin'*. His "Standing in the Doorway" on October 1, 2000, in Munster, Germany, carried a tone of sad, baffled wonder, while during the same tune on July 2, 2004, in Stra, Italy, Dylan seemed to metamorphose into Marlon Brando in *On the Waterfront*. In New London, Connecticut, on January 14, 1998, he emphasized the hurt inside "Not Dark Yet," his singing rough, jagged, and pitched against the exalted sonic grain; yet on March 10, 2000, in Anaheim his phrasing was so smooth that the crowd applauded and howled after various individual lines. To date Dylan has only performed "Highlands" nine times, each spin a fresh departure, with perhaps the sharpest coming on March 16, 2000, in Santa Cruz, when he downshifted from Scottish ballad to an American tall tale, Robert Burns in Harvard Square by way of Mark Twain.

Perhaps because as "Jack Frost" he produced the recording sessions himself, *"Love And Theft"* live was less of a free-for-all. This time responsible for the album along with "the sound in the room," Dylan didn't need to recover the gist of his new songs. They entered his repertoire sooner, and he featured all of them. Until his *Rough and Rowdy Ways* tour of 2021, *"Love And Theft"* often furnished a concert's peak spots, his most incisive singing, and his band's boldest playing. Sometimes he approached the lyrics as strings of jokes—stinging jokes, of course, about power, violence, slavery, minstrelsy, and the Civil War. Other times they resonated as slightly daft Shakespearean soliloquys, as though Lear, his Fool, and Julius Caesar are all talking at the same time. The diversity of arrangements and instrumentation was startling. Dylan regularly performed against his studio versions—accenting noir over burnish, for instance, in "Bye and Bye" on March 10, 2004, in St. Paul, Minnesota. He declined the rockabilly of "Tweedle Dee & Tweedle Dum" for a jazzed-up romp on October 27, 2012, in Las Vegas, but veered melancholy and ruminative on July 16, 2015, in Lorrach, Germany. Some of the innovations tracked differences in a song's primary instruments, such as his own piano after 2002, but also demonstrated the impact of his versatile supporting musicians—signally Campbell, and later Donnie Herron. (Herron's pedal steel all but conducts "Bye and Bye" in St.

Paul on July 12, 2005, and his violin leads "Floater (Too Much to Ask)" in Toledo on July 12, 2007.) Compared to *Time Out of Mind*, there were fewer live lyric improvisations, though at some point along the way he stopped singing the line about his departed mother in "Lonesome Day Blues," replacing the second part of "Set my dial on the radio, I wish my mother was still alive" with "I'm telling myself I'm still alive."

In five years Dylan toured North America, South America, Europe, Asia, and Australia. Iconic world cities. Overlooked towns. The most powerful Dylan concert I attended during this resurgent period took place on November 19, 2001, at Madison Square Garden in New York City. He was sixty years old. His band was the Campbell, Sexton, Garnier, and Kemper band. Over two-and-a-half hours and twenty-two songs, he delivered covers—"Wait for the Light to Shine," and "Searching for a Soldier's Grave"; early 1960s acoustic—"It Ain't Me, Babe," "A Hard Rain's A-Gonna Fall," "Don't Think Twice, It's All Right," and "John Brown"; mid-1960s electric—"Just Like a Woman," "Just Like Tom Thumb's Blues," "Rainy Day Women #12 & 35," and "Like a Rolling Stone"; and more. He introduced to New York six songs from *"Love And Theft"*: "Tweedle Dee & Tweedle Dum," "Lonesome Day Blues," "High Water (For Charley Patton)," "Summer Days," "Sugar Baby," and "Honest With Me." (Nothing, however, from *Time Out of Mind.*) Mastery, but also magic for Dylan and his band that night. Fierce, notably the three electric guitars on "Drifter's Escape" and "Honest with Me." Vulnerable, too: the three acoustic guitars on "Don't Think Twice, It's All Right" and "Tangled Up in Blue," or the ghostly delicacy of "Sugar Baby." Garnier swung between an electric and a stand-up bass, and Campbell floated to bouzouki, mandolin, banjo, and pedal steel (both *Blonde on Blonde* songs tendered pedal steel where originally was organ). Dylan frequently took the lead, whether his guitar was electric or acoustic, and injected gorgeous harmonica solos into "Drifter's Escape" and "Just Like a Woman," among others.

Magic, though, wasn't incidental to Dylan's performance that night, but needed, even urgent. This Madison Square Garden concert was

Dylan's first New York City appearance since September 11, two months earlier. He directly invoked 9/11 just once, as he introduced the band—"Most of the songs we're singing tonight were written right here in this city, New York City, and the ones that weren't written here were recorded here. No one has to ask me how I feel about this town." Yet for all of us there, every song seemed steeped in 9/11, from the opening prayer of his cover of Fred Rose's "Wait for the Light to Shine" to the wild apocalypse of his final encore. His songs seemed to coalesce into an opera that advanced, retreated, and then advanced again as an insistent, restless, irreconcilable conversation, one song challenged and contradicted by the next, the way "It Ain't Me, Babe" talked back to "Wait for the Light to Shine," or "Honest with Me" refuted "Forever Young." Counterpoint themes, contrapuntal motifs—violence, war, and empire; elegies for personal relationships; end times; benediction and healing. He sidestepped foolproof, cheering epiphanies. Just when it looked like "Blowin' in the Wind" was the final encore, Dylan returned one more time for "All Along the Watchtower."

Dylan's Madison Square Garden concert was political and spiritual. Never mind that among the large group I sat with, some friendships were about to implode, and marriages disintegrate. Late in *The Philosophy of Modern Song* Dylan recounts a story about performing and faith:

> Someone once told me about a faith healer who had clean-cut confederates standing at the door of his revival meetings to offer a complimentary wheelchair to anyone who had difficulty walking—anyone on crutches, with a cane, a walker, or even a pronounced limp. They were told there was a wheelchair section near the side of the stage. The faith healer would come out and recognize his chairs and have one of those people brought onstage. He tells the crowd that person doesn't need the wheelchair. In fact, he already knows it. He tells the person to get up and walk. When the person does, the people cheer, believing they've seen a miracle, not knowing that person was already walking in under their own power. That's the way the hustle works.

> But the interesting thing is, you talk to the guy in the wheelchair, and he believes it, too. It's powerful medicine to be onstage and have people cheering for you . . . And real hustles, the really good ones, have to have a little faith in them.

The summer following that Madison Square Garden concert, Dylan returned to the Newport Folk Festival after an absence of thirty-seven years. More powerful medicine—yet now he wore a blonde wig and a false beard, as though the boos and brouhaha of his "going electric" in 1965 mandated a mask, a disguise. What was he *thinking*? *Who* was that man?

K

VICE AND THE TRAPPINGS

"Kiss you, or kill you. . . ." The only options Dylan allows himself for "Standing in the Doorway" hiss—what else?—film noir, and late in 2021 as I walked the galleries of his *Retrospectrum* at the Frost Art Museum of Florida International University, everywhere there were hints of '70s neo-noir homages to those classic films. His raffish palette, at once irradiated and inscrutable. The empty rural vistas, wayward city streets, and all those solitary interiors. History assaults you. Two late painting series particularly, *The Beaten Path* and *Deep Focus*, recreate the high-contrast lighting and blind alleys of neo-noir, and numerous Dylan paintings in fact originate in such poignant movie stills and frames. Some culled from vintage noir—*Touch of Evil*, *The Set Up*, *The Crimson Kimono*, *Force of Evil*, *Rear Window*, *Border Incident*, *Fallen Angel*, *Clash by Night*, *The Pawn Broker*, *I Want to Live*, *Where the Sidewalk Ends*, *The Manchurian Candidate*, and *Blast of Silence*. Others from crime films—*The Friends of Eddie Coyle*, *French Connection*, *The Landlord*, *To Live and Die in LA*, *Taxi Driver*, *Barton Fink*, *Shaft*, *Dog Day Afternoon*, *Pretty Poison*, *Bonnie and Clyde*, *Down by Law*, *Matewan*, *Lone Star*, *Killer Joe*, *Fat City*, *Paris Texas*, *Black Widow*, *Prince of the City*, *Massage Parlor Murders*, and *Fleshpot on 42nd Street*. Many more, including experimental New York City documentaries—*In the Street* and

News from Home. "All these images come from films," Dylan observed in his gallery note for *Deep Focus*, before individuating the specific appeal of the source imagery. "They try to highlight the different predicaments that people find themselves in. Whether it's Jimmy Cagney or Margaret Rutherford, the dreams and schemes are the same—life as it's coming at you in all its forms and shapes." His earlier intro to *The Beaten Path* roamed farther. "The works were done from real life, literature, films, songs, poems and poetry and a certain outlook all scrambled together in one form or another."

That "certain outlook" of Dylan's just might be—or at least spans—noir. Everyone will have heard the legend of the French critics who, viewing some American films for the first time after the Second World War, *The Maltese Falcon*, *Double Indemnity*, *Laura*, *The Lost Weekend*, and *Murder, My Sweet*, concentrated on the correspondences among them, and called what they saw film noir. Approached from that angle, noir is a historical genre of psychological crime movies and analogous fiction—Dashiell Hammett, Raymond Chandler, and James M. Cain to Jim Thompson, David Goodis, Patricia Highsmith, and Chester Himes—performing inside a distinctive matrix of artistic conventions. In contemporary nostalgic colloquy, noir is sometimes reduced to fedoras, wide ties, moody illumination, and rote invocations of guns and shadows. Dylan's art instead plays up the insistent formal experimentalism of noir, the tilt towards surrealism, fragmentation, and self-consuming narratives, notably in Thompson, Goodis, or Highsmith. And I recall that the only other American writer Gertrude Stein wanted to meet during her exultant tour after the triumph of *The Autobiography of Alice B. Toklas* was Dashiell Hammett.

From other vantages, noir is as traditional as America—our illustrious novels, for instance, commence with Charles Brockden Brown's *Wieland* (1798) and a man hearing voices commanding him to kill his family. Think of Poe, whom Dylan summons in "I Contain Multitudes" on *Rough and Rowdy Ways*. Or Melville, whom he referenced as he introduced his band at New York's Beacon Theatre on his 2021 tour. Beneath these stars is a universe of gliding monsters. "I was born in 1941, that was the year they bombed Pearl Harbor," Dylan remarked from the concert stage in Minneapolis on November 4, 2008, the night Barack Obama was elected president. "I've been living in a world of darkness ever since." As Suze Rotolo, his girlfriend during the early '60s, wrote in her memoir, *A Freewheelin' Time*, "Bob had an aura of darkness and intensity that enveloped me when I was near him. I couldn't stay in that cold, dark air."

On my initial visit to his Tulsa archive, I found a Ritz Carlton envelope with the names James M. Cain and Jim Thompson in Dylan's handwriting, bracketed alongside a spate of disconnected, vaguely hardboiled speech:

> "All kinds of people around here—even an Honest Man." | "The man you killed were you in love with him" | "The first rule around here is watch your"

This seemingly impromptu hotel room manuscript dates to the early '90s. Yet noir is a throughline as far back as the early '60s—the murder ballads and death-centric tunes Dylan first covered; and his own songs rooted in them, including over the decades hymns, laments, and elegies as variegated as "The Ballad of Hollis Brown," "The Death of Emmett Till," "Only a Pawn in Their Game," "The Lonesome Death of Hattie Carroll," "George Jackson," "Joey," "Hurricane," "Beyond Here Lies Nothing," "Scarlet Town," "Tin Angel," and "Pay in Blood." On *Highway 61 Revisited* the dolls, blackmailers, mystery tramps, and junkyard angels of his cascading dictions all mimic crime fiction. The carny fantastics of "Ballad of a Thin Man"—the geek, the sword swallower, and the one-eyed midget—mirror William Lindsay Gresham's *Nightmare Alley* and *Monster Midway*, along with Dylan's childhood memories and fantasies. "Desolation Row," if affixed on a map, might border territory that encloses T. S. Eliot's "The Waste Land," Jack Kerouac's *Desolation Angels*, and Hammett's Poisonville. *Blonde on Blonde* is still bleaker, if more atmospheric—"With her fog, her amphetamine, and her pearls," and "Ain't it just like the night to play tricks when you're trying to be so quiet?"

Classic film noir operated directly on other Dylan creations along the way. He constructed songs for *Empire Burlesque* (1985) and *Knocked Out Loaded* (1986) from movie dialogue, many of those films crime and noir. (In retrospect, this stylistic move appears a trial run for his later collaged literature lyrics from Ovid, Virgil, and Timrod, etc., for *"Love And Theft," Modern Times*, *Tempest*, and *Rough and Rowdy Ways.*) On *Empire Burlesque*, a couplet of "Tight Connection to My Heart"—"What looks large from a distance / Close up ain't never that big"—originated in a line Gary Cooper applied to cops in *Now and Forever* (1934): "Close up they don't look as large as they do from a distance." "Seeing the Real You at Last," a song about reality and projection, ingeniously refracts nearly all its language from movies, including *Double Indemnity*, *To Have and Have Not*, *Rear Window*, *The Big Sleep*, *Key Largo*, and *The Maltese Falcon*:

> *Rear Window*: I thought the rain would cool things down—all it did was make the heat wet.
>
> *Key Largo*: Didn't I take chances?
>
> *The Big Sleep*: What's wrong with you? Nothing you can't fix.
>
> *The Maltese Falcon*: I don't mind a reasonable amount of trouble.

The Maltese Falcon also cycles through "Tight Connection to the Heart" and "When the Night Comes Falling from the Sky."

Noir violence suffused Dylan's twenty-first-century music videos—strikingly those directed by Nash Edgerton, "Beyond Here Lies Nothing" (2009), "Must Be Santa" (2009), "Duquesne Whistle" (2012), and "The Night We Called It a Day" (2015). For "Beyond Here Lies Nothing" (from the album *Together Through Life*) Edgerton translated the Ovidian loss of the lyric into a kitchen sink opera of love, addiction, and domestic savagery, with actors Joel Stoffer and Amanda Aardsma. "Must Be Santa" (*Christmas in the Heart*) slants the polka party drive of the Mitch Miller original into a manic brawl, where a reveler swings from a chandelier and Dylan in a blonde wig and top hat alternately dances and shrugs. Set along Broadway in downtown Los Angeles, "Duquesne Whistle" (*Tempest*) double plots a rom-com stalker parody—with Dylan leading a posse that includes a figure dressed as Gene Simmons in full Kiss regalia—and a gangster kidnapping, stocked with pepper spray and a brutal kneecapping by baseball bat. "The Night We Called It a Day" (*Shadows in the Night*) distills a sort of mini-noir, right down to a love triangle, a burlesque dancer, murders, and more totemic LA settings. When Dylan was asked whether a younger listening audience might find his Great American Songbook covers "corny," his reply seethed with noir inflections:

> These songs, take 'em or leave 'em, if nothing else, are songs of great virtue. . . . But people's lives today are filled on so many levels with vice and the trappings of it. Ambition, greed and selfishness all have to do with vice. Sooner or later, you have to see through it or you don't survive. We don't see the people that vice destroys. We just see the glamour of it on a daily basis—everywhere we look, from billboard signs to movies, to newspapers, to magazines. We see the destruction of human life and the mockery of it, everywhere we look.

In July of 2021, as a COVID lockdown project, Dylan released *Shadow Kingdom: The Early Songs of Bob Dylan*, a black-and-white noir-tinged concert film of him covering himself—his sixties self—with a small band. For the fictional setting of the Bon Bon Club in Marseille, he and director Alma Har'el fabricated a claustrophobic Virgilian afterlife where the time on the stopped clock is always 10:12, and the pervasive smoke could be cigarettes, or might just indicate the halls of Dis. All the musicians but Dylan are masked. Stage angles fluctuate from song to song, as do the audiences, so that the Bon Bon Club can seem simultaneously vast and a void; ghosts of Billie Holiday and Mildred Bailey loom in the crowd, and a sort of sculptured bust. "You in Marseille among the watermelons," Apollinaire wrote in *Zone*. "You are under arrest you are a criminal now." Noir swirls through the next world scenery. Of the thirteen cuts here, three are from *Highway 61 Revisited*, two from *Blonde on Blonde*. He revises a passage in "Watching the River Flow"—"People disagreeing on just about everything, yeah"—so that the song now circles death: "People disappearing everywhere you look / Only yesterday I seen somebody who said goodbye." Think of the people Dylan's buried. Furthermore, "To Be Alone with You," once a toss-away country love ditty from *Nashville Skyline*, reemerges here as a murder ballad reminiscent of Jim Thompson's genial psychopathic killers:

I'm collecting my thoughts in a pattern
Movin' from place to place
Steppin' out into the dark night
Steppin' out into space
What happened to me, darlin'?
What was it you saw?
Did I kill somebody?
Did I escape the law?
Got my heart in my mouth
My eyes are still blue
My mortal bliss
Is to be alone with you

With this provocative recasting of his past, Dylan is showing us some ways of revisiting our own. History assaults you. I never got over my first reading of Thompson's *The Killer Inside Me*, so much so that I needed to research and write a book about him, to see where in an individual's life and American history and popular culture a novel that weird, intractable, and apocalyptic would originate. His Oklahoma Communist Party comrades, I discovered, included Woody Guthrie and Sis Cunningham, later of the Almanac Singers. Thompson intended to audition as a writer for *Back Where I Come From*, one of Guthrie's CBS radio programs, directed by future noir director Nicholas Ray, and Dylan's template for *Theme Time Radio*. With her husband Gordon Friesen, Cunningham later founded the mimeographed folk magazine *Broadside*, and in May of 1962 they published "Blowin' in the Wind" on the cover. Once I moved to New York City, Sis and Gordon proved kind, supportive friends. Guthrie, Thompson, Ray, the Oklahoma Federal Writers Project, *Broadside*: all along a subterranean vein. With the *Shadow Kingdom* version of "To Be Alone with You," Dylan finally fleshes out the phrases he penned next to Thompson's name on that Ritz Carlton envelope some twenty-five years prior, and fleshing out much more, too. To accent the self-estrangement, among the oddest—ultimately eeriest—touches of *Shadow Kingdom* is that everyone here, the singer, his band, is visibly miming to prerecorded tracks. Right at the start of the opening song, "When I Paint My Masterpiece," there's a burst of harmonica yet no one in sight is playing one, and the entire hour cycle is dreamy, startling, and spectral.

As though this were the play inside the play of *Hamlet*, another crime drama, the final credits designate the band as "Players," and the distinguished musicians on film, Buck Meek, Joshua Crumbly, Shahzad Ismaily, Janie Cowan, and Alex Burke, apparently didn't even record what they're represented as almost but not quite playing. According to guitarist Tim Pierce, the secret actual players included Don Was, Greg Leisz, Jeff Taylor, T Bone Burnett, and Pierce himself, who rehearsed together with Dylan for nearly two months, and prepared more songs than appear in *Shadow Kingdom*. Pierce also recalled:

> Bob's songs are living breathing organisms. And whether he recorded it in the 60s or last week, whatever version he does at a particular time is only like a photograph, it's a snapshot, and the next time he does that song it's a different animal—in a different key, at a different tempo, with a different arrangement, different musicians. I had the privilege of watching him write lyrics in front of me. So he's got a sheet of paper in his hands, and we were all sitting around between songs, and because of the arrangement of the song, because it was different, he had to change some things. He just stream-of-consciousness started writing and rhyming and writing stuff down. So he's reciting these new lyrics, and these new rhymes, and he starts

> to smile and laugh, and it starts to flow. And it's all virtuoso stuff, it's like whoa, whoa, and at a certain point he says, "I don't know where this stuff comes from," and he laughs. To me I was seeing the gift that was given to the world from his poetry, and where it comes from, and I watched it happen in front of me.

Was "To Be Alone with You" the song Pierce saw Dylan rewrite, and laugh? As likely as not, Dylan named *Shadow Kingdom* after a story of masks, deceptions, and multiple identities by Robert E. Howard (also the creator of Conan the Barbarian), and published in the August 1929 issue of *Weird Tales*. The earliest of Howard's Kull fictions, "The Shadow Kingdom" originates in the Thurian age, in Valusia, a nation ruled from the shadows by a race of prehuman Serpent Men. Here Howard moves in and out of Kull's consciousness in "Masks," the final chapter of "The Shadow Kingdom":

> No, that was no dream, that monstrous interlude. As [Kull] sat upon his throne in the Hall of Society and gazed upon the courtiers, the ladies, the lords, the statesmen, he seemed to see their faces as things of illusion, things unreal, existent only as shadows and mockeries of substance. Always he had seen their faces as masks, but before he had looked on them with contemptuous tolerance, thinking to see beneath the masks shallow, puny souls, avaricious, lustful, deceitful; now there was a grim undertone, a sinister meaning, a vague horror that lurked beneath the smooth masks . . . Valusia—land of dreams and nightmares—a kingdom of the shadows, ruled by phantoms who glided back and forth behind the painted curtains, mocking the futile king who sat upon the throne—himself a shadow . . . How could a man be so many different men in a lifetime? For Kull knew that there were many Kulls and he wondered which was the real Kull. After all, the priests of the Serpent went a step further in their magic, for all men wore masks, and many a different mask with each different man or woman; and Kull wondered if a serpent did not lurk under every mask.

The boat sail behind Dylan on some of the songs in *Shadow Kingdom* also might intimate an association with Joseph Conrad's *The Shadow-Line* (1915), a novel where a sea captain revisits his distant past—"Only the young have such moments," as Conrad launches his retrospective. (Is Dylan's hallucinatory Bon Bon Club in Marseille—white sail, thick nautical ropes—modeled after the Café Bodoul, a café in the Rue Saint-Ferreol allegedly frequented by Conrad after he left Poland for the French seaport in 1874? Improbably, but possibly frequented, too, by Rimbaud. *The Shadow-Line* is also set during a pandemic: malaria.) The expanded online version of his 2009 interview with *Rolling Stone* indicates Dylan was planning *Shadow Kingdom* for over a decade. "At a certain point we'll take the songs into the studio," he told Douglas Brinkley. "We'll do a television show. Television. [Laughs] Like that still exists—with this band performing some kind of repertoire of these particular songs. And they'll be recorded properly."

Once live touring was possible again a few months after *Shadow Kingdom*, Dylan's half-lit stage at the Beacon Theatre arranged a color version of the Bon Bon Club, another noir nightspot for still more of his shadow selves. Details in his stage set for the *Rough and Rowdy Ways* tour—red curtains, crepuscular lighting, and a chiaroscuro floor—appeared specifically intended to conjure up the Red Room/Black Lodge of David Lynch's *Twin Peaks*. The Black Lodge/Red Room entered *Twin Peaks* via a dream of agent Dale Cooper. As Cooper (Kyle MacLachlan) converses with Deputy Tommy "Hawk" Hill (Michale Horse):

> **Hawk:** Cooper, you may be fearless in this world. But there are other worlds. Worlds beyond life and death. Worlds beyond scientific reality.
>
> **Cooper:** Tell me more.
>
> **Hawk:** My people believe that the White Lodge is a place where the spirits that rule man and nature reside. There is also a legend of a place called the Black Lodge. The shadow self of the White Lodge. Legend says that every spirit must pass through there on the way to perfection. There,

you will meet your own shadow self. My people call it The Dweller on the Threshold.

Cooper: Dweller on the Threshold.

Hawk: But it is said that if you confront the Black Lodge with imperfect courage, it will utterly annihilate your soul.

For the finale of *Twin Peaks*, the Black Lodge/Red Room evolved into the "waiting room," an extra-dimensional space for the transition between life and death. Inside his Red Room at the Beacon, the eight gorgeous, devastating *Rough and Rowdy Ways* songs Dylan performed each night sounded as if they too radiated from a twilight realm, as he referenced the *Egyptian Book of the Dead*, entreated "fleet footed guides from the underworld," and spoke of having "already outlived my life by far."

Noir in late Dylan can be personal. "Long and Wasted Years" distills a noir marriage:

I think when my back was turned
The whole world behind me burned
It's been a while
Since we walked down that long, long aisle
We cried on a cold and frosty morn'
We cried because our souls were torn

How little we know of ourselves, and how perplexing. Yet Dylan's noir also is intrinsically political, an interrogation of capitalism, and enmeshed in the legacies of the Civil War and slavery. As he sings on "Pay in Blood":

Night after night, day after day
They strip your useless hopes away
The more I take, the more I give
The more I die, the more I live
I got something in my pocket make your eyeballs swim

I got dogs that could tear you limb to limb
I'm circling around in the southern zone
I pay in blood, but not my own

To return to *Retrospectrum*, and the galleries of Dylan's art at the Frost Art Museum in Miami that I walked through those first few sun-soaked days of December 2021: There's "Twilight After Dusk"—after a frame of Robert Wise's 1949 noir, *The Set Up*, a study of corruption in boxing. And "Sugar Torch"—after a frame of Samuel Fuller's 1959 noir, *The Crimson Kimono*, a probing of race and interracial marriage. (Sugar Torch is the murdered stripper in Fuller's film.) Plus "Del Rio"—after a frame of Anthony Mann's 1949 noir, *Border Incident*, an account of gang exploitation of Mexican immigrants in Southern California.

Movie frames. Movie stills. According to writer and curator Raymond Foye, Dylan is "a great fan" of David Hockney's *Secret Knowledge*. "The thesis I am putting forward here," Hockney wrote, "is that from the early fifteenth century many Western artists used optics—by which I mean mirrors and lenses (or a combination of the two)—to create living projections. Some artists used these projected images to produce drawings and paintings, and before long this new way of depicting the world—this new way of seeing—had become widespread . . . All I am saying here is that long before the seventeenth century, when there is evidence Vermeer was using a camera obscura, artists had a tool and that they used it in ways previously unknown to art history." Dylan acknowledged various lenses in his "Foreword" to the catalog for *The Beaten Path*:

> . . . in some cases my hand couldn't do what my eye was perceiving. So I went with the camera obscura method. The camera obscura was a primitive camera invented in the 1600s which projected an image upside down so the painter could work from it. This was a real camera but the image was not printable. It could only be seen and filled in. Caravaggio used this in about all of his paintings and so did Van Eyck and Vermeer. These days you don't have to go to all that

> trouble. You can use a real camera. I put a 58 mm 0.43x wide-angle conversion lens onto a used Nikon D3300 Af-p on quite a few paintings . . . If that didn't work, I used a convex Plexiglass RCA 24 x 20 television screen that can be found in old junk shops and looked at the world through that.

So, finally, then, three paintings in intensive colloquy with Orson Welles's 1958 film noir *Touch of Evil*. In "Oil Riggers Shack," Dylan chases the corrosive loneliness, strangeness, and casual malice of border town industry. For "Nightmare from a Hotel Window" he transforms the original advertisement for STEAKS into a word that wittily approximates NOIR. More boldly, he titles another *Touch of Evil* painting "Philadelphia, Mississippi," thereby repositioning the image—and the evil—as the town where in 1964 the civil rights activists James Chaney, Andrew Goodman, and Michael Schwerner were abducted and murdered during "Freedom Summer."

Dylan's visual sources might call back to films made sixty or seventy years ago, but what he has said of his music holds true for his paintings, too: "My music is always speaking to times that are recent." History assaults you. As Frank Bidart once proposed, "Again and again, insight is dramatized by showing the conflict between what is ordinarily seen, ordinarily understood, and what is now experienced as real. Cracking the shell of the world; or finding the shell is cracking under you." Noir in Dylan is one of the sounds that shell of the world makes as it is cracking under us. Noir in Dylan is also—as his "Philadelphia, Mississippi" dramatizes—the sound of a nation that originated in genocide, sustained itself through slavery, yet earnestly proclaims: This is God's country.

L

POLITICS OF RELATIONSHIPS

Latin at Boston College High School hovered between sophistication and slapstick. Offering the language was intrinsic to all ceremonial ambitions for the school—core and key. Without classic languages, Greek and Latin, but especially Latin, how could BC High vindicate its mission as a college preparatory commuter high school for poor and middle-class Boston Catholic boys (and only boys, then and now; and then mostly Irish or Italian, and I was some of both), commensurate in quality, but at a fraction of the tuition, to the WASP-y bastions of the privileged, Phillips Exeter Academy, Choate Rosemary Hall, and Milton Academy?

BC High required Latin for three years. Freshman year was given over to grammar, conjugations, declensions, vocabulary, and sentence structures. As sophomores we translated Caesar's *De bello Gallico* ("Gallia est omnis divisa in partes tres . . ."), and as juniors, Cicero's "First Oration Against Cataline," Sallust's *Histories,* and the Pyramus and Thisbe episode of Ovid's *Metamorphoses.* In the optional senior year, those of us who continued the study of Latin concentrated on the first six books of Virgil's *Aeneid.* Sounds fantastic!—right?—though practice tended to scupper aspirations. This was after the liturgical changes of the Second Vatican Council (1962–1965), which banned the Tridentine Mass, thereby removing for my pious Irish Nana, who was paying for my schooling, the chief motivation for Latin, as presumably I was on a one-way street to the Catholic priesthood. Moreover, the Jesuits at BC High sold Latin to us—and our working-class parents—not as a ticket into world high culture, literature, and art, but for its hard-nosed and supposedly commonsensical benefits. By enlarging our English vocabularies, nothing could get us "in shape" (and sports imagery dominated such discussions) "stronger and faster" than Latin for "the big game" of the College Board Scholastic Aptitude Test. So except for a few Honors classrooms each year, pretty much any Jesuit was deemed capable of instructing resistant teenagers in Latin, and the courses often marked the first step down in their own sad declivities. When an exhausted or ailing priest proved inadequate to his professional field of study—history, math, physics—the rector would reassign him first to Latin, later religion, and ultimately to the guidance department, where he might say such things to us about carnal knowledge as "Your father took a seed and placed it under your mother's heart."

I'm quoting from memory. Only in one class, and with one teacher, Bill Collins, was the study of Latin ever presented to us as having anything to do with reading literature. Collins, my freshman English and senior Asian studies instructor—and a newly married "lay teacher," as the Jesuits tagged him—immersed us in modern writing, much of it palpably over our heads. To the agitation of parents, in fact, the first novel he assigned was Ian Fleming's *From Russia with Love*, and our attentions caught by sex and the Cold War, he could then transport us anywhere: Shakespeare, Milton, Donne, Whitman, Browning, Tennyson, Sandburg, T. S. Eliot, Virginia Woolf, Frost, Faulkner, William Carlos Williams, John Barth, James Baldwin, Robert Lowell, and Elizabeth Bishop. On alternate weekends we were assigned critical essays and creative writing, our own stories and poems in tandem with literary analysis. Collins taught us about the dynamics of tradition and literary allusions through such models as *The Waste Land* and Lowell's early poems, with their shards, respectively, of Ovid and Virgil. In subsequent years, my friends and I took to hanging out in his classroom after school hours. When he heard us grumbling about Pyramus and Thisbe, he urged us to read all of the *Metamorphoses* for "context," and showed us how Shakespeare adapted the tale for *Romeo and Juliet* and *A Midsummer Night's Dream*, and even mentioned that the Beatles had parodied it during a television special, *Around the Beatles* (1964). Collins instructed us in what I only later learned to call "close reading," registering yet another boon of Latin, the tangible link of studying the language to that close reading of literature, a facet I wouldn't fully appreciate until graduate school, when amid music nights at local Boston and Cambridge clubs I fleshed out a degree in the English Renaissance with courses on Horace and Catullus, Petronius and Seneca, and Virgil's *Eclogues* and *Georgics*. For a Latin poetry seminar a student might translate two lyric poems a week, something like twenty-five short pieces a semester max, which meant we almost inadvertently memorized them in both Latin and English, and could see how they worked—diction, meter, allusions, tone, voice—from the inside out. You saw through the craze of their own creation into another life.

But Latin wasn't the puzzle—at least at the outset—when Dylan released *Modern Times* on August 29, 2006. The recording would be his first number 1 album in the United States since *Desire* (1976) over three decades prior, and at age sixty-five Dylan became the oldest person ever with an album that debuted at the top of the Billboard charts. *Modern Times* was—if anything—even bleaker than *Time Out of Mind*: sort of his *Death on the Installment Plan* as electric blues. The album opens with a raucous invocation of Armageddon and Judgement Day—"Thunder on the Mountain," where, incidentally, he observes Louis-Ferdinand Celine's novel; and closes with the apocalypse—"Ain't Talkin'," where he sings from "the last outback at the world's end." In between, Dylan calls up biblical floods: "Nettie Moore," and "The Levee's Gonna Break." Hellish fires: "Rollin' and Tumblin'," and "Workingman's Blues #2." His disasters, moreover, include their own immanence.

The album title inevitably recalls Charlie Chaplin's 1936 silent film, and Dylan parallels Chaplin's black comedy of industrialization and economic alienation in "Workingman's Blues #2" with a faux paean to contemporary global capitalism: "It's a new path that we trod / They say low wages are a reality / If we want to compete abroad." But Dylan's *Modern Times* is also the Fallen World through all its degenerate guises; economic, romantic, and spiritual estrangement all blur together into End Times. Religion and sex, crises of faith and crises of politics, vengeance and mercy insistently fork and converge. "Spirit on the Water," "When the Deal Goes Down," and "Beyond the Horizon" might address a lover, yet might address God, too. He folds a love story into "Workingman's Blues #2," and "Thunder on the Mountain" fuses carnality and faith such that the promised "hot stuff" is at once fucking and Dante's *Inferno*. The "you too shall burn" of "Rollin' and Tumblin'" similarly merges eternal damnation and thwarted desire. In "Ain't Talkin'" the recurrent refrain—"Heart burnin', still yearnin'"—encodes love and punishment. Figures here ricochet from corporeal temptations to transcendent discipline, from blessed trust to despair. As Dylan sings in "Nettie Moore": "I'm standing in the light / I wish to God that it were night."

Across *Modern Times*, songs arrange noirish hints of past crimes, mistakes, and regrets which sometimes demand forgiveness, and other times are assessed as beyond forgiveness. As he sings in "Rollin' and Tumblin'"—"Let's forgive each other darlin', let's go down to the greenwood glen." Or in "Beyond the Horizon"—"My repentance is plain." Yet more impatiently in "Thunder on the Mountain"—"I've already confessed, no need to confess again." Then, in "When the Deal Goes Down"—"I'm haunted by / Things I never meant nor wished to say." And darkest of all, in "Spirit on the Water":

I wanna be with you in paradise
And it seems so unfair
I can't go back to paradise no more
I killed a man back there

Love mistaken for justice; justice for violence; violence for love. "I'm all worn down by weeping," someone mourns on "Ain't Talkin'," but then, as though that someone can't help it: "If I catch my opponents ever sleeping / I'll slaughter 'em where they lie." What could be more Old Testament—and more classic American? The stuff of Winthrop, Mather, Edwards, Brown, Hawthorne, Poe, and Melville. The alienations throughout *Modern Times* shade a world pillaged of meaning. On "Ain't Talkin'" Dylan sings, "I practice a faith that's long abandoned / Ain't no altars on this long and lonesome road." His fate, anyone's fate, is a mode of eternal exile. "The place I love best is a sweet memory," as "Working Man's Blues #2" phrases it, and "Sleep is like a temporary death." People do onto others as was done to them: "I'm gonna drive you from your home, just like I was driven from mine." As for God? "There's no one here, the gardener is gone."

In *Chronicles*, Dylan recorded his impressions of Archibald MacLeish's *Scratch*, based on "The Devil and Daniel Webster," as "full of midnight murder," and indicated his emotional resistance to collaboration:

> This play was dark, painted a world of paranoia, guilt, and fear—it was all blacked out and met the atomic age head on, reeked of foul play . . . The play spelled death for society with humanity lying face-down in its own blood. MacLeish's play was delivering something beyond an apocalyptic message. Something like, man's mission is to destroy the earth. . . . The play was up to something and I didn't think I wanted to know.

"A world of paranoia, guilt, and fear" might have been *Scratch* back in 1968, but it's also Dylan's vision in 2006 for *Modern Times*, and here he *does* want to know. Even the rare sweet twinklings on the record skirt anguish, ferocity, and menace. "Spirit on the Water" suddenly tips into cataclysm, and the penitent resolutions of "When the Deal Goes Down" and "Beyond the Horizon" will occur only after his life, even all earthly life, is over. Dylan is again a medium for the dead—"I've been conjuring these long dead souls from their crumbling tombs"—and a spectral presence, "pale as a ghost," already wandering the underworld. Deaths are traumatic. Few remember them.

But the darkness of *Modern Times* also wasn't the puzzle, or a problem. On September 14, barely two weeks after the album's release, the *New York Times* published an article that demanded, "Who's This Guy Dylan Who's Borrowing Lines from Henry Timrod?" Scott Warmuth, identified in that article as "a disc jockey in Albuquerque," had discovered through "some judicious Google searches" what the *Times* designated "concordances" between "Mr. Dylan's lyrics and Timrod's poetry." Warmuth—who over the years would emerge as the most tenacious lyric annotator of twenty-first-century Bob Dylan—elaborated in an interview, "I initially got drawn into all of this with *"Love And Theft"* in 2001. I still remember putting it into the CD player for the first time and just being knocked out by what a fantastic record it is, and then seeing the components and learning more about how musically it's built, because a lot of the songs have got an antecedent." Warmuth then veered from the music to Dylan's words:

> So I just started mapping out the musical connections, and then seeing where people were writing about the lyrical bits. That bit from the Great Gatsby was easy to spot, then a few others bubbled up. And then Dylan's use of material from the oral history of a Japanese gangster turned up, so I was fascinated by all of that. . . . Now the resources have certainly changed. . . . Google books has played a huge role in the ability to search for phrases. . . . I love to go to a library and sit and do research. Now you can just do that faster.

From the start, Warmuth circulated his finds in a spirit of wonder, awe, and admiration. "You could give the collected works of Henry Timrod to a bunch of people, but none of them are going to come up with Bob Dylan songs." Yet the *Times* cited a fan from a Dylan chat room—"Bob really is a thieving little swine"—and an Albuquerque high school teacher who averred, "If I found out that he had done this in a research paper, he'd be in big trouble." Soon after the news article the *Times* printed an op-ed by singer-songwriter Suzanne Vega, who earnestly supposed Dylan probably hadn't evoked Timrod "on purpose." *Really*?

As a culture we seem to have forgotten how to experience works of art, or at least talk about them plausibly or smartly. Given the dust-up in the *Times*, you might not guess that we'd just lived through some three decades of hip-hop sampling, not to mention a century of literary modernism. That our most ambitious and celebrated songwriter would revive Timrod on a best-selling CD across America and Europe might prompt a lively concatenation of responses—such as "Huh?" and "Who's he?"—but to narrow the Dylan-Timrod phenomenon into a news story about possible plagiarism is to confuse art with, well, that Albuquerque high school term paper.

New ways of entering and leaving the archives. You could almost fancy them covers, these fragmentary echoes of Timrod's poems Dylan slipped into *Modern Times*. The "laureate of the South"—an honorific conferred on him reputedly by none other than Tennyson—Timrod was, prior to his reintroduction to contemporary literary currency by Dylan, a nearly vanished nineteenth-century American poet, essayist, and Civil War newspaper correspondent. He still shows up in the occasional anthology because of the poems he wrote in celebration—and later, in mourning—of the new Southern nation, particularly "Ethnogenesis" and "Ode Sung on the Occasion of Decorating the Graves of the Confederate Dead at Magnolia Cemetery." Early on, Whittier and Longfellow praised Timrod, and his "Ode" lurks behind Allen Tate's "Ode to the Confederate Dead" (and thus in turn behind Lowell's "For the Union Dead"). But as Dylan later told Mikal Gilmore in *Rolling Stone*, "as far as Henry Timrod, have you even heard of him? Who's been reading him lately? And if you think it's so easy to quote him and it can help you with your work, do it yourself and see how far you get."

Timrod was born in Charleston, South Carolina, in 1828, his arrival coming two years after Stephen Foster's and two years before Emily Dickinson's. His writing, too, might be styled as falling between theirs: gloomy and skeptical at times, other times mawkish, antique. Dylan recast passages from five Timrod poems for "When the Deal Goes Down."

From "Retirement":

There is a wisdom that grows up in strife,
And one—I like it best—that sits at home
And learns its lessons of a thoughtful ease.

From a sonnet, "I Thank You":

If I, indeed, divine their meaning truly,
And not unto myself ascribe, unduly,
Things which you neither meant nor wished to say,
Oh! tell me, is the hope then all misplaced?

From "Two Portraits":

Still stealing on with pace so slow
Yourself will scarcely feel the glow . . .

From "A Rhapsody of a Southern Winter Night":

These happy stars, and yonder setting moon,
Have seen me speed, unreckoned and untasked,
A round of precious hours.
Oh! here, where in that summer noon I basked,
And strove, with logic frailer than the flowers,
To justify a life of sensuous rest . . .

From "A Vision of Poesy":

. . . and at times
A strange far look would come into his eyes,
As if he saw a vision in the skies.

Dylan—I'm guessing—is fascinated by both aspects of Timrod, the vintage as well as the brooding. The nineteenth-century "poesy" phrasings recall parlor and minstrel songs by Foster, Marshall S. Pike, and Dan Emmett, and bits of at least ten poems sweep through *Modern Times* lyrics: "Spirit on the Water," "Rollin' and Tumblin'," "Working Man's Blues #2," "Beyond the Horizon," along with "When the Deal Goes Down." The pining strains of Timrod's inflections complement the '20s, '30s, and '40s popular singers Dylan also summons, such as Bing Crosby, and a reference in "Beyond the Horizon" to "The bells of St. Mary, how sweetly they chime" precisely fuses Timrod's "Katie" ("The chime of old St. Mary's bells, / . . . as sweet as when in distant years") and Crosby's 1945 film.

On *Modern Times* Dylan mostly shuns anthology favorites for pieces about love, friendship, loss, death, and poetry. "Workingman's Blues #2" circumnavigates "Two Portraits"—"a temporary death"; "To Thee"—"to feed my soul with thought"; and "A Vision of Poesy"—"Old memories of you to me have clung." "Spirit on the Water" also encompasses "Two Portraits"—"explain / The sources of this hidden pain." "Rollin' and Tumblin'" juxtaposes "The Cotton Ball"—"The landscape is glowin', gleaming in the golden life of day"—to "Our Willie"—"The night's filled with shadows, the years are filled with early doom." Besides "Katie," "Beyond the Horizon" crisscrosses "A Rhapsody of a Southern Winter Night"—"an angel's kiss"; "Our Willie"—"mortal bliss"; and "A Vision of Poesy"—"in the long hours of twilight." Dylan often deflects Timrod by reversing or otherwise varying the original sense. "But *not* to feed my soul with thought," Timrod wrote in "to Thee," and sleeping "virtues" rather than sleep itself intersected a "temporary death" in "Two Portraits." As Dylan told Robert Hilburn in a 2004 interview about songwriting, "I always try to turn a song on its head. Otherwise, I figure I'm wasting the listener's time."

Through Timrod, and also Sidney Lanier—another Confederate poet evoked on "Beyond the Horizon"—Dylan continues from *"Love And Theft"* his insistence on the centrality of slavery and the Civil War in American life. (In fact, for "Tweedle Dee & Tweedle Dum" on that 2001 album, he already had explored "A Vision of Poesy.") For *Modern Times*, Timrod and Lanier accent atmosphere, tone, and texture. Dylan again accelerates creative tactics of what artist John Akomfrah—summarizing his own compilation, editing, and remixing of images—called "affective proximity." The songs exhibit a bold *what if* calculation: What if, for instance, in "Rollin' and Tumblin'" you tip "The Cotton Boll," a poem that fetishizes slavery ("Small sphere! / By dusky fingers brought") and glorifies the Civil War ("while our banners wing / Northward, strike with us!") into a blues expressive of Muddy Waters, a sharecropper who picked cotton alongside his family on Stovall Plantation in the Mississippi Delta, moreover a blues singer who was first recorded there by Alan Lomax in 1941? As Waters told Lomax about "Country Blues (Number One)," one of those first recordings, "This song comes from the cotton field." And what if you then, across *Modern Times*, link the "laureate of the South"—and thus implicitly the Civil War and Jim Crow—to other tainted interchanges of business and entertainment such as minstrelsy, but also minstrelsy's legacy in parlor songs, country and western classics, Hollywood musical films, the Great American Songbook, and rock 'n' roll? Dylan's affective proximities dislodge slavery from a distant, settled historical past of individual enlightened or deplorable citizens. Slavery here registers instead as inherent in the vital, ongoing heritages and structures of American culture—the violence social, collective, and inside a network of implication and complicity, including Dylan's own.

That social implication is the devastating and brilliant burden of "Nettie Moore," the eighth track on *Modern Times*. What does it mean to return? Here Dylan forgoes Timrod in favor of a direct line to nineteenth-century minstrelsy, his title and the opening couplet of his chorus harking back to "The Little White Cottage, or Gentle Nettie Moore," Marshall S. Pike and James Pierpont's popular 1857 song from the perspective of a male slave whose love, "charming Nettie Moore," was sold away to a Louisiana Bay trader who "gave to Master money and then shackled her with chains / Then he took her off to work her life away." Only death can reunite them—"But when weary life is past / I shall meet you once again, / In Heaven, darling, up above the skies."

Pike's performing career included stints with the Albino Family, the Harmoneons, and Ordway's Aeolians, and combined blackface and cross-dressing. In 1847 he appeared as Fanny in *Carolina Melodies* with the Harmoneons at the White House before President James K. Polk. Pike was drum major of the Twenty-Second Massachusetts Volunteer Infantry, and after he was captured in 1861 during the Battle of Gaines's Mill he formed a glee club at Libby Prison in Richmond, Virginia. Pierpont's journey is yet more checkered. Although his father was a celebrated Boston abolitionist, pastor, and poet, Pierpont joined Lamar's Rangers, later part of the Fifth Georgia Cavalry of the Confederacy, and while in service wrote "Strike for the South," "Our Battle Flag," and "We Conquer or Die." His most famous song, published the same year as "The Little White Cottage," is "Jingle Bells," then designated "The One Horse Open Sleigh." Twentieth-century singers of "Gentle Nettie Moore" include Sons of the Pioneers, featuring Leonard Slye, aka Roy Rogers (1934).

The untitled manuscript page in Dylan's Tulsa archive that would ultimately coalesce into "Nettie Moore" is a scattershot of verses and variations, but while many of the final lines are already in place, there is no chorus, and no clear indication or acknowledgment of Pike and Pierpont's minstrel sally. Of the songwriting on *Modern Times*, this lyric "troubled me the most," Dylan told Edna Gunderson, "because I wasn't sure if I was getting it right." In the draft, his verses haphazardly circle love, loss, and aging, passing from angry rants to protestations of eternal devotion, and are stuffed with similarly hit-or-miss folk and blues refractions—including from "Ragged and Dirty," the Willie Brown song he covered on *World Gone Wrong*, or for a verse Dylan didn't retain, Mississippi Fred McDowell's "My Baby Has Eyes Like an Eagle":

Words of fire can break your heart / blow you apart
I'll be loving you when my whiskers drag the ground
Even when you die, I'll keep hanging around

Only when Dylan annexed the "Gentle Nettie Moore" chorus would his sketchy lines and obscure blues signals cohere. With Pike and Pierpont's song as his prompt and frame, his opening verse, although word-for-word intact from the draft, suddenly tilts randomness to reveal a template:

Lost John's sittin' on a railroad track
Something's out of whack
Blues this mornin' fallin' down like hail
Gonna leave a greasy trail

Instead of the rhyming pile-up of his draft, "Nettie Moore" now advances a sort of call-and-response. Someone is struggling to sing—sing *and* write—a folk blues song. Frustrated, obstructed, and stymied, they begin to mull, fret, and complain about the impasse. In the first line, the song is Papa Charlie Jackson's "Long Gone Lost John," but no, "Something's out of whack." In line three, the song is Robert Johnson's "Hellhound on My Trail," but the implications of slipping into Johnson's words don't feel right either: "Gonna leave a greasy trail."

Dylan's aspiring singer-songwriter—a would-be modern minstrel who recognizes too much about the cruel pain of the music he adores—later attempts songs that span blues, folk, country, and rhythm and blues: "Yellow Dog Blues" (W. C. Handy); "Frankie and Albert" (a traditional song Dylan covered on *Good as I Been to You*); "The Moonshiner" (a nineteenth-century song he recorded but left off of *The Times They Are A-Changin'* in 1963); "Two Soldiers" (a song he covered on *World Gone Wrong*); "I'll Never Get Out of This World Alive" (Hank Williams's final single); "I Like My Baby's Pudding" (Wyonie Harris); and more Papa Charlie Jackson, including "Bad Luck Woman," and multiple dips into "Look Out Papa Don't Tear Your Pants." But these songs too are disrupted and blocked, and the rueful commentary overlays defensiveness, aggression, apology, and self-reproach:

- If I don't do anybody any harm, I might make it back home alive
- Got a pile of sins to pay for and I ain't got time to hide
- I'm going to make you come to grips with fate / When I'm through with you, you'll learn to keep your business straight

- The bright spark of the steady lights / Has dimmed my sights
- Everything I've ever known to be right has proven wrong

Our blighted minstrel mocks his own arcane studies—"The world of research has gone berserk / Too much paperwork." Attacks his critics—"Before you call me any dirty names you better think twice." Throws up his hands in bewilderment—"It's either one or the other or neither of the two." And fancies a swift death—"I wish to God that it were night."

Across a dozen verses, "Nettie Moore" whirls a drama of love, resistance, and refusal, but an ethics, and a politics, too. That past—but not yet past. After every three verses, as if set off in counterpoint at a nexus of race, subjugation, and performance, Dylan arrays a melancholy, shattering chorus:

Oh, I miss you Nettie Moore,
And my happiness is o'er
Winter's gone, the river's on the rise
I loved you then and ever shall
But there's no one here that's left to tell
The world has gone black before my eyes

Who's the author—the plaintive "I"—of this chorus? Who's staging the suffering? That anonymous enslaved person, himself like his beloved Nettie Moore a captive body, chattel, property, their desires dispossessed of will and agency? Blackface Pike, who disseminated their stories, voices, and anguish for his own artistic and financial gain? Or our belated minstrel, now presupposing both of them? The afterlife of slavery is *a greasy trail*. Something was—and is—*out of whack*.

Yet if *Modern Times* is Dylan's *Civil War Revisited*, the album is also his *Ovid on Ovid*. Timrod, Pike, and Lanier, I might suggest, only inscribe another deep-cover operation; they are a deflective gesture intended to divert scrutiny from the actual priority of Ovid. On at least eight of the ten songs on *Modern Times*, he refocuses language from the Roman poet, all translations by the British classicist Peter Green. He registers erotic poems—*Amores*, *The Art of Love*, and *Cures for Love*—but especially *Tristia* and *Black Sea Letters*, poems Ovid ostensibly wrote after his exile by Augustus to Tomis, on the shores of the Black Sea, perhaps because of his scandalous verses, perhaps because of enigmatic offenses against the empire, and perhaps he wasn't banished at all, that spikey detail a necessary fiction for the poetry.

Ovid, more than Timrod, furnishes essential architectural scaffolding for songs on *Modern Times*, yielding transitions and decisive structural images. That crushing final tag of the "Nattie Moore" refrain—"The world has gone black before my eyes"—issues from "a nightmare / That scared me silly" in *Amores*, about oppressive heat, a white heifer, a bull, and a carrion crow. Ovid asks his "unseen expounder of dreams . . . what does mine portend?" and is told the nightmare is an allegory of desire and adultery, "so you too will be left / Alone in your own cold bed." Dylan's chorus rises from the dream's denouement:

There
His interpretation ended. At those words the blood ran freezing
From my face, and the world went black before my eyes.

To his song about the afterlife of slavery, and the double binds of representing that afterlife for a modern folk blues, Dylan fastened an Ovidian nightmare of lost love, betrayal, and grievous interpretation.

Once noticed—and noticed initially, I believe, by the New Zealand poet and musician Cliff Fell in his essay, "An avid follower of Ovid," for the *Nelson Mail* on October 7, 2006, just a few weeks after the *New York Times* piece on Timrod—Ovid surges through *Modern Times*, inspiriting "Nettie Moore," "Workingman's Blues #2," and "Ain't Talkin.'" The Roman poet's verse also pulses in "Thunder on the Mountain," "Spirit on the Water," "Rollin' and Tumblin'," "Someday Baby," and "The Levee's Gonna Break." Some chapters back I mentioned stumbling upon the command "Read Ovid," in Dylan's hand among the early 1990s drafts in the Tulsa archive, and plainly he did. Anatomizing his reading in *Chronicles*, Dylan remarked that on the shelves of Ray Gooch's New York City library, "Ovid's *Metamorphoses*, the scary horror tale, was next to the autobiography of Davy Crockett."

Classical mythology jostles American legend. Ovid—Publius Ovidius Naso—was born into a landed-gentry family at Sulmo (now Sulmono) in central Italy in 43 BC. As Green observes in his introduction to *The Poems of Exile*, this was the "year after Caesar's assassination," and Ovid "grew up during the violent death throes of the Roman republic." He published a version of *Amores* as early as 15 BCE, soon followed by *Heroides*, *The Art of Love*, *Remedia Amoris*, *Metamorphoses*, and *Fasti*. Augustus exiled him—*if* Augustus exiled him—to Tomis (now Constanta) in AD 8. "It was two offenses undid me," Ovid alleged in *Tristia*, "a poem and an error: on the second, my lips are sealed." A possible genealogical angle on the Dylan-Ovid connection is that in *Chronicles*, Dylan traces his own family back to the cities and towns along the Black Sea. "My grandmother's voice possessed a haunting accent," he tells us, "face always set in a half-despairing expression . . . Originally, she'd come from Turkey, sailed from Trabzon, a port town across the Black Sea." He links Odessa, the city his grandmother traveled to America from, with Duluth, where he was born. "The same kind of temperament, climate and landscape and right on the edge of a big body of water."

I imagine Green's translations appealed to Dylan because Green is himself so mercurial a verbal trickster. Amid variations for his own metrical designs, Dylan wittily evolved locutions no songwriter would need a classical poet for, since they already sound like they spring from old blues, country, and rockabilly lyrics—"the face begs for love," "This girl's got me hooked," "that I'm wrong in thinking you've forgotten me," "making you wish you'd never had a woman / And swear you won't touch one again for years," and "I want to be with you any way I can." There are passages in Green's translation where Ovid appears to be channeling early Dylan. "You better think twice," he warns on a page that impacted "Ain't Talkin'." As with Timrod, the kernels might be inverted. For "Rollin' and Tumblin'" *Amores* might have influenced that "houseboy" and "well-trained maid," but whereas Ovid originally advised a Roman gentleman intent on seduction, "You must get yourself a houseboy / And a well-trained maid, who can hint / What gifts will be welcome," now it's the singer who's "nobody's houseboy," and "nobody's well-trained maid."

The apotheosis of Ovid—really the apotheosis for all the spiraling obsessions on *Modern Times*—is "Ain't Talkin'," the final song. Rhythmically, vocally, and lyrically, "Ain't Talkin'" impels a drive unique in late Dylan, a sonic intensity probably unmatched since "Idiot Wind" from 1975's *Blood on the Tracks.* Some of its force emanates from the chorus Dylan seemingly transformed from "Highway of Regret," the 1959 single by the Stanley Brothers. Here's theirs:

Ain't talking, just walking
Down that highway of regret
Heart's burning, still yearning
For the best girl this poor boy's ever met

Here's his:

Ain't talkin, just walkin'
Through this weary world of woe
Heart burnin', still yearnin'
No one on earth would ever know

For the Stanley Brothers, "burning" and "yearning" measure out only wasted love and infidelity. But in Dylan, the words—through his many variations—will syncopate lust, vengeance, and apocalypse. Other songs he revitalized into the B and D lines of the refrain aggravate the sorrow, and accelerate the propulsion. "World of woe," for instance, echoes the nineteenth-century hymn, "The Wayfaring Stranger," which in some versions has the sad pilgrim meeting his mother after death; and presumably that's why Dylan sings "So pray for me mother" in the next verse. Later, "toothache in my heel"—from minstrel Dan Emmett's "Ole Dan Tucker"—augments the sense of restless motion, and "Hand me down my walkin' cane"—the title of an 1880 song by James A. Bland, a Black musician who performed with the Georgia Minstrels—similarly embellishes another minstrel tune Dylan adapts here, the ribald "Hog-Eye Man."

Part of the song's force is biblical—"It's bright in the heavens and wheels are flying," out of Ezekiel; plus a fragment of the commandments, and scintillas of Samuel, John, James, and Timothy. But the primary force inside "Ain't Talkin'" ultimately transmogrifies Ovid, who loops through the song as insistently as the Stanley Brothers:

If I ever catch my opponents sleepin'
I'll just slaughter them where they lie

They will tear your mind away from contemplation

They will jump on your misfortune when you're down

I'll make the most of one last extra hour

All my loyal and much-loved companions
They approve of me and share my code
I practice a faith that's long abandoned

Who says I can't get heavenly aid

The suffering is unending
Every nook and cranny has its tears

I'm not nursing any superfluous fears

In the last outback, at the world's end

All these vivifying moments arise from *Amores*, *Tristia*, and *Black Sea Letters*, and have been skillfully calibrated for elisions and rhythmic accommodations, with consecutive threads of the song often far apart in Ovid. Across the multiple drafts of "Ain't Talkin' " in Dylan's Tulsa archive, the Latin poet—as far as I can tell—is largely absent. The axis on these handwritten pages is bitter remorse and—fury at falsehoods—"Sometimes I think that people would have practically nothing to say to each other / If there were no more lies to tell." Disgust with greed—"She wants everything she can see / Locomotives, bouquets of flowers, a jewelry shop / fountain pens, a pressing plant, a chocolate factory." As on *Modern Times*, a "mystic garden" opens every draft, but any sense of Eden soon shrinks into a "False Paradise that tempted me."

On the next available incarnation of "Ain't Talkin'," an alternate take released in 2008 on *Tell Tale Signs*, caricature slakes. As the lyric tightens, the vision enlarges; Dylan is a ferocious and masterly reviser, and as Elizabeth Hardwick argued, "writing includes the ability to edit yourself." On the outtake he tries out an Ovid adaptation—as the sequence reads in Green's translation of *Amores*, "Night attacks are a great thing. Catch your opponents sleeping / And unarmed. Just slaughter them where they lie." He experimented, too, with nods to Chaucer, Spenser, and Ginsberg, which he later dropped, also excising a reference to a 1940s Albert E. Brumley hymn, "It's a Grand and Glorious Feeling," that reflected the Stanley Brothers refrain. (Brumley: "It's a grand and glorious feeling / To be walking and talking with my king.") If Dylan had halted his tinkering at these revisions, the outtake could have graced his new album as a vague if overwrought ramble "down the primrose path," as he sings there, of minor key romantic dejection and disillusion. Only on *Modern Times*—and after those wily conjurations of Ovid—will "Ain't Talkin' " encompass what Greil Marcus lauded as "a complete world." The drafts exude individual gall and grumbling. Now the lyrics manifest a historical command, a metaphysical spine, and quickened Dylan's access to that pull, that lure, that whiplash recoil he appears to have found first in the music. For "Ain't

Talkin'," and across *Modern Times*, Ovid mirrored back to him a geography and a language of civil exile for erotic and spiritual desolation. Individual disperses into multitude, into history. The Roman poet also yielded Dylan a destination for his song, and his album. As Ovid wrote in *Black Sea Letters*:

Some places make exile
milder, but there's no more dismal land than this
beneath either pole. It helps to be near your country's borders:
I'm in the last outback, at the world's end.

Here and throughout, Ovid heightens the scale. A Katrina-esque detail from "The Levee's Gonna Break"—"Some people got barely enough skin to cover their bones"—emanated amid Ovid's discussion in *Tristia* of his harsh times in Tomis; Ovid was describing his own body, a self-portrait Dylan generalizes. Likewise, "I'm gonna drive you from your home just like I was driven from mine" from "Someday Baby" concentrates a contrast Ovid posed between his own fate on the Black Sea and the journey of Odysseus: "He was making for his homeland / A cheerful victor: I was driven from mine, / fugitive, exile, victim."

Odysseus, and the anti-Odysseus. "Ain't Talkin'" shades an elegy for a life, a planet. Manuscript fragments in his Tulsa archive surrounding *Modern Times* show Dylan toying with a succession of Louis Jordan songs, "Saturday Night Fish Fry," "Blue Light Boogie," "Nobody Here but Us Chickens," maybe nine or ten Jordan songs in all. But scattered among these miscellaneous papers, not attached to any specific lyric, are sundry jottings of variant styles that might intimate the scope of his thinking and planning towards the album. *Animus brincandi*, a bouncing mind. On one page he scribbled phrases from John Milton's "Lycidas," arguably the greatest pastoral elegy in English, alongside a reference to *Platinum Blonde*, Jean Harlow's 1931 film, and a line from Ernest Renan's 1863 *The Life of Jesus*. (The dates of Ovid and the historical Jesus overlap.) On a nearby page is a sliver of *Areopagitica*, Milton's attack on censorship during the English civil war. Dylan mentions nursery rhymes—*Peter the Pumpkin*

Eater, *Humpty Dumpty*, *Little Jack Horner*—and quotes Churchill ("fighting wars with other people's blood"), Woody Guthrie ("Crawdad Song"), and Yeats ("looking for the face I had before the world was made"). He scatters religious threats, "Got my own particular brand of hell fire." Politics, from Franklin D. Roosevelt's 1930s to current social relations, roils through these stray, inchoate notes and sketches.

Politics, particularly economics, is Dylan's fraught cargo for "Workingman's Blues #2," his trenchant reply to Merle Haggard's 1969 country hit. The musicians toured together in the spring of 2005, but as Dylan would suggest during his MusiCares talk a decade later, "Merle Haggard didn't think much of my songs . . . Now I admire Merle—'Mama Tried,' 'Tonight the Bottle Let Me Down,' 'I'm a Lonesome Fugitive.'" Note that Dylan doesn't mention "Workin' Man Blues," for Haggard's song *is* maudlin, cliched, and presumptuous: "You know I've been a workin' man dang near all my life . . . never been on welfare." Dylan, instead, opens large, yet matter-of-fact—

There's an evening's haze settling over the town
Starlight by the edge of the creek
The buying power of the proletariat's gone down
Money getting shallow and weak
The place I love best is a sweet memory
It's a new path that we trod
They say low wages are a reality
If we want to compete abroad

—before zeroing in on the repercussions of this "new path" (*Modern Times*, indeed) for a worker, and for his family. He shapes another seamless web of musical and literary intimations, Woody Guthrie's "Hobo's Lullaby," June Christy's "June's Blues," and Big Joe Williams's "Meet Me at the Bottom." The resonances of Timrod speak to the worker's anxiety, sadness, and isolation—"I'm trying to feed my soul with thought . . . Old memories of you to me have clung"—whereas the resonances of Ovid speak to his bewilderment, loss, and alienation: "My cruel weapons have been put on a shelf . . . Tell me now, am I wrong in thinking / That you have forgotten me . . . I'm all alone and I'm expecting you / To lead me off in a cheerful dance."

Some of Dylan's invocations of Ovid in "Workingman's Blues #2" are from episodes in *Tristia* where the Roman poet is addressing his wife, still in Rome, and tacitly chart the family disruptions and breakdowns of this neoliberal, globalized "new path." The fractured love story inside the song is romantic, but also fiscal. A glimpse of Chaucer's "The Monk's Tale"—"I'm just trying to keep the hunger from / Creepin' its way into my gut"—similarly calls up a starving child. In the interview with Mikal Gilmore where he addresses the Timrod question, Dylan passionately and stylishly vindicated his new songs as an amplification of folk process. "In folk and jazz, quotation is a rich and enriching tradition," he countered. "It's an old thing—part of the tradition. It goes way back. These are the same people that tried to pin the name Judas on me . . . Yeah, and for what? For playing an electric guitar? . . . All those evil motherfuckers can rot in hell." Folk process, just add books.

Modern Times is hardly a celebration of tradition, as Dylan is alert to contradictions, embarrassments, and checkmates. Nor is it a celebration of the classical world, though admirers sometimes confuse his Ovid, Virgil, and Homer for nostalgic homage. Assassinations, slavery, empire, and Civil Wars—Dylan's Rome is at least as violent, shamed, and devastated as Dylan's America. Archives of disaster. All times are modern to those trapped inside them. Dylan's beloved New Lost City Ramblers also titled an album *Modern Times*. As John Cohen concluded his liner notes, "The study of folklore is not simply to preserve the past, but to make the present more comprehensible." On his *Modern Times* all Dylan's first-person voices are suspect, dubious, even that vivid, overwhelmed workingman's: "I say it, so it must be so." Auditors? Locutors? Any difference? Here only vestiges and ruins; yet urgent, angry, heartbroken, far-reaching, and beautiful. A space of immersion in multitude, and as Saidiya Hartman once framed the procedures for her own writing, "History is how the secular world attends to the dead."

When ghost to ghost Dylan haunts Ovid and Timrod, or they him, the flickers often involve corridors and alleys where the poets were reflecting on their art. That "cheerful dance" is an item in Ovid's reply to a friend who urged him to "divert these mournful days with writing." When Dylan sings, "I practice a faith that's long abandoned," he mobilizes a section of *Tristia* where Ovid is tolling the quandaries of keeping his Latin alive in Tomis:

Yet, to prevent my voice being muted
in my native speech, lest I lose the common use
of the Latin tongue, I converse with myself, I practice
terms long abandoned, retrace my sullen art's
ill-fated signs. Thus I drag out my life and time, thus
tear my mind from the contemplation of my woes.
Through writing I seek an anodyne to misery: if my studies
win me such a reward, that is enough.

Even when Ovid exclaimed, "I want to be with you any way I can," he wasn't beckoning a lover, but beseeching his audience back in Rome reading the new poems he sent them from the Black Sea. Timrod's "A Vision of Poesy" etches in fanciful, mythic modes the curious route that might guide a boy born of "humble parentage" in Charleston, South Carolina, say, or Duluth, Minnesota, to poetry.

For Dylan, too, studied Latin, at Hibbing High School. As his senior-year entry in the 1959 *Hematite* famously runs:

Robert Zimmerman: to join "Little Richard"—
Latin Club 2; Social Studies Club 4.

And, yes, there in one of the group photos of the Latin Club, aka "Societas Latinas," for the *Hematite* of his sophomore year, is "Bob Zimmerman," seated between Mike Minelli and Frank Sherman, right in the front row. As that 1957 write-up summarizes:

Latin Club

Students Promote Study of Roman Culture and Life

Initiation of new members and a tea in November began the year's activities of the Latin Club. During the year the group published a newspaper, containing articles written by many of the Latin students.

The club's main purpose is to further interest in the Latin language and promote study of Roman life and customs. Membership consists of students taking Latin and students with two years of Latin. Miss Irene Walker is the group's adviser and Mary Ann Peterson and Joe Perpich are the consuls.

The next year's *Hematite* is flashier: "Societas Latinas Learns to Live as Romans." And for Old World context of a rival slant, directly under Robert Zimmerman's individual portrait in the sophomore yearbook there's a photograph of a classmate on a pay phone, apparently Hibbing High's first: "With the installation of a telephone booth in the lower hallway this year, the students have been able to enrich their learning of oral communication. Al Vranesh portrays the typical caller who fails to make connections."

When I visited Hibbing some years ago during a Dylan symposium in Minneapolis—searching for clues, I guess, in that fatuous way you intend to resolve the inexplicable—I was surprised and seized by Dylan's high school, the scale, the splendor, and the seriousness. Hibbing High was built in the early 1920s at a cost of nearly four million dollars after the Oliver Iron Mining Company entered into an agreement with progressive Mayor Victor Power to pay for a school, the Androy Hotel, and the Hibbing City Hall (modeled on Boston's Faneuil Hall), contingent on the town's relocating a few miles south so that the ore under the original settlement could be mined and sent by rail and barge to Eastern steel mills. Homes, stores, and theaters, whole or piecemeal, were jacked up and rolled on a cribbing of timbers.

Hibbing High School is beyond the New England college style grandeur of an Eastern prep school: Kasota marble, brass rails, molded plaster, cut glass chandeliers, and a set of six murals by David Ericson at the entrance depicting United States and Minnesota history, with another sixty-foot mural on the Iron Industry in the school library. The school was designed to serve Hibbing-area students from kindergarten through the first two years of community college, and everything is outsized. Over a hundred rooms, three gyms, two running tracks, an auto shop, and an 1,800-seat auditorium, where in 1958 Dylan performed with the Golden Chords, perhaps his largest indoor concert venue until well into the sixties. During this visit I met B. J. Rolfzen—Dylan's own Bill Collins; his English teacher junior year for American literature, and senior year for British literature. Smart, lively, warm, and obsessed with poetry, Rolfzen discussed, read aloud, or circulated some of the poems he introduced to "Robert," as he called him, by Donne, Tennyson, Whitman, Williams, Sandburg, and Frost. Close reading. Rolfzen distributed a poem that he'd written, "My Student," featuring, among other stanzas:

He quietly chose an unassigned seat,
Talking to no one
And acknowledging no one
With a mind attuned
To the world which lay before him.

Rolfzen's language, much like that of the future songs of his "attuned" prize student, is tricky, and double-edged. That great world and life beyond Hibbing, of course; but *Paradise Lost*, too. "The world was all before them," as Milton says of Adam and Eve near the end of his poem. Robert's initiation into literature. Epic ambitions in a fallen world, in *Modern Times.* His coeval initiation into capitalism probably would have been the Hill—Rust—Mahoning Open Pit Iron Mine, that vast gash in the Mesabi Range over two miles wide and three miles long and hundreds of feet deep. For subsequent rounds of expansion, the Oliver Mining Company wasn't so cooperative or genteel, seizing Hibbing residences and businesses far below their value. After Mayor Power's death in 1926, his coalition of immigrant Socialists and anti-KKK reformers was no match for United States Steel.

Homer, Virgil, Ovid, Shakespeare, Milton. The classic allusive arc of Dylan's twenty-first century albums can intimate the aspirational curriculum of a phantom high school of the American 1950s and 1960s. But more than Hibbing High, Latin Club, and B. J. Rolfzen, or the Pit, or even peering out a window from his bedroom in the family home at 2425 Seventh Avenue, the place that, for an instant, most seemed the shadow of Robert Zimmerman, were some streets that I walked along in North Hibbing, by the edges of the mine, and a short bicycle ride from the main drags. All the buildings were gone, moved or torn down. No houses, but here and there clearly a long-ago street, sometimes with an overgrown sidewalk, a corner gas lamp, and the rectangular footprint of a once-upon-a-time stone foundation.

> Waiting to be swallowed by that hole in the ground.
>
> So, *why not* the shadow of Robert Zimmerman?
>
> Since Hibbing, since Hibbing is a ghost town.

M

. . . FOLLOWED THE PATH . . .

Memento mori. Remember death, and—more literally—remember to die, as in, remember that you die; as in, that you *will*, that you *must*, die. Socrates and Plato. The Stoics. Centuries of paintings of skulls, hourglasses, and (of course) flowers, as Dylan sang in "I Contain Multitudes" on *Rough and Rowdy Ways*, "The flowers are dying, like all things do." Cicero's account in *de Oratore* of the lyric poet Simonides of Ceos and the banquet where the roof collapses is *memento mori* of another, more literal kind, as Simonides invents the method of *loci* and the memory palace, reconstructing the places—*loci*—where the now dead guests once sat, so that their smashed, unrecognizable bodies might be identified, buried, and mourned, before the final coming to rest. *Ecclesiastes* 9:5–6: "For the living know that they shall die: but the dead know not any thing, neither have they any more a reward; for the memory of them is forgotten."

Bob Dylan's tributes to his dear dead friends, and to the dead musicians, writers, and artists who stirred him, are among the most glorious *loci* in his memory palace. His vast spectral networks of musical, literary, and historical allusions across *Time Out of Mind*, *"Love And Theft," Modern Times*, *Tempest*, and *Rough and Rowdy Ways*, all those shadow hauntings, could be approached as memento mori, as implicit memorials of the great dead. Same for many of his live song covers, and his albums of covers, too. But I'm thinking here more of homages on albums, in concerts, and occasionally even in his rare written public statements that are *specifically* elegiac.

In 1996 Dylan founded Egyptian Records, a label imprint at Columbia/Sony. The following year he curated there the release of *The Songs of Jimmie Rodgers—A Tribute Album*, which convened a diversity of contemporary singers performing classic Rodgers: Bono, Mary Chapin Carpenter, Jerry Garcia, Alison Kraus, John Mellencamp, Van Morrison, and Willie Nelson. Dylan himself contributed a spare, solemn rendition of "My Blue Eyed Jane," a 1930 Rodgers song he first attempted in the studio in 1994 and revisited during his *Time Out of Mind* sessions. He would play Rodgers's original recording on a *Theme Time Radio Hour* episode focused on "Eyes." As Dylan observed in his album liner notes:

> Jimmie Rodgers of course is one of the guiding lights of the Twentieth Century whose way with song has always been an inspiration to those of us who have followed the path . . . Jerry Lee Lewis once said there are only four stylists—Jimmie, Al Jolson, Hank Williams and himself . . . If we look back far enough, Jimmie may very well be "the man who started it all" for we have no antecedents to compare him. His refined style, an amalgamation of sources unknown, is too cryptic to pin down. His is a thousand and one voices yet singularly his own . . . We love the man and we love what he did in the short time he was here . . . His is the voice of the wilderness of your head. . . .

The only other Egyptian Records release would be another Dylan-curated anthology tribute in 2011, *The Lost Notebooks of Hank Williams*, including this time Norah Jones, Jack White, Lucinda Williams, Sheryl Crow, Levon Helm, Merle Haggard, and his son Jakob Dylan. In 1963 for his LP jacket poem on *Joan Baez in Concert, Part 2*, he claimed "my first idol was Hank Williams." A spring, a source, and as he expanded in *Chronicles*:

> In time, I became aware that in Hank's recorded songs were the archetype rules of poetic songwriting . . . You can learn a lot about the structure of songwriting by listening to his records, and I listened to them a lot and had them internalized. In a few years' time, Robert Shelton, the folk and jazz critic for the *New York Times*, would review one of my performances and would say something like, "resembling a cross between a choirboy and a beatnik . . . he breaks all the rules in songwriting, except that of having something to say." The rules, whether Shelton knew it or not, were Hank's rules, but it wasn't like I ever meant to break them. It's just that what I was trying to express was beyond the circle.

Live on stage, and for people he knew personally, his encomia were more direct. In 1990 guitarist Stevie Ray Vaughan was killed in a helicopter crash, and Dylan performed "Moon River" for the first time in concert, dedicating the Johnny Mercer and Henry Mancini standard to Vaughan. "Everyone here knows about Stevie . . . so this one's for Stevie, wherever you are." Allen Ginsberg died on April 5, 1997, and Dylan was playing at the Moncton Colosseum in New Brunswick, Canada. After he sang "Desolation Row," he paused: "A friend of mine passed away, I guess this morning . . . That was one of his favorite songs, poet Allen Ginsberg." Minnesota senator Paul Wellstone perished in a plane crash in 2002, and Dylan dedicated to him an acoustic reading of "The Times They Are A'Changin'." When Warren Zevon was ill and dying of cancer, Dylan covered his songs during his fall 2002 tour, sometimes as many as three a concert—including "Mutineer" at the show I attended at Madison Square Garden on November 13. That night he encored with "Something," by George Harrison, who had died a year earlier, on November 29, 2001. "There's a tribute coming," he said by way of a preamble. "I guess it's next week, or the week after, over in England for George Harrison . . . But we can't make it, and that's why I'm going to do this song now in remembrance of George, because we were such good buddies."

Perhaps most poignant of all, though, are his little prose reflections on the passing of intimate friends, such as Harrison, Muhammad Ali, Robbie Robertson, Paul Butterfield, and Jerry Garcia, or his beloved mentors, Johnny Cash, Carl Perkins, and Little Richard. On Harrison, he writes:

> He was a giant, a great, great soul, with all of the humanity, all of the wit and humor, all the wisdom, the spirituality, the common sense of a man and compassion for people. He inspired love and had the strength of a hundred men. He was like the sun, the flowers and the moon and we will miss him enormously. The world is a profoundly emptier place without him.

On Ali, alluding to *The Sayings of Muhammad*:

> If the measure of greatness is to gladden the heart of every human being on the face of the earth, then truly he was the greatest. In every way he was the bravest, the kindest and the most excellent of men.

On Perkins:

> He really stood for freedom. That whole sound stood for all degrees of freedom. It would just jump off the turntable. We wanted to go where that was happening.

On Cash:

> Truly he is what the land and country is all about, the heart and soul of it personified and what it means to be here; and he said it all in plain English. I think we can have recollections of him, but we can't define him any more than we can define a fountain of truth, light and beauty. If we want to know what it means to be mortal, we need look no further than the Man in Black. Blessed with a profound imagination, he used the gift to express all the various lost causes of

the human soul. This is a miraculous and humbling thing. Listen to him, and he will always bring you to your senses.

On Robbie Robertson:

This is shocking news. Robbie was a lifelong friend. His passing leaves a vacancy in the world.

On Butterfield:

Today (December 17, 2024) is Paul Butterfield's birthday. He would have been 82. We miss you Paul.

Finally, his prose poem on Garcia:

There's no way to measure his greatness or magnitude as a person or a player. I don't think any eulogizing will do him justice. He was that great, much more than a superb musician, with an uncanny ear and dexterity. He's the very spirit personified of whatever is Muddy Waters Country at its core and screams up into the spheres. He really had no equal. To me he wasn't only a musician and friend, he was more like a big brother who taught and showed me more than he'll ever know. There's a lot of spaces and advances between the Carter Family, Buddy Holly and, say, Ornette Coleman, a lot of universes, but he filled them all without being a member of any school. His playing was moody, awesome, sophisticated, hypnotic and subtle. There's no way to convey the loss. It just digs down really deep.

Really deep . . . As late as his *Rough and Rowdy Ways* tours of Japan and Europe in 2023, and of America in 2024, Dylan was still performing Dead covers, "Truckin'," "Friend of the Devil," "Brokedown Palace," and "Stella Blue."

Dylan dedicated *The Philosophy of Modern Song* to Doc Pomus, the songwriter whose "Boogie Woogie Country Girl" he recorded for another valedictory album, *Till the Night Is Gone: A Tribute to Doc Pomus*. "I was listening to Son House, Lead Belly, the Carter Family, Memphis Minnie, and death romance ballads," he told Bill Flanagan in a 2009 interview. "As far as songwriting, I wanted to write songs like Woody Guthrie and Robert Johnson. Timeless and eternal. Only a few of those radio ballads still hold up and most of them have Doc Pomus' hand in them. . . . Doc was a soulful cat."

As Dylan's riff—a riff also on his own apprentice songwriting aspirations against the backdrop of folk and blues musicians—clarifies, his interviews are intrinsically memorial, too, and vital *loci* of his memory palace. As he talks to Flanagan, the monumental names spin and reel, seemingly not to impress but as a show of respect, and deference: from Son House to Pomus, Dylan is observant, discerning, celebratory, instructive, and commemorative. His '60s interviews often constituted trickster put-ons, but after 1991 they're characteristically thoughtful, and, if scant on confidential details, illuminating and useful to an appreciation of his art. Still, Dylan's late interviews are performative, and some even partake of the same collage strategies as his late songs—Juvenal, Woody Guthrie, Marcel Duchamp, Joyce Carol Oates, among other mementos, provocations, affinities, taunts, and panegyrics.

Obit. Past participle of *obire*, to go forward, to die. Dylan—and maybe also Patti Smith—just might be the closest we now have to a modern public intellectual, at least a public intellectual with any authority, gravitas, and cultural reach. *Memento mori*. When Joan Didion died, the celebration of her life and work at Saint John the Divine on September 21, 2022, for all the gifted and celebrated speakers, Hilton Als, Calvin Trillin, Jia Tolentino, David Remnick, Susanna Moore, Griffin Dunne, Kevin Young, and Shelley Wanger, concluded with Smith singing Dylan's "Chimes of Freedom."

You can almost track the gyrations that led there. How might we most honor her? How can we end this?

Ah—no other choice—*Patti* doing *Bob*. . . .

N

. . . DON'T SEPARATE IT BY STYLE . . .

Night—it is always at night. Igneous night. "I liked the night," Dylan wrote in *Chronicles*. "Things grow at night. My imagination is available to me at night. All my preconceptions of things go away." Over two (of ultimately three) seasons, each episode of *Theme Time Radio Hour*—including episode 78, on "Night"—opened with a short, lyrical invocation, *It's night time in the big city*, spoken by actress Ellen Barkin (except for "Halloween," when comedian Steve Wright strolled up the trick-or-treat lane instead). The city's electric grid of currents. Such openings oozed film noir, and not just because of Barkin; they also signaled everyday absurdist USA, too. From episode 1, on "Weather":

It's night time in the big city
Rain is falling, fog rolls in from the waterfront
A night shift nurse smokes the last cigarette in a pack

Episode 8, on "Weddings":

It's night time in the big city

A man buys a pack of gum, steals a nail clipper
Two pairs of sneakers are strung over a phone line

Episode 66, on "Lock & Key":

It's night time in the big city
A school teacher drinks alone
They're finally tearing down the old shoe factory

Episode 88, on "Something":

It's night time in the big city
A man falls asleep far from home
There's a strange car parked outside

Every week another fresh, home-spun American haiku—hey, who's counting syllables?—along with an archivist's ebullient array of songs; biographies of neglected musicians; far-flung, outlier facts (did you know about the harness Gus Cannon fashioned so that he could wear his jug around his neck and play banjo at the same time?); vintage jokes ("A giraffe can go a long time without water, but he wants to see a menu right away"); alleged listener emails; shards of TV and movie dialogue; bygone jingles, classic poems and novels; celebrity drive-bys; and lots of rambling, seductive talk. For that episode on "Night," for instance, Dylan dropped a pocket lecture on noir and Cornell Woolrich:

> These films were fatalistic, a small step in the wrong direction, a tiny lie, a petty crime, you could be sent into a quicksand of obliteration. . . . The whole thing painted a picture of a nocturnal, claustrophobic city, subterranean and unreal. . . . The idea of film noir was taken partially from the books of Cornell Woolrich. . . . He was protégé of F. Scott Fitzgerald, but after a couple of novels found his own true calling, dark crime fiction. He wrote a whole cycle of books

with the word black in them, *The Bride Wore Black*, *The Black Curtain*, *The Black Alibi*, *The Black Angel*, *Rendezvous in Black*, and *The Black Path of Fear*. . . . Cornell Woolrich Father of Darkness.

Theme Time Radio Hour debuted on May 3, 2006, and aired until April 15, 2009. After he launched his distillery, "Heaven's Door," Dylan returned on September 21, 2020, for a special double episode on "Whiskey." During interviews and for *Chronicles*, Dylan reiterated the notion that for him growing up in northern Minnesota music was synonymous with radio, particularly late-night radio, and that radio was tantamount to his survival. "Back then," he recalled in *Chronicles*, "when something was wrong the radio could lay hands on you and you'd be all right." On *Theme Time Radio Hour*, he celebrated radio before rock 'n' roll (episode 16, on "Dogs") and the radio stations that broadcast from across the Mexican border, "these early hothouses of modern music," which "did not have to obey the same laws as their American counterparts. They were able to broadcast deep into the United States." For Dylan radio was more than music; really, it was all popular culture. "Radio shows had been a big part of my consciousness back in the Midwest," he continued in *Chronicles*, "back when it seemed like I was living in perpetual youth. *Inner Sanctum*, *The Lone Ranger*, *This Is Your FBI*, *Fibber McGee and Molly*, *The Fat Man*, *The Shadow*, *Suspense*. . . ." Radio also led to his earliest songwriting. "We'd listen to songs at night on AM radio from down south," said LeRoy Hoikkala, Dylan's childhood friend and the drummer in his high school band, the Golden Chords. "And we had a reel to reel tape recorder that we'd tape some of those things, and he'd change them to his liking. I mean it wasn't copying. He'd just say, 'You know that should really be a little different.' And he'd pick with his guitar and he'd start playing almost the same song, but it would actually be, I would think, better."

Radio for Dylan was at once somewhere out there and interior. Sam Shepard once recast a conversation with him into a play, *True Dylan*. Here they compare their earliest experiences with music and radio:

SAM: Did you dream about music back then?

BOB: I had lotsa dreams. Used to dream about things like Ava Gardner and Wild Bill Hickok. They were playin' cards, chasin' each other, and getting' around. Sometimes I'd even be in the dreams myself. Radio station dreams. You know how, when you're a kid, you stay up late in bed, listening to the radio, and you sort of dream off the radio into sleep. That's how you used to fall asleep. That's when disc jockeys played whatever they felt like.

SAM: I used to fall asleep listening to baseball.

BOB: Yeah. Same thing. Just sorta dream off into the radio. Like you were inside the radio kinda.

Inside the radio. *Kinda.* Transmitting from Studio B of the fictional Abernathy Building, according to show credits, *Theme Time Radio Hour* obviously was a real broadcast, entertaining, instructive, and with a large audience on XM Satellite Radio (later Sirius XM Radio), organized around shifting weekly song "themes"—"Mothers," "Drinking," "Baseball," "Coffee," and "Jail," to list five episodes from the first season; "Smoking," "Dreams," "Party," Cadillac," and "Walking," for five more from the second; and "Work," "Nothing," "Cats," "Truth & Lies," and "Madness" for still five more from the third. Yet *Theme Time Radio Hour* was also a reverie deep inside Dylan's head. Here was a fiction on a mission. Three seasons, 101 episodes, more than 1,800 songs by nearly 1,160 different artists across blues, soul, country, jazz, R&B, Broadway, and rock 'n' roll, spanning the 1920s to the 2000s: the vastest of the *loci* of Dylan's memory palace.

Dreams, schemes, and themes, as Dylan cast the show. The dreams and schemes are relatively easy to suss out—radio for Dylan was already a sort of dream; and the "show itself is kind of a scheme," he remarked in episode 59, on "Dreams." Yet what did all those *themes* get him? Pretty much everything, I'd argue, certainly everything distinctive and daring.

The glory—and also the dubious challenge—of *Theme Time Radio Hour* was the apparently inexhaustible variety of the songs Dylan played—Judy Garland right after Jimi Hendrix for episode 1, on "Weather"; Lefty Frizzell just before Lightnin' Hopkins for episode 6, on "Coffee"; Frank Sinatra between Big Joe Turner and Charlie Poole for episode 8, on "Weddings"; or an exhilarating run for episode 46, on "More Trains," comprising Jimmy Bryant and Speedy West, Curtis Mayfield, Papa George Lightfoot, Captain Beefheart, Jimmy Lunceford, Lord Kitchener, Sister Rosetta Tharpe, Johnny Cash, Muddy Waters, Los Lobos, Little Eva, Louis Armstrong, Jimmy Martin, Randy Newman, Furry Lewis, and the O'Jays.

God's plenty, but maybe—potentially, precariously, perilously—Tower of Babel, too. The weekly themes stipulated a point of connection and commonality in his implacable panopticon that subtly organized a musical diversity that might otherwise have registered as chaos. For all their differences, Garland's "Come Rain or Come Shine" and Hendrix's "The Wind Cries Mary" do join up around "Weather." Certain literary forms can perform that same variation/reiteration, repetition/revelation two-step—sonnets, villanelles, and sestinas—or the way a prose abecedarium sanctions chronology inside an asynchronous topicality, at once an estranging device and a nurturing ritual. Dylan joked about this in episode 75, on "Cold," before he played "So Cold, So Dead, So Soon" by Roy Hogsed. "He's one of those guys that you don't know where to put his records," he pretended to complain of Hogsed. "Are they country boogie? Are they early rockabilly? Are they country and western? That's why I file everything alphabetically. I don't separate it by style. That's why you find Thelonious Monk right next to the Monkees." Put another way, the themes were the bass that counted off the pace, and Dylan then could chase any solo flight of his musical fancy.

His tone on *Theme Time Radio Hour* was wry and personable. Yet Dylan was his sly twenty-first-century self from his first song on that first show on "Weather," and not just because that song was Muddy Waters' "Blow Wind, Blow," or that he followed it with "You Are My Sunshine" by

James Houston Davis. Introducing "the great Muddy Waters," he silently echoed Pope's "Essay on Criticism"—"one of the ancients by now whom all moderns prize." The "Weather" show installed other templates and sparkling patterns. Movies—here Robert DeNiro in *Taxi Driver* (on later episodes, *The Wild Bunch*, *Gaslight*, *The Godfather*, *42nd Street*, *Chinatown*, and *Strangers on a Train*). Poets—here Saint Basil, identified as "def poet" (on later episodes, Ferlinghetti, Ginsberg, Sandburg, Poe, Crane, Dickinson, Coleridge, Yeats, Eliot, and Shakespeare). Quirky, *almost* random info—is Chicago actually the windiest city? Quirky, *almost* personal disclosures—when he says of Garland, "Just like Prince, she's from Minnesota." His charged rhetoric on the "catastrophe" and "apocalypse" of the Santa Anna winds, collaged from Raymond Chandler and Joan Didion. Dylan routinely repeated lyrics he adored, and by his fifth song, "Just Walking in the Rain" by the Prisonaires, he asserted his anger about race in America: "Lead singer, Johnny Bragg, was sentenced to 99 years for rape . . . But you know for a Black man in Tennessee in the '40s, rape could have just been looking at the wrong white woman in the wrong way."

The inventory, the ledger, the list. His many homages on *Theme Time Radio Hour* to favorite artists—some famous, many obscure—seemed to clear Dylan to wax personal, an autobiography of a refracted, oblique cut. Always allegedly remembering and describing someone else, he joked about his vocals in episode 13, on "Rich Man, Poor Man":

> [Tom] Waits has a raspy, gravelly singing voice, described by one fan as how you'd sound if you drank a quart of bourbon, smoked a pack of cigarettes, and swallowed a pack of razor blades, after not sleeping for three days. Or as I like to put it, beautiful.

Discussed his astrological sign in episode 26, on "Halloween":

> He was born on May 25th which makes him a Gemini. Geminis are curious, good multi-taskers, and, in Albert King's case, they play guitar left-handed.

Ran down the prison-house of fan expectations in episode 40, on "Laughter":

> One thing that's no laughing matter is pigeon-holing. Sometimes people think you can do one thing and they trap you there. They don't let you grow. Case in point: Gene Chandler.

Winked at his rep for making records fast in episode 96, on "Family Circle":

> You know, people used to go into the studio when they had a song or two, when they had something to say. Nowadays, people just go into the studio 'cause they got time to kill. They sit around, they order sushi, get some Starbucks, wait for inspiration to hit, and the records sound like that. There's some records that take two years to make and you listen to 'em, and there's nothin' on 'em! This record, I guarantee you, took less than two hours to make, and wasn't even the A side. You be the judge. What would you rather listen to? A whole record about nothin'? Or a 45 called "Little Sister"?

Glanced at the composite musics behind his album *"Love And Theft"* in episode 99, "Clearance Sale":

> The sweet, gentle sounds of Mississippi John Hurt. You can hear elements of the songster tradition, the music that came before the blues, carrying elements of minstrel songs and other Native American forms.

And explained how influences and traditions work in the guise of celebrating The Ink Spots for episode 65, on "Traveling Around the World Part 2":

> Everybody wanted to sing like Bill Kinney. You can hear him in Clyde McFadder, Jackie Wilson, Elvis Presley, and a host of others who

> don't even know they're trying to sing like Bill Kinney, who try to sing like Clyde McFadder, Jackie Wilson, Elvis Presley, etc., etc., and so it goes, down the lines of history.

Other homages look forward to his own distant recordings—for *Rough and Rowdy Ways* via Jimmie Rodgers (in episode 7, on "Fathers," and in episode 45, on "Trains") and Charlie Poole (in episode 52, on "Young & Old," and in episode 68, on "Presidents"); for *Shadows in the Night, Fallen Angels,* and *Triplicate* via Frank Sinatra (also in episode 68, on "Presidents") and Johnny Mercer (in episode 1, on "Weather").

"Jerry Lee Lewis singing Shakespeare!—that's what this show is all about," Dylan testified in episode 80, on "Blood," after spinning Lewis's "Lust of the Blood" from *Catch My Soul*, a rock 'n' roll musical adapted from *Othello* in 1968, where "The Killer" originally portrayed Iago. "Ya know if anybody ever asks me why I do this radio show I can just play 'em that."

Why? Perhaps this. *Theme Time Radio Hour* is a memory palace with another memory palace stashed inside of it; Dylan's radio show about remembering was itself a remembering. In 1940 Alan Lomax, then assistant in charge of the Archive of Folk Song of the Library of Congress, presided over *Back Where I Come From*, a CBS radio program that broadcast for fifteen minutes three times per week—Monday, Wednesday, and Friday—at 10:30 p.m. Lomax's slant, as host Clifford Fadiman announced at the conclusion of the pilot on August 19, was the "rich treasure house of American folk material, music, legend, song, stories, American Stuff in general." Directed and cowritten by Nicholas Ray, *Back Where I Come* ultimately ran for twenty-one weeks. The episodes were organized around themes, or "topics," as Lomax styled them: "each will take a single topic and develop it . . . topics on which everyone has an opinion."

Just as for *Theme Time Radio Hour* forty-six years ahead, the topic for the initial episode of *Back Where I Come From* was "Weather." Lomax was concurrently producing for CBS an educational folk music radio series, *American School of the Air*, also built on topics. Beyond "Weather," other subjects of *Back Where I Come From* overlap with Dylan's, though not always under an identical title: "Traveling," "War & Soldiers," "Work," "The Jailhouse," "New Year's," "Animals," "Railroads and Railroad Men," "Religion," "Money," "Food," and "Christmas." During the pilot, singer Josh White delivered a long sermon on Noah, and for his third radio season Dylan would devote two episodes to "Noah's Ark." *Back Where I Come From* similarly featured songs, skits, monologues, jokes, and "American Stuff" facts, and the Black and White cast clustered a radiant who's who of Dylan's future life, actual and mythic, in Greenwich Village: White, Lead Belly, Woody Guthrie, Willie Johnson, Pete Seeger, and Burl Ives, along with Sidney Bechet and Bunk Johnson, and of course Lomax himself. In 1961, when Carla Rotolo was Lomax's assistant, Dylan was living with her sister Suze. In *Chronicles* he describes attending the folk music concert parties Lomax staged twice a month in his loft at 121 West Third Street: "You might see Roscoe Holcomb or Clarence Ashley or Dock Boggs, Mississippi John Hurt, Robert Pete Williams or even Don Stover and The Lilly Brothers—sometimes even real live section gang convicts that Lomax would get out of state penitentiaries on passes. . . ."

Did Dylan also first hear *Back Where I Come From* on ancient recordings archived by Carla Rotolo at that loft? Lomax met Guthrie when they both performed at a benefit for Spanish Loyalist Refugees at the Mecca Temple on Fifty-Sixth Street on February 25, 1940. Many cast members then participated in a "Grapes of Wrath" benefit for farm workers on March 3. According to Lomax's biographer, John Szwed, "Alan would later proclaim this the moment when the folk revival in America was born." For all that, *Back Where I Come From* abruptly vaporized soon after Guthrie threatened to quit when Nick Ray persuaded Lomax to drop Lead Belly "because listeners would have trouble understanding his southern accent." Guthrie meanwhile had joined the CBS show, *Pipe Smoking Time,* sponsored by the Model Tobacco Company, before leaving for Los Angeles at the turn of the year.

Dreams, themes, and schemes—sometimes even dreams are full of prisons. Dylan's restless collecting of songs led in 2022 to a book that shaded a parallel foray to *Theme Time Radio Hour*, *The Philosophy of Modern Song*, although the intonations and emphases now were far darker. He apparently started writing in 2010, soon after his final radio season; the jacket copy positioned the book as an insider's scrutiny across "a series of dreamlike riffs" on sixty-six songs, stretching from Uncle Dave Macon's "Keep My Skillet Good and Greasy" (1924) to Warren Zevon's "Dirty Life and Times" (2003). His map of America in sixty-six songs? His Route 66? *The Philosophy of Modern Song* is another ostensibly sideline Dylan operation that occupies a surprisingly vital wing in his late memory palace. One wonder of the book is that Dylan is often more autobiographical in it than for *Chronicles*, his presumed memoir. Since the priority is the songs of other songwriters, he can—just as on the radio—address matters mostly absent in *Chronicles* from inside this façade of disinterest, even objectivity. Singers who, for instance, changed their names, such as Townes Van Zandt: "It is prescient that John Townes Van Zandt dropped his most prosaic given name early in life, whittling his identity down to an unforgettable run of syllables." Or Johnny Paycheck: "And then there are those who change their own names, either on the run from some unseen demon or heading toward something else." Singers who invent themselves, as he remarks of Bobby Darin:

> Bobby Darin could sound like anybody and sing any style . . . Darrin was more than a chameleon, for each of his guises he inhabited with verve and gusto . . . Some people create new lives to hide their past. Bobby knew that sometimes the past was nothing more than an illusion and you might just as well keep making stuff up.

Singers who radically change their styles and were booed, such as the Osborne Brothers, or here Rick Nelson in 1971 at Madison Square Garden:

> Bo Diddley, Chuck Berry, the Coasters, Bobby Rydell, a bunch of others. They were all good, did their hits. Rick was the only one out there trying to do new material. Oh, he did a couple of familiar songs. But he also did some of his newer songs. People booed.

As he veers from Poole to Garcia, John Prine, and Joni Mitchell, Dylan could diagnose his own artistic crisis after 1966: "But if your dreams are fulfilled at twenty, what do you do with the rest of your life?"

More than on *Theme Time Radio Hour*, Dylan in *The Philosophy of Modern Song* digs into songs that—as he invokes "Mack the Knife"—travel "that dark road." Each of the inaugural five songs for *The Philosophy of Modern Song*—Bobby Bare's "Detroit City," Elvis Costello's "Pump It Up," Perry Como's "Without a Song," Jimmy Wages's "Take Me from This Garden of Evil," and Webb Pierce's "There Stands the Glass"—are brutal; incandescent, but still brutal. His five commentaries are, too—"You're the Prodigal Son . . . You've learned to look into every loathsome nauseating face and expect nothing . . . And without this song he has nothing, and this is the song that he sings . . . This record presses the panic button . . . It's hard to be on the losing end of a lost cause, a lost enterprise, a cause with no object or purpose, unequivocally false from start to finish, the man is in mental bondage."

Some of this dark road shades a vision of noir—cheerless, sinister, and desperate where Ellen Barkin sounded whimsical. "A serial killer could sing this song," Dylan says of Eddy Arnold's "You Don't Know Me." Or of Rosemary Clooney's "Come On-A My House": "This is the song of the deviant, the pedophile, the mass murderer. The song of the guy who's got thirty corpses under his basement and human skulls in the refrigerator." Or of Johnny Cash's "Don't Take Your Guns to Town":

> Stories are simple. We all know them. Boy meets girl. Boy loses girl. Boy steals crust of bread. Boy gets gunned down in town square. Girl kills boy's wife. Child grows up searching for father's murderer. Girl marries boy. Boy burns down town.

Some of this dark road is Dante, or alternately Zen Buddhism. As he concludes of John Trudell's "Doesn't Hurt Anymore"—"In a real sense the only thing that truly unites us is suffering and suffering only." Presumably that's the "philosophy" of the title, as much as his disquisitions on song craft. The odd marvel in the book is Dylan's voice at those ghostly moments when he vanishes into whatever song he is exhibiting, a minor miracle of empathy that pivots on a slippery, elusive "You" reminiscent of Lorrie Moore's story collection *Self-Help* and John Ashbery's *Self-Portrait in a Convex Mirror.* Here's a bit more of Dylan's commentary on Wages's "Take Me from This Garden of Evil":

> What you'd like to see is a neighborly face, a lovely charming face. Someone on the up and up, a straight shooter, ethical and fit. Someone in an attractive place, hospitable, a hole in the wall, a honky-tonk with home cooking. Nobody needs to be in a quick rush, no emphasis on speediness, everybody'd going to measure their steps. Your little girl will support you; she'll wait on you hand and foot, and she sides with you at all times.
>
> But you're in limbo, and you're shouting at anyone who'll listen, to take you out of this garden of evil. Get you away from the gangsters and psychopaths. . . .

Dylan's merging into the songs means he reproduces deleterious aspects of them, too, including such dated misogyny and toxic masculinity. Notably, only four of the sixty-six songs were performed by women. Of the roughly fifty artists played more than five times on *Theme Time Radio Hour*, just seven were women.

Inside the radio. Inside the song. Two tiny interlocking memories of my own. Pretty much every day of my junior and senior years at BC High I woke up to Charles Laquidara's morning program on Boston's WBCN, *The Big Mattress*. Along with the latest music, Laquidara introduced song parodies created by Eddie Gorodetsky—the hilarious send-up, for instance, of Steppenwolf's heavy metal anthem "Born to Be Wild" as "Born to Be Mild," with the refrain, "Like George Gobel's child I was born, born to be mild." Gorodetsky would go on to produce *Theme Time Radio Hour*, and also served as the voice of "your announcer" Pierre Mancini. Years later, after I published my biography of novelist Jim

Thompson, one of my sources, Sis Cunningham of the Almanac Singers, suddenly recalled the name of a radio program Thompson hoped to write for in 1941 only to discover after he reached New York City that the gig was already gone—*Back Where I Come From*.

"This is your man in the moon welcoming you to sixty minutes of lunar melodies," Dylan ventured as he introduced "Moon," episode 32 of *Theme Time Radio Hour*. "In the background, Charlie Parker playing 'Ornithology.' Based on the chord structure of 'How High the Moon,' which tells ya the moon is far away and love is far away, too . . . Wow, that one sure knocked some heads together."

O

. . . THE MOVING FINGER WRITES; AND HAVING WRIT . . .

"Oh! I have suffered / With those I saw suffer . . . ," Miranda cries out to Prospero, her father, the former Duke of Milan, in Shakespeare's *The Tempest*, after witnessing the "wild" storm he conjured with "my Magick" and "mine Art" to shipwreck his "perfidious" brother Antonio. She bemoans her inability to assist, relative to the "god of power," whom she doesn't yet recognize as Prospero:

> *Had I been any god of power, I would*
> *Have sunk the sea within the earth or ere*
> *It should the good ship so have swallowed, and*
> *The fraughting souls within her.*

Miranda's *empathy*—though that word wasn't in circulation at Shakespeare's moment; empathy was coined as recently as 1908, just three years before Bob Dylan's father was born in Duluth. Contemporary English-speaking psychologists needed a translation of the German term *Einfuhlung* (literally *in*-feeling, or feeling-*into*), a concept that surfaced initially in aesthetic philosophy but quickly infiltrated the dynamics of mental processes. Empathy, from *empatheia*, presumably was modeled on *sym-*

pathy from *sympathia* (*with*-feeling), yet proved somewhat more uncanny, or—to cite another translation from the German—*unheimlich*, that is, *not from* the home. Empathy designated the ability to project one's own internal feelings and movements into objects or creatures; as Nuar Alsadir writes in *Animal Joy*, empathy is "feeling into the shape of another" and a "shapeshifting of emotion as it passes between people" during which "we are able to experience what happens outside of ourselves as part of our subjective experience."

Prospero has cast up Antonio and his other enemies, including the king of Naples and his son Ferdinand, on an island Shakespeare positions only vaguely. The terrain registers differently on different characters, appearing "lush and lusty" and "green" to the Naples court, but arid, rocky, and "hard" to its original inhabitants, Caliban and Ariel. The ostensible Mediterranean trade-route isle setting was likely impacted by the wreck of the *Sea Venture*, en route to the Virginia colonies, off the coast of Bermuda in 1609. For Prospero also is a silver-tongued European colonialist, and a slave owner, too—he excoriates Caliban as "thou most lying slave," or "abhorred slave," and Ariel enters the play by greeting Prospero with "all hail, great master . . . to thy strong bidding task / Ariel and all his quality." Amid the interlocking plots of *The Tempest*—Prospero's revenge and restoration; Miranda's falling for Ferdinand—is Caliban's slave rebellion and his desire to kill Prospero and reclaim his native home.

The Tempest was Shakespeare's final play, at least the final drama he wrote alone, and few listeners could resist the allure of dubbing Dylan's *Tempest* his own valediction and farewell at the age of seventy-one. During an interview with Mikal Gilmore in *Rolling Stone* shortly before the release of the album on September 10, 2012, though, he attempted to shut down comparison. "Shakespeare's last play was called *The Tempest*," he objected. "The name of my record is just plain *Tempest*. It's two different titles." The hubris implied by such a flagrant bardic parallel might provide explanation sufficient for Dylan's demurral, if not exactly for his curt insistence on the decisiveness of a missing definite article. I suspect he was suggesting that on *Tempest* he aimed for something more than a nostalgic "Our revels now are ended" exit; so long, and have a nice afterlife. And although making art is one of his conspicuous subjects here—nearly every major song revisits and transforms a specific traditional folk song—his album, much like Shakespeare's play, is agitated by domestic betrayals, civic and family violence, abuses of public and intimate power, and the havocs of colonialism, empire, and war (notably, if surprisingly, the War of 1812). His *Tempest,* again like Shakespeare's *The Tempest,* tracks back to still earlier storms, particularly Homer's in Book 5 of *The Odyssey* and the "whirlwind" and "commotion" of the Book of Revelation, commonly ascribed to Saint John of Patmos.

Not so much a last album, then, as a ritual in transfigured time. Right from "Duquesne Whistle," the almost jaunty opener—that is, jaunty-sounding, if you're only half-listening—*Tempest* tilts toward apocalypse. Speeding along on a tune evocative of "Each Day," Jelly Roll Morton's 1930 recording with his Red Hot Peppers, "Duquesne Whistle" is a train song with headlong railroad rhythms inside the piano, steel guitar, and an implacable chug-chug of a refrain. Dylan's verses rotate tender and abrasive, his encounters baffling ("You say I'm a gambler, you say I'm a pimp"), dreamy ("You smiling through the fence at me"), obsessive ("Everybody telling me she's gone to my head"), and idealized ("Must be the Mother of our Lord"). Across a progression of casually dead-end phrases, "Duquesne Whistle" emphasizes that our train will be stopping at just one station, and that's for the Final Judgement:

Blowin' like it's gonna sweep my world away . . .

Sound like it's on a final run . . .

Blowin' like she ain't gonna blow no more

Blowin' like the sky's gonna blow apart . . .

Blowin' like it's gonna kill me dead . . .

Dylan snappily slides Poe's "The Raven" into one of his variations on this terminal hook, "Blowin' like she's at my chamber door," and we semiautomatically complete the negative-space rhymes, "and nothing more . . . Nevermore." In Poe's poem the bird perches on a bust of Pallas Athene, the Greek goddess of wisdom, war, crafts, and skill, whose marble face—from a statue outside of the Austrian Parliament in Vienna—Dylan put on the cover of *Tempest*, and whose bust he would display on stage as he toured his album of fierce End Times songs. Lyrical images of a self in conflict, sure, but not so much the artful magician rehearsing his proud good-byes. Still, Dylan on *Tempest* rakes his complicated past for a scrap of wisdom against immanent death, just as Prospero did. When on "Duquesne Whistle," he sings, "I'll lead you there myself at the break of day," Dylan is renewing Eidothea's offer to Menelaus in *The Odyssey* to take him to Proteus, her father. Menelaus has just asked her how he might force the truth from the immortal shape-shifter. Her solution: sneak up on Proteus while he's sleeping, and cling to him through his many guises:

> *That's your moment. Soon as you see him bedded down,*
> *muster your heart and strength and hold him fast,*
> *wildly as he writhes and fights you to escape . . .*
> *And when, at last, he begins to ask you questions—*
> *back in the shape you saw him sleep at first—*
> *relax your grip and set the old god free*
> *and ask him outright. . . .*

Memory in "Duquesne Whistle" can be wistful—"I wonder if that old oak tree's still standing." But memory is also hazardous. "You're like a time bomb in my heart."

For *Tempest*, Dylan enlarges his conversation with Ovid from *Modern Times*. "Pay in Blood" parallels the Roman poet's alienated meditations on his exile—first, "Nothing more wretched than what I must endure," redolent of *Tristia*; and then, "They strip your useless hopes away," redolent of *The Black Sea Letters*. Later, in "Early Roman Kings" and "Tempest" he accents sardonic episodes from Juvenal's *Satires* (respectively that "Sicilian court," and that pimp who "dismissed his girls"). Other writers descant as well: Edward FitzGerald's nineteenth-century translation of the *Rubaiyat* shades "Tempest," and also "Narrow Way." Chaucer's *The Canterbury Tales* figures in "Tin Angel." Dylan refashions as many as a half-dozen different John Greenleaf Whittier poems, poetry impinging on slavery, throughout "Tin Angel," "Pay in Blood," and "Scarlet Town." Sir Walter Scott contributes a "helmet and cross-handled sword" to "Tin Angel," and various Tennessee Williams plays—*Battle of Angels*, *Orpheus Descending*, and *The Rose Tattoo*—ruffle "Long and Wasted Years" and "Early Roman Kings." Blake rides out "Roll on John," and Dylan tempers one of Yeats's last poems, "Under Ben Bulben," for a crucial pivot in "Tempest." Even scurrilous Joseph Moncure March manages sundry assignations: "The Set Up" in "Tin Angel," and "The Wild Party" in "Pay in Blood" and "Scarlet Town." But the sentinel—part guardian angel, part neighborhood watch—for *Tempest* is Homer, by way of Robert Fagles's 1996 translation of *The Odyssey*. Beyond "Duquesne Whistle," Homer breathes through at least six other songs here, including "Pay in Blood," "Early Roman Kings," "Narrow Way," "Long and Wasted Years," "Tempest," and "Roll on John."

Homer? In *The Nobel Lecture*, his official response to his 2016 Nobel Prize in Literature, Dylan named *The Odyssey* among just three books for his extended scrutiny (*Moby-Dick* and *All Quiet on the Western Front* were the others). His account is a mostly deadpan recap of the epic: "He finds deserted caves, and he hides in them. He meets giants that say, 'I'll eat you last.' And he escapes from giants. He's trying to get back home, but he's tossed and turned by the winds." The crux, though, is Dylan's poignant identification with Odysseus:

> Some of these things have happened to you. You too have had drugs dropped in your wine. You too have shared a bed with the wrong woman. You too have been spellbound by magical voices, sweet voices with strange melodies. You too have come so far and have been so far blown back. And you've had close calls as well. You have

angered people you should not have. You too have rambled this country all around. And you've also felt that ill wind that blows you no good. And that's still not all of it.

All the old men begin at the beginning. Dylan's Stockholm precis encapsulates the scope of his homages to Homer on *Tempest.* Often local—"Someone must have slipped a drug in your wine," from "Pay in Blood," which echoes Book 4 of *The Odyssey*; and other times sweeping—"I'll strip you of life, strip you of breath / Ship you down to the house of death" from "Early Roman Kings," which contemplates Book 9. Inevitably many of these involve Odysseus; are spoken by him, to him, about him, or surrounding him. Homer offered Dylan a charged language that mirrors back the turbulence and cruelties of his own subjects, whether political or personal. That "house of death" curse is hurled by Odysseus to Polyphemus the Cyclops after our hero gouged out his eye, blinding him. Polyphemus then prays to Poseidon that Odysseus, "raider of cities," never arrives home, or returns "broken" to "a world of pain." Helen drugs Menelaus and his retinue, but it's for "heart's-ease . . . magic to make us forget our pains." Later on *Tempest* when Dylan in "Roll on John" sings, "Rags on your back just like any other slave," he's appealing to Helen, right after her wine trick, and her account of how Odysseus in disguise roamed enemy cities. Similarly, Homer bedrocks the fierce domestic duplicities in "Long and Wasted Years," and the international treacheries of the War of 1812 and the Compromise of 1850 in "Narrow Way." Dylan angles the multiple violences of *The Odyssey* into his restless apprehension of living in End Times. When he sings, "Your bones are weary, you're about to breathe your last," he's remembering Odysseus after the storm, as—"desperate"—he reaches shore in Book 5, talking to himself:

Man of misery, what next? Is this the end?
If I wait out a long tense night by the banks,
I fear the sharp frost and the soaking dew together
will do me in—I'm bone-weary, about to breathe my last. . . .

But Dylan also sifted the Homeric past for purposes of his own artistic future. On an album critical to his self-reinvention as a writer and performer, he scrutinized at least six phrases for three songs—"Pay in Blood," "Tin Angel" and "Narrow Way"—from a speech in Book 8 where Odysseus agrees to a challenge in an athletic contest. The performing self. His revival of the speech for *Tempest* characteristically heightens "the long-suffering hero's" verbal prowess as much as his manifest skills with a discus. During an incident Dylan modernized for "Pay in Blood," Odysseus answers his antagonists, "Nevertheless, despite so many blows / I'll compete in your games, just watch. Your insults / cut to the quick—you rouse my fighting blood!" As Richard F. Thomas reminds us in *Why Bob Dylan Matters*, Pallas Athene is Odysseus's patron goddess, too—and Homer, as Thomas proposes, is yet another reason for that album cover, and that onstage bust. On *Tempest*, as we'll again see, Dylan seems to love double allusions. And just as in "The Raven," Pallas Athene often lurks just out of bounds, close by sequences from *The Odyssey* that Dylan retrofits. She's all over that storm from Book 5 that so agitates "Tempest," and she's hidden in plain sight for the song after the storm on *Tempest*, "Roll on John," the album's finale. When there Dylan sings, "They tied your hands and they clamped your mouth," he's smartly telescoping an action by Odysseus in Book 4:

> *He was hot to salute you now*
> *but Odysseus clamped his great hands on the man's mouth*
> *and shut it, brutally—yes he saved us all,*
> *holding on grim-set till Pallas Athene*
> *lured you off at last.*

Proteus, too, is often nearby. In the groundwork, as we saw, of "Duquesne Whistle," at the opening of *Tempest*, and also in "Roll On John," which at its close reviews and renews that same Proteus episode from *The Odyssey*, resuming the story after Eidothea led Menelaus to her father, and he clung to the "quick-change artist / the old wizard" as demanded. When in "Roll on John" Dylan sings, "You been cooped up on an island far too long," and "They'll trap you in an ambush 'fore you know," his observations favor the conversation between Proteus and Menelaus that immediately followed:

> *"Which god, Menelaus, conspired with you*
> *to trap me in ambush? seize me against my will?*
> *What on earth do you want?"*
> *"You know, old man."*
> *I countered now. "Why put me off with questions?*
> *Here I am, cooped up on an island far too long,*
> *with no way out of it, none that I can find,*
> *while my spirit ebbs away. . . ."*

According to the classic Homeric epithets, Odysseus is famously "wily" and "wise." Yet for *Tempest*—whether on account of his links to Proteus or Pallas Athene, and despite all Dylan's own wily but wise objections to the Shakespeare analogy—Odysseus tends to blur into the magus Prospero. In "Tempest" a storm replaces the iceberg that wrecked the *Titanic*, a storm invoked as a "wizard's curse" that "played on" as though this were a theatrical as well as a magic performance. Prospero also shadows the recurrent watchman figure in the song, who "dreamed the Titanic was sinking," and ultimately "Of all things that can be." Dylan may have dashed the "Our revels now are ended" strain, though hardly this idea: "We are such stuff / As dreams are made on, and our little life / Is rounded with sleep." Prospero's cave is also in "Roll on John," and Shakespeare more generally circles "Soon After Midnight" (*A Midsummer Night's Dream*) and "Pay in Blood" (*Julius Caesar*).

The situation—the conceit—of Dylan's *Tempest* moreover remains powerfully aligned with Prospero. Five of the album's ten tracks circumnavigate folk and blues songs Dylan would have learned in the West Village during the early 1960s. "Scarlet Town" explores "Barbara Allen"; "Tin Angel," "Gypsy Davy"; "Roll on John," "Roll On, John"; "Tempest," "The Titanic"; and "Narrow Way," "You'll Work Down to

Me Someday." Some of these songs Dylan previously performed, even recorded—"Roll On, John" on Cynthia Gooding's WBAI radio show, *Folksingers Choice*, in January of 1962; "Barbara Allen" at the Gaslight Café in October of 1962 (and taken up again in concerts during the 1980s and into 1991); "Gypsy Davy" at the home of Bob and Sid Gleason in 1961, and eventually as "Blackjack Davey" on *Good as I Been to You* (1992) and for live shows in 1993.

The twilight speech, then, of an old man to a boy. Probably the most ambitious of these musical recursions is "Scarlet Town." Child Ballad 84, "Barbara Allen," dates back to at least mid-seventeenth-century Scotland and England, and likely far earlier. In Scarlet Town, a dying young man, Sweet William, calls for Barbara Allen. Remembering that he once slighted her in the tavern, Barbara Allen resists—but upon hearing the bells knelling his death she remorsefully resolves to "die for him tomorrow." She and Sweet William are buried side by side, and the rose growing from his grave and the briar from hers intertwine into "a lover's knot," an earthly symbol of their steadfast union through eternity.

For "Scarlet Town" Dylan retained "Barbara Allen" as a rhythmic architecture. His song also starts off, "In Scarlet Town where I was born . . . Sweet William on his deathbed lay." But Dylan inverts—steadily sabotages, then shatters—the traditional drama of love, death, and ultimate redemption. In his rendering, money, not love, binds everything together, sex, politics, and religion. Sweet William likely is a slave holder, as "Uncle Tom [is] still working for Uncle Bill." The Mistress Mary who sits beside Sweet William on his deathbed is "Kissing his face, heaping prayers on his head," as though both kisses and prayers are commercial inventory. Grief, too, is on the commodities exchange, "I'll weep for him as he'd weep for me." So is private morality: "I'm making amends / While the smile of heaven descends." Is Mistress Mary Barbara Allen in disguise? (And is that "mistress" as in a woman in position of authority? An extramarital lover? A dominatrix?) Other than the versatile Mistress, the dearest approximation to Barbara Allen is identified in the song as "my flat-chested junkie whore." If the citizens of Scarlet Town are shifty and puzzling, the times are, too. To the "Beggars crouching at the gate . . . Help comes but it comes too late." Even feuds run out-of-synch, since "In Scarlet Town you fight your father's foes." (What about your own? Those battles, anyway, sound like substance abuse: "You fight 'em with whiskey, morphine and gin.") Too late here skids into End Times, for "In Scarlet Town the end is near." The Bible can be invoked, but the *Gospels* and *Epistles* are dead on arrival. Dylan's Scarlet Town lies "under the hill" of Calvary—not good; and when "You make your humble wishes known," you might in good faith touch Christ's garment, yet "the hem was torn." Myriad voices, repellently familiar. The future concord of "Barbara Allen," even if only as a bittersweet posthumous resolution, is everywhere here insistently checked and denied.

For "Scarlet Town," Dylan also engages a trio of Whittier poems—"The Wish of Today," "To Avis Keene on Receiving a Basket of Sea-Mosscs," and "Thc Chapcl of thc Hcrmits" and hc's ncarly as dryly feral with them. A politician and journalist as well as a celebrated poet, Whittier could be tagged the antithesis of Henry Timrod, for both American poetry and Dylan's twenty-first century songwriting. Born on a farm near Haverhill, Massachusetts, in 1807, he was a friend of William Lloyd Garrison, editor of the antislavery Boston newspaper *The Liberator.* In 1833, the Quaker Whittier published a pamphlet, *Justice and Expediency; or, Slavery Considered with a View to Its Rightful and Effectual Remedy, Abolition*, written in response to the Colonization Society, then led by Henry Clay, which wanted to send Black Americans back to Africa. Whittier helped found the American Anti-Slavery Society, and his first collection of poetry, assembled in his honor by antislavery allies, was titled *Poems Written During the Progress of the Abolition Question in the United States, Between the Years 1830 and 1838.*

Whittier was a surprisingly varied writer, surprising particularly for those forced to listen to "Snow-Bound: A Winter Idyll" during grammar school but might not have grasped that even in this allegedly insipid chestnut "the whirl-dance of the blinding storm" is an emblem for the psychic traumas of the Civil War, or that the poem acknowledges "Slavery's shaping hand" and "the red scourge of bondage." (On *Tempest*, Dylan spotlights a line about the Civil War from "Snow-Bound" for "Pay in Blood"—"Low circling round its southern zone"—and those comforts of family, home, and art in the Whittier original fall among the old-line values the singer of that song rejects for his doomed blaze of violence and retribution.) Besides his abolitionist poems, Whittier pursued folklore, legends, myths, the regional history of New England, and the supernatural. Some of his pieces later were set as hymns, and his mixed meters, smooth rhymes, prose syntax, and forceful dictions can actually sound a lot like Bob Dylan. Try singing along with these couplets from "The Chapel of the Hermits" to the music of "Scarlet Town":

For still the new transcends the old,
In signs and tokens manifold . . .
Through clouds of doubt, and creeds of fear,
A light is breaking, calm and clear. . . .

For "Scarlet Town" the present-day Bob Dylan again strips away the affirmations, certainties, trust, and hope in Whittier, much as he did with the eternal devotion of "Barbara Allen." Some of these moves are more of his double allusions. Those "Beggars crouching at the gate" arrive from Luke 16:20; and the garment hem he touches is from Mathew 9:20; but they both also were adapted by Whittier for "The Chapel of the Hermits," although there the beggar Lazarus is "blessed," and the hem is intact, exactly as avowed in the New Testament. Similarly, when Dylan sings about exposing his "humble wishes," the gesture for him clearly is hopeless, while in Whittier's "The Wish of Today," such desires are sure to be granted: "I make my humble wishes known; / I only ask a will resigned, / O father, to Thine own." The "maple wood" setting of "Scarlet Town" harks back to Whittier's "The Chapel of the Hermits," but for Whittier the trees forecast a far different end, one he styles a "golden-spired Apocalypse." His gilded apocalypse isn't at all Dylan's feverish intimations of terminal doom; instead, Whittier is celebrating the demise of slavery in

America: "Yon maple wood the burning bush. . . . Slaves rise up men." In the final verse of "Scarlet Town" when Dylan sings "All things are beautiful in their time," his sentiments are disrupted and tainted by the prior integer of the couplet, "If love is a sin then beauty is a crime." The notion is tainted further when we flip back to Whittier's "To Avis Keene," where the beautiful actually is at hand, and not just a sardonic if-clause, and half of a nasty rhyme with "crime":

In unison with His design
Who loveth beauty everywhere;
And makes in every zone and clime,
In ocean and in upper air,
All things beautiful in their time.

When earlier for "Scarlet Town" Dylan sang, "All human forms seem glorified," he was also recalibrating "The Chapel of the Hermits." But Whittier's emphasis was on "glorified," whereas Dylan makes us hear *seem.* In "Barbara Allen" death harmonizes all contradictions, and for Whittier the agency of God inside human history will ultimately reconcile everything. During Dylan's "Scarlet Town," nothing ever resolves—"The evil and the good" by contrast live "side by side." We're left only with shards of savage complexity: "The black and the white, the yellow and the brown / It's all right there for ya in Scarlet Town."

The reconstructions of "Barbara Allen" and Whittier across the multiple Tulsa manuscripts of "Scarlet Town" are even more ferocious. For one draft Dylan writes, "Sweet William on his deathbed lay / Bleeding from the mouth face up in bed / His Lovesick Harlot heaping prayers on his head / Lazarus crouching outside the gate / Couldn't care less about church or state." For another: "They shut down the factories—closed the school / In Scarlet Town the devil rules." As for Whittier's confidence in the ministrations of history, Dylan counters, "Scarlet Town was built to last / Nobody accepts any account of what happened in the past / Who said what and what said where. . . ." And as for Whittier's reliance on the healing powers of art: "In Scarlet Town you save your breath / The price for speaking the truth is death."

Pitiless drafts. Endangered insights. Consuming passions. Dylan recast "Barbara Allen" and Whittier for effects simultaneously political, moral, and aesthetic. "Tin Angel," a companion piece to "Scarlet Town" on *Tempest*, tips those same impulses into acid humor. Over nine minutes, twenty-eight quatrains, and a single repeated chord, he rewires a tangle of traditional songs—"Gypsy Davy" and "Blackjack Davey," but also "Love Henry," which he covered in 1993 on *World Gone Wrong*—for a serpentine murder-suicide ballad.

The plot? Well, as in "Gypsy Davy" and "Blackjack Davey," a man known only as "the boss" returns home to discover that his wife has disappeared with a charming man, in "Tin Angel" named Henry Lee after "Love Henry." The boss tracks them down, but from there on "Tin Angel" is all convolutions inside convolutions. The song jumbles centuries, as helmets, swords, golden chains, coats, ties, and electric cords stock a compound era at once medieval and 1930s. Dylan compounds dictions too—Homeric ("You too shall meet the lord of death"), pulpy ("And she raised her robe and she drew out a knife"), biblical ("He renounced his faith, he denied his lord"), and self-help ("Insomnia raging in his brain").

The tonal fireworks spiral out of a fiendishly dazzling mash-up: Chaucer's *The Canterbury Tales*; Sir Walter Scott's "The Fire-King"; Joseph Moncure March; and Whittier, too, with a phrase from "Brown of Ossawatomie," a response to the raid on Harper's Ferry published in the New York *Independent* three weeks after John Brown's execution in 1859. The Tulsa drafts for "Tin Angel" are supremely eclectic. On a Crowne Plaza pad page, Elvin Bishop's "Rock Bottom" sits next to "The Fire-King," and two more Scott narratives—"Rokeby" (set during the English civil war) and "The Bridal of Triermain" (a King Arthur epic)—along with a slice of Juvenal that will wind up in "Early Roman Kings," and a bit of Elliott Blaine Henderson's "The Soliloquy of Satan." (Scott, knights, and cavaliers were significant, too, in Confederate self-mythologizing, as Wolfgang Schivelbusch demonstrates in *The Culture of Defeat*, a book that seems to backdrop *Tempest* much as it did *Modern Times.*) On a later sheet, "Long Black Veil" is close by "Snow-Bound," among other Whittier glimpses, "Marguerite" and "Barclay Ury."

Throughout "Tin Angel" Dylan dislocates points of view as well as voices. The boss dissolving into his wife. His wife calling Henry Lee her husband. Henry Lee dissolving back into the boss. Conspicuously, when the boss creeps up on the lovers in the dark, "It was hard to tell for certain who was who." His confusion is a listener's, too, as the three of them talk, accuse, argue, and try to explain themselves. Any stray phrase rings plain and vivid, only to atomize against a blizzard of indecipherable pronouns. On a draft, Dylan mentions "Hearing old voices in the wind," and it's as though the import of what they're each saying is hiding just out of reach. As "Tin Angel" continues, who's talking, and to whom, disposes a vexing teaser; their actions, too: Who shoots first, and who dies first? "Tin Angel" closes on an image that slyly, cruelly mocks the timeless repose of the cemetery in "Barbara Allen":

All three lovers together in a heap
Thrown into the grave forever to sleep
Funeral torches blazed away
Through the towns and the villages all night and all day

Dylan's title perhaps opens up the riddle, if that's what this is. The Tin Angel Café was the name of the restaurant above and next door to The Bitter End on Bleecker Street: "where it's happening . . . Gourmet Food at Reasonable Prices . . . After Dinner, See the Show." Both venues were owned by Fred Weintraub. Dylan hung out at The Bitter End during the early 1960s with Victor Maymudes and other friends, and musicians often drifted into the restaurant for food. Joni Mitchell's song "Tin Angel" is set there, and in the next decade the Rolling Thunder Revue would emanate from The Bitter End. Concluding with those histrionic "funeral marches" that "blazed . . . through . . . the villages," is Dylan's "Tin Angel" his mischievous glance at the Greenwich Village folk scene? Are those droll, slippery convolutions how an endless murder ballad might sound upstairs, overheard through the walls and floor?

On one draft of "Tin Angel" the figure who later became "Henry Lee" is called "Henry Clay," after the nineteenth-century politician and orator—and the catalyst for Whittier's antislavery pamphlet. Henry Clay is urgent to another song on *Tempest*, "Narrow Way," a devastating metamorphosis of "You'll Work Down to Me Someday" by the Mississippi Sheiks. The original focused on spurned love and the afflictions of class: "Oh, baby, you treats me in a dirty way / And if I can't work up to you / You will really work down to me, someday." Dylan's "Narrow Way" widens the heartbreak angle of that "dirty way" to span the sorrows of two centuries of American history—a history that begins not with the Civil War, but the War of 1812, often dubbed the Forgotten War. Indeed, *Tempest* was released on September 10, 2012, during the bicentennial of the War of 1812. When in "Narrow Way" Dylan sings, "Ever since the British burned the white house down / There's a bleeding wound in the heart of town," he is referencing that war, and in particular the night of August 24, 1814, when British troops invaded Washington, setting fire to the Capitol and the so-called President's Mansion. (This battle famously prompted Francis Scott Key to write a poem that would soon be retitled "The Star-Spangled Banner," and adopted as the national anthem.)

The War of 1812 was the first American conflict for which Congress issued a formal declaration of war, and Henry Clay was instrumental in securing that declaration. Early in the war, the British recruited slaves to fight against the US Army with promises of freedom and land. Many Indigenous nations also fought for the British, in the hope of halting further American expansion. American leaders refused to enlist even free Blacks until September of 1814, when General Andrew Jackson invited "the free colored inhabitants of Louisiana" to join the US Army, pointedly excluding slaves. Blacks thus fought on both sides of the war. Signed on December 24, 1814, the Treaty of Ghent essentially restored the prewar status quo, including all property, slaves as well as territory. America exited the conflict a military power on the road to empire, especially after the Monroe Doctrine of 1823, which redefined any interference by European powers in the western hemisphere as a hostile act against the United States. The War of 1812 accelerated westward expansion and an epoch of Indigenous American annihilation, spurring the Indian Removal Act and the Trail of Tears. Slavery expanded, too, after the war. In the seldom-sung third verse of "The Star-Spangled Banner," Francis Scott Key—himself a slaveholding lawyer who later as a district attorney in Washington prosecuted a doctor for possessing abolitionist literature—menaces Blacks who fought with the British:

No refuge could save the hireling and slave
From the terror of flight or the gloom of the grave,
And the star-spangled banner in triumph doth wave
O'er the land of the free and the home of the brave.

Nasty rhymes again: slave/brave. Henry Clay was among the delegation that negotiated the Treaty of Ghent, and Dylan's couplet on the War of 1812 in "Narrow Way" invokes him. The near cliché of "bleeding wound" is, in fact, a direct reference to a speech Clay later gave in the Old Senate Chamber on January 29, 1850, when the issue was whether the territories admitted to the nation would be "slave" or "free." Stretching out his hand, he said there were "five bleeding wounds" related to slavery that needed healing if the United States were to survive. Healing for Clay meant a toughening of the Fugitive Slave Act, such that national and local officials were *required* to arrest suspected fugitives, and anyone who aided in the escape of a slave could be imprisoned. This, in exchange for California entering the Union as a free state; referendums on slavery in Utah and New Mexico; new boundaries between Texas and the United States; and slavery permitted in Washington, though no slave trade. So goes the Compromise of 1850.

Dylan's "bleeding wound" at the heart of everything American once again, then, is race, and slavery reappears in the song as via some Bessie Smith he glances at the satirical cakewalks on plantations. "Narrow Way" moves out from the War of 1812 through imperialism ("We looted and we plundered on distant shores"), and also assails the domestic extermination of Indigenous peoples. The line "This is a hard country to stay alive in," recalls John Sturges's *Escape from Fort Bravo*, a 1963 Civil War Western with William Holden, Eleanor Parker, and John Forsythe. The fictional Fort Bravo is a Union prison camp for Confederate soldiers, but North and South can unite against their common enemy: "the deadly Mescalero Indians." Dylan coordinates touching vestiges of the *Rubaiyat*, one on spiritual abandonment ("Even death has washed his hands of you"), and another about forgiveness ("a voice at the dusk of day / Saying, 'Be gentle brother, be gentle and pray.'" And when he sings, "The moving finger is moving on," he's recollecting the *Rubaiyat* on history:

> *The Moving Finger writes; and having writ,*
> *Moves on: nor all the Piety nor Wit*
> *Shall lure it back to cancel half a Line,*
> *Nor all thy Tears wash out a Word of it.*

Wizardry among the ruins—on *Tempest*, Dylan emerges as a virtuoso of infernal subtext. "Soon After Midnight," in fact, nearly is all subtext, as a surface sweetness—"It's soon after midnight / And I don't want nobody but you"—implacably digs into passions more sinister. He opens with a familiar, self-effacing nod to Johnny Mercer's "Too Marvelous for Words"—"I'm searching for phrases / To sing your praises." But what about the "phrases" that he not only searches for, but sings here for her elusive praises? His melody shades "A New Shade of a Blue," a song by the Bobby Fuller Four, where we'd hear:

> *Now I know what it's like to cry,*
> *What it's like to want to die*
> *Painted on my heart is a new shade of blue*

When Dylan croons in his second verse, "A gal named Honey / Took my money," he's probably sending us back to "Money Honey" by Clyde McPhatter and the Drifters, a song where love pretty much *is* money. The genial, gracious cynicism persists through the next phrase he finds to praise her, "And the moon is in my eye," a fillip from "The Moon Got in My Eyes." For as Frank Sinatra sang there, "I guess I should have seen right through you / But the moon got in my eyes." In the third verse, although our singer is acutely trying to reaffirm just how "cheerful" he now is, despite some past spells "down on the killing floors," he's nevertheless reminding us of the Howlin' Wolf song, "Killing Floor," which starts off starkly, "I should have quit you, a long time ago."

After this, the story inside the story veers still more contrary, and ugly. Dylan sings, "Charlotte's a harlot / Dresses in scarlet," and the razz there is to "Charlotte the Harlot," a scurrilous tune Oscar Brand recorded for a 1964 album, *Bawdy Hootenanny*, and that runs, "She'll lay for a dollar, take less or take more . . . It's Charlotte the harlot, the girl we adore / The pride of the prairie, the cowpuncher's whore." Similarly, in the next verse, he asks, "Two-Timing Slim / Who's ever heard of him?" Well, one possible reply is anyone who's heard "Two Time Slim," on *Johnny Otis Presents: Snatch and the Poontangs*:

Say, baby, do you know who I am?
I'm Bam Bim, Two Time Slim,
The High Sheriff sent from Hell

Nick Cave snagged lines from "Two Time Slim" for his X-rated impersonation of "Stagger Lee" on his 1996 album *Murder Ballads*, where he recorded a variant duet of "Love Henry" with P. J. Harvey under the title "Henry Lee." Fuller, McPhatter, Sinatra, Wolf, Brand, Otis, Cave, and Harvey. Dylan on "Soon After Midnight" seems to be avouching none of these relationships, and all of them. "I needed to learn how to telescope things, ideas," as Dylan wrote in *Chronicles*. Our increasingly fraught singer never cracks his debonair cover, even as he fantasizes a "date with a fairy queen," pictures those who gossip about him "dying in their blood," or pledges to "drag" Slim's "corpse through the mud." Who's singing "Soon After Midnight," to whom, and why? The song is vintage teen idol, and classic pulp psychotic killer. Incidentally, in 1966 Bobby Fuller wound up in a car parked outside his Hollywood apartment, pustules all over his face and chest, his body and clothes soaked in gasoline, the cause of death by some accounts suicide, by others accident, his family contending murder.

"It's now or never, more than ever," Dylan wisecracks on "Soon After Midnight." Violence radiates through *Tempest* as a second language, whether spoken privately at home or shouted in the public arena. "Pay in Blood" stalks conversations between a master and a slave, a soldier and a politician, their fervid talk tightening to a caustic refrain: "I pay in blood, but not my own." "Long and Wasted Years" profiles a brutal marriage, and was originally titled "The Girl with the Rose Tattoo," likely after the 1950 Tennessee Williams play, *The Rose Tattoo*, in which a widow, Serafina, discovers that her late husband was an adulterer, a dope smuggler, and not at all who she believed he was. Set in a village populated by transplanted Sicilians along the American Gulf coast, *The Rose Tattoo* also inflames the "trial in a Sicilian court" of "Early Roman Kings," a song that combines a South Bronx youth gang and the earliest patrician rulers of Rome. More double allusions. When in "Early Roman Kings" Dylan sings, "Fly away little bird, fly away, flap your wings," he's simultaneously rousing another Williams play, *Orpheus Descending*, and "Pretty Bird," the Hazel Dickens song. Dickens optimizes: "Fly away, little pretty bird / And pretty, you'll always stay." Williams is more intimidating: "Well, then, little bird, fly away before you—get broke." From *Battle of Angels*, an early draft of *Orpheus Descending*, Dylan also revamped a pivotal couplet for "Long and Wasted Years": "I wear dark glasses to cover my eyes / There are secrets in them that I can't disguise."

Any studied calculations—secrets, disguise—are impossible to isolate from the improvised associations of his memory, as Dylan's manuscripts rarely gloss or distinguish. For "Tempest"—the song—he obviously started with "The Titanic" by the Carter Family. "I was fooling with that one night," Dylan told Mikal Gilmore in *Rolling Stone*. "I liked that melody—I liked it a lot. 'Maybe I'll appropriate this melody.' But where would I go with it?" Well, anywhere, pretty much anywhere, even as he retains many distinctive Carter Family hallmarks. The Titanic's captain; a mysterious dreaming watchman; that major key melody, and half of an introductory verse. A version in his Tulsa archive suggests that initially Dylan contemplated a Modernist hallucination in the style of "Desolation Row": a swirl of fantastic figures, spanning Count Dracula, Edith Piaf, Nero, and someone named Protoculus, inside a cycle of circuitous stanzas, each maybe twelve, even fourteen lines long; and a flexible refrain, "The Watchman was a dreaming. . . ." ("Desolation Row" of course lists the *Titanic*, and Nero, too.) As he advanced through drafts, Dylan compressed his surreal cast, and shifted to ballad stanzas, forty-five in all, but phantasmagoric brio still prevailed. Dylan's "Tempest" exists in a world of facts, where money and class are paramount, but useless. For instance, while down in steerage "Dead bodies [are] already floating," far above them:

The rich man, Mr. Astor
Kissed his darling wife

Yet a world of facts that can absorb the fancies of a mainline movie:

Leo took his sketchbook
He was often so inclined
He closed his eyes and painted
The scenery in his mind

A movie the song casually deforms:

Leo said to Cleo
"I think I'm going mad."

But he'd lost his mind already
Whatever mind he had

And a world of facts that also is a dream:

The watchman he lay dreaming
As the ballroom dancers twirled
He dreamed the Titanic was sinking
Into the underworld

Beyond the fatal storm that at least in Dylan's retelling of "The Titanic" sinks the great ship, his "Tempest" clocks surprising categories of violence. This is a transatlantic shipwreck that somehow also is the American Civil War: "Brother rose up against brother . . . They fought and slaughtered each other." A Civil War that, in turn, summons the War of 1812: "There were traitors, there were turncoats." What is Wellington, the Iron Duke, doing on the *Titanic*? Or Calvin, Blake, and Wilson, the sixteenth-century theologian, a Romantic poet, and a future president? On an early draft, the *Titanic* "struck an iceberg" but a "tempest" soon takes over—albeit, a tempest that acts a lot like a drifting mountain of sea ice: "Tempest blew a hole . . . Tempest made a 300 ft gash." Here, "Death is on the rampage," and love is an attack. "Cupid struck his bosom / And broke it with a snap."

The guiding figure of "Tempest" is Prospero, despite Dylan's reproofs, and the storm his "wizard's curse." Across *his* drama attending to last things, Shakespeare periodically nodded to the Book of Revelation, including for Miranda's "any god of power" speech. Dylan's own nods to Revelation in "Tempest" are pervasive: "The promised hour . . . The universe had opened wide . . . the judgement of God's hand . . . All things had run their course." One of his verses even paraphrases the Greek roots of *apocalypse* in "disclosure," or a "lifting of the veil":

The veil was torn asunder
'Tween the hours of twelve and one

No change, no sudden wonder
Could undo what had been done

For the captain, "kneeling" by his ship's futile wheel as his *Titanic* goes down, there's nowhere to turn but to Revelation:

In the dark illumination
He remembered bygone years
He read the Book of Revelation
And he filled his cup with tears

End of a life, end of the world. The fusion—*con*-fusion—is understandable, widespread. Dylan was seventy years old when he recorded *Tempest* at Groove Masters Studio in Santa Monica, California. Abe, his father, died at fifty-six; his father's father, Zigman, at fifty-eight. The Book of Revelation: "Write the things which thou hast seen, and the things which are, and the things which shall be hereafter." As I write, I'm now the age Dylan was then. Since my diagnosis, my treatments and surgery, I live from CT scan to CT scan. Every three months, so far. Perhaps four months soon. Maybe even six. At the time of my diagnosis, I was told that "as many as 20 percent" of the people who undergo my operation will be alive two years later. Note the ingenious phrasing. Nobody remarked on the 80 percent who weren't. The tension of scan to scan, and my two time zones—daily life almost as always here; yet over there I'm dying—readily is deflected into other angers, other fears. Who wouldn't look down at their aging, infirm body and suspect the end of the world?

On *Tempest*, "Roll on John," the final track, is what happens next, after death. This marks another Dylan redux of a traditional song, the mountain ballad "Roll On, John." His version is, first, a tribute to John Lennon, replete with gems of a Liverpool adolescence, various Beatles lyrics, onstage quips, and 1980 assassination at the age of forty. A few years prior to writing the song, Dylan apparently boarded a public bus for a tour of the house where Lennon grew up. "He took one of our general minibus tours," a National Trust representative recounted, "and no one recognized him." During the song, he references the Quarrymen, an early skiffle band incarnation of the Beatles, apparently named after the Quarry Bank Grammar School that Lennon attended. Beyond the Woolton sandstone quarries, Dylan also acknowledges Liverpool as the capital of the European slave trade, deftly correlating dashes of *The Odyssey*: "Rags on your back like any other slave / They tied your hands and they clamped your mouth." Similarly, Beatle John's life in New York is depicted as Homeric exile—"You been cooped up on an island far too long"—while Dylan's chorus accents Lennon's classic incandescence: "Shine your light / Move it on / You burned so bright / Roll on John." Yet much as in "Tempest," any personal or nostalgic elegy, whether for *Sgt. Pepper*—"Another day in the life on your way to your journey's end"—or even Lennon's shocking murder, "They'll trap you in an ambush before you know"—evanesces, and sharpens into myth, and End Times. "Too late now to sail back home."

For "Roll on John" isn't only about John Lennon. As the too-late scenarios intensify, Beatle John starts to converge with Saint John, also John the Revelator, author of the Book of Revelation. "Doctor, doctor, tell me the time of day," the song starts, reiterating Lonnie Johnson—for *when* exactly is this? The twentieth century bumps up against the first century, and more double allusions. That "island" is Manhattan, maybe England, but also Patmos in the Aegean Sea, where John was banished by the Roman emperor Domitian, and sentenced to live out his days laboring in the stone quarries. That "deep dark cave" is the Cavern Club in Liverpool, birthplace of the Beatles, and the damp cave on Patmos where John received his visions. The "city gone dark" is New York, and Rome. As for Lennon's "light," Apostle John already talked about that in *Revelation*: "The city had no need of the sun, neither of the moon to shine in it: for the glory of God did lighten it, and the Lamb *is* the light thereof." Dylan projects Saint John of Patmos onto John Lennon—and vice versa. "Whether in art or writing, I'm drawn to these projections," novelist Amina Cain writes in *A Horse at Night*, "when one thing is placed on top of another without eclipsing it. Like two different time periods: both are present, and together they form something new. Or two different cities . . . What we see in our minds we make real."

Shapeshifting. Possession. Any god of power, and this God of Light. Miranda's empathy. Dylan's empathy. Feeling *into* Blake, and a seventeenth-century child's bedtime prayer, maybe also T. S. Eliot's "Came Christ the Tiger," *Tempest* coils, and unwinds, as "Roll on John" lodges a last wish for both Johns: "I pray the Lord my soul to keep . . . Cover him over and let him sleep."

P

. . . COULD GO ANYWHERE . . .

Piano. *Who's playing that?* The next phase of Dylan live. Opening night, the Key Arena in Seattle Center on October 4, 2002, and virtually every concert after that, piano now for more than twenty years. Someone new always will ask, *who*? Then, *why*? Bob Dylan and his guitar: archetypal. Iconic. What you did yesterday stays with you today, though actually many younger fans now have never seen him on an acoustic or electric guitar live and in person. Does that matter? How does it matter? That night in Seattle it was almost as if he wasn't there, and the piano was playing all by itself. Is that it? Maybe. But the story of Dylan live in the twenty-first century is a *piano* story. For Seattle and until at least 2006 and the release of *Modern Times*, this was an electric keyboard, perhaps a Korg Triton on a distinctly piano setting; after that on a distinctly organ setting at least until 2012 and the release of *Tempest*. More or less. Later a grand piano, later still a baby grand—though these distinctions and this chronology aren't absolute either. The Seattle show was his first public performance on piano since Stuttgart, Germany, in 1991, the year of his Grammy Lifetime Achievement Award ("*. . . so defiled in this world . . .* "), his sporadic self-rescue tour sorties including stints at the keyboards. So, then, *why piano*? Shadows fell across the keys, as rumors circulated of arthritis, or a finger injury on his left hand that according to Duke Robillard necessitated surgery; yet if there's a solid physical basis for the switch to piano it's as likely Dylan's chronically aggrieved back. Electric guitars are heavy. Illness, or estrangement? Invariably, Dylan emphasized music grounds. As he told Bill Flanagan after *Triplicate* in 2017, "I play [guitar] at sound checks and at home, but the chemistry is better when I'm at the piano. It changes the dynamic of the band if I play guitar . . . I'm strictly a rhythm [piano] player anyway. I'm not a solo player and when the piano gets locked in with the steel guitar, it's like big band orchestrated riffs. That doesn't happen when I play guitar." With David Gates at *Newsweek*, he was still more detailed. "He told me a lot about that," Gates recounted. "Basically it has to do with his guitar not giving him quite the fullness of sound he was wanting at the bottom. Six strings on guitar, ten fingers on a piano. He's thought of hiring a keyboard player so he doesn't have to do it himself, but hasn't been able to figure out who. Most keyboard players, he says, like to be soloists, and he wants a very basic sound." Concert hall, but also the tavern on the corner: a Lindy Hop concert pianist pounding out honky-tonk.

Dylan's 1959 high school yearbook holy-grail ambition to "join Little Richard," of course, designated a rock 'n' roll piano maestro, plaintive and dreamy, not a guitarist, right from his outset, *before* the outset. As far back as the summer of 1954 at Camp Herzl in Webster, Wisconsin, he swayed at the piano for a performance of "Annie Had a Baby" with his friend Larry Kegan. As Elston Gunnn he and his piano backed up Bobby Vee. On *Theme Time Radio Hour* Dylan lingered over pianists—Moon Mullican (episode 77, "Money, Part 2"); Otis Milburn (episode 79, "Beginnings, Middles & Ends"); Fats Domino and Jerry Lee Lewis (episode 95, "Truth & Lies")—unto a thumbnail lecture:

> Everybody always thinks of rockabilly as being a guitar-based music, but you can't imagine that record [Carl Perkins's 'Your True Love'] without Jerry Lee Lewis pumpin' the piano all over it. During the '60s and the '70s the guitar hero became popular, but for my money

> give me that pumpin' piano. The only reason the guitar became so popular is because you could wear it around your neck and stand in the middle of the stage. The poor guy playin' the piano was stuck in one spot, and unless you were Little Richard or Jerry Lee Lewis you were relegated to the background. I feel we lost something when it became all guitars and no piano.

That night in Seattle his keyboard was positioned close to center stage. Dylan could deprecate his own skills—"very, very elementary," he told Adrian Deevoy in 1989, but to hear him talk on *Theme Time Radio Hour*, you might think that for him those past five decades or so on various guitars were just a long, deluded detour away from and back to piano.

A strange bird. Dylan maybe also was bored. His concerts with his Charlie Sexton, Larry Campbell, Tony Garnier, and David Kemper band—depending on which song, as many as three viable lead guitarists—peaked after the release of *"Love And Theft,"* yet there were popular traditions and sounds inside his new album beyond the chime, chug, and jangle of strings. That show I saw at Madison Square Garden in 2001 landed in the vicinity of totally perfect. *Why* wallow in such evidently automatic finesse? *Why not* push past guitar virtuosity and try for something even harder? Unlike Dylan's awkward, gradual return to live form during the early 1990s, the shift to piano was a shock tactic that instantly lodged a strange new zone of energy. While on that initial fall 2002 foray with Campbell and Sexton he moved around from keyboards to guitar, the first five songs each night found him at the electric piano. His set lists expanded as if by sleight of hand—those opening five songs in Seattle: "Solid Rock," "Lay Lady Lay," "Tombstone Blues," Warren Zevon's "Accidentally Like a Martyr," and "I'll be Your Baby Tonight." And for the show I attended on November 13 at Madison Square Garden: "Seeing the Real You at Last," Van Morrison's "Carrying a Torch," "Tombstone Blues," "You Ain't Goin' Nowhere," and "Things Have Changed." Just a single duplication, and throughout that fall something close to half of his set list on any given night consisted of songs he hadn't presented the concert before.

Dylan's piano, as he claimed, was *rhythm* piano, and that's what I heard at the Garden, mostly chords with flourishes. His new incarnation was now as an ensemble, and suddenly despite the guitar skills of Sexton and Campbell there was no lead instrument, no consistent lead beyond his voice, and sometimes his harmonica. Although driven by *"Love And Theft,"* his strategy touched and transformed his past catalog. In Seattle, Dylan's piano on "Love Minus Zero" did *lock* into the pedal steel—as he hoped to Flanagan—for a pre-rock ambiance, elegant, intense, and mysterious. At the Garden, the propulsive tunes among his five openers—"Seeing the Real You at Last," "Tombstone Blues," and "Things Have Changed"—resurfaced as a lost collaboration between Jerry Lee Lewis and Count Basie, timeless and indifferent to the calendar, albeit with idiosyncratic undercurrents of contemporary menace. "You Ain't Goin' Nowhere" mixed traditional dance band with traditional country, shredding at the finish into a flurry of sad harmonica. From inside the spins and curves and coils of his words, Dylan was singing magnificently, and that fall songs could drop from anywhere—prior to Seattle, for instance, he hadn't picked up "Solid Rock" since the *Shot of Love* tours of 1981.

Modern song covers, too, were the story of those first surprise piano shows. His tributes—"Something," for George Harrison, as his final Madison Square Garden encore; and earlier that night a devastating "Mutineer" for Warren Zevon. (Other shows included Zevon's "Accidentally Like a Martyr," "Boom Boom Mancini," and "Lawyers, Guns and Money.") In *The Philosophy of Modern Song* Dylan probed "Dirty Life and Times," from *The Wind*, an album Zevon released a few weeks before his passing in 2003, and his commentary there intimates some of the reasons for his concert testimonials, and perhaps also for his return to piano:

> The braggart, the roué, the ironic observer, and the inebriated fool were all roles Zevon chose to play in his songs. And possibly at times

in his life. But stripped to the bone, as in this song, the artistry jumps out at you like spring-loaded snakes from a gag jar of peanut brittle.

Being a writer is not something one chooses to do . . . Warren was a writer till the very end.

But the writing part only was there to serve his brilliant piano playing. In other words, Warren's lyrics and piano playing were two parts of the same thing.

For his many covers that tour—the Rolling Stones' "Brown Sugar," Neil Young's "Old Man," Don Henley's "End of the Innocence," and Van Morrison's "Carrying a Torch"—Dylan wasn't just incising homages to beloved artists and mortal friends; he was scrutinizing and appraising the circuits of his new ensemble sound. What *couldn't* he—they—play?

His piano—overall—made for softer, more easygoing rhythms than in 2001, at least up to the departure of Sexton in the spring of 2003. Sexton was replaced first by Bill Burnette (son of Dorsey, nephew of Johnny), until the guitarist he apparently really wanted, Freddy Koella, was available. Koella stayed almost exactly a year, and left only when struck down by kidney failure; nevertheless, the year of Koella restored drive and intensity, though power itself was only half the tale. Once again it was as if Dylan had reached a fork in the road, and, as Yogi Berra urged, he took it. Two allegedly contrary, even irreconcilable tacks: a pre-rock breadth, richness, and nuance; and the smashed atoms of hard rock. Scruple, and thunder; rumble, and swing. Dylan's new guitarist was equally fluent in the idioms of these divergent American vernaculars. During the 2003 shows I saw—Atlantic City's Hilton Hotel on May 9 and 10; the Hammerstein Ballroom on West Thirty-Fourth Street on August 12, 13, and 20—Koella inclined towards volume and vehemence even as he occasionally accented that street corner jazz tavern vibe Dylan appeared to desire, too. (At Hammerstein there was a puzzling run of accessory guitarists to Koella and Campbell: Nils Lofgrin, Tommy Morrongiello, Andy York, and Chuck Loeb.) Bootlegs from later that year and early 2004 point to far bolder and tonally shaded concerts, particularly from Europe in

November—Zurich, Amsterdam, Dublin, Sheffield, Birmingham, and London—and across North America the following March and April: Chicago, Detroit, Toronto, Boston, Washington, DC, and Asheville. On these you can hear Koella as perhaps Dylan's most inventive guitar foil to his piano, and a beguiling sonic mirror.

Dylan with Sexton and Campbell on guitars presided over an ace machine, masterful to the point of dazzle, possibly his greatest live band. Koella in 2003–2004 sounded as proficient as Sexton, yet he also seemed more intrigued by spontaneity, contrasts, even dissonance. Born in Mulhouse, France, Koella had collaborated previously with Cajun and Zydeco songwriter Zachary Richard before joining Willy DeVille. With Koella, Dylan was ready again to make it all up night to night, and the guitarist later remarked that he was reminded of jazz. "I really love Thelonious Monk," Koella told Frank Moriarity of *Vintage Guitar* magazine. "To me it's his musical language . . . And it's funny, because when I jammed the first time with Bob, the way he played the piano reminded me of him . . . he could go anywhere." Dylan with Koella now could reimagine *Highway 61 Revisited*, *The Basement Tapes*, *John Wesley Harding*, *Nashville Skyline*, and *Blood on the Tracks*, whether as nods to the Clash or Jelly Roll Morton. Set lists will jolt and cheer—"Romance in Durango" in London live for the only time since 1976; or "Hazel" in DC live for the only time since *The Last Waltz*. One of Dylan's savviest versions of "Desolation Row" since the mid-'60s at Wembley Arena in London; fierce renditions of "Quinn the Eskimo (The Mighty Quinn)" and "Down Along the Cove" at Shepherd's Bush Empire theater; jazzy pre-rock stylings for "If Dogs Run Free" in DC, "Dear Landlord" at Carling Apollo Hammersmith, "Tangled Up in Blue" at Brixton Academy, and "To Be Alone with You" in Toronto.

For all Dylan's inspired refractions of the back catalog, the nightly standouts often evolved out of recent albums, *Time Out of Mind* and *"Love And Theft."* His year with Koella probably is the closest Dylan came to realizing live his corrosive revision of *Time Out of Mind*. Their tense, bluesy reciprocation on "Million Miles" at Brixton Academy in November of 2003, and again in Chicago the following March, surpasses any studio recording of the song I've heard. The same goes for "Can't Wait" in October in Berlin, and November in Zurich; "Tryin' to Get to Heaven" in Amsterdam in November; and "Not Dark Yet" in Asheville. On stage, Koella stood to Dylan's immediate left. "I really like to improvise, so that was ideal for me," he recalled. "Especially being on Bob's side, you can feel him and you can do the connection. It was great." Eventually someone would post at Expecting Rain a nine-volume compilation of Koella's brief transit with Dylan, under the title *Freddy Or Not.* (Another fan affixed a "gift" tenth CD, *Fuzzy Cats Vol. 1.*)

Time Out of Mind that Koella year sounded like a pledge Dylan was finally delivering on. Remarkably, he approached *"Love And Theft"* in a spirit of deconstruction, too, though of course he had produced the record himself. His relocation to piano, as he implied to Flanagan and Gates, was at least partially demanded by what he was discovering as he tried to stage *"Love And Theft"* without one. From Gatsby, Virgil, and *Confessions of a Yakuza* to nineteenth-century minstrelsy, the histories, musical and literary, inside those songs outstripped even his most sophisticated guitar designs with Sexton and Campbell. As exemplary as that 2001 Madison Square Garden concert I heard was, *"Love And Theft"* would not fully arrive live until 2003, or 2004, perhaps as late as 2005, long after Sexton and Campbell departed. On *Freddy Or Not* some of the slyest tracks hail from *"Love And Theft"*—"Lonesome Day Blues" (Toronto), "High Water" (Niagara Falls), "Floater (Too Much to Ask)" (Hammersmith), "Cry A While" (Wembly), "Summer Days" (Detroit), "Moonlight" (Hamburg), "Honest With Me" (Houston), "Bye and Bye" (New Orleans), and "Tweedle Dee & Tweedle Dum" (Dallas). And I'd want to add a parallel "gift" set list of "Floater (Too Much to Ask)" (Chicago), "Moonlight" (Chicago), "Honest With Me" (Boston), "Bye and Bye" (Toronto), "Tweedle Dee & Tweedle Dum" (Detroit), "Sugar Baby" (Pittsburgh), "Po' Boy" (Rochester).

There I almost inevitably slip. . . . For by Pittsburgh and Rochester, Freddie Koella already was ill and gone, and, after just ninety-three concerts, supplanted by Stu Kimball. Still, Dylan was now able to advance the contrary strands of his piano ensemble sound—more syncopation; *and* more rock—without any obvious rupture, no matter who was on guitar. (Koella would recover, but Kimball was ensconced.) With Kimball by his side now, *"Love And Theft"* continued to sparkle and deepen. I heard Kimball in the early 1980s at The Channel, a Boston music club as famous for reputed mob ties as for the superlative Dinky Dawson sound system, when he was a member of the local new wave band Face to Face. He later worked with Peter Wolf and Carly Simon, and contributed guitar to many tracks produced by Arthur Baker and Jimmy Iovine. Kimball would go on to back Dylan at over 1,300 shows.

But Dylan the pianist was still an experiment. As late as early 2005 he briefly engaged Elana Fremerman, later Elana James, of Hot Club of Cowtown on violin, for a sound that combined piano, violin, and pedal steel. At the time he was reconsidering concert venues, along with testing his band, and his audiences. Instead of the vast arenas of 2001 and 2002, increasingly he opted for mid-size halls in a city over multiple nights: six nights in Los Angeles, five in Chicago, five in New York. For a three-night residency in Boston, he sang some forty-two songs—forty of them different, just two on repeat. The shows I saw spanned the Borgata Hotel Casino & Spa in Atlantic City on June 6, 2004, and three (of his five) nights at the Beacon Theatre in April of 2005. The evening after the Borgata, Dylan moreover joined Wynton Marsalis and his Septet for two songs at the Jazz at the Lincoln Center's Spring Gala at the Apollo Theater. Then, during the summers he teamed up with Willie Nelson for tours of minor league baseball parks. The first year I caught Cooperstown and Fishkill. The next, Yogi Berra Stadium in Montclair. Forks in the road?

Take them. This first phase of Dylan's piano experiment culminated in the fall of 2005 at his shows in London and Dublin: five nights at Brixton Academy, and two nights at the Point Theatre. *"Love And Theft"* was close to the center certainly, and over the concerts he profiled nearly the entire album—"Honest With Me" (London nights 1, 2, 4, and 5); "Moonlight" (London, night 2), "Tweedle Dee & Tweedle Dum" (London, night 2; Dublin, night 2), "Lonesome Day Blues" (London, night 3), "Mississippi" (London, night 3), "Summer Days" (London, nights 3, 4, and 5,

Dublin night 1), "Po' Boy" (London, night 3), "Cry A While" (London, night 4; Dublin, night 1), "High Water" (London, nights 4, and 5; Dublin night 2), "Sugar Baby" (London, night 5), and "Floater (Too Much to Ask)" (Dublin, night 1)—every song but "Bye and Bye." But his mission in London and Dublin appeared more a piano-based reconnaissance of his entire back catalog from the vantage of *"Love And Theft"*—"Every Grain of Sand" (Dublin, night 2), "Positively 4th Street" (London, night 3), "Maggie's Farm" (Dublin, night 1), "Million Miles" (London, night 4), "Highway 61 Revisited" (London, night 1), "Cold Irons Bound" (Dublin, night 1), "Shelter from the Storm" (London, night 4), and probably his strongest "Visions of Joanna" (Dublin, night 2) since, well, 1966. Dylan would in 2006 enthuse of this touring outfit to Jonathan Lethem, "This is the best band I've ever been in, ever had, *man for man*. When you play with guys a hundred times a year, you know what you can and can't do, what they're good at . . . I got guys now in my band, they can whip up anything, they surprise even *me*."

Hundred shows? Good guess. In 2005 Dylan dispatched 113 shows in all, and 111 in 2004. From that Seattle concert back in the fall of 2002 through the end of 2005, he played more than 350 piano shows. But as Dylan was remaking his songs at the piano that was hardly—as other letter chapters track—all he was doing. The premiere of *Masked and Anonymous* at the Sundance Film Festival, and of the Scorsese documentary, *No Direction Home*, on PBS. The publication of *Chronicles*, *Lyrics 1962–2001*, and *The Bob Dylan Scrapbook*. The release of *The Bootleg Series Vol. 5—Bob Dylan Live 1975: The Rolling Thunder Revue*; *Live at The Gaslight, 1962*; and *The Bootleg Series Vol. 7: No Direction Home: The Soundtrack*. An interview on *60 Minutes* with Ed Bradley, and print interviews with *Rolling Stone*, the *Los Angeles Times*, the *Sunday Telegraph*, NPR, *USA Today*, and *Newsweek*. The opening of an exhibition, *Bob Dylan's American Journey 1956–1966*, at the Experience Music Project in Seattle . . . his future Tulsa archive as a miniature curiosity cabinet of 150 objects.

During those London and Dublin concerts you can also start to hear what might be a consequence of all this singing, touring, and work: a wheeze, a growl, a rasp that listeners will start to dub the Wolfman, the Circus Barker. Some up-singing, too, his voice rising mechanically at ends of phrases. Portents of something . . . ominous. But meanwhile, back in Seattle, October 4, 2002. *Who's playing that?* After Al Santos's mordant intro, Dylan, standing and facing the keyboard, aimed a dim and faraway smile at nothing in particular, hit a few chords, and started a tune.

Q

. . . A STRANGENESS THAT WAS US . . .

Quotations—a too partial smattering:

I am sad and weary
Far away from home
Miss the Mississippi and you, dear
Days are dark and dreary
Everywhere I roam
Miss the Mississippi and you

—JIMMIE RODGERS, "MISS THE MISSISSIPPI AND YOU"

. . . the darkness does not lift but becomes yet heavier as I think how little we can hold in mind, how everything is constantly lapsing into oblivion with every extinguished life, how the world is, as it were, draining itself, in that the history of countless places and objects which themselves have no power of memory is never heard, never described or passed on.

—W. G. SEBALD, *AUSTERLITZ* (TRANS. ANTHEA BELL)

. . . for Bruno's art of memory is a magical art, a Hermetic art. . . . The Roman orators used a mnemonic which is described in the Ad Herenium and referred to by Cicero and Quintilian. It consisted in memorizing a series of places in a building, and attaching to these memorized places, images to remind of the points of the speech. The orator when delivering his speech, passed in imagination along the order of memorized places, plucking from them the images which were to remind him of his notions. Not only buildings could be used as a memory place system: Metrodorus of Scepsis is said to have used the zodiac as the foundation of his memory-system. . . . The Hermetic experience of reflecting the universe in the mind is, I believe, at the root of Renaissance magic memory, in which the classical mnemonic with places and images is now understood, or applied, as a method of achieving this experience by imprinting archetypal, or magically activated, images on the memory. By using magical or talismanic images as memory-images, the Magus hoped to acquire universal knowledge, and also powers, obtaining through the magical organization of the imagination a magically powerful personality, tuned in, as it were, to the powers of the cosmos.

—**FRANCES A. YATES,** ***GIORDANO BRUNO AND THE HERMETIC TRADITION***

Remorse—is Memory—awake—
Her Parties all astir—
A Presence of Departed Acts—
At window—and at Door—
It's Past—set down before the Soul
And lighted with a Match—
Perusal—to facilitate—
And help Belief to stretch—
Remorse is cureless—the Disease
Not even God—can heal—
For 'tis His institution—and

The Adequate of Hell—

—EMILY DICKINSON

And I saw an angel come down from heaven, having the key of the bottomless pit and a great chain in his hand. . . .

And I saw the dead, small and great, stand before God; and the books were opened: and another book was opened, which is the book of life: and the dead were judged out of those things which were written in the books, according to their works.

And the sea gave up the dead which were in it; and death and hell delivered up the dead which were in them: and they were judged every man according to their works.

And death and hell were cast into the lake of fire. This is the second death.

And whosoever was not found written in the book of life was cast into the lake of fire.

—REVELATION TO JOHN, 20:1, 12–15

You may bury my body
Down by the highway side
So my old evil spirit
Can get a Greyhound bus and ride

—ROBERT JOHNSON, "ME AND THE DEVIL BLUES"

. . . I think that it was Freud who suggested that the presence of the black man in America foreshadowed America's doom—which America, if it could not civilize these savages, would deserve: it is certainly the testimony of such disparate witnesses as William Faulkner and Isadora Duncan. For Marx and Engels, the presence of the black man in America was simply a useful crowbar for the liberation of whites: an idea which has had its issue in the history of American labor unions. The Founding Fathers shared this view, eminently, Thomas Jefferson, and the Great Emancipator freed those slaves he could not reach, in order to create, hopefully, a fifth column behind the Confederate lines. This ambivalence contains the key to American literature—all the way from *The Scarlet Letter* to *The Big Sleep*.

—JAMES BALDWIN, *THE DEVIL FINDS WORK*

Underwritten by envy as well as repulsion, sympathetic identification as well as fear, the minstrel show continually transgressed the color line even as it made possible the formation of a self-consciously white working class . . . The moment of minstrelsy's greatest popularity (1846–1854) was marked by a variety of bitter political controversies: labor struggles in New York and other major cities, the Wilmot Proviso debates over the extension of slavery, the Seneca Falls women's rights convention, the Astor Place theater riot, the fugitive slave law and its aftermath, the Kansas-Nebraska bill, and others. In significant ways this historical moment suddenly made the misappropriations and distortions committed in minstrelsy politically dangerous. The conflictual character of minstrelsy only deepened with the approach of the gravest pre–Civil War threat to the social order of the Union, the debates over slavery that led to the Compromise of 1850. Stephen Foster's "Plantation Melodies" unwittingly conjured up the hydra-headed conflicts; these melodies, and the vast dissemination of *Uncle Tom's Cabin* in various politically divergent blackface theatrical productions—a kind of prelude to civil war on the stage—offer a lens through which to read a political crisis. . . .

—ERIC LOTT, *LOVE AND THEFT*

Only Malcolm X's autobiography seemed to offer something different. His repeated acts of self-creation spoke to me; the blunt poetry of his words, his unadorned insistence on respect, promised a new and uncompromising order, martial in its discipline, forged through sheer force of will.

—**BARACK OBAMA,** ***DREAMS FROM MY FATHER***

It's so hard to describe what I feel when I feel I really exist and my soul is a real entity that I don't know what human words would define it. I don't know if I have a fever, as I feel I do, or if I've stopped having the fever of sleeping through life. Yes, I repeat, I'm like a traveler who suddenly finds himself in a strange town, without knowing how he got there, which makes me think of those who lose their memory and for a long time are not themselves but someone else. I was someone else for a long time—since birth and consciousness—and suddenly I've woken up in the middle of a bridge, leaning over the river and knowing that I exist more solidly than the person I was up till now. But the city is unknown to me, the streets are new, and the trouble has no cure. And so, leaning over the bridge, I wait for the truth to go away and let me return to being fictitious and non-existent, intelligent and natural. It was just a brief moment, and it's already over. . . .

—**FERNANDO PESSOA,** ***THE BOOK OF DISQUIET*** **(TRANS. RICHARD ZENITH)**

And here was I, or what was left of me.
Feared and rejoiced in, chafed against, held cheap,
A strangeness that was us, and was not, had
All the same allowed for its description,
And so brought at least me these spells of odd,
Self-effacing balance. Better to stop
While we still can. Already I take up
Less emotional space than a snowdrop.

My father in his last illness complained
Of the effect of medication on
His real self—today Bluebeard, tomorrow
Babbitt. Young chameleon, I used to
Ask how on earth one got sufficiently
Imbued with otherness. And now I see.

—JAMES MERRILL, "THE BOOK OF EPHRAIM"

'Scuse me while I disappear . . .

—MATT DENNIS AND EARL BRENT, "ANGEL EYES"

How do the living lie with the dead? Until the dehumanization of society by capitalism, all the living awaited the experience of the dead. It was their ultimate future. By themselves the living were incomplete. Thus living and dead were interdependent. Always. Only a uniquely modern form of egotism has broken this interdependence. With disastrous results for the living, who now think of the dead as eliminated.

—JOHN BERGER, "ON THE ECONOMY OF THE DEAD"

. . . All that is left is a mosaic of facts—and points of view, which are mistaken for facts.

The past is now "pasts": a co-existing layering of versions, often with only one or two points of contact. Hard facts soften to modeling clay and can be molded into a shape. The desire to remember, to recreate and fix in place, goes hand-in-hand with incomplete knowledge and partial understanding of events. Units of information can be lined up in any formation, any order, like in a children's game. . . .

—MARIA STEPANOVA, *IN MEMORY OF MEMORY* (TRANS. SASHA DUGDALE)

I probably never would have become America's leading fire-eater if Flamo the Great hadn't happened to explode that night in front of Krinko's Great Combined Carnival Side Shows. The tragedy—if such it may be called—took place at eleven o'clock when there's only time for one more show before the carnival closes for the night, so all the concessions compete for the late crowd at the same time. The side show had a bad location, being next to the Oriental Dancing Girls ("Fugitives from a Life of Shame in the Sultan's Harem") and it's pretty hard to compete with ten naked girls for the public's interest. But a good side show can compete with anything. . . .

—DAN MANNIX, *STEP RIGHT UP!*

The thing most people don't realize about Bob Dylan is that he has a kind of photographic memory for things. He literally remembers everything he's ever heard or seen. I've had him recall to me conversations we had years earlier word for word. So he has a wealth of material to draw from in his songwriting. It's how he gleans from this, how he synthesizes all this, how he puts it together that is his real talent, I think. He was unique from the get-go. He was like a great big sponge. He absorbed everything and I don't know how aware he was that he was doing it. He would come into the Kettle of Fish and say to us, "I wrote this new song or at least I think I wrote it. Maybe I heard it somewhere."

—SYLVIA TYSON, OF IAN AND SYLVIA

In Bob Dylan's memory palace
Echoes of the past remain,
Each room filled with vivid imagery,
Tales of joy, loss, and pain.

—CHATGPT, "BOB DYLAN'S MEMORY PALACE"

Bob Dylan, killed by a discarded Oedipus
who turned around to investigate a ghost
& discovered that the ghost too
was more than one person

—BOB DYLAN, *TARANTULA*

R

. . . A GOD OF TIME AND SPACE . . .

Rewrite O. It was to be the section golden with twilight. *Tempest*, and *The Tempest*. Prospero. Melted into air. But impossible. Along the way religion—faith, but also religion—took hold, overwhelmed my other stories. Dylan told Mikal Gilmore for *Rolling Stone* in 2012 that *Tempest* was "not the album I wanted to make, though. I had another one in mind. I wanted to make something more religious. That takes a lot more concentration—to pull that off 10 times with the same thread—than it does with a record like I ended up with, where anything goes and you just gotta believe it will make sense." Modesty? Or reflexive subterfuge? For song by song that demurral is essentially the album he gave us. Across the record Dylan referenced the Old and New Testaments. "Early Roman Kings," for instance, cited Genesis and Exodus; "Narrow Way" recalled Matthew; and intimations of Final Judgement and apocalypse are everywhere. Predestination even entered "Tempest" through a mix of Revelation and the Rubaiyat.

Let it stand? Revise? "I'm a religious person," as Dylan would a decade later distill his situation to Jeff Slate in the *Wall Street Journal*. "I read scriptures a lot, meditate and pray, light candles in church. I believe in damnation and salvation, as well as predestination. The Five Books of

Moses, Pauline Epistles, Invocation of the Saints, all of it." I have no idea at all of course what Bob Dylan's precise religious beliefs and practices might aspire to, beyond his own sparse words, his words that over the years covered by this book often, perhaps inevitably, are self-revising, so for me to attest anything more definite is projection, presumptuous. One specific: I can note that whenever the word *God* appears in a song lyric draft, he tends to write G-d, following Jewish custom, an interpretation of Deuteronomy 12:3. Yet for this book, his entire reinvention after 1991 originates in that public testimony of intensive spiritual despair at the Grammys. At least on that night of his Grammy Lifetime Achievement Award, he seemed to view his artistic lapses during the 1980s as a spiritual failing: the misery and ruin of the soul.

His art. His life. Mutual defilements. Dylan's most persistent modern statements of his beliefs locate religion inside music he loves. "I find the religiosity and philosophy in the music," as he told David Gates for *Newsweek* in 1996. "I don't find it anywhere else. Songs like 'Let Me Rest on a Peaceful Mountain' or 'I Saw the Light'—that's my religion. I don't adhere to rabbis, preachers, evangelists, all of that. I've learned more from the songs than I've learned from any of this kind of entity. . . . I believe the songs." The following year, he expanded on that to Jon Pareles in the *New York Times*, "Those old songs are my lexicon and my prayer book. All my beliefs come out of those old songs, literally, anything from 'Let Me Rest on a Peaceful Mountain' to 'Keep on the Sunny Side.' I believe in a God of time and space, but if people ask me about that, my impulse is to point them back towards those songs. I believe in Hank Williams singing 'I Saw the Light.' I've seen the light, too."

Dylan, as far as I know, has never performed live Ralph Stanley's "Let Me Rest on a Peaceful Mountain," Hank Williams's "I Saw the Light," or Ada Blenkhorn and J. Howard Entwisle's "Keep on the Sunny Side." But as I noted previously, he opened his first concert in New York City after 9/11—and nearly every show that fraught autumn of 2001—with "Wait for the Light to Shine," a Fred Rose song first recorded in 1945 by Roy Acuff and His Smoky Mountain Boys. (Hank Williams later covered it.

An extraordinary Tin Pan Alley and Nashville songwriter, Rose was Williams's producer.) On that and subsequent 2002 tours, Dylan might alternate "Wait for the Light to Shine" with other country spirituals: "Somebody Touched Me" (Traditional), "Hallelujah, I'm Ready to Go" (Traditional), "I Am the Man, Thomas" (Ralph Stanley and Larry Sparks) and "Humming Bird" (Johnnie Wright, Jim Anglin, and Jack Anglin). Earlier in his Never Ending Tour he also performed Anglin's "This World Can't Stand Long," Williams's "House of Gold," and Christian hymns—Thomas A. Dorsey's "Peace in the Valley," Francis J. Crosby and William H. Doane's "Pass Me Not, O Gentle Saviour," and "Rock of Ages" (Traditional).

Dylan's own songs sometimes shadowed spiritual transcendence, notably "Highlands," "Ain't Talkin'," "Roll on John," and "Key West (Philosopher Pirate)." Yet the contrasts between the "lexicon and prayer book" songs he commended and his dark homilies of judgment, vengeance, and apocalypse on *Time Out of Mind*, *"Love And Theft," Modern Times*, and *Tempest* are harsh. Here's "Let Me Rest on a Peaceful Mountain":

Let me rest on a peaceful mountain
When the seeds for the harvest is sown
Where the wild birds nest in the good old summer time
On a mountain near my home sweet home

There's Dylan in "Tempest":

The ship was going under
The universe opened wide
The roll was called up yonder
The angels turned aside

Sweet, charming, serene nature vs. the storms, injuries, and punishments of an evil and unreasonable world. During a 2001 interview in *Rolling Stone*, Dylan was asked about his "so defiled" speech at the Grammys. His response first spoke of "living in a Machiavellian world, whether we like it or we don't. Any act that's immoral, as long as it succeeds, it's all right." But he soon pivoted to God:

> You hear a lot about God these days: God, the beneficent; God, the all-great; God, the almighty; God, the most powerful; God, the giver of life; God, the creator of death. I mean, we're hearing about God all the time, so we better learn how to deal with it. But if we know anything about God, God is *arbitrary*. So people better be able to deal with that, too.

So, God is *arbitrary*, in Dylan's italics. As likely as not he was recalling "Sinners in the Hands of an Angry God," the Great Awakening sermon that Jonathan Edwards preached in Enfield, Connecticut, in 1741. Edwards recurrently asserted God's "arbitrary" mercy, and "arbitrary" will:

> They deserve to be cast into hell; so that divine justice never stands in the way, it makes no objection against God's using his power at any moment to destroy them . . . The sword of divine justice is every moment brandished over their heads, and it is nothing but the hand of *arbitrary* mercy, and God's mere will that holds it back. . . .
>
> So that, thus it is that natural men are held in the hand of God, over the pit of hell; they have deserved the fiery pit, and are already sentenced to it . . . neither is God in the least bound by any promise to hold them up one moment; the devil is waiting for them, hell is gaping for them, the flames gather and flash about them . . . all that preserves them every moment is the mere *arbitrary* will, and uncovenanted, unobliged forbearance of an incensed God.

My italics. Edwards rides closer than "Let Me Rest on a Peaceful Mountain" and "I Saw the Light" to the tone of *Modern Times* and *Tempest.* As Dylan sings in "Early Roman Kings," breathing hellfire into Homer, "I'll strip you of life, strip you of breath / Ship you down to the house of death."

For a 2007 interview with Jann Wenner in *Rolling Stone*, Dylan distinguished between faith and religion. "Religion is supposedly a force for positive good. Where can you look in the world and see that religion has been a force for positive good? . . . Corporations are religions. . . . Religion is something that is mostly outward appearance." But faith "is a different thing. . . . Faith doesn't have a name. It doesn't have a category. It's oblique. So it's unspeakable. We degrade faith by talking about religion." A list at the top of one page of his drafts towards "Narrow Way" in the Tulsa archive frames the vicissitudes of Dylan's thinking there about religion and faith, and his backdrops veer from the legend of Robert Johnson selling his soul to the devil to David Koresh's violent spin on the Seven Seals of Revelation for the Branch Davidians, with pauses for 9/11, Jack White and Dead Weather's "Blue Blood Blues," and the Sermon on the Mount. And it's worth noting, too, that "Narrow Way" likely adapts its title from Matthew 7:14: "Because strait is the gate, and narrow is the way, which leadeth unto life, and few there be that find it." In *The Philosophy of Modern Song*, Dylan's philosophy stresses pain. "In a real sense the only thing that truly unites us is suffering and suffering only," as he writes about "Doesn't Hurt Anymore" by John Trudell. "We all know loss, whether you're rich or poor."

Me? I was raised Catholic, really Irish Catholic, in Boston, so most of my associations with organized religion match Dylan's dismissal to Wenner. Along with sin and guilt, I experienced a small-minded, mean-spirited Catholic Church steeped in bigotry and often overt racism. I eventually attended BC High, a Jesuit prep school tainted by priests who abused boys. Dominated by my mother, and her mother—my Nana—the eyes our family set on the outside world radiated distrust. Their morning masses at St. Mark's Church around the corner from our house in Dorchester; their milky tea and soda bread; the South Boston St. Patrick's Day parades and memories of Eire; the visiting florid priests and pale sisters—all directed a social order compact and impervious. Ethnic identities sustained an almost occult importance. A typical conversation satisfied a scrutinizing "What's he like?" with totemic classifications: "Oh, he's a Swede," or "She's German." The Bible receded on this mixed current of suspicion and self-content to its remote upper storage shelf in the kitchen pantry, adjoining cookbooks no one consulted, either. Although invoked periodically as a sort of triumphant last word, usually against sin, the Bible came to be linked with a breed of godforsaken sinners called "Protestants" who, as the nuns at St. Mark's explained, revolted against the Church and were condemned by God to hell. The Bible figured obscurely in that doom, but since we didn't know any Protestants, it hardly mattered.

Thus most of my impressions of the New Testament arrived secondhand, through the rhetorical filter of the Baltimore catechism. Unlike some later Protestant or Jewish friends who would retain the inflections of the King James or the Hebrew Bible as a kind of communal interior melody, the enduring tune from my religion classes pitched insistent questions against pat answers:

1. Who made us?
   God made us.

2. Who is God?
   God is the Supreme Being who made all things.

The drawings and sketches scattered throughout the catechism—famously the full and empty milk bottles tracking the debasement from a pure to a wicked soul—furthered this domestication of the Bible. A distinctly European Christ preached and performed miracles surrounded by European disciples, and, often, a small troupe of American schoolchildren: our time-transported stand-ins mingling among the mourners at Christ's crucifixion. The catechism urged us to identify with the apostles and saints. My late aunt was a nun, Sister Mary Dionetta, and Nana displayed a pair of relics on her bedroom dresser, chips of bone encased in glass and bronze. Her miniature reliquaries housed the partial remains of Pope Pius X and another saint whose long name started with the letters

D-I-O-N before fading into illegibility. For many years, I believed that smear of bone and glue was my aunt.

Still, bits of magic stuck. Whenever I thought—and think—about an afterlife, or an alongside, otherworldly life to the one we live every day, it is as a communion of the dead, a conversation among and with dead friends and family: my "saints," my Higher Power. Mom, Dad, Nana, my younger brother Jim, and my comrades and soul mates Mark and Mark, Lucy and Lucie, Jason, Liam, and Arthur. James Merrill's convocation of his familiars over a Ouija board with his partner David Jackson for *The Changing Light at Sandover* probably re-exposed this surmise when I first read "The Book of Ephraim" in *Divine Comedies*, and eventually I wrote a book about it. Now, two books. As Merrill recorded late in *Sandover*:

Night. Two phantoms out of Maeterlinck
Stand on a terrace watching the full moon sink.
DJ: It's almost as if we were dead
And signaling to dear ones in the world.

Louise Glück in her essay "The Education of a Poet" describes writing poetry as "attempting dialogue with the great dead."

On *Rough and Rowdy Ways*, Dylan's reflections on his art from inside his art focus on faith and religion. "I've Made Up My Mind to Give Myself to You" appears to zero in on a crisis of faith; "I've traveled the long road of despair." He's surrounded by deaths, in nature ("I saw the flowers come and go"), and among his friends ("A lot of people gone, a lot of people I knew"). He laments his abandonment, his isolation, "I don't think I could bear to live my life alone," and he's wary of the Last Judgement: "I hope that the gods go easy with me." For all that, the song, one of Dylan's loveliest, with a melody reminiscent of an Offenbach barcarolle, "Belle Nuit, Ô Nuit D'Amour," moves towards resolution, invoking Easter ("I'll see you at sunrise, I'll see you at dawn") and, as he signs off, hope: "I knew you'd say yes, I'm saying it too." Yet what exactly is resolved here? When Dylan mentions "the gospel of love / A love so real a love so true," is the crucial word "gospel" or "love"? When he invokes various American locales, Birmingham, San Antoine, and Salt Lake City, and refracts Jimmie Rodgers, Johnny Cash, and Ricky Nelson on "traveling, I'm a traveling man," is he a pilgrim, a wayward husband, or a touring musician? Finally, how hopeful is he? In his opening line, "Sitting on my terrace lost in the stars," Dylan casually touches on "Lost in the Stars," yet that classic Maxwell Anderson and Kurt Weill tune will wonder, "And sometimes it seems maybe God's gone away / Forgetting the promise that we've heard him say / And we're lost in the stars."

"Black Rider," the next song on *Rough and Rowdy Ways*, shapes a devil's-bargain version of that same elusive redemption, listing from spiritual calm ("My heart is at rest, I'd like to keep it that way") to spiritual anguish ("My soul is distressed, my mind is at war"), and aspirational prayer slides into brutish revenge. "Goodbye Jimmy Reed," Dylan's tribute to Jimmy Reed, and to Van Morrison and James Baldwin, too, mounts a sardonic lampoon of "that old time religion," blurring church and sex. Finally, on "Crossing the Rubicon" Dylan arranges a series of gestures and moments where everything is double—a dawning day, and the end of the world; expiation and retaliation; love, and misuses of love; the Holy Spirit, and someone named Mona Baby. His echoes are also double—Dante and *Paint Your Wagon*; the Red River of the Roman poet Lucan and Howard Hawks. Set on the day before the Ides of March, the geography of "Crossing the Rubicon" is at once the historical classical world ("The Rubicon is the Red River, going gently as she flows") and the allegorical Christian world ("Three miles north of Purgatory, one step from the great beyond"). Across Dylan's verses, the civil wars and future assassination of Julius Caesar merge with the cup and cross of Jesus Christ. Straddling all these oppositions and convergences is the imago of the divided singer who, as he recounts, "stood between heaven and earth and . . . crossed the Rubicon."

Christ and Caesar also stir Dylan's extended parley on "transfiguration" during a 2012 interview with Mikal Gilmore in *Rolling Stone*. He showed Gilmore a dog-eared book, *Hell's Angel: The Life and Times of Sonny*

Barger and the Hell's Angels Motorcycle Club, coauthored by Barger with Keith and Kent Zimmerman, a team of twins ("Bio Brothers") who also worked with John Lydon, Alice Cooper, and David Hilliard. Dylan paused over the cowriters—"Do those names ring a bell?"—but directed Gilmore to a passage about yet another Zimmerman:

> One of the early presidents of the Berdoo Hell's Angels was Bobby Zimmerman. On our way home from the 1964 Bass Lake Run, Bobby was riding in his customary spot—front left—when his muffler fell off his bike. Thinking he could go back and retrieve it, Bobby whipped a quick U-turn from the front of the pack. At that same moment a Richmond Hell's Angel named Jack Egan was hauling ass from the back of the pack toward the front. Egan was on the wrong side of the road passing the long line of speeding bikes just as Bobby whipped his U-turn. Jack broadsided poor Bobby and instantly killed him. We dragged Bobby's lifeless body to the side of the road. There was nothing we could do but send somebody on to town for help.

Dylan had glanced at the death of this Bobby Zimmerman in *Chronicles* for his "The Lost Land" chapter. With Gilmore, though, he linked Bobby to two archetypal moments in his own life. The earlier occasion involves his change of name from Bobby Zimmerman to Bob Dylan, most likely while he was still a student at the University of Minnesota, sometime during the 1959–1960 academic year. Barger—or the Bio Brothers—got the date of the accident wrong, as Bobby Zimmerman actually died on September 3, 1961, the year Dylan arrived in New York and, in fact, just a few weeks before John Hammond offered him a contract with Columbia Records. Speaking to *Rolling Stone*, it is as if Dylan were the Bobby Zimmerman Barger saw die. "Bob Dylan's here! You're talking to him," Dylan apprised Gilmore. "I couldn't go back and find Bobby in a million years. Neither could you or anybody else on the face of the earth. He's gone. If I could, I would go back . . . At this point in time, I would love to go back and find him, put out my hand. And tell him he's got a friend. But I can't. He's gone. He doesn't exist."

The other, later episode is Dylan's own motorcycle accident, by most accounts on July 29, 1966. "I had a motorcycle accident in 1966," Dylan continued to Gilmore. "Now you can put this together any way you want. . . . Transfiguration: You can go and learn about it from the Catholic Church, you can learn about it in some old mystical books, but it's a real concept. Nobody knows who it's happened to, or why." Among others who possibly were transfigured, he speculated, "Maybe Julius Caesar . . . I have no idea. Maybe Shakespeare. Maybe Dante. Maybe Napoleon. Maybe Churchill. You just never know, because it doesn't figure in the history books."

Dylan told Gilmore that he found a book about transfiguration at a library in Rome. In her 2004 study, *Transfiguration*—and might that be the book Dylan read in Rome?—theologian Dorothy Lee writes that, "given its dramatic and theological import, it is strange that the transfiguration should be one of the most neglected stories in the New Testament." Differing accounts of the transfiguration of Jesus appear four times there, in the Gospels of Mark, Matthew, and Luke, and in 2 Peter, along with briefer allusions in John. This is the Book of Matthew:

> And after six days Jesus taketh Peter, James, and John to his brother, and bringeth them up into an high mountain apart,
>
> And was transfigured before them: and his face did shine as the sun, and his raiment was white as the light.
>
> And behold, there appeared unto them Moses and Elias talking with him. . . .
>
> While he yet spake, behold, a bright cloud overshadowed them: and behold a voice out of the cloud, which said, This is my beloved Son, in whom I am well pleased; hear ye him.
>
> And when the disciples heard it, they fell on their face, and were sore afraid.

> And Jesus came and touched them, and said, Arise, and be not afraid.
>
> And when they had lifted up their eyes, they saw no man, save Jesus only.
>
> And as they came down from the mountain, Jesus charged them, saying, Tell the vision to no man, until the Son of man be risen again from the dead.

Lee glosses the transfiguration as an epiphany—"Jesus is shown in his true self, hidden from the eyes of the world"—as well as "an apocalyptic vision of the end time." When Dylan sings of that Caesar-Christ figure in "Crossing the Rubicon," "I stood between heaven and earth," he just might be paralleling Lee when she writes: "The transfigured Jesus on the mountain, therefore acts as the bridge between heaven and earth. . . . As the point of connection between heaven and earth, the incarnate Son entices human beings into his glory, a divine glory manifest in and through his flesh."

In his interview with *Rolling Stone*, Dylan cautioned Gilmore, "So when you ask some of your questions, you're asking them to a person who's long dead. You're asking them to a person that doesn't exist. . . . Have you ever heard of a book called *No Man Knows My History*? It's about Joseph Smith, the Mormon prophet. The title could refer to me. Transfiguration is what allows you to crawl out from under the chaos and fly above it. That's how I can still do what I do and write the songs I sing and just keep moving."

Theological intricacies to the side, my guess is that "transfiguration" for Dylan is also one of the many ways he accounts for the strangeness of being Bob Dylan. As he intimates to *Rolling Stone*, his life must be at least as mystifying to him as for the rest of us, even in crude outline. From Hibbing High to the Nobel Prize in Literature, by way of folk music and rock 'n' roll? His early 1960s songs? Arguably the most celebrated star in popular music? His lost years, and a return to form? Fifty, now sixty-plus years later? "I don't know how I got to write those songs," Dylan told Ed Bradley on *60 Minutes*. "Those early songs were almost like magically written."

For *Poems Without Titles*, a short, penciled collection of his poems in 1959, this was what he could do—zeitgeist poems; anyone's, or almost anyone's:

I thought she
Was hip
When we sat and
Drank
Coffee
And I flipped when
She
Recited
All of Prufrock
By Heart

Yet within three years he would be singing "A Hard Rain's A-Gonna Fall."

Transfiguration?

. . . words, and a holy flash past words.

S

. . . ALMOST LIKE FOLK MUSIC . . .

Sinatra, and not just once, but three distinct spins, and since one of those threes involves a three-record set, maybe the right aggregate is five. Sinatra, five times. Five sides. Scale is telling. "You know, when you start doing these songs," as Bob Dylan instructed Robert Love, editor-in-chief of—how was this possible?—*AARP The Magazine* about his Great American Songbook albums, "Frank's got to be on your mind. Because he is the mountain. That's the mountain you have to climb even if you only get part of the way there. And it's hard to find a song he did not do. He'd be the guy you got to check with." Of the fifty-two songs across his Great American Songbook albums, *Shadows in the Night* (2015), *Fallen Angels* (2016), and *Triplicate* (2017), Sinatra recorded fifty of them, and performed another, "Skylark," on at least three bandstand occasions in 1942, leaving perhaps only "Braggin'" as a tune the original Old Blue Eyes apparently never touched. "The Great American Songbook" tends to summon the diverse legacy of songs, jazz standards, and Broadway show tunes from the 1920s into the 1950s: twentieth-century American popular music before rock 'n' roll. But for Dylan, the Great American Songbook seems all but synonymous with Frank Sinatra. "He was funny," Dylan later recalled of a dinner at Sinatra's he attended with Bruce Springsteen in 1995. "We were standing out on his patio at night and he said to me, 'You and me, pal, we got blue eyes, we're from up there,' and he pointed to the stars. 'These other bums are from down here.' I remember thinking he might be right."

The guy you got to check with? According to Al Schmitt, Dylan's recording engineer on the albums, that check with was constant, literal. "We did two three-hour sessions every day, for three weeks, five days a week," Schmitt told Paul Tingen. "Dylan had this small music player, and at the start of each session we'd all be there in the live room to listen to the old Frank Sinatra recording of the song we were going to record, not to approach it in the same way, but to get an idea of the interpretation. We then would talk for maybe a couple of hours about how we were going to do the song." Schmitt also engineered Sinatra's *Duets*, and that "live room" happened to be Capitol Studio B, the fabled Hollywood recording studio that Sinatra himself christened in February 1956, when he conducted a sixty-piece orchestra for *Tone Poems of Color*. "A lot of other people recorded them as well," Dylan acknowledged. Lee Wiley, Mildred Bailey, Ella Fitzgerald, Louis Armstrong, Sarah Vaughan, Ray Charles, Peggy Lee, Fred Astaire, Jo Stafford, Tony Bennett, and the singer Sinatra loved most of all, Billie Holiday. Still, Sinatra. "It just so happens that he had the best versions of them," Dylan continued. "When I recorded these songs I had to make believe that I never heard of Sinatra, that he didn't exist. He's a guide. He'll point the way and lead you to the entrance but from there you're on your own." *Shadows in the Night* opens on spectral Sinatra, "I'm a Fool to Want You," and one of his few songwriting credits, and "The Best is Yet to Come," the last song Sinatra sang in public, haunts Dylan's *Triplicate*.

Dylan had been thinking about making an album of standards "for a while," or as he told *AARP*, "ever since I heard Willie's [Willie Nelson's] *Stardust* record in the late '70s." But when Dylan approached Walter Yetnikoff, the president of Columbia Records, the response was inauspicious, even hostile. "What he said was, 'You can go ahead and make that record, but we won't pay for it, and we won't release it. But go ahead and make it if you want to.' So I went and made *Street Legal* instead." As far back as

The Basement Tapes, Dylan improvised with the Band a song called "One for the Road," part Johnny Mercer, part Hank Williams, part random rhymes, and he included the Rodgers and Hart ballad "Blue Moon" on *Self Portrait.* He sang "Lucky Old Sun" at Farm Aid in 1985, "Soon" at the Gershwin Gala at the Brooklyn Academy of Music in 1987, and "Some Enchanted Evening" during his sessions for *Oh Mercy* in 1989.

Dylan recorded *Shadows in the Night* and *Fallen Angels* together in the fall of 2014, though the albums would appear over a year apart, *Shadows in the Night* issued on January 20, 2015, during the centenary of Sinatra's birth, and *Fallen Angels* on May 20, 2016. He returned to Studio B for *Triplicate* in February of 2016, the focused trio of records he released the following March presumably an echo of Sinatra's *Trilogy: Past Present Future* (1980). Throughout the musical core was his five-piece touring band—Charlie Sexton and Stu Kimball on guitars, George Receli on drums, and especially Tony Garnier on double bass and Donnie Herron on pedal steel—supplemented discretely by trumpet, trombone, and French horn. In between, Dylan received the Nobel Prize for Literature, though of course not for Sinatra covers. He actually wouldn't record a new song of his own between *Tempest* (2012) and *Rough and Rowdy Ways* (2020), nearly eight years. Only the Sinatra songs. Yet fascinatingly his Nobel citation *almost* references the Great American Songbook—"for having created new poetic expressions within the great American song tradition."

Heights up there beyond the heights of self. But Dylan put it clearest in 1985 during his interview with Cameron Crowe for *Biograph.* "Tin Pan Alley is gone. I put an end to it. People can record their own songs now." For many fans, though, didn't Frank Sinatra stand for pretty much everything Bob Dylan was put on this earth to eradicate? Starting with all those well-made professional songs that at least in theory emanated from music publishers on West Twenty-Eighth Street in the Flower District, and later the Brill Building? The Great American Songbook? My father—born the same year as Sinatra—flung Frank and Tony Bennett back at me when I played the Beatles, the Kinks, the Rolling Stones, and Dylan. My father and Frank then were roughly fifty years old, hardly aspirants for AARP.

From the ardent tone of my father's gossip about Sinatra, he was the hippest and sexiest man he ever witnessed. My music was "garbage," he'd shout, compared to theirs. Still, the Sinatra I observed in college would endorse Richard Nixon, and play golf with Spiro Agnew. I didn't know then about his campaigning for Roosevelt, Stevenson, and Kennedy, his admiration when young for Henry Wallace, or his work to desegregate Las Vegas hotels, and *The House I Live In*, his 1945 anti-bigotry short film, the Earl Robinson title song covered by Paul Robeson, Mahalia Jackson, and Sam Cooke. But I did read an amazing interview with Ray Davies where he explained his song "Sunny Afternoon" as somehow a mash-up of Dylan and Sinatra. "At the time of 'Sunny Afternoon' I couldn't listen to anything," Davies disclosed. "I was only playing *The Greatest Hits* of Frank Sinatra and Dylan's 'Maggie's Farm'—I just liked its whole presence. . . . I thought they all helped one another." And an extraordinary young teacher at Boston College, the poet Mark Gibbons, guided me and my friends to Cole Porter, Rodgers and Hart, George and Ira Gershwin, and Sinatra's 1950s albums for Capitol Records, *In the Wee Small Hours* (1955), *Only the Lonely* (1958), *Close to You* (1957), *Where Are You* (1957), and *No One Cares* (1959).

In the 1960s, as Dylan acknowledged to *AARP*, "I myself never bought any Frank Sinatra records back then . . . I never listened to Frank as an influence." My sense, though, is that for twenty-first century Dylan, Sinatra evidently came to signify blues. Novelist Marlon James glossed Dylan's Nobel Prize citation in this spirit when asked by Griffin Ondaatje about some writers' reactions to the award for a songwriter:

> You know I found very few, if any, Black writers who had a problem with Dylan winning the prize. And I think it's not necessarily a racial point so much as two things I don't think happen with black artists. I don't think we rank art. I don't think because you are a folk singer you're more important than me a rapper who's more important than me a poet . . . I also think that there's no separation with us between the so-called Great American Songbook—which is mostly

> people singing *blues*—and everything else . . . Also, you know the Nobel was pretty clear that it was for how he *expanded* the American songbook . . . And he's had a profound impact on literature. He's had a profound impact, certainly, on black literature.

Mostly people singing blues. Across *Shadows in the Night*, *Fallen Angels*, and *Triplicate*, Dylan fixed on songs that mention blues—"The blues walked in and met me" ("Stormy Weather"), and "Maybe I'm in for crying the blues" ("Nevertheless")—or rouse classic blues tropes: "To share a kiss the Devil has known" ("I'm a Fool to Want You") and "I go out walking after midnight" ("Maybe You'll Be There"). In interviews he linked early rock 'n' roll to big band blues. "Rock and roll was indeed an extension of what was going on—the big swinging bands—Ray Noble, Will Bradley, Glenn Miller, I listened to that music before I heard Elvis Presley . . . Rock and roll was atomic powered, all zoom and doom. It didn't seem like an extension of anything but it probably was."

For twenty-first century Dylan, Sinatra is also noir, his whole plot of song covered with scandal and incident and change. The jackets of his Capitol LPs might as well have decorated 1950s crime novels by Jim Thompson, David Goodis, and Patricia Highsmith: Frank alone with a cigarette under a streetlamp against a garish and distorted cityscape for *In the Wee Small Hours*; Frank drinking alone in a lively crowd for *No One Cares*; Frank as a tawdry clown for *Only the Lonely*. Sinatra, moreover, played a terrifying Thompson figure in *Suddenly* (1954), the psychopathic killer and failed presidential assassin John Baron, a heap of anxious bravado. He was Major Bennett Marco, a disintegrating Korean War vet in *The Manchurian Candidate* (1962), another presidential assassination film that Dylan thought enough of to redraw a key scene for inclusion in *Mondo Scripto*, a book of illustrated lyrics. (The drawing is paired with "I Want You.") In *Some Came Running* (1958), his Dave Hirsh character is a World War II vet and writer who marries a woman he doesn't love because, as he says, "I'm just tired of being lonely, that's all." In *The Man with the Golden Arm* (1955) he's junkie ex-con Frankie Machine. And for films that aren't so somber, Sinatra still looms a dark presence. In *Young at Heart* (1955), a Doris Day vehicle, his Barney Sloan, an insecure, suicidal music arranger, initially seems as out of place there as, well, a wise-cracking noir tragedian in a Doris Day vehicle. Sinatra's is the filmography a musician such as Dylan might have wished was *his*. Sinatra even made a noir musical, *Meet Danny Wilson* (1952), directed by Joseph Pevney, with Shelley Winters, Raymond Burr, and Alex Nicol. Filmed as his career was crumbling, the storyline hugs his own life: early assists from mobsters to bobbysoxer stardom, along with a creepy best friend/best girl triangle and a shootout at Wrigley Field. Stray facts, manic theories, and well-told lies. Dylan sings three of the songs Danny Wilson performs: "How Deep Is the Ocean?," "That Old Black Magic," and "She's Funny That Way" (as "He's Funny that Way" on *Universal Love*). The year after *Meet Danny Wilson*, Sinatra would be cast as Private Angelo Maggio in *From Here to Eternity*, the onset of his many comebacks.

During his talk with Bill Flanagan on bobdylan.com, Dylan situated the Great American Songbook as hard-edged and desperate, not at all a nostalgic moon-June frolic. "These songs are cold and clear-sighted, there is a direct realism in them," he argued. "I hadn't realized how much of the essence of life is in them—the human condition. . . . These songs are some of the most heartbreaking stuff on record and I wanted to do them justice." Particularly for *Shadows in the Night* and *Triplicate*, but also on *Fallen Angels*, he is pulled to Sinatra songs that reenact miniature noir scenarios—loss, infatuation, ruin, regret, projection, and solitude. On *Shadows in the Night*: "I'm a Fool to Want You," "The Night We Called It a Day," "Autumn Leaves," "Full Moon and Empty Arms," "What'll I Do," and "Where Are You?" On *Fallen Angels*: "Maybe You'll Be There," and "Melancholy Mood." On *Triplicate*: "I Could Have Told You," "Once Upon a Time," "Stormy Weather," "This Nearly Was Mine," "It Gets Lonely Early," "But Beautiful," "Here's That Rainy Day," and "Why Was I Born?" Over and over, the singer is alone, baffled and alone. Love whether glorious—"Some Enchanted Evening"—or catastrophic—"Melancholy Mood"—or some slippery median zone—"That Old Black

Magic"—oozes as an addiction, mysterious, troubling, but irresistible, as though a word from Eros made it all worthwhile. Romantic desolation declines into a spiritual vacancy, God and the imagination as one. Noir devastation here doesn't so much depend on any intricate transformations of the Sinatra originals as on Dylan listening to what the words say: *I can't believe we're parted. . . . Take me back I need you. . . . Must I go on pretending. . . . Paradise once nearly was mine. . . . Dwelling in my personal hell. . . . All I see is grief and gloom till the crack of doom. . . . So weary all the time.* "I don't see myself as covering these songs in any way," as he teased in a brief explanatory note that accompanied *Shadows in the Night.* "They've been covered enough. Buried, as a matter of fact. What me and my band are basically doing is uncovering them. Lifting them out of the grave and bringing them into the light of day."

Blues as noir; noir as blues. Dylan's selections span Sinatra's sessions with Harry James and his Orchestra in 1939, and the Tommy Dorsey Orchestra in the early 1940s; his Columbia 78s and LPs of the later 1940s and early 1950s; his 1950s Capitol LPs; and even into his early 1960s Reprise albums. Starting with *The Voice of Frank Sinatra* (1946), Sinatra's Columbia and Capitol LPs famously originated the concept album, a cohesive sequence of songs around a lyrical and musical theme. Thus, each of Dylan's five Sinatra discs is a microcosm, rather than a miscellany of stray outings. *Shadows in the Night*, as already suggested, is the most strictly noir, closest in tone to Dylan's own bleak *Time Out of Mind* and *Tempest*, but also to Sinatra's brooding heartbreak Capitol masterworks, his sources for six of the ten songs. *Fallen Angels* is musically and lyrically the most motley, shuffles and swing countering the downcast melodramas, and chases a complex vision of the transformative powers of love as redemptive fantasy and mournful chastening. *Triplicat*e is the most systematic, the most designed, and each of the three CDs carries a subtitle—*'Til the Sun Goes Down*; *Devil Dolls*; and *Comin' Home Late.* Each CD is built around a key song. For *'Til the Sun Goes Down* that song is "This Nearly Was Mine," and the disc tracks instances of paradises lost. For *Devil Dolls* the song is "Imagination," and the disc probes vanities of human wishes through songs about projected futures, lost futures, dreaded futures. For *Comin' Home Late*, the song is "Sentimental Journey," and this final CD is hopeful, verging on reconciled, verging on resolved, yet the tardy homecomings are full of troubled memories and ghosts. Dylan's 1960s songs found renown for the hard questions they posed, yet many of the Great American Songbook standards he takes on comprise nothing but unanswerables: "Where Are You?" "Where Is the One?" "What'll I Do?" "How Deep Is the Ocean?" "Why Was I Born?"

For all that, though, Dylan likely turned to Sinatra to remedy issues in his own voice, much as he had back in the early 1990s with the folk, country, and blues songs on *Good as I Been to You* and *World Gone Wrong.* During the years after *Modern Times* and *Tempest*, his vocals calcified into a rough bark. This enhanced the ferocity of "Pay in Blood" and "Long and Wasted Years," yet overall tended live to bulldoze nuance. Perhaps as tactical compensation he'd elevate his pitch at the conclusion of phrases such that anything might now sound as if he were pressing a query—"Don't think TWICE? It's all RIGHT?" Fifty-plus Sinatra songs were an intensive discipline for a singer in his mid-seventies, and over on the other side his vocal chords emerged responsive and flexible. His voice cracked a bit on "I Guess I'll Have to Change My Plans" and "September of My Years," but his engagement of the lyrics was surprisingly convincing, surprisingly beautiful, and as he parried to Flanagan, "My voice cracking here or there wouldn't bother me, bum notes or wrong chords would bother me more."

Still, there's an intriguing contrast, though, if you put his Sinatra cycle close by his nineties covers. On *Good as I Been to You*, and particularly on *World Gone Wrong,* Dylan was resolute to affirm the creators as songwriters, as artists, and as Modernists, "all Shakespeares." Yet for the songwriters trailing Sinatra, he downplays their individual roles in the music he's excavating and celebrating. On *Triplicate*, for instance, there aren't writing credits for the thirty songs, the artisans and technicians silent, inherent, apparitions. Contemporary recordings of standards, including by such astute and diverse singers as Willie Nelson, Bryan Ferry, Joni

Mitchell, Harry Nilsson, Sinead O'Connor, Amy Winehouse, and Diana Krall, accent virtuosity: songwriting wizardry, interpretive panache, vocal bravura. Dylan instead isn't flaunting anything, at least anything personal—even swaggers he might have by rights indulged, his latest new voice, or his intelligence over a lyric, and all these overlooked song craftsmen. As he sings on *Triplicate*, "You got no cause for braggin' / When your barn needs mendin' / And your lawn needs mowin'." His insight into the songs is at once modest and far grander. For someone growing up around the middle of the twentieth century, Dylan's Sinatra sets suggest, the Great American Songbook is a primeval circulatory system, our emotional and metaphysical collective unconscious, and the language for better and worse of our interior lives—for love, certainly, and sex, but also for all those daily pressures of reality he designated to Love and Flanagan as "realism." Describing his Sinatra versions to Love, he said, "It's almost like folk music in a way." And to Flanagan: "You start out wondering why you bought those blue pajamas and later you're wondering why you were born. You go from the foolishly absurd to the deadly serious and you've passed through the gaudy and the nasty along the way. You get to the edge and you're played out and you wonder where's the good news? Isn't there supposed to be good news?"

All the possibilities in the middle of the story, America's, our own. Dylan's COVID lockdown concert film, *Shadow Kingdom*, is the inverse of his Sinatra sets. There he circles his own early songs as though they were bygone standards, and as how a vintage hipster such as Sinatra might cover them. *Shadow Kingdom* also is only questions. Who's playing these songs? Where are we? And maybe memories and ghosts, too. During "I'll Be Your Baby Tonight," could that be Mildred Bailey? Isn't that Billie Holiday?

Where's Frank? On *Shadows in the Night*, *Fallen Angels*, and *Triplicate*, Dylan can't always do Sinatra's transitions and modulations, and he plays against Sinatra's smoothness and ease so we can experience the songs again. I don't so much hear Sinatra in the singing as across the arrangements. No strings, no piano, brushed snare drum, guitars, bass, pedal steel, Dylan's touring quintet is virtually an Oulipo action: How small can a big band get? Even with the occasional horns. Yet he records all the now rare song intros, and they recreate the extended bandstand instrumental passages along the way. "The original arrangements were for up to 30 pieces," Dylan told Love. "What we had to do was fundamentally get to the bottom of what makes these songs alive."

Mildred Bailey and Billie Holiday—of course—shared a producer: John Hammond, the Columbia Records executive who would go on to sign and produce Bob Dylan. Accounts differ, but according to some it was in fact Bailey who urged Hammond to catch Holiday at Monette Moore's new speakeasy at 148 West 133rd Street in Harlem where *Shadow Kingdom* is—and isn't—set, that February 1933 night he "discovered" her.

But that was once upon a time, as Dylan sang on his Sinatra sets, *once upon a time very long ago.*

T

. . . OPENED / BEFORE MY TIME . . .

Trial runs, false starts. For someone whose street rep is for spontaneity and for making himself up as he rolls, the secret magic word for Dylan's operations since 1991 was patience. The surprise isn't so much his ongoing high-wire improvisations. (Just this week in Japan, as I write this, he ventured to play a Grateful Dead song, "Brokedown Palace," over two concerts, before getting the words right on a third try in Nagoya. "I thought I knew this song," he admitted to the crowd after his initial Tokyo go.) The surprise is how someone so seemingly impulsive can always take a distant view: many decisions, much work framed ahead for years, maybe decades. "Read Ovid," his to-do note from the early 1990s ran, long before *Modern Times*. (See chapter L.)

Patience. I don't so much mean such crucial circumstances as his seven years of touring between original songs—*Under the Red Sky* to *Time Out of Mind*—when night after night on stage after stage he struggled to reinvent his art, dubious, confident, or indifferent about any specific creative consequences, though there was plainly lots of that kind of patience, too. (See chapter D.) I also don't so much mean the multiple pencil drafts and studio outtakes for his late-twentieth- and twenty-first-century songs in his Tulsa archive, patient attention for a songwriter once notorious for composing as fast as he could type. (See chapter Y.) I mean—for instance—circumstances like this: in 1985, some sixteen years prior to his lyrics for *"Love And Theft"* (see chapter G), Dylan created songs on *Empire Burlesque* rooted in film dialogue, over sixty films in all, a gaggle of them film noirs (see chapter K and chapter S), anticipating not only *"Love And Theft,"* but also *Modern Times* (see chapter L), *Tempest* (see chapter O), *Chronicles* (see chapter I), *Masked and Anonymous* (see chapter H), and even his paintings that draw on noir stills and screen shots (see chapter K). For decades, right from the outset of the 1960s, Dylan had deflected vestiges of folk, country, and blues into his songs—so why not, as an experiment, expand that to movies? Then, in the twenty-first century, why not intensify his trial run with movies still further into books, poems, novels, and histories? Designs. Orderings of experience. Tricks of the teller.

Once there was only—or so it appeared—inspiration; now along with inspiration there is deliberation, craft, sleight of hand. Just as vital—but patient—forms of inspiration. "You can't do something forever," Dylan all but shrugged to Ed Bradley on *60 Minutes*. "I did it once, and I can do other things now." (See chapter C.) His 1963 poem, "Yes, I am a thief of thoughts," from "11 Outlined Epitaphs," was also an oblique trial run for his twenty-first century art: "I have built an' rebuilt / upon what is waitin' / on what has been opened / before my time / a word, a tune, a story, a line." (See chapter I.)

A few more trial runs, false starts, across his late performing and writing:

- On March 11, 1987, Dylan performed "Soon" at the Gershwin Gala in Brooklyn, New York, his rendition on acoustic guitar and harmonica one of his deftest live recitals of that decade, and in retrospect an obvious trial run for his ruminations on the Great American Songbook in *Shadows in the Night* (2015), *Fallen Angels* (2016), and *Triplicate* (2017). (See chapter S.)
- Dylan's 1989 album, *Oh Mercy*, could be viewed as a trial run for *Time Out of Mind*, as each represented a career revival produced by Daniel

Lanois. Yet if so, *Oh Mercy* is a trial run that soon proved a false start when he followed this comeback record with a rearguard slide, *Under the Red Sky*, in 1990. (See chapter E.)

- Dylan executed an instrumental rendition of Dan Emmett's "Dixie" at the Beacon Theatre in New York City on October 16 and 18, 1990; again in Charlotte, North Carolina, on October 31; and at least once more in Amherst, Massachusetts, on May 12, 1991. Years later, he would repurpose further instances of Emmett's Confederate minstrelsy on *"Love And Theft"* in 2001 (See chapter G), and then perform "Dixie" itself in *Masked and Anonymous*, his film about the next American Civil War, in 2003 (See chapter H).
- Dylan's tours with Tom Petty and the Heartbreakers (1986–1987), the Grateful Dead (1987), and G. E. Smith (1988–1990) were false starts towards his finally organizing his own band in 1991. (See chapter D.)
- Beginning on February 8, 1991, in London, Dylan sporadically abandoned guitar for electric piano during his sometimes fickle European and American concerts that year, the year of his desperate "so defiled in this world" confession at the Grammys. From inside the shambles, he must have marveled at the musical transformation, including a powerful "Shooting Star" the next night at the Hammersmith Odeon, another trial run, as a decade down the line, during his fall 2002 tour, he near-permanently shifted to keyboards, with only rare and incidental guitar. (See chapter P.)
- His four-hour, fifty-song show at Toad's Place in New Haven on January 12, 1990, and his performances at Supper Club in New York City on November 16 and 17, 1993, were trial runs and false starts for his celebrated MTV Unplugged appearance, recorded at Sony Music Studios on November 17 and 18, 1994. (See chapter D.)
- In June of 1992, Dylan developed an album's worth of still mostly unreleased covers with David Bromberg at Acme Studios in Chicago, a false start towards *Good as I Been to You*, the covers record he started solo in July at his own Garage Studio in Malibu. (See chapter C.)
- During rehearsals for *Infidels* in April of 1983, Dylan and his studio band

tried out some Christmas carols, including "Silent Night" and "The Christmas Song (Chestnuts Roasting on an Open Fire)." Over twenty-five years later, in 2009, he would record *Christmas in the Heart*, proceeds designated for various homeless charities. "These songs are part of my life," he told Bill Flanagan, "just like folk songs." (See chapter B.)

- On November 4, 1995, during a tour stop in Austin, Texas, Dylan introduced local guitarist Charlie Sexton, boasting, "We're gonna have one of Austin's finest guitar players sitting in with us right now." Sexton would also play guitar with Dylan at two future Austin shows in the fall of 1996, those casual guest appearances all a trial run for his joining the band in 1999; and the Charlie Sexton/Larry Campbell guitar combination would then spur Dylan's strongest backing band. (See chapter J.)
- Among his drafts for "High Water (For Charley Patton)" on *"Love And Theft"* (2001) are multiple variations of a verse about Mary Shelley's *Frankenstein*. In one: "Dr. Frankenstein still up there at his castle on the hill / They say he's comin' down today, but I don't think he will." In another: "Doctor Frankenstein still up there in his castle on the hill / The monster he created he just know how to kill." In another still: "The butcher in his killing clothes / Looking for a hog to kill / Dr. Frankenstein still up there / At his castle on the hill / Like a nightmare up there / High water everywhere." Was "My Own Version of You," on *Rough and Rowdy Ways*, already in Dylan's sights? (See chapter A.)
- On February 6, 2015, Dylan accepted the MusiCares Person of the Year Award in Los Angeles. Introduced at the ceremony in the West Hall of the Convention Center by former president Jimmy Carter, he surprised the music industry audience by delivering from notes a detailed account of the traditional origins of his songs. His forty-minute speech that night might be judged a trial run for his Nobel Lecture of 2016—except that MusiCares is actually the superior talk: smarter, funnier, more probing and revelatory. . . .

I get ahead of myself (see chapter U). Dylan's late patience parallels, in a way, the "then/now," "occasion/outcome" dynamic novelist Vivian

Gornick once dubbed the situation and the story. "Every work of literature has both a situation and a story," Gornick submitted. "The situation is the context or circumstance, sometimes the plot; the story is the emotional experience that preoccupies the writer: the insight, the wisdom, the thing one has come to say . . . Inevitably, it's a story of self-discovery and self-definition."

Trial runs, false starts: déjà vu all over again.

U

. . . BRING ME THE SCRIPT OF THE POET . . .

"Unless, of course, he dies first." Czesław Miłosz smiled as he said this. Back then, I wasn't at all sure why he was smiling, though pretty much the whole shebang Miłosz put forth on any subject that afternoon left me feeling like I had failed a test, or several. Not that he was mean or condescending. He was, far from it, almost fiercely gracious, present, kind.

This was the spring of 1999. I was a visiting poet at Berkeley that semester, the Holloway Lecturer in Residence (as the fellowship for young and emerging poets is officially dubbed), on the recommendation of Thom Gunn. Miłosz had officially retired decades earlier, shortly before he was awarded the Nobel Prize in Literature in 1980, and he still divided his time between Berkeley and Krakow, teaching occasional seminars. I was introduced to him by Gunn and Robert Hass at some English department social event, and he cordially invited me to lunch. We were at Chez Panisse, the Alice Waters restaurant that served as an informal Berkeley cafeteria, at least for the writers and art historians I was meeting. At that lunch, which wouldn't ever be repeated, during a silence after my shy small talk in response to his questions about what I was reading, who were my favorite poets, and my teaching at the New School in New York

City, I asked him about something a mutual friend had told me. I heard Miłosz was telling people that based on what he was *gleaning from Stockholm* that Bob Dylan was in serious contention for a Nobel Prize. He sighed, as though the question was another remark of mine that faintly disappointed him, yet suddenly Miłosz was impassioned. "Yes, yes," he retorted, "all those other writers"—as I remember, he opened with Philip Roth, but also mentioned John Updike, Norman Mailer, and Joyce Carol Oates—"they all think they're going to get it, but they're wrong. Dylan is the only one I hear." He continued with the notion that the Swedish Academy doesn't think most American writers are "serious," but that Dylan is "different," and giving him the Nobel Prize would also amount to a "fuck you gesture" to contemporary American fiction. His tone suggested he shared this criticism, but I didn't press him, as I imagined that absent seriousness also encircled me, though I didn't write fiction, our American prattle no end beyond itself. "They won't give it to him now," Miłosz concluded. "He's too young. But he'll get it." He paused. "Unless, of course, he dies first. . . ."

What kind of prophet was he? Later that spring, Dylan would turn fifty-eight. Was Miłosz's smile only his dry acknowledgment that anyone's death, his own, mine, Dylan's, is—well, arbitrary? Or was he assuming I recalled that when he received *his* Nobel Prize in Literature he was already approaching seventy, so Dylan must similarly wait his turn—wait, in fact, until he was seventy-five? Or was Miłosz anticipating the literary impact of that "fuck you gesture," and not just on *American* novelists? Among the future grumblers:

- Irvine Welsh—"An ill-conceived nostalgia award";
- Hari Kunzru—"lamest Nobel win since they gave it to Obama for not being Bush";
- Margaret Atwood—"For what? . . . These things are often political."

Yet not Salman Rushdie, who tweeted, "From Orpheus to Faiz, song & poetry have been closely linked. Dylan is a brilliant inheritor of the bardic tradition. Great choice." And not Toni Morrison, the last American Nobel laureate, from as far back as 1993, who praised Dylan as "an impressive choice."

Then Dylan, himself, at least in the guise of aging and addled rock star Billy Parker in *Hearts of Fire*: "I guess I was never one of those rock 'n' roll singers that was gonna win any Nobel Prize." That hilarious riposte (who were the other rock 'n' roll Nobel laureates?) isn't his only instance of Stockholm agnosticism prior to 2016. During a press conference in Rome in 2001, he was asked about the rumors that he was under consideration, and his reply was skeptical, thoughtful. "I've heard about that," he rejoined. "But to what company does that bring me? In the one of people like Hemingway and Steinbeck? I don't know if I fit in this category." In an interview with National Public Radio in 2004, when Steve Inskeep wondered aloud what bothered him about such vintage testimonials as "voice of your generation," Dylan generalized his resistance to awards. "Having these colossal accolades and titles, they just get in the way," he countered, "especially if someone just wants to keep it simple, write songs and play them." Still, Dylan, as far as I know, is the only beneficiary of a Nobel Prize in any of their six categories who performed in Las Vegas the night his award was announced. A video screen outside the Chelsea in the Cosmopolitan on the Las Vegas Strip congratulated him, but onstage he never acknowledged the news, except *maybe* when he picked up an electric guitar in concert for the first time in nearly four years, for "Simple Twist of Fate." To look at yourself the way one looks at unfamiliar things.

Some awards honor the recipient, some awards honor the presenters. From the outset, Dylan was mysteriously prone to awards, honors he obviously merited but honors also intended to communicate the aspirational coolness of his distinguished benefactors, starting with his first honorary doctorate in music at Princeton in 1970, and the university's tone-deaf citation: "Although he is approaching the perilous age of 30 his music remains the authentic expression of the disturbed and concerned conscience of Young America. . . ." Following his Grammy Lifetime Achievement Award in 1991, Dylan received all possible musical garlands: Grammys for

World Gone Wrong (Best Traditional Folk Album), *Time Out of Mind* (Album of the Year), *"Love And Theft"* (Best Contemporary Folk Album), *Modern Times* (Best Contemporary Folk/Americana Album), *Together Through Life* (Best Americana Album); and nominations for Best Traditional Pop Vocal Album for *Shadows in the Night*, *Fallen Angels*, and *Triplicate*. He was inducted into the Nashville Songwriters Hall of Fame, and in 2003 accepted something called the Golden Plate Award for "visionaries and achievers" from the American Academy of Achievement, with none other than Chuck Berry handing him his framed dish. Perhaps presciently, he was awarded the Polar Music Prize, founded by Stig Anderson, manager of ABBA, and sometimes styled the Nobel Prize of Music; at the gala in Stockholm, Princess Christina read the citation, King Carl XVI Gustaf presented the diploma, and Bryan Ferry performed. Movie laurels, too: a Golden Globe and an Oscar for "Things Have Changed." Even his website bobdylan.com garnered a Webby nomination in 1999.

His honors outside music and film are inevitably more striking. In 1990 Dylan was named a Commandeur dans l'Ordre des Arts et des Lettres by the French minister of culture; previous Commandeurs ranged from T. S. Eliot and Jorge Luis Borges to Stevie Wonder, Jerry Lewis (of course), and Audrey Hepburn. Dylan was among the honorees at the Kennedy Center in 1997, his cohort that year including Lauren Bacall, Charlton Heston, Jessye Norman, and Edward Villella; and he was awarded the Dorothy and Lillian Gish Prize, the fourth recipient after Frank Gehry, Ingmar Bergman, and Robert Wilson. He accepted another honorary doctorate of music in 2004, this time from St Andrews University in Scotland. In 2007, he was presented the Prince of Asturias Award for the Arts, and not only with a commemorative medallion but also a Joan Miró sculpture. Perhaps presciently, too, Dylan in 2008 received a Pulitzer Prize Special Citation "For his profound impact on popular music and American Culture, marked by lyrical compositions of extraordinary poetic power." In 2009, he was awarded a National Medal of Arts, his class spanning Maya Lin, Frank Stella, Michael Tilson Thomas, John Williams, Clint Eastwood, and once more Jessye Norman. In 2012 President Obama presented him with the Presidential Medal of Freedom, America's highest civilian honor, alongside Toni Morrison, Madeleine Albright, Dolores Huerta, John Paul Stevens, and John Glenn. And in 2013 he accepted the Legion of Honor, France's highest honor, in Paris.

Dylan was present on most of these honorific occasions—though hardly all, and tellingly he tended to avoid the explicitly literary ones, such as the Pulitzer—so the Nobel Foundation might plausibly have assumed he would attend the award ceremony on December 10, 2016, in the Stockholm Concert Hall. In his letter to the Swedish Academy, Dylan cited "pre-existing commitments," and as the Academy announced in their public statement: "That laureates decide not to come is unusual, to be sure, but not exceptional. In the recent past, several laureates have, for various reasons, been unable to come to Stockholm to receive the prize, among them Doris Lessing, Harold Pinter, and Elfriede Jelinek. The prize still belongs to them, just as it belongs to Bob Dylan." Yet as a reminder, and presumably also a warning, even a taunt, the Academy appended what reads as a tart, irritated flourish. "We look forward to Bob Dylan's Nobel Lecture, which he must give—it is the only requirement—within six months counting from December 10, 2016."

No lecture, no check. No 8 million Swedish crowns, or $930,000. Dylan submitted *The Nobel Lecture*, the official version, to the Swedish Academy just five days ahead of his June 10 deadline, recording his speech over Alan Pasqua's piano, the set up reminiscent of Jack Kerouac's 1959 appearance on *The Steve Allen Show*. As I started to say (see chapter T), Dylan delivered his Nobel Lecture two, perhaps three times. His point-blank prose picked up the conversation almost right where he stopped it at his 2001 Rome press conference. He opens:

> When I received the Nobel Prize for Literature, I got to wondering exactly how my songs related to literature. I wanted to reflect on it and see where the connection was. I'm going to try to articulate that to you. And most likely it will go in a roundabout way, but I hope what I say will be worthwhile and purposeful.

"Roundabout" designates the best of *The Nobel Lecture*, his introductory pages on seeing Buddy Holly, first listening to Lead Belly, and then his deep absorption ("You internalize it") of folk and blues, "all the vernacular . . . the devices, the techniques, the secrets, the mysteries." Yet most of the lecture really isn't roundabout enough. When Dylan turns to some crucial books he read in grammar school, *Moby-Dick*, *All Quiet on the Western Front*, and *The Odyssey*, and what he calls the "principles and sensibilities and an informed view of the world" also inside those songs, his lecture can sound like a book report: long on plot summary, and sparse on any intimate literary "connection." His repurposing of Homer on *Tempest* is far more canny and original than his droll thematic precis in *The Nobel Lecture* might indicate: "You too have had drugs dropped in your wine. You too have shared a bed with the wrong woman. . . . "

In 2004 a handwritten 1958 Hibbing High School essay by Bob Zimmerman—"Does Steinbeck Sympathize With His Characters?"—came up for auction. Why not now tell people about John Steinbeck, Woody Guthrie, and the dynamics of empathy from the vantage of his songs? Similarly, Arthur Rimbaud translations by Louise Varese, Daisy Aldan, Stephen Stepanchev, and Kenneth Koch, among others, in Angel Flores's influential *An Anthology of French Poetry from Nerval to Valery*, also from 1958, could be swapped (their dictions, their rhythms) into various early Dylan songs, such as "Chimes of Freedom," or "A Hard Rain's A-Gonna Fall." For instance, read and *listen* to their Rimbaud:

Through the furious ripping of the sea's mad tides . . .

In the wails of the tree and the sighs of the night . . .

I know skies splitting into light, whirled spouts / Of water . . .

Is it in depthless nights you sleep your exile, / A million golden birds. . . . ?

Why not now talk about that?

Dylan obviously hates repeating himself. Part of the snag in *The Nobel Lecture*, I'm guessing, is that he already had already delivered that retrospective address, touching on the legacies that informed his own creative practices, with his MusiCares speech the previous year. That night Dylan was candid, speculative, and far-reaching, as well as generous to those who had assisted him. He could go wide: "These songs of mine, they're like mystery stories, the kind that Shakespeare saw when he was growing up. I think you could trace what I do back that far. They were on the fringes then, and I think they're on the fringes now."

Yet he could also zero in on the technicalities:

> These songs didn't come out of thin air . . . It all came out of traditional music: traditional folk music, traditional rock 'n' roll, and traditional big band swing orchestra music . . . I learned lyrics from listening to folk songs . . . Sang nothing but these folk songs, and they gave me a code for everything that's fair game, that everything belongs to everyone. For three or four years all I listened to were folk standards . . . I could learn one song and sing it next in an hour if I heard it just once.

Dylan's 2016 Nobel Prize citation closely parallels Samuel Beckett's in 1969. Here's Beckett's: "for his writing, which—in new forms for the novel and drama—in the destitution of modern man acquires its elevation." Here's Dylan's: ". . . for having created new poetic expressions within the great American song tradition." *New* forms, *new* expressions. Beckett, too, fled in the days and weeks after the announcement of his Nobel Prize, and when Swedish television requested an interview he reluctantly assented, but only with the stipulation that he couldn't be asked questions, and the clip aired silent. The author of *Molloy* and *Waiting for Godot* was "a real big Dylan fan," according to D. A. Pennebaker—the director of *Dont Look Back*, who also filmed a documentary about Beckett's *Rockaby*. "Samuel Beckett, before he died, asked me for a script of *Dont Look Back*," Pennebaker told Ron Rosenbaum. "Beckett never referred to Dylan by name. He always called him 'the Poet.' He'd say, 'Could you bring me the script of the Poet.' "

The mention of Beckett stirs the question of Dylan's peers. Who are they? Can you imagine a Nobel Prize for, say, Paul McCartney? Mick Jagger? Joni Mitchell? Bruce Springsteen? The scale? Sweep? Historical and literary reach? Ardent critics and biographers who recurrently compare Dylan to Homer, Virgil, Dante, and Shakespeare don't do him any favors. To quote Ovid isn't strictly to be Ovid, and Dylan's supposed veneration of the classical world allows for the bitter recognition that Greece and Rome were also Southern slave civilizations with violent designs on empire, and doleful rearview mirrors of America's ongoing civil tumult. And note that when Dylan summons Shakespeare in proximity to his own songs, he cites the mystery and morality dramas the young Bard probably experienced in Coventry, such as *Everyman* and *Mankind*, and not *Hamlet* or *King Lear*.

But *peers*. Across my lifetime I would want to mention as his peers the poets I grew up on, such as Robert Lowell and the personal and historical revolutions for American poetry in his *Life Studies* (1959) and sonnet books, *Notebook* (1969 and 1970) and *History* (1973); and Elizabeth Bishop, for the oblique, sometimes hallucinatory autobiography and internalized violences of *Geography III* (1976). Allen Ginsberg, inescapably, for *Howl* (1956) and *Kaddish* (1961). James Merrill, for *The Changing Light at Sandover* (1976–1980), and notably the spirits and mediums of the first volume of that Ouija board trilogy, "The Book of Ephraim," whose sly abecedarium (and much more) underpins every chapter of this Bob Dylan memory book. The John Ashbery of *Three Poems* (1972), *Self-Portrait in a Convex Mirror* (1975), *A Wave* (1984), and *Flow Chart* (1991). Amiri Baraka, for his poems, such as *Preface to a Twenty Volume Suicide Note* (1961), his plays, such as *Dutchman* (1964), and his prose meditations, such as *Blues People* (1963) and *Black Music* (1968).

Closer in age to Dylan is Toni Morrison, of course: her novels, *The Bluest Eye* (1970), *Sula* (1973), *Song of Solomon* (1977), *Tar Baby* (1981), *Beloved* (1987), and *Jazz* (1992), as well as her nonfiction, *Playing in the Dark: Whiteness and the Literary Imagination* (1993), and her early collaged compendium, *The Black Book* (1974). As I write this, an exhibition about Morrison at the Princeton University Library, "Sites of Memory," focuses the spirited research behind her books, arguing "her creative process was a deeply archival one." And Michael Ondaatje, with *Coming Through Slaughter* (1976) and *In the Skin of the Lion* (1987). In roughly Dylan's generation, there's Susan Howe, and her poems and essays of montage scholarship, especially *My Emily Dickinson* (1985), which reanimates the poet through her reading, Jonathan Edwards, Mary Rowlandson, Shakespeare's history plays, captivity narratives, Thomas Wentworth Higginson, and Emily Brontë. "Forcing, abbreviating, pushing, padding, subtracting, riddling, interrogating, rewriting, she pulled text from text," as Howe evokes *her* Dickinson. Sound familiar? Then, there's Frank Bidart, and *Desire* (1997), his diverse and comprehensive lyric anatomy of desire in the world, "fate embedded in the lineaments of desire," where virtually every line of the long poem, "The Second Hour of the Night," adapts, translates, quotes, paraphrases, or otherwise recasts another written work: Ovid, Plotinus, Shakespeare, Keats, and Marcus Aurelius, but also John Wayne Gacy and a Dinu Lipatti LP liner note. When Bidart writes, "We fill pre-existing forms, and when/ we fill them, change them and are changed," he could be speaking for Dylan, too.

Perhaps the most exciting advance of contemporary poetry is the surprise merging of once rival, even incompatible traditions: confessional poetry, experimental poetry, and political poetry. Yet Dylan was already there, at least by *"Love And Theft."* Some recent books you could place in charged conversation with *"Love And Theft"* might include Jen Bervin's *Nets* (2003) and *Silk Poems* (2017), also her exhibitions, *Shift Rotate Reflect* (2020) and *Source* (2023); Claudia Rankine's *Don't Let Me Be Lonely* (2004) and *Citizen: An American Lyric* (2014); Maggie Nelson's *Bluets* (2009), and *The Argonauts* (2015); Fred Moten's *The Little Edges* (2015); Solmaz Sharif's *Look* (2016); Tyehimba Jess's *Olio* (2016); John Keene's *Counternarratives* (2016) and *Punks* (2022); Layli Long Soldier's *Whereas* (2017); Jos Charles's *feeld* (2018); Terrence Hayes's *American Sonnets for My Past and Future Assassins* (2019); Tina Chang's *Hybrida* (2019); Jericho Brown's *The Tradition* (2019); Natalie Diaz's *Postcolonial Love* (2020); Kaveh Akbar's *Pilgrim Bell* (2021); Monica Youn's *From From* (2023); Diane Seuss's *Modern Poetry* (2024); Anne

Carson's *Wrong Norma* (2024); Victoria Chang's *With My Back to the World* (2024); and Reginald Dwayne Betts's *Doggerel* (2025).

As I've suggested across this book, I believe Dylan's third and ultimate Nobel Prize Lecture is *Rough and Rowdy Ways*, every song touching on his art and his life in his art. Perhaps he even started writing the album that April night in 2017 when—in a private ceremony at a "secret location" prior to a concert in Stockholm—he finally accepted his Nobel Prize. "Spirits were high," Sara Danius, the Swedish Academy's permanent secretary, later recounted. "Champagne was had. Quite a bit of time was spent looking closely at the gold medal, in particular the beautifully crafted back, an image of a young man sitting under a laurel tree who listens to the Muse."

Classical ghost writing. A scribe sits by, and invisible guests come and go. "Mother of Muses sing for me," as Dylan implores Mnemosyne, the goddess of memory, on *Rough and Rowdy Ways*. "Take me to the river and release your charms . . . I'm travelin' light, and I'm slow coming home."

V

. . . THE SAME LITTLE BOY . . .

Venice. The Grand Canal. The Palazzo. Chandeliers. Mirrors on mirrors down a long hallway.

An angel in silk panties and matching bra spirals across a table, as if in anticipation, her movements, her wings, and the cloth under her metallic heels vibrating to the song that simultaneously galvanizes and enervates the scene. An older man with a pencil mustache and a stare, his features suffused in blue light, strolls past, and tosses the black Stetson he's holding. When next we see the angel, as the song twists on—"I'm sick of love / I wish I'd never met you"—she's now wearing his hat. "Just don't know what to do / I'd give anything to be with you."

In 2004, Dominique Issermann shot *Angels in Venice*, a terse film of desire and memory, with Bob Dylan and Adriana Lima. Choreographed to "Love Sick" from *Time Out of Mind*, the film was contemplated as an ad for Victoria's Secret. Desire and memory? My Venetian language here is Proust's: "But all of a sudden the scene changed; it was the memory, no longer of old impressions but of an old desire, only recently awakened by a Fortuny gown in blue and gold, that spread before me another spring, a spring not leafy at all but on the contrary suddenly stripped of its trees and flowers by the name I had just murmured to myself: 'Venice.' " Dylan's Victoria Secret ad, though, probably cants closer to Thomas Mann's *Death in Venice*: "Yes, this was Venice, this the fair frailty that fawned and that betrayed, half fairy-tale, half snare; the city in whose stagnating air . . . musicians were moved to accords so weirdly lulling and lascivious." As far back as 1965, Dylan joked that the only commercial interest he might be tempted to sell out to was "ladies' garments." *Angels in Venice* is erotic, and a little creepy. So too, of course, are Proust and Mann.

Dylan's body, his look, even his clothes, are among the surest indicators of his art, his innovations as well as his lapses. In the 1960s that body, that look, and those clothes convened entire musical eras for him, and ultimately for America and Europe, that might last a year, a few months, a day or two, then disappear to stick around forever, as no longer does anything actually go away. A man of the moment, inventing his moment. Another batch of images: John Cohen's 1962 photograph of Bob Dylan performing on an oversized acoustic guitar atop Cohen's East Village apartment building in a work shirt and Huck Finn cap; Richard Avedon's 1963 photograph of Bob Dylan in a plaid flannel shirt, jeans, and work boots, with his weather-beaten guitar case at his feet, the East River and the Metro-North Bridge as backdrops; Don Hunstein's 1963 photograph of Bob Dylan in a camel corduroy bomber jacket with a sherpa collar huddling with Suze Rotolo at the snowy intersection of West Fourth Street and Jones, for the cover of *The Freewheelin' Bob Dylan*; Avedon's 1965 photograph of Bob Dylan strolling on the paving stones of Central Park in a full-length black belted raincoat and mod boots; Liza Law's 1966 photograph of Bob Dylan in Wayfarers, and a polka-dot shirt just purchased at Fred Segal in Hollywood; Jerry Schatzberg's 1966 photograph of a blurry and bleary Bob Dylan in a suede jacket and checkered scarf, leaning against a brick building on New York's West Side for the cover of *Blonde on Blonde*; Ken Regan's 1975 photograph of Bob Dylan in carnivalesque silk scarves and a feathered hat for *The Rolling Thunder Revue.*

Then, turn again, his lost years, gloom coupled with artifice. Once Dylan ceased anticipating and transmitting the spirit of the age, he occasionally chased the latest as though desolate to recall where he had left behind something crucial. His faux *Saturday Night Fever* tight white vests and shiny trousers of 1978. Those flash shirts, and muscle shirts, a leather vest and no shirt, gloves, dangly earrings, and perfect bouffant curls during the 1980s: someone trying hard not to be Bob Dylan. It got worse. In 1990 Allen Ginsberg photographed him sad and puffy in hipster finery around Tomkins Square Park. Those shapeless check sport jackets of 1991—ready for another round of golf, anyone? Finally, he just hid out on stage under random hats and a bulky hoodie.

Over the decades, then, Dylan's succession of bodies, looks, and clothes, prophetic or miserable, somehow also was his art, his career, and even this book, all in miniature. Whether mirror, or engine, spookily accurate: the secret world of the body. Inevitably his reinvention after 1991 coincided with another shift in clothes, look, and body, the shift I'll call—and have been calling "timeless." The body's resurrection. Elegance aslant eras, and aslant music styles. Some '20s, some '50s. A little Western, a little early rock 'n' roll, a little noir, a little vaudeville, a little commedia dell'arte. Formal, but relaxed formal. Natty frocks and jackets, dress shoes or dress boots, and sometimes a Stetson with a gambler-style flat crown. Yet nothing so specific that you can pin him down. Streamlined from conception. Like his new writing and his new music, Dylan's stage appearance after 1991 is another brilliant collage that summons ghosts of singers and players across the nineteenth and twentieth centuries, the body as temple, as haunted house.

In movies, Dylan can loom a self-conscious and awkward actor. But on stage, inhabiting a lyric not only through his vocals but also through his mouth, his eyes, the slant of his head, and the pitch of his shoulders, the empathy—the embodiment, his disappearance—is total. Again, as he wrote of Perry Como in *The Philosophy of Modern Song*, "When he stood and sang, he owned the song and he shared it and we believed every single word." Similarly, Dylan's impromptu dance steps, if that's what they are, his leg shakes, back bends, and dips, or his advances and his retreats around a microphone: everyone calls them Chaplinesque, and everyone is right.

For his Hibbing High senior yearbook, where Robert Zimmerman identified his life ambition "to join Little Richard," notice the white, straight 1950s rock 'n' rollers he didn't name, from Elvis and Buddy and Jerry Lee to Bill Haley, Wayne Cochran, Ricky Nelson, and the Everly Brothers. His yearbook aspiration was Black, and also queer. His earliest song of which a recording exists is "Hey Little Richard" from 1958, and after Little Richard died on May 9, 2020, Dylan drafted and circulated a tender memorial:

> I just heard the news about Little Richard and I'm so grieved. He was my shining star and guiding light when I was only a little boy. His was the original spirit that moved me to do everything I would do. . . .
>
> In his presence he was always the same Little Richard that I first heard and was awed by growing up and I was always the same little boy. Of course he'll live forever. But it's like part of your life is gone.

His reflections on his own complex associations with Blackness, particularly earlier American Black musicians, went into *"Love And Theft."* Yet queerness is the motor that drives his study of Little Richard's "Tutti Frutti" in *The Philosophy of Modern Song*:

> Little Richard is the master of the double-entendre. "Tutti Frutti" is a good example. A fruit, a male homosexual, and "tutti frutti" is "all fruit." It's also a sugary ice cream. A gal named Sue and a gal named Daisy and they're both transvestites. Did you ever see Elvis singing "Tutti Frutti" on Ed Sullivan? Does he know what he's singing about? Do you think Ed Sullivan knows? Do you think they both know? Of all the people who sang "Tutti Frutti," Pat Boone was probably the only one who knew what he was singing about. And Pat knows about speaking in tongues as well.
>
> There's a lot of people in Little Richard's songs. All the stereotypes: Uncle John, Long Tall Sally, Mary and Jenny, Daisy, Sue, and Melinda. They are all slipping by in the shady world of sex and dreams and giving you a run for your money.

Some of Dylan's other decisive influences were queer: Arthur Rimbaud, Paul Clayton, Allen Ginsberg, James Baldwin. Probably as homage to Rimbaud, Dylan told biographer Robert Shelton that upon his arrival in New York he worked as a hustler. "Sometimes we would make one hundred a night, really, from four in the afternoon until three or four in the morning. . . . Cats would pick us up and chicks would pick us up. And we would do anything you wanted, as long as it was paid. . . . I almost got killed. . . . I didn't come down to the Village until two months later. Nobody knew I had been hustling uptown."

Dylan's body and mien in 1966 are almost startlingly androgynous, a quality director Todd Haynes accented when he cast Cate Blanchett as Jude Quinn, one of his six Bob Dylans in *I'm Not There.* (Of his hair that year, Dylan said to Bill Flanagan, "I was trying to look like Little Richard, my version of Little Richard.") In 1966 he also told Shelton, "Sex and love have nothing to do with female and male. It is just whatever two souls happen to be. It could be male or female, and it might not be male or female. It might be female and female, and it might be male and male." And in 1984, when another interviewer, Kurt Loder, asked Dylan, "doesn't the Bible say that homosexuality is an abomination?" he recoiled. "That's no reason for me to condemn anybody . . . It certainly doesn't matter to me."

Queer subtexts infuse his lyrics. For *Blood on the Tracks,* when encapsulating his past "relationships" and "situations" on "You're Gonna Make Me Lonesome When You Go," Dylan wittily rallies essential nineteenth-century queer icons: "Mine have been like Verlaine's and Rimbaud's." (Paul Verlaine also famously shot Rimbaud in the wrist at a Brussels hotel in 1873.) On *Rough and Rowdy Ways*, the Whitmanesque "I Contain Multitudes" is casually queer, punning on queens ("All the old queens, from all my past lives") and invoking the Bowie anthem, "All the Young Dudes."

During the first days of 2024 Pride Month, more than 540 anti-LGBTQ+ bills were introduced in state legislatures, with at least 220 bills specifically targeting transgender and non-binary people. Among the most frequently "challenged" books in America are Maia Kobabe's memoir *Gender Queer,* George Johnson's *All Boys Aren't Blue*, Toni Morrison's *The*

Bluest Eye, Ashley Hope Perez's *Out of Darkness*, Mike Curato's *Flamer*, Ellen Hopkins's *Tricks*, and Angie Thomas's *The Hate U Give*. Book-banning accelerated after the 2024 election. Books by Margaret Atwood, Khalid Hosseini, and Jodi Picoult. On Easter Sunday 2025, Trump's secretary of defense Pete Hegseth would post on X about the Democratic Party: "Your agenda is illegals, trans & DEI—all of which are no longer allowed @ DoD." Queerness, Blackness; often Queerness and Blackness. Homophobia, white supremacy, and an embargo on knowledge and memory.

In "Mother of Muses" on *Rough and Rowdy Ways*, Dylan sings, "I've already outlived my life by far," and the mortal body shadows his records from *Good as I Been to You* and *World Gone Wrong* on, especially after *Time Out of Mind*. He still operated in culture domains that insisted on youth, but the songs refused to forget age, decline, and death. Dylan was fifty-five when he recorded *Time Out of Mind*, and already he was "strolling through the lonely graveyard of my mind," visualizing his physical decay—"even if the flesh falls off of my face"—and his imminent passing, "Now I feel like I'm coming to the end of my way." On *"Love And Theft,"* recorded when he was sixty, he revisited sexual impotence riffs out of Bo Carter blues: "I got my hammer ringing, pretty baby, but the nails ain't goin' down." On *Modern Times* and *Tempest* his direst intimations of ultimate apocalypse were personal, wrapped inside his human mortality, "When the Deal Goes Down," "Ain't Talkin'," and "Roll on John."

The timeless body eventually is also the aged body. When he resumed touring in the fall of 2021 after the COVID lockdown, Dylan at eighty seemed frail. For the three shows I attended at the Beacon Theatre in New York, he mostly stayed on his seat behind the piano, and his tentative movements around center stage suggested balance issues. (His post on Instagram in 2022 about his use of an autopen would mention "a bad case of vertigo" that "continued into the pandemic years.") Yet his voice was powerful, even stronger than at his gorgeous last shows at the Beacon in December 2019—maybe due to the rare, extended rest? Again, I was reminded of Beckett, particularly those late plays, "Not I," "That Time," and "What Where," where nothing remains of the body but a head, or a mouth, and a voice.

Inside my own aging, mortal body, little works as it once did, yet you learn to run with and around that internal not-working. The most visible exterior sign of the surgeries is a bulge in my abdomen the shape of a baseball that won't recede, an "incisional hernia," apparently among the most common "complications" of my specific procedures, that expanded as I regained some of the pounds I lost to my illness. There's a lot of inevitable scarring, too; still, shirts cover that. During discussions at a recent follow-up with my doctors, one reason for the hernia suddenly clarified: I wasn't expected to live as long as I have after the surgeries. Why bother at the end of an intricate fourteen-hour operation with a cosmetic fine point that won't trouble all that many patients?

Shakespeare in *Richard II* linked the human body to the body politic. Donne in his "Holy Sonnets" linked the human body to the spheres, the zodiac. Writing at age eighty-one about the Who's "My Generation" for *The Philosophy of Modern Song*, Dylan wasn't so allegorical, or cosmic, more (as he says there) "Straight talk, eyeball to eyeball." As he slid his voice on the page into the voice of Pete Townsend's song:

> You're hoping to croak before senility sets in. You don't want to be ancient or decrepit, no thank you. I'll kick the bucket before that happens. You're looking at the world mortified by the hopelessness of it all.
>
> In reality, you're an eighty-year-old man, being wheeled around in a home for the elderly, and the nurses are getting on your nerves. . . .

W

. . . MAGIC SHADOWS INTO BEING . . .

Where were we? After a nearly two-year suspension during COVID-19, Dylan resumed live shows in the fall of 2021. What distinguished this tour from all prior outings was that it appeared to carry an expiration date: "Bob Dylan '*Rough and Rowdy Ways* World Wide Tour' / 2021–2024." Weird. Was this, then, his spoof on the notion of a Never Ending Tour? Or, still weirder, his . . . farewell? Dylan would turn eighty-three in May 2024. It *almost* seemed to fit. But would anyone even approximating his renown conclude six decades of public performances without a glorious victory lap of vast arenas? But—instead—a multiyear circuit of small and mid-size halls in favorite cities across America, Asia, and Europe, and, moreover, a set list where ultimately more than half the songs came from his most recent albums? No hits, few obvious classics, and one of the rare tunes that perhaps hued closest to a Dylan standard, "To Be Alone with You" from *Nashville Skyline*, now rewritten so that it apparently enlisted the voice of a psycho killer?

Maybe. Starting in Milwaukee on November 2, amid a mirage of such claims and counterclaims, Dylan took *Rough and Rowdy Ways*, his rogue Nobel Lecture, on the road for a proposed three years. Two hundred thirty-one such shows in all. America in November and December of 2021; March, April, May, and June of 2022; and October, November, and December of 2023. Europe in September, October, and November of 2022; and June and July of 2023. Japan in April of 2023. Finally, the American South in March and April of 2024, and back to Europe for the fall. (During the summer of 2024 Dylan would join the Outlaw Music Festival Tour, alongside Willie Nelson, Robert Plant and Alison Krauss, John Mellencamp, Billy Strings, Brittney Spencer, Celisse, and Southern Avenue, but with a very different, *almost* retrospective set list, galvanized by surprise, beautiful covers—Chuck Berry, Hank Williams, Dewayne Blackwell, Robert Hunter, and Jerry Garcia.)

From the vantage of the mutually reflecting and contrasting songs of *Rough and Rowdy Ways*, Dylan could in his live shows of 2021–2024 circle his musical and literary traditions. He could address his audience for "I've Made Up My Mind to Give Myself to You." He could engage specific aspects of his craft—his multiplicity and artistic ventriloquism for "I Contain Multitudes," and his innovative collages for "My Own Version of You." For "Mother of Muses" he could inscribe his epic ambitions by invoking Calliope, and signal the history behind his songs, notably slavery and the Civil War, for "I Contain Multitudes," "My Own Version of You," and "Crossing the Rubicon." In the Trump era he could summon earlier American presidents, Lincoln for "I Contain Multitudes," McKinley, Truman, and Nixon for "Key West (Philosopher Pirate)," and Kennedy for "Murder Most Foul," which so far he has never performed live, and throughout track the role of crime in empire. He could press the spiritual dimensions of his art, too. Manifold religions: Jewish, Christian, Native American, Hindu, Egyptian, Zen.

But *Rough and Rowdy Ways* is neither reductive autobiography nor rote reportage. All here is fluid, multi-angled, and alert to oppositions and contradictions. That spiritual impulse won't stop Dylan from viewing religion as salacious showbiz in "Goodbye Jimmy Reed." "My Own Version of You" is both horror and love story. Forgiveness vies with and transforms into vengeance for "False Prophet," "I Contain Multitudes," and "Goodbye Jimmy Reed." His are "songs of love" and "songs of betrayal." His "heart is at rest" and his "soul is distressed," his "mind is at war." Dylan's stance on time is volatile and intricate. Songs obsess over change, the irrevocable, death, and mortality, yet as he sings, "Everything's flowin' all at the same time." He allegorizes the ancient worlds of Greece, Rome, and the Bible, such that Julius Caesar will merge with Christ, the Augustan Empire meld into contemporary America, and the end of any life insinuate apocalypse. He stages his past in "Crossing the Rubicon" as a succession of decisive junctures of no return, but the inspirational pivot of "Mother of Muses" is Mnemosyne, or memory, a looping back.

Still, *Rough and Rowdy Ways* isn't only a celebration of what he did, and how he did it. Dylan also reckons the costs, sacrifices, and losses, the pains in his pleasures. The tacit boast inside "I Contain Multitudes" assesses the price of his "songs of experience" and the deprivations of living such a fragmented mode. Whatever else "My Own Version of You" encompasses, the spur is a fear of death, and moreover there Dylan of course reclaims Alfred Nobel's stated criterion for his annual awards—"the greatest benefit on mankind"—as the cry of a mad scientist desperate for his own immortality. "I've Made Up My Mind to Give Myself to You" in turn glances at the isolation and self-sacrifice of yielding to any audience. Similarly, that nourishing, even buoyant sensation of all times simultaneously present-time that the record holds dear. The recurrent underworlds—Homer, Virgil, Ephesians, Dante, *The Egyptian Book of the Dead*—slant the perspective as poised between life and death. And in concert Dylan only reinforced those liminal underworld vistas with a stage set derived from *Shadow Kingdom*, along with the songs he chose from albums other than *Rough and Rowdy Ways*.

His rogue Nobel Lecture live was thus embedded inside the conceptual frame of *Shadow Kingdom*. Of the seventeen songs he initially performed most nights on the "*Rough and Rowdy Ways* World Wide Tour," first eight, then nine of the songs originated in *Rough and Rowdy Ways*. (During the inaugural leg, he included "Early Roman Kings" from *Tempest*, but soon after Russia invaded Ukraine he swapped "Crossing the Rubicon" into its place.) Of the residual eight, five migrated directly from *Shadow*

Kingdom, "Watching the River Flow," "Most Likely You Go Your Way and I'll Go Mine," "I'll Be Your Baby Tonight," "To Be Alone with You," and "When I Paint My Masterpiece." That left a pair of songs with salient if antithetical religious arcs, "Gotta Serve Somebody" and "Every Grain of Sand." Most nights early on, too, in the fourteenth slot, there was a rotating cover, sometimes "Melancholy Mood" or "That Old Black Magic" from his Sinatra albums, but increasingly a shifting assortment of songs associated with the Grateful Dead.

Dylan's piano was the lead instrument, his reconfigured band circled around him, rapt on his every instrumental and vocal tack. This was essentially a jazz combo, sometimes a miniature big band of the '30s and '40s on the verge of inventing rockabilly, but characteristically more austere, angular, pointillistic, and redolent of Thelonious Monk. For *Chronicles*, Dylan recounted an afternoon he visited Monk at the Blue Note on West Third Street. "Just to listen—told him that I played folk music up the street. 'We all play folk music,' he said. Monk was in his own dynamic universe even when he dawdled around. Even then, he summoned magic shadows into being."

After his Sinatra recordings, and some twenty-plus months at home, Dylan's voice was clear—sharper, perhaps, than at any moment since 2012, perhaps even 2006—and he opted for an expressive Sprechstimme, half croon, half recitation. The consistent set lists of his *Rough and Rowdy Ways* tour was another Oulipo experiment: Over multiple years of the same songs night after night, what could he discover and pull out of them? A lot, as it proved, short term and long. At the Beacon a song might reconstruct and renew concert to concert. On Friday "I've Made Up My Mind to Give Myself to You" was a ravishing lilt, enlivened by his piano trills. For Saturday, he cut against that lilt with dissonant runs, and accented as well the mortal anxieties inside the lyric. On Sunday his arrangement was just as lovely as Friday's, yet mournful and elegiac, caught up in the compromises and wastes of living for an audience, for anyone else. Or "Goodbye Jimmy Reed"—Friday was all Jerry Lee Lewis swagger, but the next night Dylan's piano rolled more than rocked, his vocal at once playful and vigilant to the cynical revivalist preacher subtexts. Or "I Contain Multitudes"—on Friday he held back, spare and soft, as if merely recapitulating the factual affirmations in his Whitman title; Sunday those same facts arrayed an emotional inventory of the casualties and salvations of a creative life. Or "Black Rider"—Friday, Dylan sounded like a man earnestly trying to talk himself into something he really doesn't want to do; Saturday, the song was more about transience and hurt and a craving for the certainty that might come with death; by Sunday, the Black Rider was an irritant the singer hoped to swat away—"One of these days I'll forget to be kind." Or "False Prophet"—the crowd loved the looming vengeance in Dylan's words Saturday and Sunday, but Friday he managed to signal the anguish and insecurity in his triple negatives. His songs from other albums veered at least as radically. He completely rewrote "Gotta Serve Somebody," extending the servitude across jobs, personal relationships, and history. One night "Every Grain of Sand" might chart a straightforward declaration of faith, but the next lodge his tentativeness: "Sometimes I turn, there's someone there, other times it's only me."

The Beacon was my first real foray since my surgeries and treatments of the past year and a half. For others, the Dylan shows threw down a get out of COVID-19 jail free card. As respite for the fatigue I still experienced, Kristine and I booked a room at the Hotel Beacon over the theatre, and each of the three nights there was an afterparty on an upper floor, thirty to forty people overflowing an infinitesimal "suite" that comfortably might have crammed ten. A chatty fantasy high school reunion of graying Dylan fans, writers, photographers, and tapers from across America, England, France, and Japan. No one there wearing a mask, of course, even those of us who dutifully masked-up for the concerts, but no reports of illness as far as I heard later. After one engagement Dylan himself was glimpsed exiting a side door in a mask. His band was staying at the Hotel Beacon. We shared an elevator ride with Tony Garnier, and spoke with drummer Charley Drayton and his family in the lobby.

On his tours since the Beacon, Dylan's frailty has intensified, and he has looked on occasions to perform in pain—for 2022 and 2023 he banned all smart phones from his shows, requiring they be locked inside Yondr pouches; the rare videos that emerged from Europe and Japan showed him occasionally resting a sore hand atop his piano. But somehow the vitality of his vocals also intensified, and so did the daring of his ambitions for *Rough and Rowdy Ways*. Night after night Dylan excavated secrets from inside lyrics that increasingly resembled Shakespearean monologues, though many nights it was as if different characters spoke them. Arrangements, too, evolved, rebounded, spiraled—spectators in Copenhagen, Berlin, London, Barcelona, or Rome now could be certain of which song only after he started singing the first lines. The transformations along his live, roadshow Nobel Lecture embodied the dynamism in *Rough and Rowdy Ways*:

- Three variations for "Crossing the Rubicon": Paris, on October 11, 2022, a spectral, postmortem rant; then Dublin, a month later on November 7, an earthy, worldly-wise boast; then Nagoya, on April 20, 2023, a tense, menacing future threat;
- Three more for "Black Rider": Nottingham, on October 30, 2022, all apocalypse, amid intimations of William Burroughs and Tom Waits, and their Robert Wilson opera, also called *Black Rider*; Nagoya, on April 20, 2023, a sardonic Brecht-Weill carnival; and then Perugia, on July 7, 2023, edgy, syncopated movie jazz;
- Two for "My Own Version of You": Manchester, on November 2, 2022, a mock-tender story of obsession with a rhythmically off-center start-and-stop vocal; in Tokyo, on April 11, 2023, full-tilt mad scientist, sweetly sung against a compulsively deconstructing musical maelstrom.

As I listened to Dylan's shows from Japan and Europe, I kept fastening on the word *abstraction*, as in early abstract versus figure painting. His Nagoya "Black Rider" wasn't exactly Brecht-Weill, but an abstraction of Brecht-Weill, just as—for another instance—"Goodbye Jimmy Reed" in Tokyo wasn't exactly rockabilly, but an abstraction of rockabilly, and so on.

At a Fort Lauderdale concert in March of 2024, after a woman shouted, "Play something we know," Dylan and his band reciprocated with a reworking of "When I Paint My Masterpiece" to the tune of "Istanbul (Not Constantinople)," the They Might Be Giants song, itself of course a reworking of Irving Berlin's "Puttin' On the Ritz"—his poker-faced surmise that, surely, she must *know* her classics and contemporaries. Anomalous covers, sometimes songs about the city where he was in residence that night or songs by writers who grew up in that city, charmed other fans during the American circuits of the "*Rough and Rowdy Ways* World Wide Tour": "Johnny B. Goode," in St. Louis; "Longest Days," in Indianapolis; "Dance Me to the End of Love," in Montreal; "On the Banks of the Old Pontchartrain," in New Orleans; "Across the Borderline," in Austin; "Big River," in Louisville; "Jambalaya," in Lafayette; even a few bars of "New York State of Mind," in Manhattan.

For the twenty-six city 2024 Outlaw Tour with Nelson and others, Dylan abandoned *Rough and Rowdy Ways* songs for a winding flux of reliable favorites ("Things Have Changed," "Simple Twist of Fate," "Ballad of a Thin Man," and "Highway 61 Revisited"), deep cuts ("Shooting Star," "Beyond Here Lies Nothing," "Under the Red Sky," and "Love Sick"), *Tempest* tracks ("Early Roman Kings," "Pay in Blood," and "Soon After Midnight"), and a vertiginous proportion of covers. Over the initial two concerts alone in Alpharetta, Georgia, and Charlotte, North Carolina: "My Babe," "Little Queenie," "Mr. Blue," "Cold Cold Heart," "The Fool," "Stella Blue," and "Six Days on the Road." After some nineteen years in Dylan's bands, multi-instrumentalist Donnie Herron (pedal steel, violin, guitar) was gone; and Jim Keltner was now on drums. The show Kristine and I saw at Bethel Woods on July 6 recalled an impromptu, often riveting rehearsal, though by then a tour set list was more or less entrenched. Mickey Raphael, from Nelson's band, guested on harmonica for "Simple Twist of Fate." My physical therapist, fresh to late Dylan, left with the confounded impression that *every* song was a cover. Only our close walk song by song through the program persuaded him that actually there were just four.

When Dylan resumed his *Rough and Rowdy Ways* cycle in Prague on

October 4, he restored all nine tracks from his latest album—once again, dodging only "Murder Most Foul"—but any reservations about the band from the Outlaw summer dispersed as he took the stage for a driving "All Along the Watchtower." Although in videos that surfaced from the fall European tour he can look frailer during some performances than at others, one surprise was the renewed energy of his vocals, as a second was the precision and dexterity of his band, Keltner still holding down the drums but attending more thoughtfully to Bob Britt and Doug Lancio's guitars and Dylan's dynamic phrasing. (At the final Outlaw show in Buffalo, Dylan demonstrated the rhythms he wanted for "Desolation Row" by tapping a small wrench against his microphone!) The eight other songs he now played that weren't on *Rough and Rowdy Ways* perhaps could indicate appreciative audience reactions to the sixties and seventies from the Outlaw cavalcade—"All Along the Watchtower," "It Ain't Me, Babe," "When I Paint My Masterpiece," "To Be Alone with You," "Desolation Row," "It's All Over Now, Baby Blue," "Watching the River Flow," and "Every Grain of Sand." Yet each lyric also intersected the reflections on his art, inspirations, losses, and identity for *Rough and Rowdy Ways* in beguiling ways. The result was an even more intensive incarnation of his traveling live Nobel Lecture. As Dylan introduced his guitarist on October 27 in Dusseldorf after "My Own Version of You": "Doug Lancio on the second guitar. Playing a serious song for serious people."

Even more intensive were the modulations of his *Rough and Rowdy Ways* rearrangements across the twenty-eight shows, with several concerts often in the same city. For "I Contain Multitudes": in Frankfurt on October 17, offered as though Dylan were confiding inside stories; in Paris on October 24, rendered with a rueful appreciation of a life's complexities—"no apologies to make"; up-tempo and cheeky for his first night in Wolverhampton on November 9, yet the very next night there delivered as though intended to impress and win someone over, a seduction; finally, in London on November 14, sung with valedictory intimations of wonder. For "False Prophet": defiant and threatening in Nurnberg on October 14; a con man's brag in Frankfurt on October 17; and flung down as though settling a controversy or a score in Wolverhampton on November 10. Correspondingly, his other songs—for "When I Paint My Masterpiece": in Saarbrucken a syncopated shuffle; tense and edgy in Wolverhampton, much as if the "masterpiece" that night must be a Jackson Pollack action painting. For "It Ain't Me, Babe": in Frankfurt, a cruel kiss-off; by Liverpool, a gracious demurral.

This on a nearly dark stage: Dylan behind his baby grand piano or a Nord Electro 6 keyboard, but sporadically prowling with a handheld mic. Early in the tour Dylan sometimes played guitar at a show's start for "All Along the Watchtower" and "It Ain't Me, Babe," facing away from the audience towards Keltner for a private jam session, or seated at the piano. Later, he took to walking on a minute or so after the band, an instrumental version of what would turn into "All Along the Watchtower" underway. The performance centers radiated from *Rough and Rowdy Ways*, particularly "Black Rider," "My Own Version of You," "Crossing the Rubicon," "Key West (Philosopher Pirate)," "I've Made Up My Mind to Give Myself to You," and "Mother of Muses," but in spirited dialogue with all the other songs about art, selfhood, loss, faith, doubt, inspiration, and last things. Despite the skills of his sophisticated backing band, the dramas song to song inhered in the sensation Dylan imparted here of thinking his life aloud—that innermost sense, as he said, of serious songs for serious people. Moreover, once he reached England and Scotland, he divested many of the full band arrangements. By his three London shows, he delivered those pivotal *Rough and Rowdy Ways* songs all but solo, some all but a cappella.

Each show opened with Dylan intoning, "There must be some kind of way out of here," and for his penultimate song, "Goodbye Jimmy Reed," valediction was forthright in the title. He would resume the Bob Dylan "*Rough and Rowdy Ways* World Wide Tour"—but without any play-by dates—the following year. But was there any lyric during the official final installment of the *Rough and Rowdy Ways* tour that didn't at least implicitly involve endings, silence, mortality? In set list order:

". . . There must be some kind of way out of here . . . It *sure* ain't me, babe . . . The flowers are dying like all things do . . . I forgot when I died . . . Yes, it sure has been a long hard climb . . . You've been on the job too long . . . I'll see you, maybe, on Judgement Day . . . What happened to me, darling . . . I crossed the Rubicon . . . Don't send me no more letters . . . Death is on the wall . . . What's the matter with me? I don't have much to say . . . It's all over now, Baby Blue . . . I saw the flowers come and go . . . I've already outlived my life by far . . . Goodbye Jimmy Reed . . . There's a dying voice within me . . ."

For all his restless, terminal articulations, each show concluded wordlessly, with Dylan on heartbreaking harmonica for "Every Grain of Sand."

Mad scientist, frail magus: presumed command; inevitable limits. At the close of his 2022 *Rough and Rowdy Ways* Nottingham show, he announced a death from earlier that day. "I don't know how many of you know," Dylan said, "but Jerry Lee is gone. So we're gonna play this song, one of his." He then led his band through the stately, plaintive, and gorgeous farewell of "I Can't Seem to Say Goodbye."

X

. . . BOB IS THE ONLY PERSON . . .

> X the unknown variable, but X rays, too;
> and X marks the spot—

Third Person

"Every night he would come in with a rolled-up bundle of paper, wrapped up with a rubber band, his lyrics that he was in the process of working on," Malcolm Burn, one of the recording engineers who assisted producer Daniel Lanois on *Oh Mercy*, recounted for *Uncut* of Dylan. "He'd go over to where we had the coffee machine and put the lyrics out on the table and start scribbling and fixing up a few lines, and then he'd say, 'Okay, let's go.'"

". . . One night, we were going to do 'Most of the Time' and he sat down with his guitar, and I actually recorded this, I still have it somewhere, and he said, 'Well, we could do it like this'—and he played the entire song, just him on acoustic guitar and harmonica, the archetypal Bob Dylan thing. He actually referred to himself in the third person, 'That would be like a typical Bob Dylan way of doin' it.' And then he did it another way, and he played it like a blues, really slow, and I recorded that, too. And then there was the version we ended up doing on the record.

"He always wore this hoodie, y'know, and he'd just kind of play and sing. For the first few days we were recording, we had the Neville Brothers rhythm section there. And the drummer, Willie Green, he came up to me, I was sitting at the mixing board, and Bob was like, four feet away. Willie says, 'Man, I've been here for two or three days. When the fuck's Bob Dylan showing up? I thought we were making a record with Bob Dylan.' And then, seriously, the bass player, Tony [Hall], he comes in, and it turns out he didn't know this was Bob sitting there either. He says, 'That Bob Dylan is some weird motherfucker, man.'

"Bob just sort of looked up and raised his eyebrow. And then he went back to working on his lyrics."

That Girl

Winston Watson was the drummer in Dylan's band during the years 1992 to 1996, nearly four hundred shows. He sometimes traveled with his wife, Deb, and their young daughter, Marcella. "She was two to six when I was with Bob," Watson told Ray Padgett. "He and my daughter always got along because both of them, they're just ridiculous together . . . I don't think he gets credit for it, but as serious as 'Masters of War' is, he's a really funny guy. . . ."

One night late in May 1995 they were all backstage at the Warfield, waiting to play. "We were getting ready to do the show," Watson continued. "I'm getting my clothes on. I see my wife in the green room, and I don't see my daughter. I said, 'Deb, where's Marcella?' She looks at me, the color drains from her face. She's like, 'Isn't she with you?' I go into a panic . . .

"Everybody helped. At one point, I'd looked everywhere except Bob's dressing room. I go up and knock on the door real quick. His assistant opens it, and there she is.

"We were already five minutes late going onstage, and the two of them were holding the show up. I said, 'Babe, come on, Bob's got to go to work now.' She says, 'Oh, okay.' He says, 'I want to talk a little more about that later, okay?' She's like, 'Okay, Bob.' And she grabs her drink and comes out and meets my wife.

"I go to stand with the band and wait for him. They bring the house lights down. Bob stops me with his arm. He says, 'We got to do something about that girl.'

"I said, 'Oh, man, I'm sorry, she just loves you. I didn't want her to disturb your show.' He goes, 'No, that girl in art class. She's real mean. We got to do something about her.'

"We'd gotten Marcella these cowboy boots and there was this mean little girl in her art class who splashed paint on them. Bob asked her, 'How'd you get that paint on your cowboy boots?' So while I'm looking for my daughter, she's telling Bob that story, and they're holding the show up.

"He stops me and says, 'Hey, we got to do something about that girl.' "

. . . cycling on level macadamized causeways . . .

Dylan is known to make impromptu pilgrimages to places associated with favorite artists, writers and musicians, John Lennon, Neil Young, and James Joyce, among others, some open to the public, others not. In October and November of 2008, he toured Canada. According to Andy Greene in *Rolling Stone*, when John Kiernan and Patti Regan returned to their home in River Heights, Winnipeg, Dylan was waiting on their doorstep. Accustomed to encountering fans who wished to see the house where Neil Young grew up, they didn't initially recognize him. Kiernan and Regan showed Dylan around, and took him into Young's old bedroom, now their daughter's. "OK, so this was his view," Kiernan quoted Dylan as he observed the room, "and this is where he listened to his music." The following November, he boarded a minibus in Liverpool for a visit to John Lennon's childhood home on Menlove Avenue. No one on the excursion recognized him, except Colin Hall, the National Trust guide, who offered a private tour that he politely refused. "This kitchen, it's just like my mom's," Dylan told Hall. In Lennon's bedroom, he noticed a volume from Richmal Compton's *Just William* schoolboy series. "Dylan was fascinated by the book," Hall recounted, "and I remember thinking, 'I'm standing in John Lennon's bedroom with Bob Dylan.' It was a totally surreal moment."

When Dylan toured the James Joyce Museum, a Martello tower in Sandycove, Dublin, where Joyce stayed for six nights in 1904, "a curator urged him to take a ride on James Joyce's bicycle. Bob was amazed at this offer, rode a few feet and stopped. The curator told him to take it for a proper ride, so Bob pedaled around Dublin a bit."

A French Dylan fan later visited the museum and inquired about other "celebrities" and the Joyce bicycle. "Oh, good God, no!" the curator responded, when asked if (for instance) Ben Affleck might ride it. "Bob is the only person who was allowed to ride the bike in some years," the French fan was advised. Why? "The curator sighed, 'Well, I like Bob a great deal, he's stopped in here a few times and is always a polite and charming fellow.'"

Normal Indicators

On July 23, 2009, some Long Branch, New Jersey, homeowners called the police about an "eccentric looking old man" in their yard. They were selling their house, a For Sale sign out front, but it was pouring rain, and his appearance and actions (he peered into their windows) spooked them. Officer Kristie Buble drove over, stopped the man. According to her description, "He was wearing black sweatpants tucked into black rain boots, and two raincoats with the hood pulled down over his head." Officer Buble asked him what he was doing there. He said that he was looking at a house for sale. She asked his name. "I'm Bob Dylan," he told her. She said no, your real name. "Zimmerman," he told her. She asked why he was in Long Branch, and he said he was touring the country with Willie Nelson and John Mellencamp.

"So now I'm really a little fishy about his story," Officer Buble reported. She asked him where he lived. He told her, "I have houses all over the place. I don't live in one place. I travel so much, I have a house in

London, I have a house in California." She asked if he had any identification, but he wasn't carrying any, he told her.

"I just put him in the car, and said, 'Okay, where are you staying, Bob?' kind of sarcastically, messing with him a little bit. 'Where's your hotel, where are your friends?' And he says, 'Oh, it's this hotel out by the ocean.' I thought it might be some guy in character, someone who might be imitating him and won't get out of character, even dealing with the police. We see a lot of people on our beat, and I wasn't sure if he came from one of our hospitals or something."

During the drive, the man kept talking. "He told me he's famous for singing," Officer Buble reported. "He told me he wrote all these songs. He's just blabbering in the back. And I wasn't even paying attention to some of the things he was saying because in my head I was wondering, 'What am I going to tell the hospital, what am I going to tell my supervisor?' I remember he said, 'Just take me over there, I'll give you tickets to my show, you can see me play.' And I thought, this guy is crazy." He also asked, "if I could drive him back to the neighborhood when I verified who he was, which made me even more suspicious. He's saying these things that are normal indicators of liars."

When they pulled up to the hotel, "I was thinking, let me check this out. Maybe it's just a coincidence there's buses here, they're not for him. And his manager came running out to us, and flipped out. I was like, 'Sorry! Sorry, Bob! I didn't mean to not believe you.' I couldn't talk to him anymore, because his manager wouldn't let me have anything to do with him. I wanted to have a normal conversation with him. I wanted to say, 'Manager, just step away from him for one minute, I promise I don't want anything from him, I don't want to bother him. I just want to have a conversation with him where I don't think he's a crazy person.'"

The more sincerely, truthfully, and literally he answered her formal questions, the more dubious and suspicious he sounded to her. Of the man who turned out to be Bob Dylan, Officer Buble reported, "It never crossed my mind that this could really be him. When you encounter someone as famous as this you expect him to be pompous: 'This is who I am, don't do this, don't you know who I am?' It was nothing like that, nothing at all. He was modest and calm and chill. He was nicer than 95 percent of the people I deal with every day."

Phone Tag

A novelist was sitting for a print interview about his new book when his cell phone chimed. He excused himself to take the call—Dylan: his current tour included the novelist's town, might he be interested in meeting up, maybe for dinner? The journalist recognized the voice on the other end of the line, obvious, unmistakable, and asked how did he know the singer? The novelist answered carefully that his agent's husband had introduced them. The phone call, and that detail entered the story, which out of respect or obliviousness didn't then connect the dots. The novelist was telling the journalist that Thomas Pynchon introduced him to Bob Dylan. "What goes around may come around," as Pynchon wrote in *Inherent Vice,* "but it never ends up in exactly the same place, you ever notice?"

Timehop

Players in Dylan's recent bands occasionally give interviews about working with him, on tour or in the studio. A few take to social media. Guitarist Charlie Sexton posted on Instagram random daytime shots from the road under the rubric, "Waiting Game." On February 18, 2020, he posted a mysterious photo of just his lower legs and shoes by a parking block: "WG undisclosed." *Rough and Rowdy Ways* emerged from those recording sessions at Sound City Studios in LA. When "Murder Most Foul" reached number 1 on the Billboard charts during early COVID lockdown, Sexton posted: "We're all in the waiting game. . . . sending out blessings to everyone as we all navigate these hard times. . . . but must humbly send out regards to this gentleman as I truly know first hand how hard he has and continues to work, god bless you sir."

Blake Mills, also a guitarist on *Rough and Rowdy Ways*, was more flamboyant, maybe a bit passive-aggressive on Instagram. Soon after the album was released on June 19, he posted videos of himself reprising his guitar parts for "My Own Version of You," "Mother of Muses," "Black Rider," "Crossing the Rubicon," "I've Made Up My Mind to Give Myself to You," "False Prophet," and "I Contain Multitudes."

Dylan, as far as I know, then wasn't an active devotee of social media. He's since, though, as of September 2024, while touring Europe, started posting on X, his initial transmissions almost startling in their outward everydayness. "Happy Birthday Mary Jo! See you in Frankfort." "Last time in New Orleans we ate at Dook Chase's Restaurant on the corner of North Miro and Orleans. If you're ever there I highly recommend it." "I ran into one of the Buffalo Sabres in the elevator at the Prague Hotel. They were in town to play the New Jersey Devils. He invited me to the game but I was performing that night." His concert in Frankfurt coincided with the international book fair, and Dylan apparently stopped by and on X recommended a book. "I didn't know there were so many publishers in the world, I was trying to find Crystal Lake Publishing, so I could congratulate them on publishing *The Great God Pan*, one of my favorite books. I thought they might be interested in some of my stories. Unfortunately it was too crowded and I never did find them." He recommended a film, Tod Browning's *The Unknown*, with Lon Chaney. Dylan would go on to post on Instagram music by Johnny Cash, Ricky Nelson, Django Reinhardt, Lorrie Collins, Paul Robeson, The Osborne Brothers, Josh White, The Shangri-Las, among many others, even Machine Gun Kelly. Clips from Westerns, sci-fi, and *The Best Years of Our Lives*. Genuine American distinction, heroism, greatness. Soon after the Trump inauguration some historical and literary ghosts started to appear—"Last Testament of Frank James," "Al Capone in his own words," "Edgar Allen Poe speaks from the grave," and "Stephen Foster speaks from the grave." Dylan's own virtual Ouija board.

Members of his family are on Instagram. In the spring of 2023, Dylan toured Japan, and a stack of vacation photos—parks, restaurants, shops, sports stadiums, temples, and an advertisement for a Bob Dylan concert—posted by a daughter-in-law would seem to indicate that the shows coincided with a family outing. One of Dylan's daughters regularly posts on his birthday, and on Father's Day. A photo of herself as a baby, next to what looks like one of his dogs, with a childhood memory; and another photo, also as a baby, plucking an acoustic guitar larger than her body ("Guitar cred: Dad"). A theater program for *Girl from the North Country*. A photo of "Grandma Beatty." A grandson on his travels posted a photo of himself outside a mansion in Abernathy, Scotland, later deleted from Instagram. A photo inside a house in Abingdon Square—acoustic guitar on the wall; boxing gloves strung from the ceiling—also taken down.

Dissolve

Although he's sometimes surprised arriving at a sound check or after a concert exiting backstage for the tour bus, Dylan is rarely photographed except when he intends to be. On May 19, 2021, the *Daily Mail* ran a photograph of him under the headline: "EXCLUSIVE: Times they are a-changing! Bob Dylan is seen in public for the first time in a DECADE while running errands in LA—just days before his 80th birthday." Journalist Karen Ruiz teased out the ostensible clues, amid disinformation. "The folk legend, who turns 80 next Monday, kept a low profile in a navy short sleeve shirt, combat-style boots, and dark aviator glasses. Dylan was also seen wearing what appeared to be a wedding ring despite supposedly being single after divorcing his second wife, Carolyn Dennis, in 1992. The sighting marks Dylan's first appearance in public since 2011—when he was photographed heading to a local synagogue in LA . . . In December, Dylan was reported to have sold his entire catalog of songs to Universal Music Publishing Group for $300M."

Low profile? Closer to hidden in plain sight. Those solitary walks, house tours, museum visits: Dylan is hardly reclusive, despite his reputation, and seems to carry on his daily life with minimal interference and celebrity hoopla, more or less on his own terms. Apparently, when he saw

Girl from the North Country no one, including cast or director, knew he was in the theater. He regularly attends concerts that his son, Jakob, performs with his band, the Wallflowers, again sans fuss or commotion. Singer Ron Sexsmith toured with the Wallflowers. "Once on the road," Sexsmith told Griffin Ondaatje, "I asked Jakob, 'Does Bob ever come to your shows?' He goes, 'Oh yeah, he comes all the time.' " After the conclusion of his fall 2024, European tour, Dylan attended a Nick Cave concert in Paris, Cave realizing this only after friends alerted him to his posting on X. "Saw Nick Cave in Paris recently at the Accor Arena and I was really struck by the song Joy where he sings, 'We've all had too much sorrow, now is the time for joy.' I was thinking to myself, yeah that's about right."

"Dissolve myself into situations where I was invisible," as he apprised Jules Siegel back in the mid-1960s. Online, a fan grumbled that Dylan's hoodie and shades were by now so familiar as no longer to constitute a disguise; he must *want* to be recognized. Well, maybe, another fan replied. But still, it wasn't until the final encore of a Wallflowers club date, he said, that he realized just who was the man dressed exactly that way standing right next to him all night.

Alone/Share

Experiment Ensam was a Swedish web film series where people experienced alone activities customarily done with others, often amidst crowds. The premise: "Do we have more fun together with others? We find out what it's like to do social activities on your own." Singing karaoke. A crosscut saw designed for two tree fellers. Comedy clubs. "Loneliness is a subject that interests Swedes. Kungsholmen, a community in Stockholm, is one of the world's loneliest islands with 80 percent of the households being single."

As a "final experiment" on November 23, 2014, *Experiment Ensam* persuaded Bob Dylan and his band to perform exclusively for Fredrik Wikingsson, a Stockholm writer, actor, and fan with a private afternoon show at the Philadelphia Academy of Music. For Wikingsson, sitting in the otherwise deserted hall a few rows back—"I thought the first row might freak him out. I was like a guy picking the next-to-most expensive bottle of wine in a restaurant, which is a very Swedish thing to do"—Dylan discarded any usual set list, and played Buddy Holly's "Heartbeat," Fats Domino's "Blueberry Hill," Lefty Frizzell's "You're Too Late," and Big Bill Broonzy's "Key to the Highway."

The song choices resembled a Dylan sound check. After "Heartbeat" Wikingsson only applauded, but soon realized "I had to say something. It was just too weird. I screamed out, 'You guys sound great! I just wanted to say that.' This caused Dylan to burst out laughing. Now, I have two kids and their births were great, but him laughing onstage at some lousy fucking comment of mine was unbelievable."

When his own personal Dylan concert was over, Wikingsson shouted, "Thank you very much . . . Take care guys," and the singer again laughed. "Thank you for coming . . . You can come anytime."

Together? Or alone? "It wouldn't have been as intense with other people there," Wikingsson concluded, or almost concluded. "But once I stepped out of the theater, all confused and dizzy, it could have been more intense if I had someone to share it with. In that way I'm torn about the experience. It was incredibly intense then and there, but after the fact and forever after, I miss having someone to share it with."

Autopen

On Instagram, Friday, November 25, 2022:

> To My Fans and Followers:
>
> I've been made aware that there's some controversy about signatures on some of my recent art prints and on a limited edition of *Philosophy of Modern Song*. I've hand-signed each and every art print over the years and there's never been a problem.
>
> However, in 2019 I had a bad case of vertigo and it continued into the pandemic years. It takes a crew of five working in close quarters

with me to enable these signing sessions, and we could not find a safe and workable way to complete what I needed to do while the virus was raging. So, during the pandemic, it was impossible to sign anything and the vertigo didn't help. With contractual deadlines looming, the idea of using an auto-pen was suggested to me, along with the assurance that this kind of thing is done "all the time" in the art and literary worlds.

Using a machine was an error in judgement and I want to rectify it immediately. I'm working with Simon & Schuster and my gallery partners to do just that.

With my deepest regrets,

Bob Dylan

Y

. . . FACTUAL TELEPATHY . . .

You walk into the room with a pencil in your hand—except it's not a pencil this time but a hatchet in your hand, or at least that's what you're carrying according to a pair of typed draft manuscripts of "Ballad of a Thin Man" in Bob Dylan's Tulsa archive. Reading draft manuscripts—and listening to studio outtakes—for songs you adore and know by heart can be hallucinatory experiences, residues of a dream. Such experiences can seem as if you've inadvertently slipped into a rival world where, as Dylan in "Ballad of a Thin Man" taunts Mr. Jones: "Something is happening but you don't know what it is, do you?"

On March 2, 2016, Ben Sisario in the *New York Times* announced the existence of "Bob Dylan's Secret Archive" that had just been acquired by the George Kaiser Family Foundation and the University of Tulsa, and would be residing in Oklahoma. In Tulsa the GKFF previously had purchased the Woody Guthrie Archive, housed at the Woody Guthrie Center. The *Times* calculated the Dylan Archive at six thousand pieces.

The lives you live, relive them? Six thousand alternatives in Dylan's "secret" archive. Alongside the melodramatic coyness of the headline, the *Times* ultimately underestimated the magnitude. Wildly. But really, what, where, how, when, and why? So, specifics and correspondences here, too. Late in 2014, Michael Chaiken was contacted by Glenn Horowitz, who told him he was working on the Dylan Archive at the request of Jeff Rosen, president of the Bob Dylan Music Company, and might Chaiken wish to help? Horowitz started at the Rare Book Room of the Strand Bookstore in New York City, and is a leading agent and broker of author papers, manuscripts, and correspondence, with such clients and estates as Vladimir Nabokov, John Cheever, Don DeLillo, Marilynne Robinson, Alice Walker, Marge Piercy, and Albert Murray, among notable others. Following a cold call to Horowitz from Chaiken in 2007, when Chaiken was working with Albert and David Maysles on the preservation of their films, Horowitz and Chaiken collaborated on the archives of the Maysles brothers, Norman Mailer's films, Nicholas Ray, D. A. Pennebaker and Chris Hegedus, Spalding Gray, and Donald Lyons. There were kindred convergent endeavors. While Horowitz did not broker the Guthrie Archive to Tulsa, he advised the GKFF on the sale. Chaiken intersected the Bob Dylan Music Company when he curated *Dont Look Back* for the Criterion Collection. (Plus another near-convergence: I wrote the essay for the booklet that Criterion included with *Dont Look Back*, though I did not then meet Chaiken.)

By the time Chaiken went into the Dylan office in Gramercy Park early in 2015, the materials of a future archive were far along in crucial identification and sorting, much of that performed by Parker Fishel, an archivist, researcher, and writer who worked with Rosen on many of the sets in *The Bootleg Series*. "Parker spent a lot of time going over every single piece of paper, essentially creating a database and organizing things," Chaiken recalled. "There were already dedicated folders." As backdrop, and perhaps as galvanizing prompts for the Dylan Music Company, fugitive song manuscripts were coming up for auction at Sotheby's and Christie's—in 2010 the handwritten lyrics of "The Times They Are A-Changin'" sold for $422,500; and a draft of "Like a Rolling Stone" on stationery from the Roger Smith Hotel in Washington, DC, sold for $2.05 million in 2014. Sally Grossman, widow of Dylan's first manager Albert Grossman, planned to sell early materials in her custody, but an arrangement was reached, and the auction pulled. All entering, or almost entering, the market as commodities. More quietly, over the years George Heckster, a serious collector also of George Bernard Shaw and Charles Bukowski, assembled a cache of manuscripts for over ninety Dylan songs, which he donated to the Morgan Library. (Specimens of these would be displayed in 2006 at the Morgan for Bob Dylan's American Journey, 1956–1966, a traveling exhibition of drafts, objects, and listening stations coordinated by Experience Music Project, and a sort of dry run for a Dylan Center in Tulsa.) A smart decision was made by the Dylan office to try to keep everything together, and to think about the dynamics of an archive. Dylan meanwhile sent in items from Malibu and Minnesota.

Chaiken's original commission was to write a fifty-page overview of the archive, a value and significance document for potential acquiring institutions. Jeff Gold appraised the collection. Horowitz, probably because of his prior involvement with the Guthrie Center, envisaged the GKFF from the outset, yet there was excitement at Harvard Library Special Collections and the Harry Ransom Center in Austin, Texas. "I called my friend Ken Levit, the head of the foundation," Horowitz told Tad Friend in the *New Yorker*, and said, 'How are things going with the Guthrie?' And he said, 'Only seventeen to twenty thousand people a year are coming through.' I said, 'The deal I'm working on would guarantee a quarter of a million visitors . . . Twenty million dollars will buy you a lousy Willem de Kooning painting—and for the same price you get *all* of Bob Dylan, American icon.'" After meetings in New York, a deal was finalized with the GKFF during the fall of 2015, with the intention of a public announcement in March. The story somehow leaked to *Times* journalists, who were promised an exclusive if they would delay until then. Since Chaiken knew the collection so intimately, the GKFF asked if he might travel along with the Dylan Archive to Tulsa for the first six months. "Those six months," as he quips, "turned into six years."

Beyond the Woody Guthrie Center, and now the Bob Dylan Center, the George Kaiser Family Foundation is an independent philanthropic organization in Tulsa with an emphasis on childhood poverty, health, and early education. Initiated by George Kaiser, heir to the Kaiser-Francis Oil Company and chair of BOK Financial Corporation, the GKFF advances programs in women's health, racial equity and health policy, HIV/Aids, teacher training, health news and information, and fellowships in health reporting. During the opening weekend of the Bob Dylan Center, I attended powerful talks by GKFF Executive Director Levit and his staff in all of these areas, notably by the program officers of ConnectFirst and the Birth through Eight Strategy for Tulsa. George Kaiser also helped create Gathering Place, a 66.5-acre space on the Arkansas River, the largest public park built with private money. For Sisaro's *Times* article, Kaiser spoke of the role of the Guthrie and Dylan archives in revitalizing Tulsa. "Portland wasn't always cool," he said, "Seattle wasn't always cool. One of the ways you can try to make your city cool is by attracting talented young people and hoping that a number of them stick."

Once I read about the Dylan Archive, I contacted Rosen, whom I had been introduced to by Greil Marcus years earlier, about possibly consulting it for this book, and we met again at his office. He put me in touch with Chaiken, and by early June of 2016 I was in Tulsa. Other writers soon followed. I returned to the Helmerich Center at the University of Tulsa as often as I could, filling notebooks in pencil with those "secret" alternatives of Dylan's songwriting. The next summer Chaiken invited me, as the first writer to experience the archive, to join a small group that would select the architects for the Bob Dylan Center. Over August 24 and 25 of 2017, at the Dechert conference center on Sixth Avenue in New York, four design teams delivered formal presentations: a Brooklyn firm; a Kansas City firm; a Manhattan firm with an Oklahoma City partner; and out of Seattle, Olson Kundig, the firm that would eventually get the nod. All demonstrated superb portfolios of museums across America. Among the gathered participants also were Chaiken; Levit and Steve Higgins of the GKFF; Rosen, Fishel, and Larry Jenkins of Dylan's office; Rosanne Cash; and writers Robert Rubin, Sean Wilentz, and Raymond Foye. A third day of revised concepts and proposals by the two finalists took place in Tulsa on October 20. Olson Kundig was our unanimous choice—their aesthetics, and a flexibility of exhibition space; their budget.

During those model sketches and mock-ups, inevitable questions inside any notion of a Bob Dylan Center—chronic questions, persistent questions, and irresolvable questions that would linger long past the official opening—propelled our deliberations. What are the connections between the Bob Dylan Center and the Bob Dylan Archive? Is the Dylan Center a shrine to Dylan, a Dylan museum, or the public face of the archive? Is the Dylan Center a tourist attraction, a source of revenue, or a vibrant cultural resource and an agent for community transformation? Do the exhibitions illustrate the standard Dylan story, or show how the archive reshuffles the plot you thought you knew? How might a Dylan Center thrive as a living, evolving entity? Much was impressive, particularly Jeff Rosen's graciousness, sincerity, and analytic cool; the shrewd clarity tendered by Alan Maskin of Olson Kundig; and the seriousness and capaciousness of Chaiken's vision. At Chaiken's urging, the GKFF would purchase the Cynthia Gooding Archive, the Mell and Lillian Bailey Archive, the Harry Smith Library, the Madison Tapes, and the Toni Mendell Tapes. Chaiken also could articulate the standing of the Bob Dylan Center among the diverse civic enterprises of the GKFF, and the problematics of erecting another temple to a white folk singer at the site of the 1921 Tulsa Race Massacre. Many specifics would change. For a while the Bob Dylan Center was slotted into the Zarrow Center—too small. Then, as a new, ground-up, stand-alone construction on the parking lot behind Zarrow—too large. Finally, only when artist Richard Prince and Robert Rubin were scrutinizing old Tulsa warehouses did attention shift to a building the GKFF already had rehabbed as the downtown site of the Philbrook Museum, formerly the Matthews warehouse for paper. The Bob Dylan Center opened inside there on May 5, 2022.

A riveting frisson of the Bob Dylan Archive is that this comprises the repository of an artist who, of course, is himself also an inveterate archivist. Dylan operated as a magpie archivist from his earliest folk days in Minneapolis, Madison, Denver, and New York, even before he wrote his own songs, running down old ballads, searching out the surviving performers of the musical eras before him, and even—notoriously—pinching rare and obscure records, as charged by Walt Conley and Jon Pankake. Once he wrote songs, there often was a template, a source, a provenance, a legacy, a tradition. This process would accelerate. Dylan in his songs, books, and films after 1991 is a supreme archivist of literature and music. For visual artists, theorists, and historians of his generation and after, the archive moreover is not so much a static reliquary as generative—for Saidiya Hartman, writing from the archive is "a kind of time travel." Archives animate artists as various as Tacita Dean, Dayanita Singh, Arthur Jafa, Zoe Leonard, Aurelien Froment, Thomas Ruff, Douglas Gordon, Thomas Hirschhorn, and Richard Prince. In 2004 for the journal *October*, critic Hal Foster traced "an archivist impulse at work internationally in contemporary art," and many of his phrases across "An Archival Impulse" effortlessly summon the Dylan of *Time Out of Mind*, *"Love And Theft," Modern Times*, *Tempest*, *Masked and Anonymous*, and *Chronicles*. "Archival artists," Foster observed, "seek to make historical information, often lost or displaced, physically present." Many archival artists "inventory, sample, and share as ways of working," in a "gesture of alternative knowledge or counter-memory," toward a "matrix of citation and juxtaposition" and "new orders of affective association." Poets were there first, T. S. Eliot and Muriel Rukeyser, but particularly such Dylan contemporaries as Frank Bidart, Susan Howe, Robin Coste Lewis, and M. NourbeSe Philip. Reflecting on her own poems involving Emily Dickinson and Jonathan Edwards, Howe characterizes the archive as "felt fact," "factual telepathy," and "chthonic echo-signals." Emily LaBarge encapsulated Howe's poetic project as a "rewarding route to how one might construct a life—and a life's work—from diving into language, the past, archival sources." Her words on Howe align as well a provocative pocket assay of Bob Dylan.

The archive of an archivist, a memory palace about a memory palace. Chaiken and I embarked on a comprehensive catalog of manuscripts and photographs in the Dylan Archive for Callaway Arts & Entertainment. To expand perspectives, and commensurate with the GKFF civic aims, we invited musicians, writers, artists, and others to Tulsa, where they would each select one item from the archive to write a short essay about for inclusion in the catalog, and also give a public performance, reading, or talk. Gregory Pardlo, Joy Harjo, Michael Ondaatje, Griffin Ondaatje, Lucy Sante, Tom Piazza, Peter Carey, Eileen Myles, The Friend, Allison Moorer, Clinton Heylin, Jeff Gold, Amanda Petrusich, Jeff Slate, Joe Andoe, John Doe, Raymond Foye, Richard Hell, Greg Tate, Larry "Ratso" Sloman, Robert Rubin, Steve Gunn, Duncan Hannah, and more. The catalog would refract Dylan through his archive, the story and the story behind the story. These visits, and the events we staged around them, prompted me to engage sectors beyond the radius of my own research. Here's a quick octave of archive favorites outside the timelines of this book:

- A draft manuscript for "Subterranean Homesick Blues," mostly typed but with ballpoint substitutions and riders, and Dylan's working title of "Look Out Kid." On the reverse, he began a new song, "Mavis."
- A draft of "Maggie's Farm," where he can't decide whether Maggie is really forty years old but claiming to be twenty-four, or twenty claiming to be sixty-four.
- The fading coffee cup—or are they red wine glass?—stains on a variant typed sheet for "Subterranean Homesick Blues."
- Lyric drafts for *New Morning* (1971) in a 39¢ BIG VALUE pad, when Dylan was envisaging the songs as interludes for *Scratch*, a stage musical by Archibald MacLeish based on Stephen Vincent Benet's "The Devil and Daniel Webster."
- An August 24, 1970, letter from Huey P. Newton to Dylan. Newton writes, "Your music has always meant a great deal to the Black Panther Party, and to us personally. I always tell people we would never have gotten out the first issue of our paper, if it hadn't been for you, and especially 'Ballad of a Thin Man.'"
- A small notebook towards *John Wesley Harding* (1967) that contains drawings and passages from the Bible.

- A Super 8 film of Dylan performing "The Groom's Still Waiting at the Altar" with guitarist Mike Bloomfield at the Fox Warfield Theatre, San Francisco, on November 15, 1980. Shot from the Warfield balcony by Bill Pagel, this was Dylan's final appearance with Bloomfield, his guitarist on *Highway 61 Revisited*, and at the 1965 Newport Folk Festival. Bloomfield would die the following February.
- Another small notebook, his "blue" one for *Blood on the Tracks* (1975) where the tiny, spidery yet always intelligible hand resembles my wife Kristine's in her daily ledger. For both Dylan and Kristine, we are verging on Robert Walser's *Microscripts*.

So much more. If a ninth—an Executive Inn jotting with further revisions to "Tangled Up in Blue," three years after release. During those early days with the archive at the Helmerich Center my immediate sense wasn't just his handwriting, all the diverse stationery, and the myriad evidences on paper and inside a studio of his sheer hard work, but what I took to calling the gaps. The gaps between a final surviving manuscript and the demo, the gaps between early takes and a finished (is it ever finished?) album. I eventually learned that these weren't gaps but leaps. For the first time it is possible to follow a song from a fancy on a scratchpad through manifold drafts and then into multiple recordings, typically with alternate lyrics and arrangements. Still, the leaps documented by the archive never—as far as I've read or listened—unmask the "secret" of a song, they only preserve, even magnify the mysteries. Ovid—for one among many such radial instances—is there, if you look closely enough, in the archive, albeit a disproportionally tacit presence inside the files around *Modern Times*. Still, "Something is happening"—so you dig deeper, as your questions coil and proliferate.

Six thousand items? The center would upgrade that to one hundred thousand, and counting. Yet how do you tally photographic negatives, contact sheets, drafts, outtakes, reshoots? For the opening of the Bob Dylan Center, I was well enough to travel to Tulsa, despite balance issues left over from my treatments. For many this was a first plane flight since

COVID lockdown, and I enjoyed catching up with Piazza, Fishel, Pagel, Wilentz, Clinton Heylin, Mitch Blank, Doug Brinkley, David Beal, Mark Davidson, and Antoinette's coffee. Some I hadn't seen since Dylan's 2021 Beacon Theatre shows, some for far longer. I talked with George Kaiser about Joe Brainard and Ron Padgett, and the three of them together at Tulsa's Central High School, class of 1960. At the launch, Joy Harjo read beautifully the essay she wrote on "Tangled Up in Blue" for our catalog.

And Bob Dylan? A few weeks before, on April 13, he played the Tulsa Theater, formerly the Brady Theater, a flaneur's stroll of a few minutes to the Bob Dylan Center, where a thirty-by-ninety-foot mural of his face by Eric Burke fronts the brick façade. Rumors circulated that he opted instead to pass his free afternoon down the street at the season opener of the Tulsa Drillers, their Double-A baseball team. Sure enough, on stage at the Tulsa Theater, a blue and white Drillers pennant hung from Dylan's piano.

Z

. . . THAT'S MY STORY . . .

Zero hour? Zero hour—Bob Dylan's late albums tend to conclude on a song that hovers around death, a song often close by End Times, too. "The End begins before you are ever aware of it," as Ling Ma starts her post-apocalypse novel *Severance*. "It passes as ordinary." For me the starkest of these late Dylan zero hours is "Ain't Talkin'," on *Modern Times*, where "tonight in the mystic garden" ultimately will pulse and snake into "the last outback at the world's end." Almost as stark is "Tempest," his sinking-of-the-*Titanic* coda to *Tempest*: "sixteen hundred had gone to rest" and "Love had lost its fires / All things had run their course." For "Highlands," on *Time Out of Mind*, the "gentle and fair" hills out of Robert Burns might refresh the singer's ideal future afterlife, but for now, "The party's over and there's less and less to say." Even on "Sugar Baby," his warm codicil to *"Love And Theft,"* Dylan admonishes, "Look up, look up—seek your Maker—'fore Gabriel blows his horn."

Zero hours, transience to cataclysm to doomsday, all through his ongoing artistic revival, and this astonishing second act as a writer and performer. But there we are. Or are we? For *Rough and Rowdy Ways*, "Key West (Philosopher Pirate)," originating in violence and civic turmoil with the 1901 assassination of William McKinley in Buffalo, obviously carries on his inclination to conclude with The End—carries this on at least halfway; and maybe literally halfway, as the song's refrain, "Key West is on the horizon line," positions him and us exactly halfway between sea and sky, earth and heaven. The agent of this horizon line, this eye-level reorientation, is paradoxically the radio, a presence in our midst, unknown, unseen, which Dylan dramatizes with the same mystic awe of his 1997 London press conference—"The radio connected everybody like Orpheus," as he marveled. Radio here too is a force simultaneously outward and inner—"Like you were inside the radio," he told Sam Shepard, and a way of dreaming, "Radio station dreams." "Key West (Philosopher Pirate)" also correlates radio to eros and art, when Dylan sings, "I'm searching for love and inspiration / On that pirate radio station / It's coming out of Luxembourg and Budapest."

The song opens with his variation on Charlie Poole's "White House Blues." First, Poole:

McKinley hollered, McKinley squalled
Doc said to McKinley, "I can't find that ball"
From Buffalo to Washington

Then, "Key West (Philosopher Pirate)":

McKinley hollered—McKinley squalled
Doctor said McKinley—death is on the wall
Say it to me if you got something to confess
I heard all about it—he was going down slow
Heard it on the wireless radio
From down in the boondocks—way down in Key West

As Dylan echoes and transforms Poole, it's as if he's actually listening to the death of McKinley—except, of course, in 1901 there was no "wireless radio," the debut public wireless broadcast occurring on Christmas Eve of 1906—although 1901 was the year Guglielmo Marconi first sent wireless signals across the Atlantic Ocean. Elegiac encoding. Dylan, moreover, is recreating a horrific event that no matter when wireless was invented couldn't have been transmitted over the radio except through his memory and imagination; just as when later in the song he claims, "I heard the news—I heard your last request," he can't have *heard* McKinley's dying song "request," those whispered final words to his doctors in the operating room of the hymn, "Nearer, My God, to Thee," the story of Jacob's dream of heaven, also the last song the ship's band performed on the *Titanic*.

In *Chronicles*, Dylan remembered that it was Izzy Young at the Folklore Center who introduced him to Poole's songs. "He played me 'White House Blues' and said that this would be perfect for me." For *The Philosophy of Modern Song*, he included a reading of Poole's "Old and Only in the Way," and associated him with his dear friend Jerry Garcia. "Poole's lyrics are incisive and inclusive," he writes. "It took a certain amount of wit for Jerry Garcia to name one of his side-projects, a long-running bluegrass band, Old and in the Way. One thing Jerry knew was his place in the universe." During his official *Nobel Lecture*, he glanced at another Poole song, "You Ain't Talkin' to Me," for his memoir of war and his early reading of *All Quiet on the Western Front*. Dylan's introduction of McKinley—later Harry Truman, and even Richard Nixon by way of "I'd like to help you but I can't," a sour echo of Deep Throat in *All the President's Men*—links "Key West (Philosopher Pirate)" to "Murder Most Foul" and the Kennedy assassination. When Dylan sings "I do what I think is right, what I think is best," a paraphrase of a maxim proverbially ascribed to Truman, it's impossible not to envision the terrible weapons with the cartoon codes, Little Boy, Fat Man, dropped on Hiroshima and Nagasaki in 1945.

Key West here is a physical place—Amelia Street, Bayview Park, Mallory Square, they're real—and a fancy, another radio station dream. There is no Mystery Street, except again in Dylan's memory and imagination; Truman's Little White House sat on Front Street. "Mystery Street," though, is a song he absorbs into "Key West (Philosopher Pirate)"—the original as recorded by Alma Cogan runs, "You may lose your heart /

And then your mind"—and the title of a noir murder film directed by John Sturges, shot around Boston the year before I was born there, and depicting Harvard Square locations I would pass every day for a decade.

Along a similar curve, Dylan's radio dream Key West all but merges into Dylan's historical Duluth. When he mentions his "Walkin' in the shadows after dark" from Amelia Street to Bayview Park, that stroll along Truman Avenue would take him by the Basilica of St. Mary Star of the Sea and the Convent of Mary Immaculate, formerly home to the Sisters of the Holy Name of Jesus and Mary. Tag it a silent pun, or an eye rhyme, but Dylan was born on May 24, 1941, in St. Mary's Hospital in Duluth's Lincoln Park, superintended by the Benedictine sisters, and built on the foundation of their convent motherhouse. "Wherever I travel—wherever I roam," as he sings here, "I'm not that far from the convent home."

His Key West allows for elemental autobiography—his Beat influences, "I was born on the wrong side of the railroad track / Like Ginsberg, Corso, and Kerouac"—and gallant reverie, as when he morphs into a Roman gladiator who signals he's decided his vanquished opponent will live: "Got my right hand high with the thumb down." He can replay his bar mitzvah as Hosea's Old Testament marriage, "Twelve years old and they put me in a suit / Forced me to marry a prostitute," and the ceremony will add a Hindu sari flourish of "gold fringes on her wedding dress." And along that "horizon line," Dylan's Key West also marks a spectral descent and return redolent of Virgil:

Key West is under the sun
Under the radar—under the gun
You stay to the left and then you lean to the right
Feel the sunlight on your skin
And the healing virtues of the wind
Key West—Key West is the land of light

In the Old Testament, the marriage of the prophet Hosea to the faithless Gomer is introduced as allegory for the broken relationship between

God and Israel: "Go, take to yourself a wife of whoredom and have children of whoredom, for the land commits great whoredom by forsaking the Lord." Hosea's prophecy is a warning of judgment for idolatry and sin—"But like Adam they transgressed the covenant; there they dealt faithlessly with me"—and retribution: "The days of punishment have come; the days of recompense have come; Israel shall know it." Still, as Dylan's tender Hindu wedding embellishment further emphasizes, Hosea's message also encompasses forgiveness, grace, and hope: "Say to your brothers, 'You are my people,' and say to your sisters, 'You have received mercy.'" God instructs Hosea to love Gomer as he has loved Israel. "And the LORD said to me, 'Go again, love a woman who is loved by another man and is an adulteress, even as the Lord loves the children of Israel, though they turn to other gods.'"

From Poole and McKinley to Hosea and Aeneas, Buffalo to the Empyrean, radio in "Key West (Philosopher Pirate)" arises as an otherworldly spirit and the medium for channeling that spirit, however glorious or cheerless the tidings, much as Dylan in turn here is somehow both a medium and our spirit guide. From inside the radio, who's the broadcaster, who's the listener? The song just might be his most brilliant account of the strangeness of being Bob Dylan.

Dylan after 1991 is—involuntarily—surely reluctantly, no doubt dismissively—a—what to call it, though, that won't distort or demean—a model? an exemplar? the embodiment? maybe just a handy for-instance—of how someone might try to keep their art alive despite aging, illness, diminishment, and the immanence of death. "I'm not what I was, things aren't what they were," as he acknowledges on "I've Made Up My Mind to Give Myself to You." Everything across the span of this book is his working always with what's left. Dylan resisted any sanctioned generational role. But for me, for my generation, his memory palace is in our collective unconscious. At BC High would I have read *Illuminations*, *Howl*, and *On the Road*, sought out in Harvard Square record shops and movie houses Woody Guthrie, Ma Rainey, Robert Johnson, *Broadside*, Marcel Carné, Federico Fellini, François Truffaut, and Jean-Luc Godard, if he hadn't talked about them, to recall only the earliest and most conspicuous autodidact forages? Politics, too. The Boston I grew up in was a racist city. The desegregation busing crisis. Louise Day Hicks. Mothers taunting Mayor Kevin White as "Mayor Black" at the annual South Boston St. Patrick's Day parade. Dylan's songs inscribed strategies for engaging, for refusal, and an alternative to the life around me. When my father bought that copy of *Highway 61 Revisited* at Jason's Luggage and Music, I'm guessing against his better judgment, he was hoping not to lose me. Your parents give you the tools to rebel, and are hurt and crushed when you do.

Over the course of this book, erosions of memory and fact, and assaults on history proliferated. The Georgia Board of Education passed a resolution opposing K-12 lessons about "divisive concepts," after Governor Brian Kemp designated critical race theory "anti-American ideology." In Florida the social studies curriculum henceforth will include a "benchmark clarification" of the ways slaves "benefitted" from slavery, and Governor Ron DeSantis barred public schools from participating in a College Board Advanced Placement course in African American studies. Florida also released a list of over seven hundred banned books in schools. Across the nation genocide denialists attributed the decimation of Indigenous North America to "the activity of microbes . . . rather than human agency." The Supreme Court granted "immunity" to American presidents for "official" crimes, as if their illegal acts had never happened.

All-American *amnesia*. Early in the twenty-first century, cognitive neuroscientist Eleanor Maguire updated, maybe literalized, certainly localized, the classical memory palace. "In a roundabout way," as her *New York Times* obit recalibrated centuries of mnemonic conjecture and metaphor, "Dr. Maguire's findings revealed the scientific underpinnings of the ancient Roman 'method of loci,' a memorization trick also known as the 'memory palace.'" Her groundwork probed the hippocampus, a five-centimeter-long structure of the temporal lobe so named in 1587 by anatomist Giulio Cesare Aranzi from the Greek words for "horse" and "sea monster" because the shape of that area in the brain suggested to him a seahorse. Her initial research tracked London cabdrivers, famous for passing "The Knowledge," an examination demanding memorization of thousands of city streets and landmarks. A paper co-authored by Maguire in 2000 concluded:

> Structural MRIs of the brains of humans with extensive navigation experience, licensed London taxi drivers, were analyzed and compared with those of control subjects who did not drive taxis. The posterior hippocampi of taxi drivers were significantly larger relative to those of control subjects. . . . These data are in accordance with the idea that the posterior hippocampus stores a spatial representation of the environment and can expand regionally to accommodate elaboration of this representation in people with a high dependence on navigational skills.

Her subsequent investigations into amnesia patients focused on the hippocampus as a point of connection for episodic memory, spatial navigation, imagination, and future thinking. Maguire advanced a Scene Construction Theory that realigned the multiple functions of the hippocampus around space. Her pivotal discovery about memory in a 2007 article for *The Proceedings of the National Academy of Sciences* involved what comes next: "If patients with hippocampal damage are impaired at recollecting past events . . . this systematic study formally documents that patients with hippocampal amnesia have a deficit in richly imagining new experiences." Cut off from the past, Maguire's amnesia patients also could not envision a future.

Meanwhile, every summer month is the "hottest on record." And as the encore scare headlines struggle to remind us, "Extreme Heat and Weather Threaten Health at Nearly Every Stage of Life, WHO"—World Health Organization—"Says." Inside my own health house, I've experienced troubling symptoms my doctors reassure me are local, and separate from my original diagnosis, at least—they caution—until my next CT scan.

A book such as this is inevitably a snapshot of a moment in time. From one slant, February 20, 1991, and his "so defiled in this world" Grammy Lifetime Achievement Award, through *Rough and Rowdy Ways* and the extensive tours for the album that followed: 1991 into the fall of 2024. From another angle, the book starts—and ends—on March 27, 2020, with the dead-of-night release of "Murder Most Foul," amid extended flashbacks and foreshadowing. Five years ago, or five years down the line—conceivably richer; perhaps impossible—different snapshots.

On "False Prophet," Dylan references Augustine's *The City of God*, Augustine's title an allusion to Psalm 46, a psalm Barack Obama chose to read in New York at a 9/11 memorial in 2011. In his *Confessions*, Augustine narrates his rise by stages towards God. After the stage of the body, "The next stage is memory, which is like a great field or a spacious palace, a storehouse for countless images of all kinds which are conveyed to it by the senses." In the "vast cloisters of my memory," he discovers, "I meet myself as well." Memory "contains my feelings," but "the mind and the memory are one and the same. We even call memory the mind, for when we tell another person to remember something, we say 'See that you bear this in mind,' and when we forget something, we say, 'It was not in my mind' or 'It slipped out of my mind.'" For Augustine, only through memory can he rise beyond memory to God. As he rhapsodizes:

> The power of memory is great, O Lord. It is awe-inspiring in its profound and incalculable complexity. Yet it is my mind: it is my self. What then am I, my God? What is my nature? A life that is ever varying, full of change, and of immense power. The wide plains of my memory and its innumerable caverns are full beyond compute. . . . I can glide from one to the other. I can probe deep into them and never find the end of them. This is the power of memory! This is the great force of life in living man, mortal though he is.

God then dwells, Augustine realizes, in his memory. "So, since the time when I first learned of you," he continues, "you have always been present in my memory, and it is there that I find you whenever I am reminded of you and find delight in you. This is my holy joy, which in your mercy you have given me, heedful of my poverty."

Back to that horizon line. "Key West (Philosopher Pirate)" is vividly alert to mortality, on a large-scale—McKinley's shooting—as well as minute, verging on incidental: the "fishtail palms" that Dylan lists in the regional landscape bloom once and die. But the core of the song is a flow of evident contradictions, at least as many oppositions and antitheses as he staggered through "I Contain Multitudes," his song on *Rough and Rowdy Ways* constructed around his own multiple lives. The contradictions are "everywhere here," as he observes of the hibiscus flowers. In the second verse he can rejoice, "I'm so deep in love I can hardly see," but in the second-to-last, "I don't love nobody—gimme a kiss." There are poisons, "tiny blossoms of a toxic plant," and antidotes, "the healing virtues of the wind." A marriage is "forced," but "She's still cute and we're still friends." His repertoire includes songs of nature—"gumbo limbo spirituals"—and religion, too, "all the Hindu rituals." Dylan may claim he's "never lived in the land of Oz," yet a few lines earlier he situates Key West as "beyond the shifting sands," precisely as L. Frank Baum located Oz on the maps for his books. Moreover, Baum's dying words to his wife were, "Now we cross the Shifting Sands." There's violence, McKinley, or the Roman gladiator, and mercy, the same Roman gladiator. There's pervasive death, and "People tell me I'm truly blessed." As Dylan sings, "I play both sides against the middle / Pickin' up that pirate radio signal."

Except—except, contrary to "I Contain Multitudes," none of these are presented as contradictions, even as alternatives, options, variances. No more so than in his memory and imagination "Mystery Street" can't really be a street, Key West can't be Duluth, and his Minnesota birth hospital can't be a convent off Truman Avenue; no more so than in the logic of his radio station dreams he can't be listening to the death of McKinley. No more so, indeed, than "on the horizon line" sea and sky, and maybe earth and heaven, too, are contradictions. All are just *there.*

Key West is the place to be
If you're lookin' for immortality
Key West is paradise divine
Key West is fine and fair
If you lost your mind you'll find it there
Key West is on the horizon line

"Key West (Philosopher Pirate)" is under ten minutes long. Yet the song shadows Ezra Pound's trajectory of the modern epic, as Pound distilled it for a letter to his father:

A. Live man goes down to world of Dead

B. The Repeat in history

C. The "magic moment" or moment of metamorphosis, bust thru from quotidian into "divine or permanent" worlds.' Gods, etc.

Pound's "Gods, etc." is priceless, hilarious, and incandescent. Dylan's strongest recreations of "Key West (Philosopher Pirate)" on tour retain that horizon-line view of heaven *and* earth, even as arrangements evolved. For the debut at the Riverside Theater in Milwaukee on November 2, 2021, his piano was lead instrument, though he and the band stumbled a bit on the song—even at the Beacon later in the month, on each of the three nights he made small mistakes with the lyrics. In Washington, DC, on December 2, Donnie Herron's accordion took the lead, as on the album, and would for the rest of the fall. For me, no live incarnation of "Key West (Philosopher Pirate)" surpasses the *Rough and Rowdy Ways* recording until the night of March 6, at the Kiva Auditorium in Albuquerque, when piano, Herron's pedal steel, and Dylan's vocal attain the "magic moment" of Pound's epic. After that, gorgeous and devastating pretty much every concert, whether led by piano, pedal steel, Bob Britt and Doug Lancio's guitars, and even by Tony Garnier's bass, as in Lyon on June 30, 2023, or a defiant, syncopated—all but solo—recasting on March 26, 2024, in Nashville.

During the official final European run of "Bob Dylan '*Rough and Rowdy Ways* World Wide Tour' / 2021–2024," few songs renewed night to night as profoundly as "Key West (Philosopher Pirate)." There were up-tempo full-band portrayals—opening night in Prague on October 4, stately, even as any assumption of inspiration and transcendence steadily was agitated by insistent cross-rhythms; or Frankfurt on October 7, where transcendence sounded like the most natural and inevitable alternative for a shattered world; or Antwerp on October 29, where he suddenly introduced harmonica solos into a song he had staged harpless for three years. Some evenings Dylan's piano dominated, other evenings Britt and Lancio's guitars. Slotted in Europe at position eleven—of seventeen songs—"Key West (Philosopher Pirate)" fell between "Desolation Row" and "Watching the River Flow," parrying against their various negations: the despairs of "Desolation Row," and the creative log jams of "Watching the River Flow." After a gorgeous delivery in Liverpool on November 3, Dylan even confided what he purported were the origins of "Key West (Philosopher Pirate)": "I wrote that song at Ernest Hemingway's house. I think there's a lot of him in that song."

A song of angles inside angles on top of more angles. As Dylan stripped down his band arrangements that November for Scotland and England, "Key West (Philosopher Pirate)" increasingly was performed solo, his spare piano approaching John Cage, his delivery close to a hushed poetry reading. Listening to his virtually a cappella final night account of the song at Royal Albert Hall on November 14, as he felt and thought his way along his raw, vulnerable phrases, I was reminded of what Dylan said of his "metamorphosis" at Locarno, Switzerland, in 1987, one of the decisive spiritual prompts of his artistic revival, and for this book:

> It's almost like I heard it as a voice. It wasn't like it was even me thinking it. I'm determined to stand whether God will deliver me or not. And all of a sudden everything just exploded. It exploded every

which way . . . After that is when I sorta knew: I've got to go out and play these songs. That's just what I must do.

Crossroads. Ghost codes. Dylan's songs resist endings, at least the convenient takeaway of singer-songwriter epiphany endings, his answers from the outset blowing closer to that last chapter of Samuel Johnson's *Rasselas*: "The conclusion, in which nothing is concluded." A number of songs on *Rough and Rowdy Ways* approach notions of transcendence: "My Own Version of You"—"I'll be saved by the creature that I create"; "Mother of Muses"—"Make me invisible like the wind"; and, particularly, "Crossing the Rubicon"—"I stood between heaven and earth and I crossed the Rubicon." Yet ultimately hesitate, demur, won't go there.

In the final chorus, Key West is still on the horizon line of sky and sea, this world and another.

Horizon line, or vanishing point? "That's my story," as Dylan sings of "Key West (Philosopher Pirate)" and his life and his life's work. "That's my story but not where it ends."

ACKNOWLEDGMENTS

For all of his life, but especially perhaps since 1991, Bob Dylan's music shaped a vast, layered conversation among the living and the dead. So, too, along far smaller contours, this book. There are many powerful accounts of Dylan, and my bibliography hints at some of this range. While I have learned from all of them, here I particularly want to recognize the music and arts writers whose friendships, personal and professional kindnesses, and creative inspirations have animated and sustained me. The matchless Greil Marcus, as well as his dear wife, Jenny. Weekly check-in conversations with Griffin Ondaatje, and The Friend. Also Clinton Heylin. Lucy Sante. James Miller. Douglas Brinkley. Robert Rubin. Michael Gray. Sean Wilentz. Amanda Petrusich. Richard Thomas.

Anyone who writes about Dylan's accomplishments over the late-twentieth and early-twenty-first centuries will be grateful to the ingenious lyric researches of Scott Warmuth, and to Ray Padgett for his engrossing interviews with various Dylan band members. We are all indebted as well to *Expecting Rain*.

At The New School, I wish to signal my abiding appreciation to John Reed, Luis Jaramillo, Laura Cronk, Lori Lynn Turner, J. Mae Barizo, Lisa Rubin, Mary Watson, Renée T. White, and Joel Towers. Also Jared Maguire, Carrie Sun, Katy Hershberger Joseph, Charlotte Slivka, Sophie Brown, Alexander Lanz, and Thomas Higgins.

I want to thank Jeff Rosen for his remarkable thoughtfulness, precision, and generosity. Also, David Beal and Parker Fishel.

At the Bob Dylan Center in Tulsa—and even before there was a fully realized Bob Dylan Center there, when the Bob Dylan Archive was initially housed at the Helmerich Center for American Research at Gilcrease Museum—I want to thank everyone involved, from then until now, but particularly Mark Davidson, senior director of Archives and Exhibitions, for his many knowledges and his deft access to all he knows; and Steven Jenkins, the elegant director of Bob Dylan Center / American Song Archives. At the George Kaiser Family Foundation, I want to thank George Kaiser and Ken Levit. I especially wish to remark here on the incomparable skills and commitment of Michael Chaiken, the first curator, one of the dedicatees of this book, whose friendship over the years is wrapped across and inside every chapter.

For that overall conversation of the living and the dead, letter by letter, A through Z, my exemplar is James Merrill's "The Book of Ephraim." But along the way there are in turn localized letter conversations with Robin Coste Lewis, Joseph Conrad, William Faulkner, Octavia E. Butler, John Donne, James Joyce, Annie Ernaux, Toni Morrison, Herman Melville, Elizabeth Hardwick, Christina Sharpe, Robert Lowell, Dionne Brand, Maya Deren, David Goodis, Jonathan Edwards, Michael Ondaatje, Czesław Miłosz, Carmen Maria Machado, Harry Smith, Walter Benjamin, and Harmony Holiday.

For their vital support, I'm also immensely grateful to Honor Moore, Fred Leebron, Mark Mellinger, and my agents, Glen Hartley and Lynn Chu.

My experience at Liveright with Haley Bracken, Luke Swann, and Bob Weil was a dream vision with only gratifying and joyful surprises. I'm beholden to the exceptional quality of their focus and care. Over at Liveright I also am grateful to Charlotte Kelchner, Steve Attardo, Don Rifkin, Rebecca Springer, Lauren Abbate, Nick Curley, Kadiatou Keita, Anna Oler, Clio Hamilton, and Peter Miller. At Universal Music Publishing Group, I want to thank Joy Murphy and Alexis Williams for their generous permissions regarding Bob Dylan's lyrics.

Without my genius medical team this book literally would have been impossible. At Lenox Hill: Dr. Elliot Newman, Joyce Aydin, and Dr. Lee Richstone. At Phelps: Dr. Anna Komorowski, Erica Bello, Chris Moon, and Dr. Peter Stein. At Northwell: Dr. Zeph Okeke. At the Institute for Family Health in New Paltz: Dr. Marek Balutowski.

In all other ways but diagnostics, surgeries, and treatments, this book also could not have been possible without the love of my wife, Kristine Harris. Read this, as Ovid *almost* wrote in *Ars Amatoria*, read this, and learn by reading how I was loved . . .

BIBLIOGRAPHY/WORKS CITED

Aeschylus. *Agamemnon*. Translated by Robert Fagles. Penguin, 1984.

Aeschylus. *The Oresteia*. Translated by Robert Fagles. Penguin, 1966.

Akbar, Kaveh. *Pilgrim Bell*. Graywolf, 2021.

Akomfrah, John. "John Akomfrah—in Conversation, *Vertigo Sea*." Arnolfini Gallery, August 21, 2016.

Alsadir, Nuar. *Animal Joy*. Graywolf, 2022.

Apollinaire, Guillaume. *Alcools*. Translated by Donald Revell. Wesleyan, 1995.

Apollinaire, Guillaume. *Zone*. Translated by Samuel Beckett. Dolmen Press, 1972.

Ashbery, John. *Flow Chart*. Knopf, 1991.

Ashbery, John. *Self-Portrait in a Convex Mirror*. Viking, 1975.

Ashbery, John. *Three Poems*. Viking, 1972.

Ashbery, John. *A Wave*. Viking, 1984.

Asbury, Herbert. *The French Quarter*. Knopf, 1936.

Asbury, Herbert. *The Gangs of New York*. Knopf, 1928.

Auster, Paul. *Moon Palace*. Viking, 1989.

Baldwin, James. *Collected Essays*. Edited by Toni Morrison. Library of America, 1998.

Baldwin, James. *I Am Not Your Negro*. Vintage, 2017.

Baraka, Amiri. *Black Music*. Morrow, 1967.

Baraka, Amiri. *Blues People*. Morrow, 1963.

Baraka, Amiri. *Dutchman*. 1964.

Baraka, Amiri. *Preface to a Twenty Volume Suicide Note*. Totem/Corinth, 1961.

Barger, Ralph "Sonny," with Keith Zimmerman and Kent Zimmerman. *Hell's Angel: The Life and Times of Sonny Barger and the Hell's Angels Motorcycle Club*, Morrow, 2000.

Bear Family Records. *A Shot in the Dark: Nashville Jumps*. 2000.

Bear Family Records. *A Shot in the Dark: Tennessee Jive*. 2000.

Beattie, Keith, and Trent Griffiths. *D. A. Pennebaker Interviews*. University Press of Mississippi, 2015.

Beckett, Samuel. *Endgame*. 1957.

Beckett, Samuel. *Film*. 1965.

Beckett, Samuel. *Krapp's Last Tape*. 1958.

Beckett, Samuel. *Molloy*. Translated by Patrick Bowles. Grove Press, 1955.

Bell, Ian. *Once Upon a Time*. Pegasus, 2014.

Bell, Ian. *The Time Out of Mind*. Pegasus, 2015.

Benitez-Eves, Tina. "Interview with Chrissie Hynde." *American Songwriter*, May 10, 2021.

Benjamin, Walter. *The Arcades Project*. Translated by Howard Eiland and Kevin McLaughlin. Harvard University Press, 1999.

Bervin, Jen. *Nets*. Ugly Duckling Press, 2003.

Bervin, Jen. *Shift Rotate Reflect*. Illinois State University Gallery, 2020.

Bervin, Jen. *Silk Poems*. Nightboat Books, 2017.

Bervin, Jen. *Source*. Catherine Clark Gallery, 2023.

Bidart, Frank. *Half-light: Collected Poems 1965–2016*. Farrar, Straus and Giroux, 2017.

Bishop, Elizabeth. *Geography III*. Farrar, Straus and Giroux, 1976.

Blake, William. *The Complete Poetry & Prose*. Edited by David V. Erdman. Commentary by Harold Bloom. University of California Press, 1982.

Bowles, Jennifer. "Interview with Bob Dylan." *New York Post*, 1993.

Bradley, Ed. "Interview with Bob Dylan." CBS, December 5, 2004.

Brand, Dionne. *No Language Is Neutral*. Coach House Press, 1990.

Brand, Dionne. *A Map to the Door of No Return*. Random House, 2001.

Brand, Dionne. *Ossuaries*. McClelland & Stewart, 2010.

Brecht, Bertolt, and Tabori, George. *Brecht on Brecht*. 1963.

Brillo, Paolo. *No Such Thing as Forever: Images from 30 Years of The Never Ending Tour 1989–2019*. Red Planet, 2020.

Brillo, Paolo. *Stolen Moments: Bob Dylan and Other Music Icons*, Antonio Colombo Gallery, 2023.

Brinkley, Douglas. "Bob Dylan Has a Lot on His Mind: Interview with Bob Dylan." *New York Times*, June 12, 2020.

Brinkley, Douglas. "Bob Dylan's Late-Era, Old-Style Individualism: Interview with Bob Dylan." *Rolling Stone*, May 14, 2009.

Brontë, Charlotte. *Jane Eyre*. 1847.

Browdie, Fawn. *No Man Knows My History*. Knopf, 1945.

Brown, Charles Brockden. *Wieland: or, The Transformation: An American Tale*. 1798.

Brown, Francis F. *Bugle-Echoes. A Collection of the Poetry of the Civil War Northern and Southern*. White, Stokes, and Allen, 1886.

Brown, Jericho. *The Tradition*. Copper Canyon, 2019.

Budge, E. A. Wallis. *The Egyptian Book of the Dead*. Dover, 1967.

Burns, Robert. "My Heart's in The Highlands." 1789.

Burroughs, William. *Naked Lunch*. Olympia, 1959.

Butler, Octavia. *Kindred*. Doubleday, 1979.

Butler, Octavia. *Parable of the Sower*. Four Walls Eight Windows, 1993.

Butler, Octavia. *Parable of the Talents*. Seven Stories, 1998.

Byron, George Gordon, Baron Byron. *Don Juan*. 1819–1824.

Cain, Amina. *A Horse at Night*. Dorothy, 2022.

Celine, Louis-Ferdinand. *Death on the Installment Plan*. Translated by Ralph Manheim. New Directions, 1966.

Celine, Louis-Ferdinand. *Journey to the End of Night*. Translated by Ralph Manheim. New Directions, 1983.

Chang, Tina. *Hybrida*. W. W. Norton, 2019.

Chaplin, Charlie. *Modern Times*. 1936.

Charles, Jos. *feeld*. Milkweed Editions, 2018.

Charles, Larry. *Masked and Anonymous*. 2003.

Chaucer. *The Canterbury Tales*. c. 1400.

Cicero. *de Oratore*. Translated by E. W. Sutton. Loeb Classical Library, 1967.

Coates, Ta-Nehisi. *Between the World and Me*. Spiegel & Grau, 2015.

Cockrell, Dale. *Demons of Disorder: Early Blackface Minstrels and Their World*. Cambridge University Press, 1997.

Conrad, Joseph. *The Secret Agent*. 1907.

Conrad, Joseph. *The Shadow-Line*. 1917.
Conrad, Joseph. *Victory: An Island Tale*. 1915.
Cooke, Lynne. *Outliers and American Vanguard Art*. University of Chicago Press, 2017.
Cott, Jonathan. "Bob Dylan: The Rolling Stone Interview." *Rolling Stone*, November 16, 1978.
Curato, Mike. *Flamer*. Henry Holt, 2020.
Dalton, David. *Who Is That Man? In Search of the Real Bob Dylan*. Hachette, 2012.
Davidson, Mark, and Parker Fishel, with additional essays selected by Michael Chaiken and Robert Polito. *Bob Dylan: Mixing Up the Medicine*. Callaway, 2023.
Deevoy, Adrian. "Interview with Bob Dylan." *Q Magazine*, December 1989.
Deren, Maya. *Divine Horsemen: The Living Gods of Haiti*. Thames & Hudson, 1953.
Dettmar, Kevin J. H. *The Cambridge Companion to Bob Dylan*. Cambridge University Press, 2009.
Diaz, Natalie. *Postcolonial Love*. Graywolf, 2020.
Donne, John. *The Complete Poetry*. Anchor, 1967.
Dos Passos, John. *1919*. Washington Square Press, 1961.
Dos Passos, John. *The 42nd Parallel*. Washington Square Press, 1961.
Dos Passos, John. *The Big Money*. Washington Square Press, 1961.
Dylan, Bob. "11 Outlined Epitaphs." 1963.
Dylan, Bob. *The Asia Series*. Gagosian, 2011.
Dylan, Bob. *The Bob Dylan Scrapbook*. Simon & Schuster, 2005.
Dylan, Bob. *The Brazil Series*. Prestel, 2010.
Dylan, Bob. *Chronicles Volume One*. Simon & Schuster, 2004.
Dylan, Bob. *Drawn Blank*. Random House, 1994.
Dylan, Bob. *The Drawn Blank Series*. Prestel, 2007.
Dylan, Bob. *Face Value*. London: National Portrait Gallery, 2013.
Dylan, Bob. *Mondo Scripto*. Halcyon Gallery, 2018.
Dylan, Bob. *Mood Swings*. London: Halcyon Gallery, 2013.
Dylan, Bob. MusiCares awards speech, February 6, 2015.
Dylan, Bob. *The Nobel Lecture*. Simon & Schuster, 2017.
Dylan, Bob. *The Philosophy of Modern Song*. Simon & Schuster, 2022.
Dylan, Bob. "Poems Without Titles." 1959.
Dylan, Bob. *Retrospectrum*. Miami: Frost Art Museum, 2021.
Dylan, Bob. *Revisionist Art*. Gagosian/Abrams, 2012.
Dylan, Bob. *Tarantula*. Macmillan, 1971.
Edwards, Jonathan. *Writings from the Great Awakening*. Edited by Philip F. Gura. Library of America, 2013.
Eliot, T. S. *The Complete Poems and Plays*. Harcourt, Brace, 1952.
Eliot, T. S. *Selected Prose*. Edited by Frank Kermode. Ecco, 2023.
Ellison, Jim. *Younger Than That Now: The Collected Interviews with Bob Dylan*. Da Capo, 2004.
Emmett, Daniel Decatur. "Dixie." 1859.
Engleheart, Murray. "Maximum Bob." *Guitar World*, March 1999.
Epstein, Daniel Mark. *The Ballad of Bob Dylan*. Harper, 2012.
Ernaux, Annie. *Exteriors*. Fitzcarraldo Editions, 2021.
Ernaux, Annie. *The Years*. Fitzcarraldo Editions, 2018.
Estanove, Laurence, Adrian Grafe, Andrew McKeown, and Claire Helie. *21st-Century Dylan: Late and Timely*. Bloomsbury Academic, 2020.
Esterhas, Joe. *American Rhapsody*. Knopf, 2000.
Farley, Christopher John. "Legend of Dylan: Interview with Bob Dylan." *Time Magazine*, September 17, 2001.
Faulkner, William. *Absalom, Absalom!* 1936.
Faulkner, William. *Light in August*. 1932.
Faulkner, William. *The Sound and the Fury*. 1929.

Fell, Cliff. "An Avid Follower of Ovid." *Nelson Mail*, October 7, 2006.
Ferrante, Elena. *The Story of the Lost Child*. Europa Editions, 2014.
Fitzgerald, F. Scott. *The Great Gatsby*. 1925.
Fitzgerald, F. Scott. *The Last Tycoon*. 1941.
Flanagan, Bill. "A Conversation with Bill Flanagan." bobdylan.com, March–April, 2009.
Flanagan, Bill. "Bob Dylan in Conversation with Bill Flanagan." bobdylan.com, February 13, 2015.
Flanagan, Bill. "Q&A with Bill Flanagan." bobdylan.com, March 22, 2017.
Foote, Shelby. *The Civil War: A Narrative Volumes 1–3*. Random House, 1958, 1963, 1974.
Foster, Hal. "An Archival Impulse." *October* 110, Fall 2004.
Gates, David. "The Book of Bob: Interview with Bob Dylan." *Newsweek*, October 4, 2004.
Gates, David. "Dylan Revisited: Interview with Bob Dylan." *Newsweek*, October 13, 1997.
Gilmore, Mikal. "Bob Dylan at 60 Unearths New Revelations: Interview with Bob Dylan." *Rolling Stone*, November 22, 2001.
Gilmore, Mikal. "Bob Dylan Unleashed: Interview with Bob Dylan." *Rolling Stone*, September 27, 2012.
Gilmore, Mikal. *Night Beat: A Shadow History of Rock & Roll*. Doubleday, 1998.
Gluck, Louise. *Proofs & Theories*. Ecco, 1994.
Goodis, David. *Down There*. Gold Medal, 1956
Gornick, Vivian. *The Situation and the Story*. Farrar, Straus and Giroux, 2001.
Goss, Nina, and Hoffman, Eric. *Tearing the World Apart: Bob Dylan and the Twenty-First Century*. University Press of Mississippi, 2017.
Gray, Michael. *The Bob Dylan Encyclopedia*. Bloomsbury, 2006.
Gray, Michael. *Hand Me My Travelin' Shoes: In Search of Blind Willie McTell*. Bloomsbury, 2007.
Gray, Michael. *Outtakes on Bob Dylan: Selected Writings 1967–2021*. Route, 2021.
Gray, Michael. *Song and Dance Man III: The Art of Bob Dylan*. Cassell, 2001.
Greene, Andy. "Bob Dylan Makes Pilgrimage to Neil Young's Childhood Home." *Rolling Stone*, November 11, 2008.
Greene, Robert. *The 48 Laws of Power*. Viking, 1998.
Gresham, William Lindsay. *Houdini: The Man Who Walked Through Walls*. Holt, 1959.
Gresham, William Lindsay. *Monster Midway*. Victor Gollancz, 1954.
Gresham, William Lindsay. *Nightmare Alley*. Rinehart, 1946.
Gunderson, Edna. "Bob Dylan—I'll Be at the Nobel Prize Ceremony . . . if I Can." *Telegraph*, October 29, 2016.
Gunderson, Edna. "Bob Dylan's *Time Out of Mind*: Interview with Bob Dylan." *USA Today*, September 28, 1997.
Gunderson, Edna. "Dylan Is Positively on Top of His Game." *USA Today*, September 10, 2001.
Gunderson, Edna. "Dylan On Dylan: Interview with Bob Dylan." *USA Today*, May 12, 1995.
Gunderson, Edna. "Dylan's Art Is Forever A-Changin'." *USA Today*, August 28, 2006.
Gunderson, Edna. "Rock Icon: Interview with Bob Dylan." *USA Today*, September 14, 1990.
Hajdu, David. *Positively 4th Street*. Farrar, Straus and Giroux, 2001.
Hampton, Timothy. *Bob Dylan's Poetics: How the Songs Work*. Zone, 2019.
Hardwick, Elizabeth. *Sleepless Nights*. Random House, 1979.
Har'el, Alma. *Shadow Kingdom: The Early Songs of Bob Dylan*. 2021.
Hartman, Saidiya. *Scenes of Subjection: Terror, Slavery, and Self-Making in Nineteenth-Century America*. Oxford University Press, 1997.
Hartman, Saidiya. *Wayward Lives, Beautiful Experiments*. W. W. Norton, 2019.
Hassabis, Demis, Dharshan Kumaran, Seralynne D. Vann, and Eleanor A. Maguire. "Patients with Hippocampal Amnesia Cannot Imagine New Experiences." *Proceedings of the National Academy of Sciences* 104, no. 5 (2007): 1726–31.
Hathaway, Henry. *Now and Forever*. 1934.

Hawks, Howard. *The Big Sleep*. 1946.
Hayes, Terrance. *American Sonnets for My Past and Future Assassins.* Penguin, 2018.
Haynes, Todd. *I'm Not There*. 2007.
Hedin, Ben. *Studio A: The Bob Dylan Reader*. W. W. Norton, 2004.
Hemingway, Ernest. *The Complete Short Stories*. Scribner, 1987.
Hemingway, Ernest. *The Sun Also Rises*. 1926.
Henderson, Elliott Blaine. "Soliloquy of Satan." 1907.
Hershey, Geri. *Nowhere to Run: The Story of Soul Music*. Penguin, 1985.
Heylin, Clinton. *Behind the Shades: The 20th Anniversary Edition*. Faber and Faber, 2011.
Heylin, Clinton. *Bob Dylan: Behind the Shades. Take Two*. Penguin-Viking, 2000.
Heylin, Clinton. *Bootleg. The Rise & Fall of the Secret Recording Industry*. Omnibus Press, 2004.
Heylin, Clinton. *The Double Life of Bob Dylan: Vol. 1: A Restless, Hungry Feeling, 1941–1966*. Bodley Head, 2021.
Heylin, Clinton. *The Double Life of Bob Dylan: Vol. 2: Far Away from Myself, 1966–2021*. Bodley Head, 2023.
Heylin, Clinton. *Dylan Day By Day: A Life in Stolen Moments*. Schirmer, 1996.
Heylin, Clinton. *Revolution in the Air: The Songs of Bob Dylan: Vol. 1: 1957–73*. Constable & Robinson, 2009.
Heylin, Clinton. *Still on the Road: The Songs of Bob Dylan: Vol. 2: 1974–2008*. Constable & Robinson, 2010.
Hibbing High School. *Hematite* (yearbook). 1958.
Hibbing High School. *Hematite* (yearbook). 1959.
Hilburn, Robert. "Dylan Now: Interview with Bob Dylan." *Los Angeles Times*, February 9, 1992.
Hilburn, Robert. "Reborn Again: Interview with Bob Dylan." *Los Angeles Times*, December 14, 1997.
Hilburn, Robert. "Rock's Enigmatic Poet Opens a Long-Private Door: Interview with Bob Dylan." *Los Angeles Times*, April 4, 2004.
Hilburn, Robert. "Sing a Song of Dylan: Interview with Bob Dylan." *Los Angeles Times*, September 16, 2001.
Hirshey, Gerri. *Nowhere to Run*. Crown, 1984.
Hitchcock, Alfred. *Rear Window*. 1954.
Hockney, David. *Secret Knowledge: Rediscovering the Lost Techniques of the Old Masters*. Avery, 2006.
Holiday, Harmony, and John Beardsley, *Lonnie Holley*. Rizzoli Electa, 2025.
Homer. *The Iliad*. Translated by Robert Fagles. Viking, 1990.
Homer. *The Odyssey.* Translated by Robert Fagles. Viking, 1996.
Hopkins, Ellen. *Tricks*. Margaret K. McElderry Books, 2009.
Howard, Robert E. "Shadow Kingdom." *Weird Tales*, August, 1929.
Howe, Susan. *My Emily Dickinson*. North Atlantic Books, 1985.
Huston, John. *Key Largo*. 1948.
Huston, John. *The Maltese Falcon*. 1941.
Igliori, Paola. *Harry Smith: American Magus*. Semiotext(e), 2022.
Ingate, Matthew. *Together Through Life: My Never Ending Tour with Bob Dylan*. Matador, 2022.
Jameux, Charles B. *Memory Palaces and Masonic Lodges*. Inner Traditions, 2019.
Jackson, Alan. Interview with Bob Dylan. *The Times*, November 15, 1997.
Jackson, Alan. Interview with Bob Dylan. *The Times*, June 6, 2008.
Jess, Tyehimba. *Olio.* Wave Books, 2016.
Johnson, George. *All Boys Aren't Blue*. Farrar, Straus and Giroux, 2020.
Johnson, Samuel. *The History of Rasselas, Prince of Abissinia*. 1759.
Joyce, James. *Dubliners*. 1914.
Joyce, James. *Portrait of the Artist as a Young Man.* 1916.
Joyce, James. *Ulysses.* 1922.

Juvenal. *The Satires.* Translated by Niall Rudd. Oxford World's Classics, 1992.
Kaganski, Serge. Interview with Bob Dylan. *Mojo*, February, 1998.
Keene, John. *Counternarratives.* New Directions, 2016.
Keene, John. *Punks.* Song Cave, 2021.
Kerouac, Jack. *Desolation Angels.* Coward McCann, 1965.
Kerouac, Jack. *On the Road.* Viking, 1957.
Khayyam, Omar. *The Rubaiyat.* Translated by Edward FitzGerald. Oxford World's Classics, 2010.
Kobabe, Maia. *Gender Queer.* Oni Press, 2022.
La Barge, Emily. "A Poet of the Archives: On Susan Howe." *BOOKFORUM*, April 11, 2018.
Lanier, Sidney. *The Poems of Sidney Lanier.* Charles Scribner's Sons, 1929.
Lee, Dorothy. *Transfiguration.* Continuum, 2005.
Lethem, Jonathan. "The Genius and Modern Times of Bob Dylan: Interview with Bob Dylan." *Rolling Stone*, September 7, 2006.
Levenson, Randal, and Spalding Gray. *In Search of the Monkey Girl.* Aperture, 1982.
Lewis, Robin Coste. *To the Realization of Perfect Helplessness.* Knopf, 2022.
Lewis, Robin Coste. *Voyage of the Sable Venus and Other Poems.* Knopf, 2015.
Lincoln, Abraham. *Speeches and Writings 1832—1858.* Edited by Don E. Fehrenbacher. Library of America, 1989.
Lincoln, Abraham. *Speeches and Writings 1859—1865.* Edited by Don E. Fehrenbacher. Library of America, 1989.
Loder, Kurt. "Bob Dylan, Recovering Christian: Interview with Bob Dylan." *Rolling Stone*, June 21, 1984.
Lomax, Alan. *Back Where I Come From.* Broadcast. CBS Radio, 1940–1941.
London, Jack. *Novels and Stories.* Edited by Donald Pizer. Library of America, 1982.
Long Soldier, Layli. *Whereas.* Graywolf, 2017.
Lott, Eric. *Black Mirror: The Cultural Contradictions of American Racism.* Harvard University Press, 2017.
Lott, Eric. *Love and Theft: Blackface, Minstrelsy and the American Working Class.* Oxford University Press, 1993.
Love, Robert. "Bob Dylan Uncut: Interview with Bob Dylan." *AARP Magazine*, January–February 2015.
Lowell, Robert. *For the Union Dead.* Farrar, Straus and Giroux, 1964.
Lowell, Robert. *History.* Farrar, Straus and Giroux, 1973.
Lowell, Robert. *Life Studies.* Farrar, Straus and Cudahy, 1959.
Lowell, Robert. *Notebook 1967–1968.* Farrar, Straus and Giroux, 1969.
Lynch, David. *Twin Peaks.* 1990–1991.
Ma, Ling. *Severance: A Novel.* Farrar, Straus and Giroux, 2018.
Machado, Carmen Maria. *Her Body and Other Parties.* Graywolf, 2017.
Machado, Carmen Maria. *In the Dream House.* Graywolf, 2019.
MacLeish, Archibald. *Scratch.* Houghton Mifflin, 1971.
Mann, Thomas. *Death in Venice.* 1912.
Mannix, Dan. *Step Right Up!* Harper, 1951.
March, Joseph Moncure. *Wild Party & The Set-Up.* Blue Ribbon, 1931.
Marcus, Greil. *Bob Dylan by Greil Marcus: Writings 1968–2010.* PublicAffairs, 2010.
Marcus, Greil. *Folk Music: A Bob Dylan Biography in Seven Songs.* Yale University Press, 2022.
Marcus, Greil. *Invisible Republic.* Picador, 1997.
Marquand, Richard. *Hearts of Fire.* Phoenix Entertainment Group, 1987.
Matthews, Harry, with Johannah Rogers, "Agent Provocateur." *Brooklyn Rail*, June 2005.
Matthews, Harry, with Susannah Hunnewell. "The Art of Fiction No. 191." *Paris Review*, Spring 2007.

McCarron, Andrew. *Light Come Shining: The Transformations of Bob Dylan*. Oxford University Press, 2017.
McDougal, Dennis. *Dylan: The Biography*. Turner, 2014.
McPherson, Conor. *Girl from the North Country*. 2017. Melville, Herman. *The Confidence-Man*. 1857.
Melville, Herman. *Moby-Dick; or, The Whale*. 1851.
Mezzrow, Mezz, and Bernard Wolfe. *Really the Blues*. Random House, 1946.
Miers, Jeff. *Bob Dylan Concert Preview*. *Buffalo News*, August 9, 2002.
Miłosz, Czesław. *The Separate Notebooks*. Translated by Robert Hass & Robert Pinsky with the author and Renata Gorczynsk. Ecco, 1984.
Milton, John. *Aeropagitica and Other Writings*. Edited by William Poole. Penguin, 2016.
Milton, John. *The Complete Poetry of John Milton*. Edited by John T. Shawcross. Anchor, 1971.
Mingus, Charles. *Beneath the Underdog*. Knopf, 1971.
Moore, Lorrie. *Self-Help*. Knopf, 1985.
Morris, Lloyd. *Incredible New York: High Life and Low Life of the Last Hundred Years*. Random House, 1951.
Morrison, Toni. *Beloved*. Knopf, 1987.
Morrison, Toni. *The Black Book*. Random House, 1974.
Morrison, Toni. *The Bluest Eye*. Knopf, 1970.
Morrison, Toni. *Playing in the Dark*. Harvard University Press, 1992.
Morrison, Toni. *Song of Solomon*. Knopf, 1977.
Morrison, Toni. *The Source of Self-Regard: Selected Essays*. Knopf, 2019.
Morrison, Toni. *Sula*. Knopf, 1973.
Morrison, Toni. *Tar Baby*. Knopf, 1981.
Moten, Fred. *The Little Edges*. Wesleyan University Press, 2015.
Muir, Andrew. *One More Night: Bob Dylan's Never Ending Tour*. CreateSpace, 2013.
Muir, Andrew. *The Razor's Edge: Bob Dylan and the Never Ending Tour*. Helter Skelter, 2001.
Muir, Andrew. *The True Performing of It: Bob Dylan & William Shakespeare*. Red Planet, 2019.
Nelson, Maggie. *The Argonauts*. Graywolf, 2015.
Nelson, Maggie. *Bluets*. Wave Books, 2009.
Nguyen, Bao. *The Greatest Night in Pop*. Netflix, 2024.
Obama, Barack. *Dreams from My Father*. Random House, 1995.
Ondaatje, Griffin. "Interview with Marlon James." June 21, 2022, New York City.
Ondaatje, Michael. *Coming Through Slaughter*. House of Anansi Press, 1976.
Ondaatje, Michael. *In the Skin of a Lion*. Knopf, 1987.
Ovid. *The Poems of Exile: Tristia and the Black Sea Letters*. Translated by Peter Green. University of California Press, 2005.
Padgett, Ray. *Flagging Down the Double E's*. Substack.
Padgett, Ray. *Pledging My Time: Conversations with Bob Dylan Band Members*. EWP Press, 2023.
Pareles, Jon. "A Wiser Voice Blowin' in the Autumn Wind: Interview with Bob Dylan." *New York Times*, September 27, 1997.
Patchen, Kenneth. *Journal of Albion Moonlight*. New Directions, 1961.
Perchuk, Andrew, and Rani Singh. *Harry Smith: The Avant-Garde in the American Vernacular*. Getty Research Institute, 2010.
Perez, Ashley Hope. *Out of Darkness*. Carolrhoda Lab, 2015.
Philip, M. NourbeSe. *She Tries Her Tongue, Her Silence Softly Breaks*. Casa de Las Americas, 1988.
Philip, M. NourbeSe. *Zong!* Wesleyan University Press, 2011.
Poe, Edgar Allan. *Poetry and Tales*. Edited by Patrick Quinn. Library of America, 1984.
Polizzotti, Mark. *Bob Dylan's Highway 61 Revisited*. Continuum, 2006.
Pound, Ezra. *Ezra Pound to His Parents: Letters 1895–1929*. Oxford University Press, 2011.
Preston, John. Interview with Bob Dylan. *Sunday Telegraph*, September 26, 2004.

Proust, Marcel. *In Search of Lost Time Volume II: Within a Budding Grove*. Translated by C. K. Scott Moncrief and Terence Kilmartin, Revised by D. J. Enright. Modern Library, 1998.

Proust, Marcel. *In Search of Lost Time Volume V: The Captive, The Fugitive*. Modern Library, 1998.

Putnam, Alfred P. *Singers and Songs of the Liberal Faith*. Roberts Brothers, 1875.

Pynchon, Thomas. *The Crying of Lot 49*. Lippincott, 1966.

Pynchon, Thomas. *Gravity's Rainbow*. Viking, 1973.

Rankine, Claudia. *Citizen*. Graywolf, 2014.

Rankine, Claudia. *Don't Let Me Be Lonely*. Farrar, Straus and Giroux, 2004.

Reid, Graham. "Dylan and the Dead Considered. 1989." *Elsewhere*, August 31, 2020.

Rimbaud, Arthur. *Complete Works, Selected Letters*. Translated by Wallace Fowlie. University of Chicago Press, 1966.

Rohmer, Sax. *The Return of Dr. Fu-Manchu*. Pyramid, 1961.

Rollins, Henry. *High Adventures in the Great Outdoors*. 2.13.61 Publications, 1990.

Rotolo, Suze, *A Freewheelin' Time: A Memoir of Greenwich Village in the Sixties*. Crown, 2009.

Rugoff, Ralph. *Circus Americanus*. Verso, 1995.

Saga, Junichi. *Confessions of a Yakuza*. Translated by John Bester. Kodanscha, 1995.

Saga, Junichi. *Memories of Silk and Straw*. Translated by Garry O. Evans. Kodanscha, 1987.

Scaggs, Austin. "Catching Up with Bob Dylan: Interview with Bob Dylan." *Rolling Stone*, December 9, 2004.

Schivelbusch, Wolfgang. *The Culture of Defeat*. Metropolitan, 2003.

Schwartz, Howard. *Leaves from the Garden of Eden*. Oxford University Press, 2008.

Scorsese, Martin. *No Direction Home*. PBS American Masters, 2005.

Scott, Sir Walter. "The Fire-King." 1816.

Sebald, W. G. *Austerlitz*. Random House, 2001.

Shakespeare, William. *The Riverside Shakespeare*. Edited by G. Blakemore Evans. HarperCollins, 1973.

Sharif, Solmaz. *Customs*. Graywolf, 2022.

Sharif, Solmaz. *Look*. Graywolf, 2016.

Sharpe, Christina. *In the Wake: On Blackness and Being*. Duke University Press, 2016.

Sharpe, Christina. *Ordinary Notes*. Farrar, Straus and Giroux, 2023.

Sheehy, Colleen J., and Thomas Swiss. *Highway 61 Revisited: Bob Dylan's Road from Minnesota to the World*. University of Minnesota Press, 2009.

Shelley, Mary. *Frankenstein; or, The Modern Prometheus*. 1818.

Shelton, Robert. *No Direction Home*. Morrow, 1986.

Shepard, Sam. *Rolling Thunder Logbook*. Viking, 1977.

Shepard, Sam. "True Dylan." *Esquire*, July 1987.

Siegel, Jules. "Rebel King of Rock 'n' Roll: Interview with Bob Dylan." *Saturday Evening Post*, July 30, 1966.

Simmons, Michael. "Interview with Larry Campbell." *Mojo*, November 2023.

Simon, Kate. *New York Places and Pleasures*. Meridian, 1959.

Sisario, Ben. "Bob Dylan's Secret Archive." *New York Times*, March 2, 2016.

Slate, Jeff. "Bob Dylan on Music's Golden Era vs. Streaming: 'Everything's Too Easy': Interview with Bob Dylan." *Wall Street Journal*, December 19, 2022.

Solnit, Rebecca. *A Paradise Built in Hell*. Viking, 2009.

Spence, Jonathan D. *The Memory Palace of Matteo Ricci*. Viking, 1984.

Stein, Gertrude. *The Autobiography of Alice B. Toklas*. 1933.

Stein, Gertrude. *The Making of Americans*. 1925.

Stein, Gertrude. *Selected Writings*. Vintage, 2012.

Stepanova, Maria. *In Memory of Memory*. New Directions, 2021.

Sterne, Lawrence. *The Life and Opinions of Tristram Shandy, Gentleman*. 1759–1767.

Stevenson, Robert Louis. *The Complete Stories*. Modern Library, 2002.

Sykes, Christopher. *Getting to Dylan*. BBC, 1987.
Szwed, John. *Cosmic Scholar: The Life and Times of Harry Smith*. Farrar, Straus and Giroux, 2023.
Szwed, John. *John Lomax: The Man Who Recorded the World*. Viking, 2010.
Thomas, Angie. *The Hate U Give*. Balzer + Bray, 2017.
Thomas, Richard F. *Why Bob Dylan Matters*. Dey Street Press, 2017.
Timrod, Henry. *Poems*. 1860.
Twain, Mark. *Adventures of Huckleberry Finn*. 1884.
Uncut.co.uk. "Bob Dylan Tell Tales Special!: Online Exclusive! Part 2," October 2008.
Virgil. *The Aeneid*. Translated by Robert Fagles. Viking, 2006.
Volo, Dorothy Denneen, and James M. *Daily Life in Civil War America*. Greenwood, 1998.
Walser, Robert. *Microscripts*. Translated by Susan Bernofsky. New Directions, 2012.
Warmuth, Scott. Bandcamp. scottwarmuth.bandcamp.com.
Warmuth, Scott. *Goon Talk*. swarmuth.blogspot.com.
Warmuth, Scott. Instagram. @scottwarmuth.
Warmuth, Scott. Squarespace. static1.squarespace.com.
Warmuth, Scott. X. @scottwarmuth1.
Warner, Michael. *American Sermons: The Pilgrims to Martin Luther King Jr*. Library of America, 1999.
Wells, H. G. *The Time Machine*. 1895.
Wells, H. G. *The War of the Worlds*. 1898.
Wenner, Jann. "Bob Dylan Like You've Never Heard Him Before: Interview with Bob Dylan." *Rolling Stone*, May 3, 2007.
Whittier, John Greenleaf. *Poetical Works*. Houghton Mifflin, 1891.
Wilentz, Sean. *Bob Dylan in America*. Doubleday, 2010.
Williams, Paul. *Bob Dylan: Performing Artist: 1960–1973*. Underwood, 1991.
Williams, Paul. *Bob Dylan: Performing Artist: The Middle Years, 1974–1986*. Underwood, 1992.
Williams, Paul. *Bob Dylan: Performing Artist: 1986–1990 & Beyond*. Omnibus Press, 2004.
Williams, Tennessee. *Battle of Angels*. 1940.
Williams, Tennessee. *Fugitive Kind*. 1937.
Williams, Tennessee. *Orpheus Descending*. 1957.
Yaffe, David. *Bob Dylan: Like a Complete Unknown*. Yale University Press, 2011.
Yates, Frances. *The Art of Memory*. Routledge & Kegn Paul, 1966.
Yates, Frances. *Giordano Bruno and the Hermetic Tradition*. University of Chicago Press, 1964.
Yeats, William Butler. *The Collected Poems*. Macmillan, 1956.
Youn, Monica. *From From: Poems*. Graywolf, 2023.
Yu, Jimmy. *Readings of the Gateless Barrier*. Columbia University Press, 2025.
Zollo, Paul. "Bob Dylan: The Interview." *Songtalk*, Winter 1991.

INDEX